Filmography of
American History

Filmography of American History

Grant Tracey

GREENWOOD PRESS
Westport, Connecticut • London

Library of Congress Cataloging-in-Publication Data

Tracey, Grant Annis George, 1960–
      Filmography of American history / Grant Tracey.
          p.   cm.
      Includes bibliographical references and index.
      ISBN 0–313–31300–8 (alk. paper)
          1. Historical films—United States—History and criticism.   2. United States—In motion
pictures.   3. Motion pictures and history.   I. Title.
      PN1995.9.H5T73   2002
      791.43'658—dc21   2001033717

British Library Cataloguing in Publication Data is available.

Library of Congress Catalog Card Number: 2001033717
ISBN: 0–313–31300–8

First published in 2002

Greenwood Press, 88 Post Road West, Westport, CT 06881
An imprint of Greenwood Publishing Group, Inc.
www.greenwood.com

Printed in the United States of America

The paper used in this book complies with the
Permanent Paper Standard issued by the National
Information Standards Organization (Z39.48–1984).

10 9 8 7 6 5 4 3 2 1

Contents

Acknowledgments

On a personal note, I would like to thank all who have helped make this project happen: Robert Baird, a great friend from my Ph.D. days at the University of Illinois, who recommended me to Greenwood; Gary Johnson, the outstanding and hard-working editor/creator of *Images: The Journal of Film and Popular Culture* (imagesjournal.com), who many years ago taught me to appreciate the American western and the films of John Wayne; Vince Gotera, University of Northern Iowa colleague and co-editor of the *North American Review*, who helped select the multicultural films included here and did more than his share of work on *NAR* so that I could be freed up to write; colleague Cheryl Roberts for suggesting films for the Viet Nam chapter, and then kindly reading it over and offering further wisdom; colleague, office neighbor, and mentor Rich Fehlman who weekly spent time delightfully listening to me ramble on about the films I was then currently engaged with; Department Head Jeffrey S. Copeland who encouraged my efforts by sharing advice and protecting my work time; David Walker, Dean of the Graduate College, who offered financial support so that I could purchase films to research; graduate assistants Nader Anis, Floyd Bumpers, Jami Cope, Nate Jones, and Chenwei Zhao for digging up background articles from the library and the Internet; Debby Adams, Nicole Cournoyer, and the people at Greenwood who have been very supportive; all my students at UNI, who have turned me on to films that I hadn't initially considered, including *Arlington Road* (1999), *Fight Club* (1999), *Girl 6* (1996), and *The Thing* (1982); and finally a very special thanks to my family—Caitlin, Elizabeth, and Devin, whose energy and love fills all of these pages, and to my wife, Karen, to whom this book is dedicated.

Introduction

The *Filmography of American History* explores the relationship between American history and American film. Its focus is on social history and how the nearly 210 films featured either retell the past from a perspective of distance (as in the case of *The Patriot* or *Glory*) or reinscribe the values of the day (*Bonnie and Clyde*, for example, says as much about a pair of 1930s bank robbers as it does about the women's rights movement in the 1960s and our growing disenchantment with authority). This book does not discuss biographical movies. Those films are usually tedious, distorted, and extremely self-serving. History isn't shaped by great men performing extraordinary or heinous acts, but instead it is shaped by the lives of ordinary men and women—hard working people—caught up in extraordinary circumstances (the story of the Joads in *The Grapes of Wrath* is much more compelling than the life and times of a famous general, glorified in *MacArthur*). History is a variety of intersections between social forces and everyday people. Alongside this interest in people, *Filmography of American History* analyzes how popular films reflect ourselves and our fears at particular points of time. *Kiss Me Deadly* (1955) and *Invasion of the Body Snatchers* (1956) speak directly to the anxieties of the atomic age and the fear of spreading communism. They are products of their Cold War period.

Overall, the book is structured around landmark events: the Civil War (1861–1865), the Way West (1840–1900), immigration (1880–1915), World War One (1917–1918), the Great Depression (1929–1941), World

War Two and the atomic bomb (1941–1945), *Brown versus the Board of Education* and the Civil Rights Movement (1954–1960s), the Kennedy assassination (1963), Viet Nam (1960s–1970s) and the accompanying counterculture rebellion, and Watergate (1972–1974) and its aftermath—a growing residual cynicism in politics. A preponderance of the entries deals with two important streams of American thought: human rights (including rights for African Americans and women) and America's position as a world power. Since 1945, this dichotomy between domestic issues (a desire for diversity, for America to embody the ideals of Thomas Jefferson and become truly inclusive) and foreign policy concerns (America's need to secure human rights abroad combined with our own fears and growing disenchantment at home over being ruled by the Joint Chiefs of Staff and living in a national security state) have dominated the post–World War Two mood. Thus many of the films in the last six chapters fit into either multicultural concerns, counterculture rebellion, or paranoid conspiracy thriller categories.

THE FILMS, THE PEOPLE, THE HISTORY

This book does not attempt to list the greatest films, or the efforts of the greatest directors and actors. Instead the focus is on breadth and representation. Certain actors, however, appear frequently because they represent so well both the past and the period in which they live—for example, Henry Fonda and Tim Robbins cross several historical epochs, and John Wayne is best associated with the American west or World War Two—and thus they appear in more entries than others do. Works of directors such as John Ford and Howard Hawks—who were directly and indirectly interested in creating a vision of the past and America—appear more often than the films of other notables, but some of their worthy films are neglected—*The Man Who Shot Liberty Valance* (1962) and *His Girl Friday* (1940)—in order to be more expansive on the films selected. In an attempt to correct some of the distortions of Hollywood films and to provide a counterpoint, several Public Broadcasting Service (PBS) documentaries are included. Six of the fourteen chapters are foregrounded by some of PBS's fine multivolumed works. The splendid *Eyes on the Prize* (1990) will give students a real foray into Civil Rights concerns and why the intervention of the federal government was necessary for justice to be carried out. And Ric Burns' *The Way West* (1995) is perhaps the most instructive of all documentaries, correcting a series of distortions and myths created by Hollywood westerns. Burns, in a very gritty and detailed way, analyzes how the philosophies of whites and of Native Americans differed, and how the whites systematically tried to destroy a race.

THE ENTRIES

Each entry begins with an angle, and then marshals scenes and filmic details to demonstrate a theme. One in six entries features a "double bill," a grouping of two movies that balance and comment on each other so well that they are paired in a single entry. As I wrote the entries, I found myself becoming an advocate for the films, finding positive points of value and interest that I hope other viewers will find valuable, too. And as I've revised the manuscript, I've noticed that several entries focus on humanity and dignity, which many of the filmic characters featured strive to attain or maintain. Sometimes the struggle, as in the case of Tom Holmes in *Heroes for Sale* (1933) or Brandon Teena in *Boys Don't Cry* (1999), is against overwhelming circumstances, cruelty, and an indifferent society.

Many entries feature a letter—W or M or a combination of the two—next to the title. These letters indicate that the film deals with woman-centered or multicultural themes. Sometimes, as in the case of *Thousand Pieces of Gold* (1990), a story about a Chinese woman coming to an American mining town in the 1880s, it's both. For films produced after 1967, their Motion Picture Association rating is included to help high school teachers discern if certain films are appropriate for classroom viewing. Also included are the running times for key scenes cited and discussed in each entry. These running times are cued from the beginning of the credits (allow for a thirty-second error before or after the listed running times), and they give viewers, students, and teachers the opportunity to cue up magical, cinematic moments for study. All of the entries conclude with suggestions for further reading, and each chapter ends with an additional list of recommended films to view. Much of the research for this book was done through the World Wide Web. I recommend several wonderful databases: Infotrac (for general articles), Silver Platter (for a wider mix of the scholarly and the popular), and ABC-Clio (a history database that provides amazing background contexts). Almost all of the films discussed are available, either through the Web at Amazon.com or the Internet Movie Database (imdb.com), or from two outstanding warehouse resources: Movies Unlimited (1–800–4–MOVIES) and Ken Crane's DVD Planet (1–800–624–3078). Those few movies that are currently unavailable (such as *Breaking Point* [1950] and *Johnny Got His Gun* [1971]) occasionally make the rounds on television, particularly on Turner Classic Movies. So keep watching those TV listings.

CRITERIA FOR INCLUSION

A combination of elements shaped the structure of this book. I wanted a mix of old (i.e., black and white) and new (i.e., color and post-*Jaws*-era films), a combination of works that reconfigured the past and those that reflected history as it occurred. I wanted films that were, for the most part, popular since it is through popular culture that we best understand and create ourselves. I also sought films that deal with social history in strikingly meaningful ways. In terms of how I structured history for this book, I considered the quality of films made. We have few entertaining or artistically fulfilling films on America in the pre–Civil War period, and thus the dearth of representation there. History was also divided to correspond to the way it is frequently presented in text books and introductory college readers for history and humanities classes. I also consulted secondary school teachers to learn what films they teach and recommend. Moreover, many of the films analyzed are readily available in video stores (important for those who need a quick turnaround on an assignment or simply want to be able to view what they read about). Most of the films are also already part of an existing canon. They have been discussed and debated by scholars, and many have been preserved by the Library of Congress' National Film Registry or have made the various top one hundred lists (American feature films, comedies, stars, etc.) of the American Film Institute. Thus, students viewing and study-ing these films will be joining in on a dialogue of ongoing knowledge. Also, many of the films featured appeal to students. I've taught many of these in my university classes and have found our discussions to be lively and en-gaging. Finally, an element of the personal and purely subjective enters into the mix, too. The works of favorite actors (Fonda, Robbins, James Cagney, Tom Hanks, John Garfield, Barbara Stanwyck, and Denzel Washington) and directors (Ford, Hawks, Samuel Fuller, and Spike Lee) are presented here. Also, several of my personal favorite films are highlighted: *The Apartment* (1960), *The Big Combo* (1955), *Billy Jack* (1971), *Double Jeopardy* (1999), *Force of Evil* (1948), *The Hudsucker Proxy* (1994), *Kiss Me Deadly* (1955), *Malcolm X* (1992), *Mayor of Hell* (1933), *Net Worth* (1995), *Rebel Without a Cause* (1955), *Rio Bravo* (1959), *sex, lies and videotape* (1989), and *Sher-lock, Jr.* (1924).

Abbreviations

Doc.	documentary film
G	film rating; General Audiences (All ages admitted.)
M	multicultural themes
PG	film rating; Parental Guidance Suggested (Some material may not be suitable for children.)
PG-13	film rating; Parents Strongly Cautioned (Some material may be inappropriate for children under 13.)
R	film rating; Restricted (Under 17 requires accompanying parent or adult guardian.)
TV	made for television or direct to cable film
W	women's themes

1

America Before the Civil War

Amistad ♦ *Beloved* ♦ *The Patriot* ♦ *Thomas Jefferson*
Young Mr. Lincoln

Amistad (1997) (R) (M)

Setting: Atlantic Ocean, Connecticut, 1839–1840

Director: Steven Spielberg

Screenplay: David H. Franzoni

Director of Photography: Janusz Kaminski

Cast: Djimon Hounsou (Cinque), Matthew McConaughey (Roger Baldwin), Anthony Hopkins (John Quincy Adams), and Nigel Hawthorne (Martin Van Buren)

Availability: DreamWorks SKG Home Video

In the middle of a torrential storm, fifty-three Africans aboard the *Amistad* break from their chains and attack and murder the slavers who are illegally bringing them to the new world (0:00–6:23). Director Steven Spielberg films the sequence in claustrophobic close-ups, mixed with blackouts from the storm and righteous indignation from the Africans' leader, Cinque. As the Africans attack the slavers and Cinque skewers one man with a sword to the floor of the ship, Spielberg veers perilously close to stereotypes of African "savagery," but his point is to throw the white audience into a state of confusion in order to more fully bring about an identification with the Africans' humanity during the course of three trials in Connecticut. Following the attack, Cinque relies on the help of a Cuban captain and his first mate to return his people to Sierra Leone. But the crooked Cubans take them to Long Island, New York, where the ship is intercepted and the Africans are captured and placed on trial for murder. In 1839 the kidnapping of Africans from Africa was illegal, but it wasn't illegal to purchase slaves who were raised on plantations in the West Indies, Cuba, or the United States. The Cubans claim that the "slaves" are Cuban. How are the Africans to speak for themselves? Their lawyer, Roger Baldwin, recognizes their humanity, befriends them, and eventually finds an African American who was a member of the Mende tribe and can translate their stories. From Cinque, Baldwin hears of the horrors of the Diaspora and how his people were kidnapped, placed in the cramped hulls of the *Temora*, and whipped. When it was discovered that there weren't enough provisions for the slaves, several were chained and dropped overboard to their deaths (1:16:52–1:25:58). Later, the survivors were transferred to the *Amistad*. Baldwin eventually wins the Africans' case by finding the ship's manifest and telling how the Africans were captured illegally. But the trial's stirring moment occurs when Cinque eloquently speaks for his people, chanting over and over, "Give us, us Free" (1:34:00–1:35:26). It is a moment of bristling humanity, but the victory is short-lived. With the 1840 election dawning, President Martin Van Buren fears a Southern backlash. The black murder of whites challenges the Southern system of hierarchy. Van Buren appeals the case to the Supreme Court, where six of the nine justices are slave holders. Baldwin, fearing his inexperience before the Court, approaches the sympathetic and crusty old former president, John Quincy Adams, to speak on behalf of Cinque and his people. Adams, a closet abolitionist, agrees to represent the Africans, and gives a rousing speech before the justices. If their freedom, Adams says, "means Civil War let it come . . . and let it be finally the last battle of the American Revolution." The justices side with the Africans. This striking decision affirms not only freedom, but the American system: our Supreme Court, on occasion, has the ability to transcend its own limitations for a path of righteousness.

Further Reading

Ansen, David and Allison Samuels. "Amistad's Struggles." *Newsweek* 130 (December 8, 1997): 64–65+.

Samuels, Allison and Jeff Giles. "Unchained Melody." *Newsweek* 129 (April 7, 1997): 70–72.

Schickel, Richard. "*Amistad*: A Paean to Past Agony." *Time* 150 (December 15, 1997): 108.

Beloved (1998) (R) (M) (W)

Setting: The antebellum South, 1855; the outskirts of Cincinnati, Ohio, 1873

Director: Jonathan Demme

Screenplay: Akosua Busia, Richard LaGravenese, Adam Brooks

Director of Photography: Tak Fujimoto

Cast: Oprah Winfrey (Sethe), Danny Glover (Paul D.), Lisa Gay Hamilton (Young Sethe), Kimberly Elise (Denver), and Thandie Newton (Beloved)

Availability: Touchstone Home Video

Set in post–Civil War Reconstruction, *Beloved* grapples with the legacy of slavery and how it affects the lives of Sethe, her daughter Denver, and Sethe's lover, Paul D. Sethe and her daughter hide out in a ramshackle house in Ohio. Denver has heard some horrible rumors about her mother and is afraid to step outdoors. Sethe is haunted by the horrors and cruelties of slavery. She has three graphic flashbacks. In one, the pregnant Sethe is attacked by some white boys who fondle her milk-filled breasts and rape her (17:09–22:04). In another, a younger Sethe watches as her mother and several other slaves are hanged because they were too "uppity" (49:50–52:57). The third flashback reveals the darkest secret: infanticide (1:47:54–1:54:39). After fleeing the South, Sethe enjoyed twenty-four days of freedom in Ohio. But on the twenty-fifth day, her Southern plantation owner, "School Teacher," arrives to reclaim his "property" under the Fugitive Slave Law. When Sethe sees him and his sons, she retreats to a horse barn and slits the throat of her young baby. Doused in blood, she stands defiant against these men, and they in turn, appalled by her violence and fearing that she may be insane, don't insist on taking her back. One of the sons spits and calls her an animal. Unfortunately, the murder was the only way that she and her children could remain safe and free. Paul D., too, is affected by the legacy of slavery. Upon hearing, in 1873, of Sethe's actions eighteen years earlier, he rejects her, using the harsh indictment of the white man: "You got two feet, Sethe, not four." Paul D. lacks the ability to empathize with the victim, and a healthy relationship is destroyed. This legacy of slavery is further complicated by an allegorical representation of the darkness: Beloved, a ghostlike, perhaps demonic figure, who has returned to the home. She can barely speak, has a slit mark on her throat, and in her needy demands for attention drains Sethe of her love and energy. She may be an apparition-in-the-flesh of the child Sethe murdered. But despite the supernatural component that signifies the dark, evil legacy of slavery, Toni Morrison's world offers hope. Denver finally does venture out and brave society (2:12:52–2:13:33). The specter of Beloved vanishes after a group of African American women arrive at the home and sing spirituals of exorcism (2:20:01–2:31:56). Paul D. redeems himself, too. He returns to a sickly Sethe, promising to take care of her and realizing her inner and outer beauty: "You, your best thing, Sethe" (2:39:29).

Further Reading

Corliss, Richard. "Bewitching *Beloved*." Review of *Beloved*. *Time* 152 (October 5, 1998): 74–77.

Denby, David. "Haunted by the Past." Review of *Beloved*. *New Yorker* 74 (October 24/November 2, 1998): 248–250+.
Morrison, Toni. *Beloved: A Novel*. New York: Knopf, 1987.
"The Web Page of Toni Morrison's *Beloved*." www.curl.utexas.edu

The Patriot (2000) (R) (M)

Setting: Battle of Cowpens, South Carolina; Yorktown, Virginia; 1776–1781

Director: Roland Emmerich

Screenplay: Robert Rodat

Director of Photography: Caleb Deschanel

Cast: Mel Gibson (Benjamin Martin), Heath Ledger (Gabriel Martin), Jason Issacs (Col. William Tavington), Lisa Brenner (Ann Howard), and Jay Arlen Jones (Occam)

Availability: Columbia Tri-Star Home Video

On the surface, *The Patriot* appears to be an overwrought epic owing more to the *Lethal Weapon* action films than to the American Revolutionary War. Mel Gibson, as South Carolina widower Benjamin Martin, no longer plays the edgy Martin Riggs of *Lethal Weapon*, but he does have a similarly shrouded past. His wife is deceased, and he exhibits a fearful savagery learned in war—French-Indian versus Viet Nam—that he can't escape. And like Riggs, Martin is comfortable around children—in this case his own. But despite obvious box-office ploys—a savage British villain, who more closely represents images of Holocaust-era Nazis and Indians in racist westerns; an underclass group of plucky rag-tags who band with Martin to wage a guerilla campaign against the crown; a second-lead, Martin's son Gabriel, who is all hunk and charm and actually the inspiration for the film's title; an incipient romance (between the hunk and a *Melrose Place*–type beauty, Ann Howard), and lots of graphic battle scenes depicting hand-to-hand carnage (along the brutal lines of screenwriter Robert Rodat's previous effort, *Saving Private Ryan*)—this film is historically accurate. The battle scenes, with armies marching in straight formation as cannon balls pound and bullets zip, reflect the colonial fighting style (2:18:59–2:33:01). Martin's militia finds this mode of fighting defeatist and opts for lightning strikes from the woods (36:24–40:59; 1:07:12–1:09:09), a form of guerilla fighting employed by many Americans during the Revolution. But perhaps the most interesting angle to *The Patriot* rests in its depiction of a slave, Occam, who becomes part of an integrated fighting army (the first and last until the Korean War). What appears to be a hokey nod to present-day political correctness—a black soldier fighting so that he can be free—is actually a fair depiction of the past. Occam fights alongside Martin so that he can integrate into the larger society. In fact, many slaves hoped that an American victory would free them from their shackles. Little did they know it would take another hundred years to gain freedom—and only then by degrees. At the end of the war, some slaves were given freedom and land in Ohio territory, then in Virginia. But, unfortunately, thousands of others were returned to bondage. Another arresting aspect to the film is how Martin and many others struggle with a concept of self. Martin doesn't want to fight because not only is he afraid of conjuring up his past warrior demons, he also doesn't know who he is: English, American, or something in between. Although opposed to "taxation without representation" (10:12–15:36), Martin is not sure about replacing the tyranny of King George III with a possible package of "elected" tyrants. What actually does it mean to self-govern? In the early days of this nation's history, many must have been presented with that paradoxical dilemma. Martin joins the cause largely to protect his patriotic son from getting killed, but after his son's death at the hands of the evil Tavington, Martin finds his vision, his love for country. Hoisting his son's tattered American flag (such a flag actually didn't exist at the time of the war, but the filmmakers wanted the imagery for symbolic purposes), Martin rides into predawn battle converted and committed (2:14:22–2:15:55).

Further Reading

Gleiberman, Owen. Review of *The Patriot. Entertainment Weekly* (June 21, 2000): www.ew.com

Mitchell, Elvis. "A Gentle Farmer Who's Good." Review of *The Patriot. New York Times* (June 28, 2000): www.nytimes.com

Moore, Lucinda. "Capturing America's Fight for Freedom." *The Smithsonian* 31 (July 2000): 44–48+.

Thomas Jefferson 2 vols. (1997) (Doc.) (M)

Setting: United States, 1743–1826

Director: Ken Burns

Writer: Geoffrey C. Ward

Directors of Photography: Allen Moore, Ken Burns, Buddy Squires, and Peter Hutton

Narrators: Ossie Davis and Sam Waterson (Jefferson)

Editors: Paul Barnes and Kevin Kertscher

Availability: PBS Home Video

Thomas Jefferson is an ambiguous American icon. He espoused small government but took it upon himself to double the size of the United States by purchasing Louisiana without consulting Congress. He owned over two hundred slaves and never freed them, but in the Declaration of Independence he wrote "all men are created equal." This documentary explores the inconsistencies between his ideals and his life. Volume one covers the early Jefferson and his important involvement in the Continental Congress where he wrote two of America's essential creeds: his belief in equality and his belief in "life, liberty, and the pursuit of happiness" (33:41–38:05). The volume also details inconsistencies in his 1782 publication, "Notes on Virginia," where Jefferson promoted an agrarian vision for America, placing power in the hands of farmers, but excluding laboring slaves from that dream. Jefferson regarded blacks as "inferior in body and mind" (1:02:22–1:10:12). Race is a strong component to volume two, as Burns speculates on Jefferson's exploitation of and affair with Sally Hemings, one of his slaves (34:02–39:45). Rumors of a relationship first circulated in the Federalist-run newspaper, *The Recorder*. Jefferson never refuted the charges. A descendent of Hemings and Jefferson, Robert Cooley, argues that he has the benefit of 200 years of oral history and knows that he's related to the former president. Several historians interviewed by Burns deny the notorious mystery to Jefferson's sexual life, but DNA evidence released a few years after the documentary was completed affirms Cooley's connection to the nation's icon. Besides issues of race, volume two covers Jefferson's election to the presidency (21:44–22:07); his unauthorized purchase of Louisiana for $15 million (30:17–31:27); his "corps of discovery" mission in which he sent Meriwether Lewis and William Clark to document the U.S. frontier (31:28–33:38); and his founding of the University of Virginia (1:01:04–1:05:32). The volume concludes with historians speculating on the ways in which Jefferson's words (his ideals of freedom for all versus individual state rights) inspired both the North and the South during the Civil War.

Further Reading

Bowman, James. "Ken Burns Does Jefferson." *New-Criterion* 15 (April 1997): 53–58.

Burstein, Andrew. *The Inner Jefferson: Portrait of a Grieving Optimist.* Charlottesville: University of Virginia Press, 1995.

Ellis, Joseph J. *American Sphinx: The Character of Thomas Jefferson.* New York: Alfred A. Knopf, 1997.

———. "Whose Thomas Jefferson Is He Anyway?" *New York Times* (February 16, 1997): II:35.

Young Mr. Lincoln (1939)

Setting: New Salem, Illinois, 1832; Springfield, Illinois, 1837

Director: John Ford

Screenplay: Lamar Trotti

Director of Photography: Bert Glennon

Cast: Henry Fonda (Abraham Lincoln), Richard Cromwell (Matt Clay), Eddie Quillan (Adam Clay), Ward Bond (John Palmer Cass), Charles Halton (Hawthorne), and Russell Simpson (Woolridge)

Availability: 20th Century Fox Home Video

John Ford's tribute to Abraham Lincoln's early days in Illinois portrays a man of the people, a crafty thinker rising to prominence. Lincoln is first introduced as a shy, modest man. "I'm plain Abraham Lincoln," he tells the citizenry, as he announces his candidacy for the legislature. "If elected, I'll be thankful. If not, all the same" (2:48–4:07). Like his forefathers George Washington and Thomas Jefferson, Lincoln appears not to thirst for power, but to be a somewhat reluctant leader. These qualities of modesty and reluctance resurface in his early days as a lawyer in Springfield, Illinois. In his meetings with clients, Lincoln, feet up on the desk or twanging a Jew's harp, uses frontier smarts to solve disputes (14:33–18:17). "Brother" Woolridge is suing "Brother" Hawthorne for $250 in damages. Lincoln looks over the report and discovers that Hawthorne owes Woolridge $245.47 in back pay. He suggests that they avoid a date in court by splitting the difference which just happens to be Lincoln's legal fee. When the "Brothers" wrangle over that decision, Lincoln tells a down home story of a fellow "butting two heads together and busting both of them." The two get the point and settle out of court. The scene marvelously shows Lincoln's ability to relate to the common man, and his own distrust of the legal system. Later in the film, Lincoln shows his cagey smarts during a picnic tug-of-war. As his team is about to be dragged through the mud, Lincoln, the team's anchor, hitches his rope around a mule wagon and wins (21:38–21:52). But the heart of the film is Lincoln's coming-of-age, his surprising success in a murder trial that is loosely based on the Duff Armstrong case tried in Beardstown, Illinois, in May 1858. At that murder trial, Lincoln discredited the testimony of an eyewitness by producing a *Farmer's Almanac* that proved that the prosecution's chief witness couldn't have seen the murder because the moon was low in the horizon and wouldn't illuminate the crime scene. The film alters the events for much greater drama. Lincoln saves his clients twice. First, a mob wants to lynch the two accused brothers, but Lincoln convinces the mob that it is against their best interests to break the law (34:41–39:22). And later in the courthouse, not only does Lincoln use the *Almanac* to prove that the night in question wasn't "moon bright," he also proves that the state's top witness committed the murder of Scrub White himself (1:28:52–1:35:19). Lincoln is lovable in Ford's film because he plays possum, downplaying his ability and catching both the prosecution and the guilty by surprise. In a sense, it is this surprising subtlety of greatness that would eventually stand him in good stead during the Civil War.

Further Reading

Gallagher, Tag. "Second Period (1935–1947): The Age of Idealism." *John Ford: The Man and His Films.* Berkeley: University of California Press, 1986. 119–243.
"John Ford's *Young Mr. Lincoln.*" *Film Theory and Criticism*, 2nd Edition, ed. Gerald Mast and Marshall Cohen. New York: Oxford University Press, 1979. 778–831.

Neely, Mark E., Jr. "The Young Lincoln: Two Films." *Past Imperfect: History According to the Movies*, ed. Mark C. Carnes. New York: Henry Holt, 1996. 124–127.

FURTHER VIEWING

Abe Lincoln in Illinois (1940)

The Crucible (1996) (PG-13)

Drums Along the Mohawk (1939)

Jefferson in Paris (1995) (PG-13)

Last of the Mohicans (1992) (R)

Lewis and Clark: Journey of the Corps of Discovery (1997) (Doc.)

Liberty: The American Revolution (1997) (Doc.)

One Man's Hero (1999) (R)

The Scarlet Letter (1926)

1776 (1972) (G)

2

The Civil War, 1861–1865

Andersonville ◆ The Civil War ◆ Glory ◆ Gone with the Wind ◆ Red Badge of Courage

Andersonville (1996) (TV)

Setting: Cold Harbor, Virginia, 1864; Andersonville (Camp Sumpter), Georgia, 1864–1865

Director: John Frankenheimer

Screenplay: David W. Rintels

Director of Photography: Ric Waite

Cast: Jarrod Emick (Cpl. Josiah Day), Frederic Forrest (Sergeant McSpadden), Ted Marcoux (Martin Blackburn), Gregory Sporleder (Dick Potter), and Jan Triska (Captain Wirz)

Availability: Turner Home Video

John Frankenheimer's *Andersonville* brutally portrays the appalling conditions at the South's prisoner-of-war camp. In Andersonville, the foppish, Prussian-born commandant, Captain Wirz, presides over the men atop a white stallion, and most of the prisoners are so badly broken that some deliberately cross the demarcated fences in order to be killed and to escape a living hell (29:30–30:48). Wirz, who was later found guilty of war crimes and executed, practiced a form of extermination seventy years before Adolf Hitler's concentration camps. Over 30,000 men were cramped into twenty-six acres of land. They weren't given shelters. Often they made ramshackle homes out of their own linen, clothes, and sticks gathered in the compound

(19:01–20:07). The drinking water caused death by dysentery (44:41). Many men feared the swamp and would only drink when it rained. Lice and scurvy were also rampant in the camp, and sick men weren't given any medical treatment. Sergeant McSpadden has a bullet removed not by doctors but by members of his own Massachusetts regiment (38:05–38:38). At one low point, nearly one hundred men a day died in Andersonville (1:31: 00–1:47:00). Frankenheimer's film reveals all of these dark conditions. Unfortunately, Frankenheimer can't quite capture the appalling images of once strong bodies wasted to ultra-thin proportions, but he does succeed in telling a stirring story of survival. Corporal Day, a Massachusetts man and the hero of the film, learns to survive in camp by heeding the warnings of his friend Dick, watching over his friends, and refusing to crack under the strain. Along with combating Wirz's cruelty, Day also has to learn to deal with cruelty within the ranks. A group of renegade union men, "the Raiders," prey upon the new "fish" brought into Andersonville. They attack the young recruits, steal their provisions, and even kill some of them in pursuit of comforts. They are outlaw scavengers. But Day and others from his regiment, including McSpadden, stand up to the Raiders and eventually launch a counteroffensive, capturing all of the offenders and placing them on trial. During the trial (1:47:00–2:15:55), the Raiders' defense lawyer claims that Andersonville has no laws and what the Raiders did, "they did to live." Day, a man of integrity, disagrees: "We do not stop belonging to the federal army because we are here. . . . We do not betray each other." The jury agrees and six of the Raiders are hanged. Although this subplot is stirring drama, the North-on-North crime within the compound deflects somewhat from the larger portrayal of Southern cruelty to Northern soldiers. However, in the end, Frankenheimer reminds us fully of the latter. The men are told that they are to be exchanged for Southern prisoners. The gates open, they are led outside of Andersonville, and hope emerges. But a final graphic provides a cruel twist. The men are not exchanged. Instead, they are shipped to other Southern prisoner-of-war camps. Although these camps are less meanspirited than Andersonville, the film's conclusion suggests a lack of closure, a battle for survival that Corporal Day and his men will have to continue to wage. Will they have the strength to survive until the end of the war?

Further Reading

Gussow, Mel. "*Andersonville*: A Symbol of Wartime Suffering and Brutality." Review of *Andersonville*. *New York Times* (March 3, 1996): XII:4.

Marin, Rick. "The Infamous Stockade." Review of *Andersonville*. *Newsweek* (March 4, 1996): 62.

Rosenberg, Howard. "Civil War POWs' Tale of Horror." Review of *Andersonville*. *Los Angeles Times* (March 1, 1996): *Calendar*:1.

The Civil War 9 vols. (1993) (Doc.)

Setting: 1861–1865

Director: Ken Burns

Writers: Ken Burns, Ric Burns, and Geoffrey C. Ward

Directors of Photography: Ken Burns, Allen Moore, and Buddy Squires

Narrator: David McCullough

Editors: Paul Barnes, Bruce Shaw, and Tricia Reidy

Availability: PBS Home Video

Ken Burns' *The Civil War* is a wonderful work of military history. Exquisitely told with old Matthew Brady photographs, voiceovers performed by famous personages (including Sam Waterson as Abraham Lincoln), and commentary primarily from historian Shelby Foote, Burns details key battles, military decisions, and Lincoln's dilemmas throughout the 1861–1865 period. Volume one, "1861: The Cause," analyzes the events leading up to the war. Burns quickly overviews the harsh lives of slaves (14:01–17:06), the reasons behind the abolition movement (18:34–23:50), the controversy over the Dred Scott decision (25:57–26:53), and the firebrand insurrection of John Brown, an abolitionist whose attack on Harper's Ferry in 1859 and his failed attempt to free the slaves in many ways precipitated the Civil War (27:01–32:51). Following Brown's failed assault a confederate army was formed. The 1860 presidential campaign became a referendum on the Southern way of life (slavery had been abolished in the North since 1793); and when Lincoln, who had received only 40 percent of the popular vote became president, the South saw his presidency as an attempt to radicalize the South. On April 12, 1861, the war began with the South shelling Fort Sumter (48:00–50:37). On July 16, 1861, the battle of Manassas, in which there were 5,000 casualties in one day, proved that this would be no "ninety-day war" (1:13:00–1:23:10). Volume two, "1862: A Very Bloody Affair," studies the maneuvers at Shiloh (31:54–43:18); the dreaded advances in technology, including the minie ball which obliterated bones and caused many deaths and amputations (45:44–46:57); and the ineffectual leadership of Union General George McClellan (10:54; 24:20–27:34; 1:01:54). Volume three, "1862: Forever Free," looks at Stonewall Jackson's Southern victories at Shenandoah (5:35–10:04), McClellan's continued ineptness as head of the Union forces (42:42–56:34), and concludes with Lincoln's controversial decision to free the slaves: "In giving freedom to the slave, we assume freedom for the free," Lincoln reasoned (1:02:46–1:08:04). Volume four, "1863: Simply Murder," looks at heavy Union losses at Fredericksburg (8:44–18:00) and General Robert E. Lee's brilliant unconventional strategies to defeat General Hooker there and at Chancellorsville (42:25–51:16). Volume five, "1863: The Universe of Battle," details the horrific three-day war at Gettysburg and Lee's hubris. His feeling of invincibility resulted in the loss of 28,000 Southern men (10:57–46:18). The volume also briefly studies the roles of women such as Clara Barton and Mary Livemore who worked in hospitals attending the wounded and dying (52:01–56:09); details the ugly draft day riots in New York, as Irish immigrants rejected conscription, refusing to fight to free blacks (1:00:34–1:05:03); glances at the new black soldier, including those who fought with Robert Gould Shaw (1:07:00–1:13:17); and concludes with a stirring rendering of Lincoln's famed "Gettysburg address" (1:29:02–1:31:16). Volume six, "1864: Valley of the Shadow of Death," gives biographical backgrounds of General Ulysses S. Grant (8:41–15:23), General Lee (15:25–20:48), and General William Tecumseh Sherman (57:06–1:04:09). It also looks poignantly at the last days of dying soldiers in hospitals and how they "fixed" themselves for death (49:50–57:05). Volume seven, "1864: Most Hallowed Ground," recognizes Lincoln's turmoil, the demands for peace in the North, and the president's doomed feeling that he would not be reelected. Former General McClellan was nominated by the Democratic party and ran an infamous campaign of race-hatred, claiming that Lincoln's goal was miscegenation (16:44–19:01). The volume also reveals the bleak conditions at the Southern prison at Andersonville, where Union soldiers were systematically starved to death, given only three tablespoons of beans and a half-pint of cornmeal per day (48:10–54:18). Andersonville commandant, Henry Wirz, would later be charged with war crimes and hanged (vol. 9, 44:46–45:01). The episode concludes with Lincoln's political woes lessening: General Sherman's victory in Atlanta betters the president's chances, and he wins reelection with 55 percent of the popular vote (55:44). Volume eight, "1865: War Is All Hell," traces the war's last days: Sherman's march through the south (5:52–15:47), Grant's victory over Lee at Petersburg (35:52–38:38), and Lee's eventual retreat and surrender at the Appomattox Court House (47:10–1:04:02). The final volume reexamines Lincoln's assassination (vol. 9, 11:29–25:59) and lists some staggering totals: 3.5 million men fought in the war, 620,000 died, and a quarter of the South's white men of military age were dead (35:22). Overall, the series is a must for those wanting a quick narrative on the epic battles of the war, but outside its excellent coverage of the military strategy and battles, the documentary is somewhat disappointing. Burns' team overlooks social history. A lot more could have been done with African American experiences (the life of slaves before and during the war). Also, the lives of white women, both Southern belles and Northern abolitionists, are given far too short shrift. What did Southern women think about defending the "peculiar institution of slavery," and how were the South's gender codes and sexual identities caught up in the very struggle that they were immersed in?

Further Reading

Edgerton, Gary. "Ken Burns's America: Style, Authorship, and Cultural Memory." *Journal of Popular Film and Television* 21 (Summer 1993): 50–64.

Thomson, David. "History Composed with Film." *Film Comment* 26 (September/ October 1990): 12–16.

Tibbetts, John C. "The Incredible Stillness of Being: Motionless Pictures in the Films of Ken Burns." *American Studies* 37 (Spring 1996): 117–134.

Toplin, Robert Brent, ed. *Ken Burns's Civil War: Historians Respond*. New York: Oxford University Press, 1996.

Glory (1989) (PG-13) (M)

Setting: Readville Camp, Massachusetts, 1862; Antietam, Maryland, 1862; Beaufort, South Carolina, 1863; Darien, Georgia, 1863; James Island, South Carolina, 1863; Fort Wagner, South Carolina, 1863.

Director: Edward Zwick

Screenplay: Kevin Jarre and Robert Gould Shaw (letters)

Director of Photography: Freddie Francis

Cast: Matthew Broderick (Col. Robert Gould Shaw), Denzel Washington (Trip), Cary Elwes (Maj. Cabot Forbes), Morgan Freeman (Sgt. Maj. John Rawlins), Jihmi Kennedy (Jupiter Sharts), Cliff De Young (Col. James M. Montgomery), and Andre Braugher (Thomas Searles)

Availability: Columbia Tri-Star Home Video

Glory tells the stirring story of the 54th Regiment, a group of black soldiers who under Colonel Robert Gould Shaw prove themselves to be free men. Their quest for manhood, as told through Gould, reveals a conquering of racism. The South proclaims that any black soldier, and any commander of black soldiers, captured on the field of battle will be summarily executed (25:01–26:37). Within the Union ranks, the soldiers also face ridicule. Shaw's left hand, Major Forbes, at first doesn't train the men as hard as he should because he assumes they'll never be given the opportunity to fight (32:30–36:48). A camp commandant refuses to issue the regiment boots until Shaw confronts and threatens him (51:01–52:02). Black soldiers are paid by the government three dollars less a month than white soldiers (54: 00–54:18), and across the ranks, the white soldiers distrust the blacks in their midst (17:38). But Shaw (somewhat cleaned up in Kevin Jarre's script; in reality he shared some of the racist thoughts of the day) gives the soldiers dignity and allows them to become men. Following the battle of Antietam where Shaw was wounded, he, under the prodding of his liberal and heavily influential political father, agrees to lead an all-black Massachusetts regiment. At first, he is overcome with doubt, but he believes that his team will fight and he trains them hard. When one soldier is too proud of how well he hit a target, Shaw seizes a pistol, orders him to reload, and blasts the pistol over his head, harrying the soldier (32:30–34:20). "Faster," he shouts. "A good man can fire three aimed shots in a minute." After chastising the soldier for his cockiness, Shaw turns to Forbes and demands that he "teach them properly, Major." He even, in a sad echo of the plantation overseer, whips one of his own men for desertion in order to enforce team unity (45:41–48:47). After discovering from Sergeant Rawlins the reason for Trip's desertion (he had gone to find shoes), Shaw can't apologize directly, but he does look in on the beaten soldier, feels pained, and then acts, demanding boots for all. The dynamics of his relationship with Trip, his inability to apologize, and Trip's inability to immediately buy into the group mindset (he refuses Shaw's request to carry the flag in battle [1:25:47–1:27:48]) is one of the deep resonances of the film. But both men respect each other and, in the end, find glory. After a stunning victory at James Island, South Carolina, where Shaw's regiment repells the enemy in hand-to-hand combat (1:17:41–1:22:44), Shaw offers to give his men greater dignity by leading the first charge on Fort Wagner. During the suicide run, Shaw is killed, but Trip, visibly moved by Shaw's courage, rallies and picks up the flag. He too is killed, and in the end, they're both thrown in a shallow grave, body upon body. A white man buried with a group of blacks was viewed by the South as a sign of degradation, but for Shaw and the men of his regiment, it becomes a slow-motion tableau of society's movement toward integration and a larger emblem of the 54th's purpose: to give blacks respect, dignity, and equality.

Further Reading

"Clouds of Glory: Can Great Cinema Be Good History?" Review of *Glory*. *The Economist* 314 (January 20, 1990): 103–105.

Correll, Barbara. "Rem(a)inders of G(l)ory: Monuments and Bodies in *Glory* and *In the Year of the Pig*." *Cultural Critique* 19 (Fall 1991): 141–177.

McPherson, James M. "The *Glory* Story: The 54th Massachusetts and the Civil War." *New Republic* (January 8 and 15, 1990): 22–29.

Gone with the Wind 2 vols. (1939) (W)

Setting: Atlanta, 1861–1870s; London, 1870s

Director: Victor Fleming

Screenplay: Sidney Howard

Director of Photography: Lee Garmes, Ernest Haller, and Ray Rennahan

Cast: Vivien Leigh (Scarlett O'Hara), Clark Gable (Rhett Butler), Leslie Howard (Ashley Wilkes), Olivia de Havilland (Melanie Hamilton Wilkes), Hattie McDaniel (Mammy), Barbara O'Neill (Ellen O'Hara), Butterfly McQueen (Prissy), and Everett Brown (Big Sam, the foreman)

Availability: MGM/UA Home Video

Gone with the Wind is a fantasy of an Old South that never existed. In the novel by Margaret Mitchell, blacks were content with their lot in the antebellum period. Getting a gold watch for years of service seems a fitting and honorable reward (vol. 2, 23:02–23:28). The blacks are also extremely loyal to their masters. Mammy, an Aunt Jemima stereotype, guides Scarlett's decisions. Big Sam, a strong buck stereotype, bravely rescues Scarlett from dastardly carpetbaggers (vol. 2, 42:10–44:02). And some, such as Prissy, are presented as lazy, ignorant children. Supposedly this film was made under the watchful auspices of the NAACP. The white men, Ashley Wilkes and Rhett Butler, believe in "lost causes." The North has the munitions, and the numbers, Rhett warns, but he and Ashley commit to some grand notion of the South and its hierarchical society. The film offers no representation of the inhumanity and violence inherent in slavery, instead suggesting that the South is morally superior; in particular, wives of plantation owners are moral arbiters. Mrs. O'Hara helps mete out justice. When she learns that her overseer, Mr. Wilkerson, is having an affair with a shantytown white woman she insists that her husband fire him (vol. 1, 13:11–14:07). Sadly, Mitchell and producer David O. Selznick's idealized visions ignore gritty issues of miscegenation. While condemning the sexual misconduct of the poor whites, the film doesn't portray the mixed offspring that resulted from white plantation owners' rape of their slaves. In fact, most of the African Americans in the cast are extremely dark skinned—no doubt an unconscious attempt to avoid the issue of rape. But in fact the position of women like Mrs. O'Hara in the real South allowed white men to absolve themselves of moral concerns and to sexually coerce their slaves. They didn't have to be moral; their women were. And the most moral woman in the film is Scarlett's close friend, Melanie. She's extremely kind and acts nobly under stressful situations. When her husband returns from a postwar raid (he was routing carpetbaggers out of Atlanta), Melanie deceives the cavalry by feigning anger at her husband and Rhett for getting drunk and going to a brothel. The officers, looking to arrest the raiding party (actually Klansmen in the novel, but muted by Selznick for the film), are convinced of Ashley's innocence, apologize, and leave. As soon as they're out the door, Melanie and Rhett drop their performances and attend to Ashley who was wounded in the raid (vol. 2, 49:34–52:40). Moreover, she truly loves her man despite his weaknesses. Scarlett can't understand deep love. Her attraction for Ashley is one of infatuation. Director Victor Fleming shows these contrasts in a beautifully shot sequence (vol. 2, 13:13–14:18). In extreme long shot, a tired soldier trudges along the dusty path fronting Tara. Scarlett assumes that it's a man in need of sustenance. But Melanie, who truly loves Ashley, recognizes him, breaks from Scarlett, and runs into his arms. Despite the film's disturbing representations of race, class, gender, and history, *Gone with the Wind* is still immensely popular, possibly because of the Old South fantasy, but possibly because of the strong, independent heroine. Scarlett begins the film as a self-centered flirt. As a volunteer nurse, she runs from the horrors of amputations she sees in the hospital (vol. 1, 1:01:47–1:04:41), but after helping deliver Melanie's baby, and in the aftermath of shooting a Union soldier who tried to rape her (vol. 2, 4:48–6:41), Scarlett succeeds, through shady business dealings and loveless marriages, in holding onto the Tara plantation. But her success is costly. Scarlett's desire for autonomy and power and her belief in the Old South create a rift in her tempestuous relationship with Rhett Butler. They're evenly matched, but his desire to make her over into the "true woman" (Melanie) and her desire to make him over into the Southern aristocratic gent, Ashley, create a tension of stylized ideals that the film refuses to falsely reconcile. It may be these gender roles, finally, that are "Gone with the Wind."

Further Reading

Campbell, Edward D. C., Jr. "*Gone with the Wind*: Film as Myth and Message." *From the Old South to the New: Essays on the Transitional South*, ed. Walter J. Fraser, Jr. and Winfred B. Moore, Jr. Westport, CT: Greenwood Press, 1981. 143–151.

Dessommes, Nancy Bishop. "Hollywood in Hoods: The Portrayal of the Ku Klux Klan in Popular Film." *Journal of Popular Culture* (Spring 1999): 13–22.

Leff, Leonard J. "David Selznick's *Gone with the Wind*: 'The Negro Problem.' " *Georgia Review* 38 (1984): 146–164.

Red Badge of Courage (1951)

Setting: Civil War, 1861?

Director: John Huston

Screenplay: Albert Band and John Huston

Director of Photography: Harold Rosson

Cast: Audie Murphy (Henry Fleming, the Youth), Bill Maudlin (Tom Wilson, the Loud Soldier), and John Dierkes (Jim Conklin, the Tall Soldier)

Narrator: James Whitmore

Availability: MGM/UA Home Video

The Red Badge of Courage had a troubled production history. Director John Huston wanted to depict not only a war between the North and South, but also the uselessness of the pursuit of courage, as he ended the film with subtle symbolism: the zealous Youth storms a Southern fortress wall that crumbles all too easily under his feet. MGM producer Dore Schary regarded Huston's sentiments about war's absurdism as blasphemous toward U.S. military history and Stephen Crane's original novel. Schary had much of Huston's film edited in order to insure a more positive representation of war, and in an attempt to further capture the mood of Crane's classic, Schary added, against Huston's wishes, James Whitmore's voiceover commentary, recreating the novel's distance between the youth's uneducated speech and the narrator's well-written literary observations of the youth's thoughts. Despite this troubled production history, however, Huston's film, like Crane's novel, still succeeds in examining the inner anxieties faced by a youthful recruit before and between Civil War battles. Young Henry Fleming and his Ohio regiment have been marching and training for months, but have seen no fighting. Most of the regiment talks big about wanting to fight, but Henry worries about being a coward in battle and dishonoring his country and family name. When the soldiers first hear that a skirmish is imminent, Huston highlights Fleming's separation from his group. As they howl, Fleming steps aside, his face pained and anxious (4:40–5:02). Moments later, Henry asks close friend Private Wilson if he wonders if any of the boys will run. "What's a matter, Henry, ya scared?" Wilson quietly questions. Nervously Henry sweats, and dismisses the doubts with a raised tone of false bravery: "What a damn fool question" (5:59–6:47). But he has reason to be scared. Americans fighting other Americans is complicated and absurd. Huston reveals this painful absurdity in a gentle moonlight scene. Henry is on watch when a Rebel soldier politely tells the youth to step out of the moonlight because he is an easy target (7:13–8:03). Henry, perplexed, slowly retreats, and thanks the enemy (7:13–8:03). The next day, at dawn, Henry experiences the hells of war (18:44–29:36). He looks ill in battle (19:48–19:59), shells pop around him, and thick plumes of smoke engulf the field with a dusty haze (20:00–25:41). During a second rebel advance, many from the regiment, including Henry himself, break ranks, stumbling through the woods (27:03–29:36). Ashamed, Henry hooks up with a group of wounded soldiers and views his second horror of the day. Good friend Jim Conklin, his mind wandering, his soul longing for tall ground, rambles to an open green pasture, turns, and falls in the "fix me" ready-for-death position (hands across chest; legs crossed) (35:50–37:42). Fleming, who had chased Conklin, cries after his death, and eventually returns to his regiment. There he finds Wilson, and the two men share how they have been changed by war. Wilson no longer brags about "licking the Rebs." Instead, he confesses, "I remember I was a pretty big fool in those days" (47:17–47:22). And after being a hero in a second battle (55:54–1:01:32), Fleming tempers the enthusiasm by telling Wilson that he had "lit out" during his first battle. Wilson confesses to having done the same (1:03:38–1:04:44). In the end, Henry becomes a man by proving his mettle under fire—no doubt the casting of Audie Murphy, America's most decorated World War II veteran, as the youth added a sheen of realism to the main character's transformation.

Further Reading

Chatman, Seymour. "The Implied Author at Work." *Coming to Terms: The Rhetoric of Narrative in Fiction and Film*. Ithaca, NY: Cornell University Press, 1991. 90–108.

Kaminsky, Stuart. "Crippled Epic." *John Huston: Maker of Magic*. Boston: Houghton Mifflin, 1978. 75–82.

Prattley, Gerald. "Final Films Under the Studio System, 1949–51." *The Cinema of John Huston*. New York: A. S. Barnes & Co., 1977. 72–87.

Ross, Lillian. *Picture*. New York: Rinehart, 1952.

Silva, Fred. "Uncivil Battles and Civil Wars." *The Classic American Novel and Movies*, ed. Gerald Perry and Roger Shatzkin. New York: Frederick Ungar, 1977. 114–123.

FURTHER VIEWING

The General (1927)

Gettysburg (1993) (PG)

Horse Soldiers (1959)

John Brown's Holy War (1999) (Doc.)

Little Women (1994) (PG) (W)

Ride with the Devil (1999) (R)

Roots (1976) (M) (TV)

3

The Way West and America's Two Solitudes, 1840–1900

*The Ballad of Little Jo ◆ Dances with Wolves ◆ The Ox-Bow Incident
Posse ◆ Rio Bravo ◆ The Searchers ◆ Thousand Pieces of Gold
Unforgiven ◆ The Way West ◆ Double Bill: High Noon and Johnny
Guitar ◆ Double Bill: My Darling Clementine and Tombstone
Double Bill: Stagecoach and Red River*

The Ballad of Little Jo (1993) (R) (W)

Setting: American frontier, a mining town, late 1880s to early 1900s

Director: Maggie Greenwald

Screenplay: Maggie Greenwald

Director of Photography: Declan Quinn

Cast: Suzy Amis (Little Jo), Bo Hopkins (Frank Badger), David Chung (Tia-Mah Wong), and Rene Auberjonois (Streight Hollander)

Availability: New Line/Columbia Tri-Star Home Video

In classical Hollywood westerns women are often portrayed in one of the following limited range of stereotypes: the schoolmarm, the nurturing settler, or the whore with a heart of gold. Maggie Greenwald's post-modernist western, *The Ballad of Little Jo*, deconstructs that sexist paradigm and gives us a strong frontier woman who can herd sheep, shoot wolves (46:23–49:23), run her own farming business, and kill no-good cattle ranchers who are trying to run the farmers off the land (1:47:27–1:47:57). But the film has a stunning catch. In order to be free and to live at peace, Josephine Monahan has to live her life in masquerade, as a man. Following an affair with a photographer and begetting a child, Josephine is banished to the west by her Bostonian father. There, the film begins, and in the opening sequence Josephine is accosted by two Union soldiers (1:43). She seeks shelter from their overtures by befriending a traveling trader who lets her help sell his wares. But later that night, the two soldiers return (7:36–9:09); the trader had sold her as property to them. Tracked through the tall grass, mud, and streams, Josephine escapes, floating downstream. In the aftermath of this attempted rape, she decides the only way to survive in the west is to become a man. She buys male trousers and shirts, and in a savage moment that says more about masculinity than femininity, Josephine marks her transformation with a long self-inflicted scar across her face (14:09). The scar is supposedly to detract any one from asking questions about her sexual identity. In her transformation, Jo (played dynamically by Suzy Amis) drops her voice to a slower, more laconic pitch, and walks with a masculine hitch. Of course, it seems absurd that a scar should deflect any questions of gender, but Greenwald's point is to illustrate just how codified western gender codes were. But an outsider, beyond the gaze of heterosexism, can see through the masquerade. Tia-Mah—a Chinese immigrant who worked on the railroads for fifteen years, was whipped and beaten by white foremen, and is now in frail health—knows her real identity within three days (1:11:55–1: 15:49). The two become lovers. After making love, however, Josephine/Jo is trapped in a liminal zone. She can't go back to being a woman. When she puts on a dress, cooks a pie, and tries to be more feminine, Tia-Mah tells her of the dangers in such posturing. The men she's developed a trust with will turn ugly and she'll lose her peace and security in a sexist world (1:32:40–1:33:14). In the end, Jo's masquerade isn't discovered by the community until her death, and sadly some make it into a mockery. But those closest to her, such as Frank Badger whose life she had saved from three hitmen, are left pondering their narrow concepts of gender construction.

Further Reading

Chen, Chiung Hwang. "Feminization of Asian (American) Men in the U.S. Mass Media: An Analysis of *The Ballad of Little Jo.*" *Journal of Communication-Inquiry* 20 (1996): 57–71.

Holden, Stephen. Review of *The Ballad of Little Jo*. *New York Times* (August 20, 1993): C9.

Kitses, Jim. "An Exemplary Post-Modern Western." *The Western Reader*, ed. Jim Kitses and Gregg Rickman. New York: Limelight Editions, 1998. 367–380.

Modleski, Tania. "Our Heroes Have Always Been Cowgirls: An Interview with Maggie Greenwald." *Film Quarterly* 49 (Winter 1995/1996): 2–11.

Dances with Wolves (1990) (PG-13) (M)

Setting: American frontier, 1866–1868

Director: Kevin Costner

Screenplay: Michael Blake

Director of Photography: Dean Semler

Cast: Kevin Costner (Lieutenant Dunbar/Dances with Wolves), Mary McDonnell (Stands with Fist), and Graham Greene (Kicking Bird)

Availability: Warner Bros. Home Video

Two-thirds of the way through Kevin Costner's dynamic revisionist western *Dances with Wolves*, the Lakota Sioux, helped by Lieutenant John Dunbar's cache of arms, repel an attack by the warring Pawnee tribe and emerge victorious, conquering the bow and arrow with the Winchester (2:06:01–2:11:14). For some critics, such a scene presented yet another Hollywood film (like the earlier *Mississippi Burning*) in which a great white hope comes to the aid of a minority culture. No doubt, such a criticism leveled at Costner's film has some merit but the overall arc to the film's narrative does celebrate the Sioux way of life as something that was sadly lost by the western migration of white settlers into Indian territory in the post–Civil War era. Moreover, Costner may be white, but his hero rejects the white ways: he is appalled at how white settlers hunt and kill buffalo for only their hides (1:21:45–1:24:31). Furthermore, during the Pawnee attack, Dunbar feels transformed. As he fights for the Sioux and in the battle's aftermath hears his Sioux name shouted by his fellow warriors, Dunbar realizes "who I really was." He's no longer John Dunbar, he is now Dances with Wolves. He confirms his new identity after being captured by the U.S. Cavalry. Ridiculed and tortured for going "Injun," Dances with Wolves refuses to acknowledge the government's authority to be in the territory or to question him. In Sioux he shouts, "I am Dances with Wolves" (2:30:50–2:31:11). They cannot understand his words, and that's just what he wants—he's no longer a part of their world. And just moments later, in a wonderful inversion of traditional Hollywood western mythos, the Native Americans rescue Dances with Wolves from the clutches of the Cavalry (2:38:30–2:42:37). In the end, the film's power resides in its belief that identity is open to transformation and that we can rename, remake ourselves. Dances with Wolves moves from seeing Native Americans as his enemies or as oddities, to embracing their customs and beliefs. And in "going native," Dances with Wolves doesn't represent the triumph of the white man, but the profound loss of cultural interaction. Because whites killed off or banished Native Americans to reservations, western civilization failed to benefit from mixing other philosophies and ways of life into those of the Republic.

Further Reading

Baird, Robert. " 'Going Indian: In and Around *Dances with Wolves*." *Michigan Academician* 25 (Winter 1993): 133–146.

Prats, Armando Jose. "The Image of the Other and the Other *Dance with Wolves*: The Refigured Indian and the Textual Supplement." *Journal of Film and Video* 50 (Spring 1998): 3–19.

Seixas, Peter. "Confronting the Moral Frames of Popular Film: Young People Re-
	spond to Historical Revisionism." *American Journal of Education* 102 (May
	1994): 261–285.
Tompkins, Jane. "Saving Our Lives: *Dances with Wolves*, Iron John, and the Search
	for a New Masculinity." *Eloquent Obsessions: Writing Cultural Criticism*, ed.
	Marianna Torgovnick. Durham: Duke University Press, 1994. 96–106.

The Ox-Bow Incident (1943)

Setting: Nevada, 1885

Director: William A. Wellman

Screenplay: Lamar Trotti

Director of Photography: Arthur Miller

Cast: Henry Fonda (Gil Carter), Dana Andrews (Donald Martin), Harry Davenport (Arthur Davies), Frank Conroy (Major Tetley), and Leigh Whipper (Sparks)

Availability: 20th Century Fox Home Video

Set in Nevada in 1885, this dark allegory taps into the mythic untamed wildness of the West. But this time, the problem isn't taming the wilderness or subduing hostile natives; the problem rests within white settlers' understanding of law and conscience. After rumors swirl that beloved landowner and rancher Larry Kincaid has been murdered by a group of rustlers, a posse forms and becomes a killing party. Allegorically the attitudes of that posse sadly remind Americans of a sordid past. From 1885 to the 1920s thousands of African Americans were brutally lynched across the deep South. Wellman hammers his allegory home, late in the film, as the posse votes on whether or not to lynch the three suspects: a Mexican, a feeble old man, and Don Martin, a young rancher. As ballots are counted, the first man to step forward in opposition to lynching is a black character, Sparks, "the preacher." Gil Carter, the film's hero, and five others follow Sparks' lead, but they can't stop the majority will (57:10–59:45). As the mob decides to execute the men, Carter vainly pulls his gun and shouts at the sadistic "Major" Tetley, "No, you stop it," but he's tackled and disarmed (1:04:04). Carter is a man echoing David Thoreau's essay "On Civil Disobedience." He realizes that the majority isn't always moral, and that individuals must make choices based on their own conscience. He also represents, perhaps, one of the westerns' first impotent heroes. He's powerless to stop the killings. But despite his impotency, Carter delivers one of the great metaphysical epiphanies in the western. After the hanging and the discovery of the men's innocence, Carter leans against a bar and reads the letter Martin wrote for his wife (1:10:20–1:13:09). Many of the guilty conspirators hover, listening to the dead man's epitaph, and Wellman daringly chooses to photograph Henry Fonda with his eyes shielded by his riding buddy's hat, so that the trembling decency of the actor's voice has to carry the scene. And carry it

Fonda does, as he speaks screenwriter Lamar Trotti's eloquent words: "If people touch God anywhere, where is it except through their conscience, and what is anybody's conscience except a little piece of the conscience of all men that ever lived."

Further Reading

Bluestone, George. "*The Ox-Bow Incident.*" *Novels into Films.* Baltimore: Johns Hopkins Press, 1957. 170–196.

Houghton, Donald E. "The Failure of Speech in *The Ox-Bow Incident.*" *English Journal* 59 (December 1970): 1245–1251.

Review of *The Ox-Bow Incident. The New Republic* 108 (May 17, 1943): 669–670.

Review of *The Ox-Bow Incident. Time* 41 (May 3, 1943): 94.

Thomas, Tony. "*The Ox-Bow Incident.*" *The Films of Henry Fonda.* Secaucus, NJ: Citadel Press, 1983. 124–126.

Posse (1993) (R) (M)

Setting: Cuba, New Orleans, western frontier, 1898

Director: Mario Van Peebles

Screenplay: Sy Richardson and Dario Scardapane

Director of Photography: Peter Menzies, Jr.

Cast: Mario Van Peebles (Jesse Lee), Stephen Baldwin (Jimmy J. Teeters), Charles Lane (Weezie), Big Daddy Kane (Father Time), Billy Zane (Colonel Graham), Richard Jordan (Sheriff Bates), and Woody Strode (Storyteller)

Availability: Polygram Home Video

One-third of the West's 8,000 cowboys were African American, and Mario Van Peebles' revisionist western celebrates that fact. In some ways *Posse*'s plot is fairly conventional: the film mixes elements of the revenge theme (Jesse Lee, a lone hero, seeks to avenge the racially motivated murder of his preacher father) with the professional plot (a band of outsiders takes on an evil, racist sheriff). But *Posse*'s emphasis on race, in both of its plot structures, explores neglected perspectives. Jesse Lee's father was murdered by Sheriff Bates because he was educating blacks to seek their own identities and economic power. Bates' gang in Cutterswood wants to run the remaining black settlement out of FreedomVille so that when the railroad runs through, white folks can reap the profits. Jesse Lee, who had been banished to the military for life because he fought against the men who murdered his father, has returned to town with his posse, ready to defend the village. Lee's posse is composed of disenchanted men who fought under the ruthless and narcissistic Colonel Graham in the Spanish-American War. Graham ridicules blacks and sends them on suicide missions because he regards them as subhuman (6:53–7:49). After successfully raiding and killing a Spanish-held supply tent, Jesse's men stumble upon a cache of Spanish gold (11:44–13:

02). Moments later, Colonel Graham crosses their path, assumes that they were going AWOL, and orders their execution. The men fight back, killing the entire unit except for Graham. The scene of stylized, slow-motion mayhem (including a character knocking out a horse with one punch) emphasizes just what kind of outlaws these men are (13:39–14:57). Unlike standard Hollywood outlaws (bank robbers, gunslingers, mercenaries), these men are rebels because of a racist power structure that regards them as inferior and subhuman. In the end, Jesse Lee's gang triumphs over Graham and Bates, but Peebles brings his mythic treatment back to a sad current reality, informing the viewer in a painful endnote that African Americans comprise 12 percent of the U.S. population but only account for one-half of one percent of its wealth. The racist structures that destroyed several black settlements of the old west are still at work, albeit less visibly, today.

Further Reading

Dash, Julie. Review of *Posse*. *Interview* 23 (May 1993): 108–112.
Review of *Posse*. *Jet* 84 (July 19, 1993): 15.
"Success of *Posse* Altered Blacks' View of Westerns" (interview with actor-writer Sy Richardson). *Jet* 84 (July 19, 1993): 15.
Travers, Peter. "*Posse* Leader Mario Van Peebles Shoots from the Lip" (interview with director-actor Mario Van Peebles). *Rolling Stone* (June 10, 1993): 76.
———. Review of *Posse*. *Rolling Stone* (June 10, 1993): 73–74.

Rio Bravo (1959)

Setting: Texas, 1870s/1880s?

Director: Howard Hawks

Screenplay: Leigh Brackett and Jules Furthman

Director of Photography: Russell Harlan

Cast: John Wayne (Sheriff John T. Chance), Dean Martin (Dude), Ricky Nelson (Colorado Ryan), Angie Dickinson (Feathers), Ward Bond (Wheeler), Walter Brennan (Stumpy), Claude Akins (Joe Burdette), and John Russell (Nathan Burdette)

Availability: Warner Bros. Home Video

Howard Hawks' feel-good western is a delightful celebration of friendship, respect, and responsibility. Sheriff John T. Chance has arrested Joe Burdette for killing a man in a saloon. But there's a problem. Prominent rancher and community power-broker Nathan Burdette wants his brother released and has hired several mercenaries to get the job done. Chance, outnumbered, counts on the support of his best friend, the recovering drunk Dude; an old cripple, Stumpy; a young gun, Colorado; and a card shark, Feathers. Director Hawks claimed that he had made *Rio Bravo* as a direct challenge to the politics of Fred Zinnemann's *High Noon* (1952), in which Will Kane surveys the town in a vain attempt to find men to help him fight Frank Miller, a man Kane sent to prison and who now wants him dead. Nobody in the town helps the sheriff and *High Noon* becomes a message film about our inhumanity. Hawks disliked the film intensely and felt that Kane acted inappropriately: a professional never asks amateurs for help; a professional is "good enough" to do the job himself or with the aid of fellow, right thinking professionals. By contrast, Hawks' Chance refuses the help of Wheeler because his men are a bunch of "[w]ell meaning amateurs. Most of them worried about their wives and kids" (24:36–25:45). So he finds help with those he trusts and respects, his friends. Midway through the film, Chance preaches some tough love: "Sorry don't get it done, Dude," he says after Dude slugged Chance for the second time out of alcoholic frustration (1:34:29). Dude worries that he's "no good" anymore, following a surprise mugging by Nathan Burdette's guns in a stable and the subsequent rescue by Chance and Colorado. Tortured with self-doubt and the d.t.'s, Dude returns to the bottle. As he sits in the jail about to imbibe, he hears Burdette's mercenaries playing the death march song, and decides against self-destruction (1:39:52–1:43:48). He asks Chance to let him rejoin the team. Chance agrees, and moments later, in an early form of a music video, Dean Martin, his black hat tucked over his eyes with Rat-pack cool, and Ricky Nelson, guitar strapped around his shoulder in Rockabilly poise, sing "My Rifle, Pony, and Me," and "Cindy (Get Along Cindy)" (1:44:43–1:48:19). Stumpy, a harmonica around his pouty gums, joins in on the merriment, and Wayne, drinking coffee and leaning with relaxed ease, smiles. A delightful aura of male camaraderie resonates. This is a pure Hawksian moment, as men stand by their friends and face possible death with grace under pressure. They have Burdette's no-good brother locked up in the jail and they won't budge. They are a group of professionals, insular and strong, standing against the void of the outside world.

Further Reading

McBride, Joseph. "Themes and Variations: Three Westerns." *Hawks on Hawks.* Berkeley: University of California Press, 1982. 130–141.

Wayne, George. "Thoroughly Modern Angie" (interview with Angie Dickinson). *Vanity Fair* 58 (April 1995): 208.

Willis, Donald C. "*Rio Bravo.*" *The Films of Howard Hawks.* Metuchen, NJ: Scarecrow Press, 1975. 54–61.

Wood, Robin. "*Rio Bravo* and Retrospect (1968, 1981)." *The Western Reader*, ed. Jim Kitses and Gregg Rickman. New York: Limelight Editions, 1998. 173–194.

The Searchers (1956) (M)

Setting: Texas and the Northwest, 1868–1874

Director: John Ford

Screenplay: Frank S. Nugent

Director of Photography: Winton C. Hoch

Cast: John Wayne (Ethan Edwards), Jeffrey Hunter (Martin Pawley), Vera Miles (Laurie Jorgensen), Natalie Wood (Debbie Edwards), and Henry Brandon (Scar)

Availability: Warner Bros. Home Video

The *Searchers* is a revenge western with a wicked twist. Ethan Edwards wants to avenge the murders of his massacred nephew, niece, brother Aaron, and sister-in law Martha (whom he secretly loved). He also seeks to rescue his nine-year-old younger niece, Debbie, from Chief Scar and his band of Indians. But after Debbie reaches adolescence and marries Scar, Ethan wants to murder her. Ethan's fear of race-mixing is perhaps one of the most disturbing themes in a Hollywood western. Out on the sand dunes, after he and the young Marty have found Debbie encamped with Scar, Ethan's viciousness registers full scale (1:25:48–1:28:03). Debbie runs toward Marty, speaking Comanche and pleading with him to leave. Ethan stands rigid in the dust, and breaks up the reunion, a gun clamped in his hand. "Stand aside, Marty," he orders. Marty nobly defends Debbie, throwing her behind him, his arms locked around her like a Christ figure. Ethan is a violent racist. Early on, he looks at young Marty, saying with some disgust, "a fellow could mistake you for a half-breed" (5:43–5:47). Later, when Ethan sees two crazed white women who had been raped by Indians, he dismisses them: "They aren't white. Not anymore." And as he exits the room, John Ford's camera rapidly tracks in on John Wayne's face to a close-up that reveals hard slits for eyes and a mean curl to his lips (1:14:45–1:15:47). His distaste even leads him to kill a bunch of buffaloes so that the "Commanch" won't have enough to eat in winter (1:09:04–1:10:25). Director Ford doesn't condone Ethan's actions, nor does he necessarily side with whites over Indians. Filmed in 1956, a time when the nation's Civil Rights Movement was advancing and two years after the *Brown vs. the Board of Education* decision was rendered in Topeka, Kansas, outlawing school segregation, *The Searchers* explores these cultural issues. Marty is really the film's moral hero. He wants to bring Debbie back no matter what, but Ethan feels that Marty doesn't belong on the quest: "She's no kin of yours." And yet, Marty, even though not blood-related, belongs more than anyone in the new community of integration. He has the American spirit of democratic acceptance. When Marty learns that Debbie is still alive, he demands to rescue her. Ethan wants to charge in and hopes she gets killed in the crossfire. Even Marty's girlfriend, Laurie, feels "Ethan should put a bullet in her brain. I tell you, Martha would want him to" (1:47:16–1:47:44). Marty vows to save Debbie from Ethan and his kind. One-eighth Cherokee, "the rest Welsh and English," Marty is a melting pot of identities, and unlike Scar he desires to fit into the mainstream. He represents the kind of integration Ford and writer Frank S. Nugent could envision in 1956. By contrast, Scar is punished for being too much of an outlaw or, in an allegorical sense, being "too black." Ethan, too, is punished. There is no space for racial hatred and segregation in a new America. At the end of the *Searchers*, Ethan returns Debbie home. He then stands at the threshold of the house, grabs hold of his right arm, turns and moves deep into the frame, wandering into the desert as the wind kicks up dust and the door closes to a fade.

Further Reading

Clauss, James J. "Descent into Hell: Mythic Paradigms in *The Searchers.*" *Journal of Popular Film and Television* 27 (Fall 1999): 2–17.

Eckstein, Arthur M. "Darkening Ethan: John Ford's *The Searchers* (1956), from Novel to Screenplay to Screen." *Cinema Journal* 38 (Fall 1998): 3–24.

Gallagher, Tag. "*The Searchers.*" *John Ford: The Man and His Films*. Berkeley: University of California Press, 1986. 324–338.

Henderson, Brian. "*The Searchers*: An American Dilemma." *Movies and Methods, Volume II*, ed. Bill Nichols. Berkeley: University of California Press, 1985. 429–449.

Thousand Pieces of Gold (1990) (PG-13) (M) (W)

Setting: Northern China and San Francisco, 1880; Oregon, 1880s

Director: Nancy Kelly

Screenplay: Anne Makepeace

Director of Photography: Bobby Bukowski

Cast: Rosalind Chao (Lalu), Chris Cooper (Charlie Beamis), Kim Chan (Li Po), and Michael Paul Chan (Hong King)

Availability: Plaza Entertainment Inc.

Thousand Pieces of Gold is a story of dislocation, cross-cultural love, and a woman's struggle for independence. Lalu is a young Chinese woman whose father sells her to a dubious man during a drought and famine (5:22–5:43). Uprooted, she's shipped to San Francisco where she is stripped naked, auctioned, and sold for gold (7:30–8:38). The man she's sold to, Li Po, takes her to Oregon. During the journey he tells her how an immigrant can make it in America: "Learn English, carry a gun, start your own business. Don't let anyone push you around" (13:02–13:04). But what he doesn't tell her is that he's sending her to a white mining settlement where she'll become a prostitute and go by the name "China Mary" or "China Polly." Naive and innocent, Lalu assumes that Hong King, her new husband, wants a wife. Her first encounter with him is shockingly brutal. He orders her to wash his feet and then savagely rapes her. While Lalu screams, Charlie Beamis plays cards with some acquaintances and disapprovingly says, "He sure knows how to show a girl a good time" (20:54–21:20). At first, Beamis exoticizes Lalu, but in time he falls in love with her. For him, Lalu is beauty and salvation. Late in the film, he tells her: "Some of us need an angel like you to save us from ourselves" (1:28:39). After the rape scene, Hong King offers to sell Lalu's services to the highest bidder, offering the "pleasures of the east" (27:43). But Lalu remembers what Li Po taught her, and when a fat, surly cowboy tries to bed her, she brandishes a knife and defends herself. Hong King is furious, but Charlie enters the back room and supports her. He tells Hong King to keep her as a wife, not a whore. "You don't own her. You can't own a person," the former Civil War veteran from Ohio says. "Those days are over" (30:06). So she stays in the dreary relationship, despondent during love making (31:54), a prisoner in America, washing clothes, baking pies, and dreaming of making enough money to go back to China. Eventually, Charlie wins Lalu from Hong King in a game of cards, and she comes to live with him. But his love for her is unrequited. She remains distant and distrusting, and he's honorable enough not to force sex (1:01:16). It's not clear if Lalu keeps her distance from Charlie because he's white, holds economic power over her, or because she desires to return to China. But by rebuffing his advances she gains in stature so that when they do unite at the end of the film they're a much more balanced and equal couple. After she first rebuffs him, she goes into business for herself, opening up a boarding house and earning capital. During a Chinese New Year festival in February, when Charlie is wounded by some miners, Lalu helps nurse him back to health. The recovering Charlie and Lalu finally kiss passionately by a stream (1:36:01). His power over her has been lessened by his wounds, her economic gains, and her learning English. They are now in a more equal partnership. After following some sage advice from a Chinese elder who tells Lalu to "eat soup of forgetfulness. Cross river to be reborn on the other side," Lalu decides to make America her "home" (1:40:23–1:41:24).

Further Reading

Cheung, King-kok. "Self-Fulfilling Visions in *The Woman Warrior* and *Thousand Pieces of Gold.*" *Biography: An Interdisciplinary Quarterly* 13 (Spring 1990): 143–153.

Hesford, Walter. "*Thousand Pieces of Gold*: Competing Fictions in the Representation of Chinese-American Experience." *Western American Literature* 31 (May 1996): 49–62.

Kim, David. Review of *Thousand Pieces of Gold*. *Village Voice* (October 1, 1991): 56.

Terry, Patricia. "A Chinese Woman in the West: *Thousand Pieces of Gold* and the Revision of the Heroic Frontier." *Literature/Film Quarterly* 22 (1994): 222–226.

Unforgiven (1993) (R)

Setting: Big Whiskey, Wyoming, 1880
Director: Clint Eastwood

Screenplay: David Webb Peoples

Director of Photography: Jack N. Green

Cast: Clint Eastwood (William Munny), Gene Hackman (Little Bill Daggett), Morgan Freeman (Ned Logan), Richard Harris (English Bob), Jaimz Woolvett (the Scofield Kid), Saul Rubinek (W. W. Beauchamp), Anna Thomson (Delilah Fitzgerald), David Mucci (Quick Mike), and Rob Campbell (Davey Bunting)

Availability: Warner Bros. Home Video

"Deserve's got nothing to do with it," William Munny spits, as he cocks a shotgun at Little Bill Daggett's head, late in Clint Eastwood's *Unforgiven* (2:01:23)—and no finer epitaph was ever spoken for this revisionist western. *Unforgiven* is dark, depressing, and full of failed figures. Munny's failure as a pig farmer mirrors his failure at reformation through the love of a good, Christian woman. In discussing the virtues of his dead wife, Munny's words sound memorized, insincere, and lacking in conviction: "My wife, she cured me of that, cured me of drink and wickedness" (12:04–12:21). But the darkness reemerges as Munny goes on a killing spree, becoming yet another one of Eastwood's avenging angel figures. Munny's two partners, close friend Ned Logan and novice killer, the Scofield Kid, also come to realize that "deserve's got nothing to do with it." The Kid wanted to become a famous outlaw, but after shooting a man sitting in an outhouse, he laughs while crying, "Three shots and he was taking a shit" (1:45:43–1:47:33). *Unforgiven* deglamorizes western-movie violence. For the Kid, there's no glory in killing, and justifications just don't fit. "Well, I guess he had it coming," the Kid rationalizes, fighting back emotion. "We all have it coming, Kid," Munny replies, refusing to absolve him (1:49:04). Ned, too, can't stomach the killing because it all seems undeserved. He rides along to help an old friend, Will, but when they shoot an unarmed kid off a horse, hit him in the belly, and watch him slowly die while he complains of an unquenchable thirst, Ned, speechless, looks at Munny and shortly thereafter abandons bounty hunting (1:30:08–1:34:19). Sheriff Daggett, too, is a failure. He rules poorly. Little Bill doesn't punish the men who cut up Delilah, a prostitute. Instead, he treats her like property, demanding that Quick Mike and his sidekick, Davey, bring in some good horses from the T-Bar ranch as reparations (3:35–5:51). The other prostitutes aren't pleased with this decision, and they place a bounty on the two men's heads (7:04–8:16). Yet that response is excessive: Do the men deserve to be *killed* for what they did? Later Bill sadistically beats an unarmed English Bob in the middle of the street (45:14–45:48), further exposing his inadequacy as a leader. That night in prison, Little Bill continues to deglamorize the old west by telling writer Beauchamp what really happened one night in Wichita (53:45–58:00). Beauchamp had written a romanticized account of English Bob's duel with the dangerous Corky. Bill revises the story, telling how there was no honor involved. Instead, the fight between the two was a matter of drunken lust, and Bob killed an unarmed man. Like the story within the filmic story, Eastwood's *Unforgiven* is a work of beauty because it revises and challenges western mythology. Thus, Little Bill's flawed, unfinished house becomes a metaphor. The house is made up of odd angles and leaking holes. So are Eastwood's characters. In *Unforgiven* nothing fits, nothing's deserved.

Further Reading

Greenberg, Harvey R. Review of *Unforgiven. Film Quarterly* 46 (Spring 1993): 52–56.

Grist, Leighton. "*Unforgiven.*" *The Book of Westerns,* ed. Ian Cameron and Douglas Pye. New York: Continuum, 1996. 294–301.

Ingrassia, Catherine. "Writing the West: Iconic and Literal Truth in *Unforgiven.*" *Literature/Film Quarterly* 26 (1998): 53–59.

Plantinga, Carl. "Spectacles of Death: Clint Eastwood and Violence in *Unforgiven.*" *Cinema Journal* 37 (Winter 1998): 65–83.

Prats, Armando J. "Back from the Sunset: The Western, the Eastwood Hero, and *Unforgiven.*" *Journal of Film and Video* 47 (Spring/Fall 1995): 106–123.

The Way West, Episodes 1–4 (1995) (Doc.) (M)

Setting: American West, 1840–1890

Director: Ric Burns

Writer: Ric Burns

Directors of Photography: Allen Moore and Buddy Squires

Editors: Bruce Shaw and Li-Shin Yu

Availability: PBS Home Video

Ric Burns' documentary is a must see for fans of the American West. Unlike the romanticized Hollywood films of the classical period (1930–1960), this series takes a stark, painful look at America's brutal past on the western frontier. In particular the series closely examines how white America, directly and indirectly, exterminated Native Americans. Volume one, "Westward, the Course of Empire Takes Its Way," establishes the hunger for land as European Americans emigrate west. In 1840, land west of Missouri and Iowa was regarded as the "Great American Desert" (15:04), but with land hunger in the East, 1,000 pioneers headed for California in 1843 (16:08). In 1846, Mormons settled in Salt Lake, and with the Gold Rush of 1849, the population of San Francisco jumped from 429 to 20,000 (18:46–19:49). By 1859, half a million Americans had flowed west. And by October 21, 1861, the transcontinental telegraph line was established between San Francisco and Washington, DC, linking the country. In the past it had taken five months to send a message East; now, it took merely seconds (50:11–51:30). But with the expansion came conflict. According to Charlotte Elk

Black, Native and Euro Americans have differing perspectives on the land. Whites, coming from a Judeo-Christian perspective, regard themselves as having fallen out of Eden and they are trying to get back to paradise. In such a paradigm, the earth becomes a tool for attaining something better. Therefore, the earth itself is not respected, but is regarded as something to be conquered. For Natives, the earth is a mother, and it doesn't need to be conquered because we are all part of its family, living in harmony (10:56–12:09). The Native people wanted to keep the land the way it was. The Euro Americans, with their mining settlements, telegraph lines, and railroads, were bringing "progress" to the plains and were changing the land. These differing philosophies (the desire to hold onto a sacred past versus the desire to build a new future) led to a series of deadly skirmishes and massacres. In September of 1855, 600 U.S. soldiers killed 86 Native Americans and captured 70 women and children in Nebraska (34:26). Several other massacres followed, most of them perpetrated by the U.S. Cavalry (31:00–33:27; 58:00–1:05:17; 1:06:21–1:10:33). Unfortunately, many officers after the Civil War believed in extermination (53:18) or forcing Indians onto special colonies or "reservations" (54:00). Also, the government, with its vast numbers of military men, made Indians sign a series of treaties that the United States would never fulfill. Volume two, "The Approach of Civilization," explores the furthering of the cultural divide as technology comes to the West. With the linking of the Union and Pacific Railroads in 1869, the conflict deepened (34:06). Native Americans knew that with the railroad came white settlements and a scaring away of the buffalo (34:34; 1:17:37). In the eighteenth century 75 million buffalo roamed the plains. By the 1880s they were destroyed. Indirectly, the extermination of the buffalo was a form of genocide, killing off the native peoples who relied on the buffalo for their clothing, shelter, food, weaponry, and heating (vol. 2, 34:45–39:56; vol. 3, 25:01–28:34). In one eight-month period, Buffalo Bill Cody killed 4,862 buffalo himself. The hides were sold to tanneries back east, and the corpses were left rotting (vol. 2, 39:42–39:56). This differing in philosophies led to more massacres, on both sides, between 1867 to 1869. The worst was perpetrated by George Armstrong Custer at the Battle of the Washataw. There, Custer's men slaughtered 800 ponies and killed 103 Native Americans (only 11 were warriors, the rest were women and children) (vol. 2, 1:04:28–1:08:34). Interestingly enough, east coast newspapers, throughout the "Indian Wars," disapproved of the brutal actions of the U.S. Cavalry and regarded the West as barbaric (vol. 3, 5:25–7:17). By contrast, Hollywood films define the savageness of the West in terms of the presence of the red man, but in historical actuality, western lawlessness stemmed from the actions of an unfettered military. Volume three, "The War of the Black Hills," covers the hubristic arrogance of General Custer and his crushing defeat at the Battle of Little Big Horn. In 1873, a wide depression had settlers demanding that the government open up lands reserved for Indians, the Lakota Sioux in particular. The Black Hills were rich with gold, and the whites wanted it. Lakota Sioux Chief Sitting Bull didn't want to give up any more land to the whites, and following an eighteen-hour dance, he had a vision of soldiers falling upside down. "These soldiers do not possess ears," a voice told him (vol. 3, 51:46–53:24), and rallying his warriors and teaming up with other tribes, Sitting Bull was ready with over 1,500 men. On June 25, 1876, Custer rode into battle, extremely confident that once the Indians heard his bugles, they would scatter and run scared, but he had no idea of their numbers. Quickly, Custer's 7th Cavalry was placed on the defensive, and he tried to retreat to higher ground, Last Stand Hill. But as he and his men reached the top of the hill, they were met by a mass of Indians, led by Crazy Horse. In all, 225 Cavalrymen were killed (vol. 3, 1:09:29–1:17:41). This massacre left a profound mark on the American psyche, and in its aftermath, the U.S. military and government were committed fully to unethical policies. All reservations were placed under military watch, and the U.S. Cavalry wanted revenge, and got it, at Wounded Knee. Volume four, "Ghost Dance", concludes with this massacre of December 29, 1890, in which 250 Lakotas were murdered— 146 of them buried in mass graves (56:51–1:09:14). Prior to this atrocity, two great Native American leaders were assassinated by government machinations: Crazy Horse was killed while being promised a place to settle (10: 01–16:00), and Sitting Bull was killed in a botched, unjustified arrest (47: 22–49:52). What led to these murders and the atrocity of Wounded Knee was a failure of whites to understand Lakota peoples. The government, in the 1880s, tried to include the Lakotas in the body politic by converting them to Christianity. But the Sioux had desired their own religion. The Sioux's need to redefine, to rediscover the past led to a religion of the "Ghost Dance," a tribal ritual that promised to bring back the dead and a Native world that existed before the onslaught of whites and industrialization. As thousands of natives "ghost danced," the military became hysterical and feared an uprising. This fear, combined with unrestrained white hatred, created the context for the tragedy of Wounded Knee, a tragedy that still haunts relations between the two races today.

Further Reading

Brown, Dee. *Bury My Heart at Wounded Knee: An Indian History of the American West*. New York: Henry Holt, 1991.

Smith, Sherry L. *The View from Officer's Row: Army Perceptions of Western Indians*. Tucson: University of Arizona Press, 1991.

Stansberry, Rhonda. "*Way West* to Debut in Lincoln." *Omaha World Herald* (April 28, 1995): 35SF.

Utley, Robert M. *Frontier Regulars: The United States Army and the Indian, 1866–1891*. Lincoln: University of Nebraska Press, 1984.

DOUBLE BILL: COLD WAR ANXIETIES ON THE RANGE

High Noon (1952)

Setting: American West, 1870s/1880s?

Director: Fred Zinnemann

Screenplay: Carl Foreman

Director of Photography: Floyd Crosby

Cast: Gary Cooper (Will Kane), Grace Kelly (Amy Kane), Ian MacDonald (Frank Miller), Sheb Wooley (Ben Miller), and Howland Chamberlain (Hotel Clerk)

Availability: Columbia Tri-Star Home Video

Johnny Guitar (1954) (W)

Setting: American West, 1870s/1880s?

Director: Nicholas Ray

Screenplay: Philip Yordan

Director of Photography: Harry Stradling

Cast: Joan Crawford (Vienna), Sterling Hayden (Johnny Guitar), Mercedes Mc-Cambridge (Emma Small), Scott Brady (Dancin' Kid), Ward Bond (John McIvers), and Ben Cooper (Turkey)

Availability: Republic Pictures Home Video

The western has always been a filmic world of allegory. Stories set in the past allow writers to displace current concerns onto a mythic landscape. In *High Noon*, Fred Zinnemann tells a misanthropic tale of a town that has lost its nerve and will not stand up to evil. As three outlaws converge on the edge of town, the locals refuse to help outgoing sheriff Will Kane. Kane, the film's laconic hero, is rebuffed first by his Quaker wife, then saloon goers, and finally members of a church. The church members feel that if Kane leaves, the problem will follow. Their gutless reaction is an allegory for communism. If, according to the filmmakers, communism goes unchecked, like falling dominoes it will take over and destroy a community. There are strong hints of this attitude in the film. When outlaw Ben Miller appears at a saloon, several of the townies greet him with kind words and look forward to a "hot time in the old town tonight" (34:43–35:19). A concierge at a hotel tells Kane's estranged wife that he doesn't like her husband: "It was always busy when Frank Miller was around." These outlaws appeal to the town's baser elements, but if unheeded, they will destroy the town. Kane, no longer a part of the town but indebted to his own sense of self-worth, stays on and tackles the gang. In the end, with the help of his wife, he saves a town that has become dead inside. In a gesture of disgust, he drops his tin star in the dust and rides away. *Johnny Guitar* is an allegorical film about the House Un-American Activities Committee (HUAC), the fear of communists, and the drive to destroy nonconformists. Vienna is disliked by the community because she runs a gambling saloon, wears pants and boots, and totes a gun. Even Sam, her croupier, comments on her difference from the norm: "Never seen a woman who was more a man. She thinks like one, acts like one, and sometimes makes me feel like I'm not" (5:54–6:02). Johnny Guitar, her former lover, is also a nonconformist. He carries a guitar instead of a gun, and during an intense rivalry between Vienna's gang and the wicked Emma, he absurdly steps between the groups and says, "There's nothing like a good smoke and a cup of coffee" (16:54). But the town, led by Emma and McIvers, lacks emotion and integrity and dislikes Vienna's style of living. She must be destroyed. And in their desire to destroy her, they force Turkey, a member of a gang of robbers, to falsely testify that Vienna was involved. "It was Vienna's idea, wasn't it? Tell us. Don't be afraid, we'll protect you," Emma promises him, decked in Salem-trial blacks and whites (1:17:01–1:18:46). But once he falsely names Vienna as the ringleader, he is lynched anyway. The film's theme of testifying, the desire to name names, clearly echoes the McCarthy witch hunts of the 1950s. And in a strange case of film echoing life, Sterling Hayden, in 1951, faced a dilemma similar to Turkey's. In order to save his livelihood, Hayden gave in to the mob-like demands of HUAC and named names. Playing Johnny Guitar must have been cathartic for the actor. Johnny's gun-crazy obsession and desire to leave the past behind (by taking up the guitar) may have resonated with Hayden's own need to find peace from his tortured conscience. Unable to accept who he is, Johnny/Hayden forges a new identity. By film's end, following his rescue of Vienna from a lynching and having reclaimed her love, he accepts his former self. The Dancing Kid exclaims, "Are you Johnny Logan?" Johnny/Hayden, no longer hiding behind a "front," acknowledges, "That's the name, friend" (1:36:08).

Further Reading

Drummond, Phillip. *High Noon*. London: BFI, 1997.
Peterson, Jennifer. "The Competing Tunes of *Johnny Guitar*: Liberalism, Sexuality, Masquerade." *Cinema Journal* 35 (Spring 1996): 3–18.
Robertson, Pamela. "Camping Under Western Stars: Joan Crawford in *Johnny Guitar*." *Journal of Film and Video* 47 (Spring/Fall 1995): 33–49.
Spoto, Donald. "Harry Cohn Steals a Masterpiece: *High Noon*, 1952." *Stanley Kramer, Film Maker*. New York: Putnam, 1978. 98–108.

DOUBLE BILL: VARIATIONS ON THE WYATT EARP LEGEND

My Darling Clementine (1946)

Setting: Tombstone, Arizona, 1882

Director: John Ford

Screenplay: Samuel G. Engle, Sam Hellman, Stuart N. Lake, and Winston Miller

Director of Photography: Joe MacDonald

Cast: Henry Fonda (Wyatt Earp), Linda Darnell (Chihuahua), Victor Mature (Doc Holliday), Walter Brennan (Old Man Clanton), Tim Holt (Virgil Earp), and Ward Bond (Morgan Earp)

Availability: 20th Century Fox Home Video

Tombstone (1993) (R)

Setting: Tombstone, Arizona, 1881–1882

Director: George P. Cosmatos

Screenplay: Kevin Jarre

Director of Photography: William A. Fraker

Cast: Kurt Russell (Wyatt Earp), Val Kilmer (Doc Holliday), Sam Elliot (Virgil Earp), Bill Paxton (Morgan Earp), Powers Boothe (Curly Bill), and Michael Biehn (Johnny Ringo)

Availability: Hollywood Pictures/Cinergi Home Video

On October 26, 1881, a feud pitting the Earp brothers (Wyatt, Virgil, and Morgan) and Doc Holliday against Ike Clanton's gang was resolved in a nasty gunfight at the O.K. Corral. Three of the Clanton gang were killed, but Ike and another member escaped. In March 1882, Morgan was killed by an unknown assassin. To avenge Morgan's murder, Wyatt and some friends killed two suspects. Wyatt, in turn, was accused of murder and fled, moving to Colorado and then on to California. John Ford's *My Darling Clementine* and George Cosmatos's *Tombstone* present strong variations on history. *Clementine* is a brooding film noir; *Tombstone* is a buddy-buddy film. In Ford's film, Wyatt Earp is a kind of Hamlet figure. First his brother James is killed, and even though all clues point to the Clantons, Wyatt fails to act. Instead of being a typical revenge western, this film seems to owe more to a post–World War Two mood of despair, alienation, and inaction. Following James' death, Earp bumps into his brother's killers in a hotel lobby (12:46–14:08). As Henry Fonda exits the frame, he says his name, "Earp. Wyatt Earp." Pa Clanton, standing at the lobby desk and looking grizzled and nasty, is suddenly taken aback, his leer straightened with fear. Ford then cuts to Fonda in the hard rain, walking down rain-splattered planks. With his back to the camera, Fonda's walk is slow and determined, his hat a strong icon of justice, but an intense mood of alienation and determination deferred resonate. That deferred determination leads to the unnecessary deaths of Chihuahua and Wyatt's brother, Virgil. Following these deaths, Wyatt is forced to act, and the film takes us to the classic showdown at the O.K. Corral (1:27:31–1:38:01). Cosmatos' *Tombstone* comes closer to accurately detailing the shootout at the O.K. Corral. But what happens in the shootout's aftermath is all Hollywood invention. Following his victory at the O.K. Corral (1:11:02–1:15:08), Wyatt witnesses the death of his brother Morgan and the maiming of his older brother, Virgil. Supposedly defeated, Wyatt leaves Tombstone to catch a train. But at the station, he kills Stillwell, and then in an intense closeup, his eyes squinting down the barrel of a shotgun, he wages war atop the train platform. "I see a red sash, I kill the man wearing it. . . . You tell them I'm coming and hell's coming with me" (1:32:54–1:34:17)—and it does. A montage of violence celebrates Earp's apocalyptic crew crashing their horses through a barber shop window, shooting a bunch of cowboys and hanging others (1:34:27–1:38:08). In a glorious moment of twisted angelic and messianic glee, Wyatt, trapped in a crossfire, boldly wades through a stream, bullets zipping by, and defiantly kills Curly Bill, the leader of the red-sashed cowboys (a kind of corporate mafia) (1:37:35). But what makes this film doubly interesting is how it expands on Howard Hawks' *Rio Bravo* and the friendship between men. Doc Holliday had always backed up Wyatt. Prior to the showdown at the O.K. Corral, he was deeply hurt when Wyatt told him that this wasn't his fight: "That is a helluva thing for you to say to me" (1:10:07–1:10:14). He had also protected Wyatt from Ringo, a deadly gun, at the Oriental Club (37:02–40:02) and later on the streets of Tombstone (1:19:33). But when Ringo challenges Wyatt to a showdown in order to avenge Curly Bill's death, Wyatt is bound by the western mythos to honor the request. In the quiet before the showdown, Wyatt and Doc have a gentle conversation that expresses their love (1:45:39–1:48:13). In words that echo his own troubled life, Holliday explains Ringo's evil: "A man like Ringo has a great empty hole right in the middle of him . . . for being born." Wyatt nods and then bluntly fears, "I can't beat him, can I?" "No," Doc admits. The two men don't overtly say how they feel, but they use the occasion of the showdown convention to express their sympathy and understanding for each other. After Wyatt departs for his probable death, Ringo waits by the assigned tree and watches a solitary figure in black lope toward him, hat down. "I'm your huckleberry," Holliday says, throwing back his cloak and lifting his chin, a teasing edge in his voice (1:49:33). He arrives before Wyatt does, and his actions illuminate larger themes of male love, friendship, and sacrifice.

Further Reading

Holden, Stephen. Review of *Tombstone*. *New York Times* (December 24, 1993): C6.
Luhr, William. "Reception, Representation, and the OK Corral: Shifting Images of

Wyatt Earp." *Authority and Transgression in Literature and Film,* ed. Bonnie Braendlin and Hans Braendlin. Gainesville: University of Florida Press, 1996. 23–44.

Marcus, J. S. "Who Was Wyatt Earp?" *American Heritage* 49 (December 1998): 76–78+.

Simmon, Scott. "Concerning the Weary Legs of Wyatt Earp: The Classic Western According to Shakespeare." *Literature/Film Quarterly* 24 (1996): 114–127.

DOUBLE BILL: JOHN WAYNE AND THE LAND

Stagecoach (1939)

Setting: American West, 1870s

Director: John Ford

Screenplay: Dudley Nichols

Director of Photography: Bert Glennon

Cast: John Wayne (Ringo Kid), Claire Trevor (Dallas), John Carradine (Mr. Hatfield), Thomas Mitchell (Doc Josiah Boone), Louise Platt (Lucy Mallory), and Berton Churchill (Gatewood)

Availability: Warner Bros. Home Video

Red River (1948)

Setting: Texas, 1850; Texas, Kansas, 1866

Director: Howard Hawks

Screenplay: Borden Chase and Charles Schnee

Director of Photography: Russell Harlan

Cast: John Wayne (Tom Dunson), Montgomery Clift (Matt Garth), and Walter Brennan (Groot)

Availability: MGM Home Video

American westerns are often interested in Manifest Destiny and the white man's relationship to the land. In John Ford's *Stagecoach* and Howard Hawks' *Red River*, John Wayne's personas create divergent aspects of this myth. In *Stagecoach,* Wayne's Ringo Kid is comfortable in the land. When he first appears in a stunning tracking shot, the Kid stands against the landscape, a saddle drooping in his left hand, a Winchester twirling in his right (18:25–18:33). He's a rough, self-reliant character, but because his horse gave out, he has to briefly abandon his quest to avenge the murders of his brother and father. He says with laconic calm, "saw a ranch house burning last night" (19:08–19:12), a subtle way of acknowledging that Geronimo is on the war path, and then decides to stay with the stagecoach to help them safely ride to Lordsburg. The members of the stagecoach represent a microcosm of society: a merchant, a banker, a southern gent, a southern belle, and drunken doctor, and a prostitute named Dallas. The latter two have been sent out of town by a Ladies Temperance Society. Ringo feels comfortable with Dallas and the Doc because he too is an outcast (he has escaped from prison). During a dinner scene, Ford showcases Dallas and Ringo's alienation from the others (27:44–31:05). They sit together at the end of the table while Ford's cutaway shots emphasize how the banker, Mrs. Mallory, and Hatfield disapprove of having to sit in their presence. Later, after Ringo watches Dallas hold Mrs. Mallory's newborn, he falls in love with her (48:02–49:16). Outside, along a wooden fence, Ringo invites Dallas to join him in paradise: "[I] got a ranch house across the border . . . trees, grass, water. There's a cabin there. A man could live there with a woman. Will you go?" (51:04–53:23). After Ringo kills the Plummer boys, he and Dallas return to an Eden, away from "civilization." In Hawks' *Red River*, hard-boiled Tom Dunson can't return to Eden so he tries to tame a land that he regards as hostile. First, he seizes the land from Mexicans, killing to keep it (15:50–18:10), then he tries to impose his will upon it through his massive and dangerous cattle drive across the Chisholm Trail. During the drive Dunson becomes bitterly paranoid, surly, and tyrannical. When Matt Garth (his adopted son, played with sensitivity by the slender-shouldered Montgomery Clift) suggests that men break for water, Dunson rancorously refuses: "I'll do the thinking. Keep them going" (45:40–46:17). Later, when a cowboy sneaks sugar from the wagon train pantry and causes a stampede, Dunson grabs a whip. The cowboy, refusing to be treated like an animal, nervously backs up and trying to preserve his dignity reaches for a gun. Before Tom can draw, Matt intervenes, shooting the cowboy in the shoulder, knocking him down. Matt, gaining distance from Tom's darkness, says, "You'd a shot him right between the eyes." "As sure as you're standing there," Dunson coldly replies as the rest of the cattlemen look on with growing displeasure (56:45–58:17). *Red River* is a tale of generational conflict: younger men are more fit to rule than their fathers. Matthew Garth is one of filmdom's first quiet rebels, a nonconformist who refuses to follow the father's law and instead is guided by a more just law. Eventually he takes over the cattle drive after Dunson, a sickened Ahab figure, decides to hang two men for deserting the cattle drive. Matt, who had previously desired his father's approval (the larger narrative arc is for Matt to add the letter "M" to his father's Red River "D" brand), has to rebel. "No, no you're not," he says, his voice full of calm trembling as he stops the hanging. Matt takes over the herd and decides not to take the men and cattle to Missouri (a dangerous land fraught with carpetbaggers and warring Indians), but instead heads on to Abilene (a wiser choice, and an option that Dunson refused to consider). Groot, a member of the older generation, represents Hawks' voice of reason: "You was wrong, Mr. Dunson."

Further Reading

Browne, Nick. "The Rhetoric of the Specular Text with Reference to *Stagecoach*." *Theories of Authorship*, ed. John Caughie. London: BFI, 1981. 251–260.

Buscombe, Edward. *Stagecoach*. London: BFI, 1992.

Mast, Gerald. "The Genre Epic: *Red River*." *Howard Hawks, Storyteller*. New York: Oxford University Press, 1982. 297–346.

Sklar, Robert. "Empire to the West: *Red River*." *American History/American Film: Interpreting the Hollywood Image*, ed. John E. O'Connor and Martin A. Jackson. New York: Continuum, 1988. 167–181.

FURTHER VIEWING

Dead Man (1996) (R)

Forty Guns (1957) (W)

High Plains Drifter (1972) (R)

The Long Riders (1980) (R)

The Man from Laramie (1955)

Man of the West (1958)

The Man Who Shot Liberty Valance (1962)

The Shootist (1976) (PG)

The Story of Elizabeth Cady Stanton and Susan B. Anthony (Doc.)

True Grit (1969)

4

The Country versus the City: The Agrarian and Industrial Conflict, 1870–1940

Citizen Kane ◆ *Elmer Gantry* ◆ *The Great Gatsby* ◆ *Meet Me in St. Louis* ◆ *New York: A Film Documentary* ◆ *Reds* ◆ *Rosewood* *Sherlock, Jr.* ◆ Double Bill: *Clarence Darrow* and *Inherit the Wind* Double Bill: *Eight Men Out* and *Matewan* ◆ Double Bill: *Our Town* and *Shadow of a Doubt*

Citizen Kane (1941)

Setting: Colorado, New York, California, 1871–1941

Director: Orson Welles

Screenplay: Herman J. Mankiewicz and Orson Welles

Director of Photography: Gregg Toland

Cast: Orson Welles (Charles Foster Kane), Joseph Cotten (Jedediah Leland), Dorothy Comingore (Susan Alexander), Everett Sloane (Bernstein), Agnes Moorehead (Mrs. Mary Kane), and George Coulouris (Walter Parks Thatcher)

Availability: MGM/Turner

When newspaper publisher Charles Foster Kane dies alone in Xanadu, he clutches in his hand a glass ball with a snow-drenched wood cabin inside. As snow falls inside the glass ball, and seemingly inside the room, he blurts "Rosebud." The snowfall resonates his yearnings. He longs for the love of his second wife, Susan Alexander (the glass ball is hers: it is first seen in her apartment, by a dressing mirror [58:13–58:37]). He also desires to return to his mother and the pastoral world of Colorado. As a young boy, Kane was yanked from the countryside. His mother, having fallen into fortune (earning the deed of the supposedly worthless Colorado Silver Lode from a defaulting boarder), decides to free her son from her abusive husband. She wants Charles to have all the advantages of the rich, so she sends him to New York, with robber baron Walter Parks Thatcher. But Thatcher is a cold, unfeeling man and gives the boy no love. The scene in which Mrs. Kane signs young Charlie over to Thatcher is heart-wrenching (17:22–22: 34). Welles, with the help of cinematographer Gregg Toland, uses a deep-focus composition: Mom and Thatcher in the foreground discuss the boy's New York opportunities. Dad, in the middle area, protests weakly, and Charlie in the vanishing point of the composition, the tip of the triangle, plays outside in the snow, framed by the window. Oblivious of what's being decided on his behalf, he shouts "the Union forever." Of course, his union with the land and his mother is about to be broken and that tension makes the scene powerful. In New York, Charles tries to find a purpose. He becomes a crusader, using his newspaper to tackle corruption on Wall Street and in government. But his promised greatness is destroyed by his own desire to control the world, to make people love him. In a telling scene with Jed Leland and Walter Bernstein (told from Bernstein's perspective), Kane puts forward his "Declaration of Principles" (37:12–39:21). "I want to make the *New York Inquirer* as important to New Yorkers as the gas in this light," he vows, but as he states his ideals, he shuts off the light, casting his own face in ambiguous shadows. A double failure occurs: first, Bernstein's idealized narrative of Kane can't be trusted (Toland's contrary compositions undercut the narrator's admiration); second, Kane's ideals will never be achieved in the city. As he strives for success in politics and love, Kane forces his will upon others. He even attempts in vain to make the talentless Susan into a grand opera singer (1:25:02–1:33:13). But he fails in all of these endeavors and eventually leaves the city for Xanadu, a mock-pastoral paradise in California. There, alone, in his pleasure dome, Kane longs for a childhood that he can no longer find.

Further Reading

Carringer, Robert L. *The Making of Citizen Kane*. Berkeley: University of California Press, 1985, 1996.

"*Citizen Kane* Remembered." *Action!* 4.3 (May/June 1969): 26–35.

Ferguson, Otis. Review of *Citizen Kane*. *The New Republic* 104 (June 2, 1941): 760–761.

Hartung, Philip T. Review of Citizen Kane. *The Commonweal* 34 (May 9, 1941): 65.

Slocombe, Douglas. "The Work of Gregg Toland." *Sequence* 8 (Summer 1949): 69–76.

Elmer Gantry (1960)

Setting: the Midwest, 1927
Director: Richard Brooks
Screenplay: Richard Brooks

Director of Photography: John Alton

Cast: Burt Lancaster (Elmer Gantry), Jean Simmons (Sister Sharon Falconer), Arthur Kennedy (Jim Lefferts), and Ed Andrews (George Babbitt)

Availability: MGM/UA Home Video

From 1870 to the 1920s revivalism expanded in the Midwest. As theological liberalism grew in influence (and Darwin's *On the Origin of Species* became popularized), industrialization changed America's economy from agrarian-based to a series of small corporate markets, and the influx of Eastern European immigrants (largely Jewish and Catholic) upset Protestant visions for America, hell became a place to consign one's enemies. Perdition was the fate of liberals, Darwinists, socialist labor leaders, and beer drinkers. In short, revivalism sought to buttress Victorian values in an era of social and intellectual turbulence. Richard Brooks' *Elmer Gantry* examines this dark side of a movement fuelled by fear and based on intolerance. Gantry, played marvelously by the bombastically acrobatic Burt Lancaster, taps into the fears of many Midwesterners who felt their way of life was losing its dominant control over the direction of East Coast (largely New York City) America. In his sermons, Gantry challenges Darwin's theory of evolution (28:01–29:21; 56:21–57:37), he rails against industrial changes such as the automobile that have brought about a sexual revolution (1:14:58–1:15:10), he makes anti-immigrant statements on radio, stating that "dirty" French postcards were "sold to me by a man with a black beard—a foreigner!" (1:34:41), and he despises intellectualism (1:35:12). Moreover, the corporate sponsors of the revival show in Zenith, led by George Babbitt, desire to maintain a Protestant outlook on their town's values. Babbitt worries that there is a lost generation out there and a Catholic (Alfred Smith) running for president. But despite Brooks' indictment of revivalism, he makes his film interesting by having the circus showman Gantry and the traveling show's main speaker, Sharon Falconer, really believe in their work. Gantry can be somewhat crude, vulgar, and hypocritical but he reveals flashes of sincerity. He tells reporter Lefferts that he truly believes in the Lord (2:08:18), and when he preaches he undergoes a transformation to a higher self, preaching the beauty of a divine love over a carnal love (3:44–5:57; 36:15–40:28). Similarly Falconer, a product of the shanty towns who changed her name from the lowly Katy Jones, sincerely feels that she is doing God's work. But whereas Gantry is transformed only during his sermonizing, Falconer exists in a constant state of transformation. "I am Sharon Falconer, now," she states boldly (1:32:15). She wants to save souls, raise a tabernacle, and open a soup kitchen for the needy. But she is not ordained, and Lefferts asks, "how did you get [God's] approval?" (1:22:02–1:22:52). In one troubling scene, Falconer seems to go too far, grasping at becoming a Christ-figure as she obsessively tries to heal a deaf man (2:15:12–2:18:20). She succeeds, but shortly thereafter her tabernacle is set aflame by a parishioner's haphazardly discarded cigarette. As the fires burn, it seems that hell and damnation may strike Falconer and Gantry for overstepping their human limits and trying too hard for Godliness.

Further Reading

Butler, Jonathan M. *Softly and Tenderly Jesus Is Calling: Heaven and Hell in American Revivalism, 1870–1920*. Brooklyn: Carlson, 1991.
Moorhead, James H. Review of *Softly and Tenderly Jesus Is Calling*. *Church History* 62 (June 1993): 292–293.
Review of *Elmer Gantry*. *Time* 76 (July 18, 1960): 76.
Weiler, A. H. "Screen: A Living, Action-Packed *Elmer Gantry*." *New York Times* (July 8, 1960): 16.

The Great Gatsby (1974) (PG)

Setting: Long Island and New York City, 1925

Director: Jack Clayton

Screenplay: Francis Ford Coppola

Director of Photography: Douglas Slocombe

Cast: Robert Redford (Jay Gatsby), Sam Waterson (Nick Carraway), Mia Farrow (Daisy Buchanan), Bruce Dern (Tom Buchanan), Karen Black (Myrtle Wilson), and Scott Wilson (George Wilson)

Availability: Paramount Home Video

F. Scott Fitzgerald's dashing novel of the jazz age was made into a somewhat ponderous film, but Robert Redford captures the charming menace of the title figure. The film explores a 1920s definition of success: an entrepreneur achieving economic wealth by taking advantage of the opportunities offered by the Industrial Age. Gatsby is a somewhat mysterious figure who represents a new kind of American aristocracy, one based not on birth or inherited wealth but on industrial enterprise comprised of self-confidence, initiative, and determination. Party-goers assume that Gatsby may have killed a man, or is connected to the government in some way (27:53–33:31). Gatsby is nothing but a "big bootlegger" (1:15:52), claims the brutal Tom Buchanan, a polo-playing racist and a man lacking in all principles—he cheats on his wife and later sets up Gatsby's murder. But Gatsby is really just a poor kid from the Midwest who, in pursuit of America's success myth, makes himself over from Jimmy Gatz to the handsome Jay Gatsby. But entrepreneurial success in Fitzgerald's novel has a price. As a child Gatsby embodied traditional values of frugality, hard work, and piety. He kept a schedule of Ben Franklin–like resolves: "Practice elocution, poise, and how to attain it" (2:16:42–2:17:52), but his entrepreneurial transformation embraces the dark side. Gatsby gets mixed up with gamblers (Meyer Wolfsheim, Gatsby's close friend, helped fix the 1919 World Series) and does some shady business. Moreover, Gatsby's desires for success are driven by a romantic idealism that is now outmoded in the jaded, thrill-seeking hedonism of the 1920s. Gatsby's dream yearns for a return to the past, an antiquated notion in a time of economic prosperity and technological progress. He tells Nick Carraway that "of course you can" repeat the past (1:18:40). Eight years ago he loved Daisy Buchanan, but she jilted him because he wasn't rich. Now a success, Gatsby wants to rekindle a prewar love with Daisy and have her admit that she never loved her husband, Tom, and that she only loves him. He ultimately fails in this adolescent dream. This fantasy is told through the eyes of Carraway, a peripheral, observing narrator who says little and judges few, but whose dispassionate looks and penetrating eyes understand all. Nick finds the rich world of Gatsby completely fascinating, from the extravagant "Charleston"-jiggling parties to the rough undercurrent in Gatsby's polished "Old Sport" sheen. Nick is pleased by Gatsby's charm. When Nick tells Gatsby that some people think that he killed a man, Gatsby disarmingly grins and says, "Just one," and Nick nods with approval (1:33:33). Finally, Carraway rejects the world of the Buchanans, but we've rejected it well before he has. When we watch Wilson, the mechanic, agonize first over his wife's affair, and then her savage hit-and-run death, the lives of the rich and privileged just don't seem very interesting at all.

Further Reading

Cawelti, John. *Apostles of the Self-Made Man.* Chicago: University of Chicago Press, 1965.
Fitzgerald, F. Scott. *The Great Gatsby.* New York: Scribners', 1925.
"Ready or Not, Here Comes *Gatsby.*" *Time* 103 (March 18, 1974): 82–91.
Simon, John. Review of *Great Gatsby. Esquire* 82 (July 1974): 144, 146.

Meet Me in St. Louis (1944) (W)

Setting: St. Louis, 1903–1904

Director: Vincente Minnelli

Screenplay: Irving Brecher and Fred F. Finklehoffe

Director of Photography: George Folsey

Cast: Judy Garland (Esther Smith), Margaret O'Brien (Tootie Smith), Mary Astor (Mrs. Anna Smith), Lucille Bremer (Rose Smith), Leon Ames (Mr. Alonzo Smith), and Tom Drake (John Truett)

Availability: Warner Bros. Home Video

Made in 1944, during the last days of the European campaign of World War II, *Meet Me in St. Louis* is a nostalgic look back at an all-American family, the Smiths, living in a supposedly simpler, preindustrial time. In the 1940s, women had swelled the work ranks for the war effort. But in preparation for the soldiers' return home, *Meet Me in St. Louis* attempts to reinscribe traditional gender roles and make Rosie the Riveter desire to become a homemaker. After all, the women are all powerful in this film. At home, Mr. Smith, a lawyer, has no control. Often, during heated family discussions, he's photographed separately from his wife and daughters, Rose and Esther (16:20–16:33; 17:02–18:13; 20:03–23:47). And when he upsets the family by telling them they will have to move to New York City with him and miss the St. Louis World Fair of 1904, his distance is further registered by director Vincente Minnelli (1:07:22–1:12:52). In medium closeup, Mr. Smith tells them of his news, and the family—Grampa and the two younger girls, Mrs. Smith, and the older daughters, Rose and Es—are photographed in separate shots (1:09:09). Home and domesticity is how the women of 5135 Kensington Avenue in St. Louis define themselves. In fact, when Esther attempts to break free of those strictures she is thwarted. In the enchanting turning-out-the-gas-lights scene (36:08–43:35), Esther attempts to break convention and make the neighborhood boy, John Truett, kiss her. But John deliberately plays the scene in a clumsy fashion to derail her attempts at romance. (According to the film's philosophy, the boy is supposed to make the first move.) As Esther cozies up, he tells her that her perfume smells exactly "like the kind my grandmother uses" (40:02). Eventually, a scene that started with Esther acting on her desires winds up with Esther standing on top of the stairs, singing, placing herself as an object for his erotic gaze. Esther's repressed desires are further championed in comical ways in the lively "Trolley Song" in which she sings about customs and manners (42:36–48:32). She belts out the tune with robust glee, but when Johnny arrives and sits next to her, she suddenly realizes that he's heard the last few bars of the tune. She is abashed for revealing her emotions too directly. The only females that seem to have freedom in terms of their self-definitions are the young girls, Agnes and Tootie. During a Halloween sequence, they cross-dress as boys and set chairs on top of a bonfire. Tootie roams up the street and "kills" Mr. Bracoff (i.e., throws flour in his face) (53:37–57:56). But their rebellion against gender codes seems temporary, a kind of child-like experimentation. Moreover, their experimentation is couched with abnormality: Tootie and Agnes are always obsessing over death. But the dark side of the younger daughters helps Mr. Smith make the right decision. On Christmas Eve, a distraught and hysterical Tootie runs outside in the cold and bashes in the heads of her snow family. She can't take them with her to St. Louis so she decides to kill them. Mr. Smith, watching from the upstairs window, is moved to a powerful epiphany, one that affirms family over career. The Smiths don't have to step forward into the industrial progress of New York. Instead, they can stay in their own backyards, a world that, with the coming of the Louisiana Purchase Exposition, rests on the cusp of change.

Further Reading

Bordwell, David and Kristin Thompson. "Form, Style, and Ideology: *Meet Me in St. Louis*." *Film Art* (Fifth Edition). New York: McGraw-Hill, 1997. 420–425.

Crowther, Bosley. Review of *Meet Me in St. Louis*. *New York Times* (November 29, 1944): 20.

Farber, Manny. Review of *Meet Me in St. Louis*. *New Republic* 111 (December 18, 1944): 837.

New York: A Film Documentary 5 vols. (1999) (Doc.)

Setting: New York City, 1609–1933

Director: Ric Burns

Co-directors: Lisa Ades and Li-Shin Yu

Writers: Ric Burns, James Sanders, and Ronald Blumer

Photography: Buddy Squires and Allen Moore

Narrator: David Ogden Stiers

Editors: Li-Shin Yu, Edward Barteski, David Hanser, and Nina Schulman

Availability: PBS Home Video

This five-part PBS documentary does more than just celebrate the greatest city in the world, it also explores the city's relationship to the countryside, and how it forged a new identity for the nation. New York City begins in 1609 as a Dutch mercantile colony (vol. 1, 12:01–25:26), and then becomes a British colony in 1664 (25:26–27:36). During the Revolutionary War it was captured by the English and transformed into a British garrison (57: 15). But before the war, and after, the city was shaped by the vision of two men: Alexander Hamilton and DeWitt Clinton. Hamilton envisioned the city as being in flux, a place where one could rise to prominence and power (46:08–48:57). After the war, New York had been devastated by the English. Hamilton, as President George Washington's Secretary of the Treasury, wanted the government to rebuild the city and to reimburse those who had lost property fighting for the Republic. Hamilton's chief rival, Thomas Jefferson, then Secretary of State, saw the nation's future in agrarian democracy. Hamilton, by contrast, believed that the city truly made you free and that the future was in commerce, labor, and immigrant toil (1:00:33–1:07:03). At the time, the Continental Congress had set up a temporary capitol in New York City. Jefferson feared the capitol becoming a permanent fixture, and thereby establishing the city as the future of America. He agreed to reimburse Hamilton's homeless, in exchange for Hamilton's promise to move the capitol to Washington, DC, which was at the time a swamp along the Potomac. Thus, very early in America's history there was a battle of

ideology between North and South, country and city, commercial manu-
facturing and farming (1:10:30). Hamilton's promise changed the destiny
of New York. No longer tied down by the notions of being a capitol city,
New York was able to pursue a purely capitalist endeavor, and within a few
short years, the Stock Exchange opened on Wall Street in 1792. The second
great visionary for New York's future was ten-term Mayor DeWitt Clinton
who in 1811 literally transformed the countryside of New York and forced
nature into his architectural designs. Under Clinton, Manhattan city plan-
ners drew up a grid that designed the future: 12 avenues, 155 streets, and
2,000 blocks across 11,000 acres. The plan sought to establish the foun-
dation for a giant metropolis of more than 1 million people. Clinton also
brought the country to the city by building a 363-mile ditch—the Erie
Canal (1:34:17–1:43:18). The canal, completed in 1825, made New York
the world's ideal harbor and port of call for goods going into the hinterland
and out to Europe. Volume two, "Order and Disorder," highlights the first
great migration to America and how the Irish suffered (26:20–36:01). From
1845 to 1855 one-eighth of the Irish nation arrived in New York. They
took unskilled jobs, experienced anti-Catholic virulence, and feared being
lower in social status than African Americans. This troubling insecurity lead
to the deadly Draft Day riots of July 1863, when the New York Irish re-
volted over conscription to a war that would free blacks. For three days New
York City burned. Nineteen African Americans were lynched, and 119 ri-
oters were killed by the militia (vol. 2, 1:18:50–1:42:52). The Irish revolt
raised the serious question of whether or not the city would represent a
thriving mix of cultures or be a segregated landscape. In order for the city
to be a multiethnic and a racially united polyglot, urban planner Frederic
Law Olmsted began to build Central Park in 1857–1858. The 840-acre
park sought to capture nature and show New Yorkers that they didn't need
to go out to the country—the country could be brought to the city (2:04–9:
37). Volume three, "Sunshine and Shadow," showcases New York during
the Industrial Age. The Brooklyn Bridge unites the five burroughs, and its
promenade allows New Yorkers to cross it and see and experience the grandeur of the city (57:52–1:09:30). Industrialist J. P. Morgan, after the re-
cession of 1873, masterminded a rebirth in the American economy, one
based on managed competition (51:32–55:02). But perhaps the greatest
question of the age is raised by Jacob Riis' *How the Other Half Lives*. The
1890 publication presents a series of haunting images of children working
in sweatshops, the deplorable conditions of tenement housing, and the hard
life on the Lower East Side. Slums are not inevitable, Riis insists. Men and
women could change these conditions (1:22:04–1:31:30). Riis demands
that New Yorkers combine the accumulation of private profits with a com-
mensurate social justice (1:32:53). Volume four, "The Power and the People," explores the vast migration of peoples from Eastern and Southern
Europe, and the continued need for social justice. In 1909 the daughters

of immigrants protested the heinous conditions in New York's sweatshops: 225,000 men, women, and children in the the garment industry worked eleven-hour days, six-day weeks, locked in small, crowded rooms. Shopkeepers fired employees who talked or demanded to go to the bathroom (1:08:41–1:12:47). A group of teenage women braved the cold to stand on the picket lines and demand their rights. This was one of the first general strikes in the history of organized labor. Unfortunately, the 40,000 workers (due to the cold and dwindling resources) were unable to win their protest (1:13:39–1:18:52). But through eventual tragedy, they did win. In 1911 the Triangle Waist Company, a miserable sweatshop, erupted in tongues of flame (1:19:59–1:34:41). Since the doors were locked from the outside (supposedly to keep union organizers out), 200 women were trapped on the tenth floor. As the fire engulfed them, several young women leaped to their deaths. In all, 146 people died, 141 of them young women. New Yorkers were outraged. Many of the dead were the same women who had picketed two years before. The time was now ripe for reform led by thirty-eight-year old Alfred Smith. Smith was a Tammany Hall protégé, but rather than support big business (as Tammany had so often done), Smith investigated several factories. He found fire escapes blocked and children hidden by management in elevators (1:37:20–1:43:50). The city took a dramatic turn toward social welfare, as Smith and his team handed down their decision. New laws were put in place (no child under fourteen could work in the factories at all), and the factories had to provide washrooms, adequate lighting, fire protection, higher wages, and a maximum fifty-four-hour work week. Smith became a popular hero of immigrants, and in 1918 the Irish-Catholic leader became governor of New York. His success was predicated upon his "us against them" mentality: the children of immigrants versus the status quo. That very support base was also to be his downfall, ten years later, when he ran for the presidency. Volume five, "Cosmopolis," looks at the birth of Harlem and the Jazz Age (12:28–45:04), the wondrous construction of the Empire State Building (erected in just thirteen months) (1:20:40–1:47:10), and Smith's doomed presidential campaign (46:25–1:00:46). The 1928 election became a dark period in American political history and signified a referendum on New York by the countryside. People in the South and Midwest found Smith's Roman Catholic religion and big city style alienating. He represented the city, which was seen as a foreign place made up of Anarchists, Jews, Italians, and other "non-Nativists" opposed to Prohibition. The people in the country didn't like the direction the city was taking, and Smith was hounded with bigotry at his speeches. The Ku Klux Klan placed burning crosses along his campaign trail, and several articles claimed that if Smith were elected, the Pope would reside in the White House. Under such hostility, Smith lost in a landslide to Republican Herbert Hoover. But in a harbinger of things to come, Smith did carry the twelve largest cities, and in just a few short years, the politics and power of the city—Smith's social welfare programs of 1911 were really the birth of the New Deal—would eventually reach the countryside and transform it under the Roosevelt administration of 1932–1945.

Further Reading

Bender, Thomas. *New York Intellect: A History of Intellectual Life in New York City from 1750 to the Beginnings of Our Time.* New York: Knopf, 1987.
Burrows, Edwin G. and Mike Wallace. *Gotham: A History of New York City to 1898.* New York: Oxford University Press, 1999.
Lebowitz, Fran. *Metropolitan Life.* New York: Dutton, 1978.
Mermelstein, David. Review of *New York: A Documentary Film. Variety* 377 (November 15, 1999): 37.

Reds (1981) (PG) (W)

Setting: Portland, Oregon, 1915; New York City, 1916; the Northeast, 1917; Russia, 1917–1920

Director: Warren Beatty

Screenplay: Warren Beatty and Trevor Griffiths

Director of Photography: Vittorio Storaro

Cast: Warren Beatty (John Reed), Diane Keaton (Louise Bryant), Jack Nicholson (Eugene O'Neill), and Maureen Stapleton (Emma Goldman)

Availability: Paramount Home Video

Reds is an evocative and ambitious film. Director Warren Beatty weaves together the documentary accounts of witnesses (those who lived during the turbulent teens), a love story between John Reed and Louise Bryant, and an accurate rendering of how the communist movement in both the United States and Russia reflected the city versus country dialectic. *Reds* is not an indictment of communism but an even-handed assessment of the movement. The first half of the film also explores a woman's quest for identity. Louise Bryant desires to escape the bourgeois trappings of her marriage to a West Coast dentist. She poses nude for paintings, runs with a Bohemian crowd, and pursues being a writer: she has had some pieces published in San Francisco's anarchist journal, *The Blast.* She meets John Reed, a writer for the leftist-leaning *Masses,* and admires his idealism. Reed strongly believes that there is nothing noble about war. If the United States is to enter World War One it is only for profits, to help defend the money of J. P. Morgan, who has invested a lot in France and England and would go bankrupt if those world powers lost to Germany (8:36; 10:10–10:53). Bryant falls in love with Reed's ideas, abandons her marriage, and travels with him to New York's Greenwich Village. But she still seeks her own identity. Prior to leaving, she wonders if she'll be perceived as his mistress, his paramour, and his concubine (17:37–18:24)? In New York and later in the lyrical retreat of Cuton, she feels immersed in his shadow and is jealous of his fame.

Reed and his friends, anarchist Emma Goldman and playwright Eugene O'Neill, discuss the working class struggles and the pressures on America to get into a world war. While Reed is in Boston, organizing workers to join the Industrial Workers of the World (IWW), Bryant indulges in free love with O'Neill (50:05–51:12). Upon Reed's return, he refuses to question her about it, and instead asks her to marry him. The marriage goes well, for a time, until Reed suspects that she's rekindled her romance with O'Neill (1:08:25–1:14:42). Angry, and wanting to hurt her, Reed says (perhaps falsely?) that he has had several affairs during his marriage. "What do you want, a list? It doesn't mean anything" (1:11:57–1:12:41). Furious, Bryant leaves to pursue her own writing career in France. The second half of the film explores their romantic rekindling in Russia. The country has had a revolution, and Reed suggests that Bryant join him and go where the real stories are (1:23:20–1:23:40). She does, but on her terms, as "Miss Bryant," not "Mrs. Reed." They sleep in separate beds, but the excitement of the revolution reunites them. They revise each other's news stories, offering equally strong constructive criticism (1:30:27–1:32:52). After Reed speaks passionately at a workers' meeting, Bryant falls in love with him again (1:39:02–1:39:15). They return to the United States as husband and wife, but when the stateside labor party splits into two socialist camps, Reed travels to Russia to get his branch of the American Communist Labor Party sanctioned by the Comintern. While working in Russia, Reed becomes slightly disillusioned with the movement. He is not allowed to go home when he wants to. His objections to the Comintern's efforts to radicalize the American Federation of Labor aren't listened to (2:42:20–2:42:47). A word in his speech is changed from "class war" to "Holy war" (2:55:08–2:55:20). Emma Goldman, who was deported by U.S. Attorney General A. Mitchell Palmer and his Red Scare brigade, tells Reed that this wasn't the dream. "If Bolshevism means peasants taking land, workers taking factories, Russia has no Bolshevism" (2:44:44–2:47:17). All of the power is held in the hands of the few. Reed, steeped too far into his beliefs, can't let them go. He tells Goldman: "It's just the beginning E.G. . . . It's happening. . . . If you walk out on it now, what's your whole life been?" *Reds* is an enthralling historical drama, capturing the politics of the 1910s, and presenting the American labor movement and commited socialists in a positive light. Moreover, the love story between activist Reed and "New Woman" Bryant—portrayed by Diane Keaton with an interesting mix of vulnerability, sexual opportunism, and intelligence—is compelling, especially in today's era of dual-career couples.

Further Reading

Crist, Judith. "Beatty's Ambitious Try." *Saturday Review* 9 (January 1982): 52–53.
Gardiner, Virginia. *"Friend and Lover": The Life of Louise Bryant.* New York: Horizon, 1982.

Rosenstone, Robert A. *Romantic Revolutionary: A Biography of John Reed.* New York: Knopf, 1975.

———. *"Reds* as History." *Why Docudrama? Fact/Fiction on Film and TV*, ed. Alan Rosenthal. Carbondale: Southern Illinois Press, 1999. 296–310.

Stansell, Christine. *"Reds." Past Imperfect: History According to the Movies*, ed. Mark C. Carnes. New York: Henry Holt, 1996. 192–195.

Rosewood (1997) (R) (M)

Setting: Rosewood, Florida, 1922–1923

Director: John Singleton

Screenplay: Gregory Poirier

Director of Photography: Johnny E. Jensen

Cast: Jon Voight (John Wright), Ving Rhames (Mann), Don Cheadle (Sylvester Taylor), Bruce McGill (Duke), Esther Rolle (Sarah Carrier), and Michael Rooker (Sheriff Walker)

Availability: Warner Bros. Home Video

This hard-hitting film is a western set in the 1920s. Director John Singleton delves once again into the issues of racism by looking at a forgotten and ghastly moment in American history when a group of rednecks deliberately destroyed a small, prosperous all-black town in Florida in 1923. The whites are envious of the blacks' success, and once a married white woman (who was having an affair with a white man) screams that she was raped by a black man (37:23–38:06), the lower-based elements of the nearby town of Sumner have their excuse and invade Rosewood. In a four-day siege, they burn churches and homes and lynch several men, women, and children. As the town burns, John Wright, a well-meaning white businessman who has made his living off of selling goods to black folks, straddles the fence between the two communities. Secretly, he helps the blacks, while appearing to Sheriff Walker and his gang as being on their side. Behind the scenes, Wright works with Mann (a kind of black Clint Eastwood figure) to hide the women and children in the woods and then set them free by helping them catch a train to Gainesville (2:05:53–2:13:23). The transformation of the West's mythic train from harbinger of civilization and western expansion to escape from a twisted civilization of gun-toting whites is a shockingly strong revision of a classic icon. Mann, a fictional invention of Singleton's and played by Ving Rhames in a soft-spoken but strong manner, is another western revision. Mann, a World War One veteran and a stranger to the town, just wants peace and a home in a postwar world, but once blacks are under siege, he becomes an Eastwood-like avenging angel of death, sporting two revolvers and protecting children from a lynch-minded white man. The third ingredient in this revisionist western is Michael Rooker, a decent-minded but weak and ineffectual white sheriff. Like Wright, he, too, tries to be fair to the blacks while also being conscious of his own place in white society. Ultimately, however, his nondecisions and inaction bring about a series of tragedies (from the death of the well-beloved Sarah to the burning of Rosewood). Although the state of Florida in 1993 granted reparations to the Rosewood families, the legislature listed the official death toll of the Rosewood Massacre at eight (six blacks and two whites). But those survivors who were interviewed by Singleton placed the number of African American dead at a disturbingly much higher number: 40 to a possible 150.

Further Reading

Dye, Thomas R. "Rosewood, Florida: The Destruction of an African American Community." *The Historian* 58 (Spring 1996): 605–622.
Guerrero, Ed. Review of *Rosewood*. *Cineaste* 23 (Winter 1997): 45–47.
McCarthy, Todd. Review of *Rosewood*. *Variety* 366 (February 17, 1997): 68.
"*Rosewood*: Tells Story of How White Mob Destroyed a Black Town in 1923." *Jet* 91 (March 24, 1997): 56–59.

Sherlock, Jr. (1924)

Setting: Midtown USA, 1924

Director: Buster Keaton

Screenplay: Clyde Bruckman, Jean C. Havez, and Joseph A. Mitchell

Directors of Photography: Elgin Lessly and Byron Houck

Cast: Buster Keaton (the boy/Sherlock, Jr.), Kathryn McGuire (the girl), Joe Keaton (her father), Ward Crane (the sheik/villain)

Availability: Kino Video

In the 1920s various cultural gatekeepers (clergy, sociologists, reformers, and politicians) feared that a second industrial revolution had taken hold in America and stripped people of their individuality. With the advent of radio, the boom of the automobile industry, and the mass marketing through advertising of consumer goods (vacuum cleaners, washers and dryers, kitchen appliances) gatekeepers assumed that the masses were being manipulated by immoral media producers. Films, the most popular of all media, also came under attack for shaping ideas and attitudes. In 1924, comic genius Buster Keaton, contrary to these concerns, celebrated the joy of the mechanical medium. A product of a mechanistic age, Keaton saw cinema as a place for grand spectacle, a kind of series of attractions that transcended an emphasis on story for a string of stunning sight gags. Keaton, in a series of audacious stunts, runs atop of a moving railroad car (13:56–15:40), rides a runaway motorcycle with his rear perched upon the handlebars (35:53–39:10), and as a movie fan, tries to jump into the film screen. First he's rejected and then he's accepted into the fictional realm, but the backgrounds keep unexpectedly changing, sending Keaton into a series of perilous predicaments

(18:40–21:48). In terms of the story, Keaton plays a projectionist who fantasizes about being a detective. He proposes to his girl, but when her father discovers that his watch is stolen, Keaton is falsely accused of the crime. Banished from the home, he returns to the theater, helpless. His girl investigates, and discovers from the pawnshop owner that it was her second suitor, and not Keaton, who had stolen the watch (16:27). The plot now is ostensibly over. The next two-thirds of the film delays the inevitable— Keaton's reconciliation with his girlfriend. In the interim, Keaton takes us on a series of spectacles, a dream-like fantasy in which he imagines himself as the world's greatest detective, Sherlock, Jr. In one brilliant sequence that toys with ranges of knowledge (what viewers know versus what characters know), Sherlock, Jr. plays a game of deadly pool (22:20–29:26). The story's villains have replaced the 13 ball with an explosive one. Sherlock, supposedly oblivious to the danger, performs a series of dangerous trick shots around ball 13, never once tapping it. And when he does finally sink it, it doesn't explode. Later alone outside, Sherlock, Jr. holds the explosive ball in his hand. He knew about the fiendish plot all the time and made a switch. Thus what had started out as a scene in which viewers knew more than the hero did (the setup to kill him) ends with the hero having known more than the audience all along. This narrative inventiveness shows Keaton's admiration for what is possible on film. Not only does he play with cinema's conventions, Keaton also celebrates the power of cinema in molding identity. In the story, the lonely hero loses himself in the film-within-a-film, becoming a second self, Sherlock, Jr., who transcends and conquers his own limitations. Also, when all is righted and Keaton is restored to his rightful place as his girl's ideal suitor, the film ends with him once again turning to the screen for advice on courtship: how to hold hands, how to kiss. But when Keaton stands with his girl in the projection booth and watches the movie stars kiss, and the scene fades, and then the male lead holds two babies on his lap, Keaton is left quizzically scratching his head. Not all experiences can be lived vicariously.

Further Reading

Karlyn, Kathleen Rowe. "The Detective and the Fool: Or, the Mystery of Manhood in *Sherlock, Jr.*" *Buster Keaton's Sherlock, Jr.*, ed. Andrew Horton. Cambridge, England: Cambridge University Press, 1997. 140–157.

Knopf, Robert. "Keaton Re-viewed: Beyond Keaton's Classicism." *The Theater and Cinema of Buster Keaton*. Princeton, NJ: Princeton University Press, 1999. 96–111.

"A Lively Comedy." Review of *Sherlock, Jr. The New York Times* (May 26, 1924): 21.

Pearson, David B. "Playing Detective: Possible Solutions to the Production Mysteries of Sherlock, Jr." *Buster Keaton's Sherlock, Jr.*, ed. Andrew Horton. Cambridge, England: Cambridge University Press, 1997. 140–157.

DOUBLE BILL: CLARENCE DARROW: A MAN OF INTEGRITY AND INTELLECT

Clarence Darrow (1974) (TV)

Setting: 1886–1926, United States

Director: John Rich

Screenplay: David W. Rintels

Scenery and Lighting: H. R. Poindexter

Cast: Henry Fonda (Clarence Darrow)

Availability: Kino Home Video

Inherit the Wind (1960)

Setting: Hillsboro, Tennessee, 1925

Director: Stanley Kramer

Screenplay: Nathan E. Douglas and Harold Jacob Smith

Director of Photography: Ernest Laszlo

Cast: Spencer Tracy (Henry Drummond), Frederic March (Matthew Harrison Brady), Gene Kelly (E. K. Hornbeck), Dick York (Bertram Cates), Donna Anderson (Rachel Brown), Claude Akins (Reverend Jeremiah Brown), and Florence Eldrige (Mrs. Sarah Brady)

Availability: MGM/UA Home Video

For nearly fifty years defense attorney Clarence Darrow, a native of Ohio, helped shape the conscience of a nation. He defended labor leaders against unjust laws, thrill-killers Leopold and Loeb from receiving the death penalty, and John T. Scopes in the famed monkey trial. Darrow, as portrayed by Henry Fonda in his one-man show, is a man of integrity who believes in representing the downtrodden and fighting for the freedom to think and change the world. In 1894, labor leader Eugene Debs was charged with "conspiracy to commit murder" after seven Pullman strikers were killed in a riot by armed troops. Darrow defended Debs because he believed that a government "of the people is better than railroad's ownership of government" (17:45). At the trial Darrow further argued that the conspiracy charge was a "Tyrant's effort to punish the crime of thought" (19:11). From 1894 to 1911 Darrow represented labor. He was appalled by the conditions of the Pennsylvania coal mines, where children worked life-threatening twelve-hour shifts, and he diligently worked to change their environment. "A laborer who asks for shorter hours asks for a better life," Darrow said (27:42). In 1910, Darrow defended another labor leader, "Big" Bill Haywood of the IWW, from a false murder rap and won (29:01–35:58). In 1925, during the Scopes trial, Darrow fought for the right to teach evolution in the Tennessee town of Dayton. Once teaching from Darwin's *On the Origins of Species* in schools is declared a crime, then the banning of many books and newspapers won't be too far behind, he reasoned with passion (1:01:44–1:05:22). But perhaps Darrow's greatest moment, and least known, was his defense in 1925–1926 of Dr. Sweet for murder (1:06:11–1:12:10). Dr. Sweet, an African American, had bought a home in a white neighborhood of Detroit. The community, in Klan-like gestures, tormented Sweet and ten other African Americans inside the house. "Get the niggers!" the mob shouted. Shots were fired, and when one white man was killed, all eleven blacks were tried for murder. Darrow, hired by the National Association for the Advancement of Colored People (NAACP), defended Sweet with dignity. Darrow challenged the jury to transcend their prejudices, to help aid social progress, and to acquit the group. After forty-six hours, the prejudices of some jury members could not be overcome and the trial was stalemated. But at a second trial, Darrow won. Stanley Kramer's socially relevant *Inherit the Wind*, adapted from the play by Jerome Lawrence and Robert E. Lee, looks back at the famed Monkey Trial in which Darrow defended Scopes' right to teach evolution, and William Jennings Bryan, the famed populist and two-time presidential nominee, argued for creationism and the expulsion of Darwin from the schools. In light of recent school board book bannings and Kansas' 1999 decision to remove evolution from its optional teaching and examination standards, Kramer's film, and the Scopes trial, still pack a real punch. In Kramer's film, the names of the central players are changed (Scopes/Cates, Darrow/Drummond, Bryan/Brady; Gene Kelly is also present as an H. L. Mencken-type of cynical, acid-tongued reporter), but the story line is faithful to history. Cates is arrested for teaching against the prescribed law that favors the book of Genesis. Drummond defends his right to think and to promote thinking in his classroom. In the film's stirring scene, Drummond examines prosecuting attorney Matthew Brady on the witness stand, challenging his literal interpretation of the Bible (1:29:27–1:45:56). How could the sun have literally stood still for Joshua? If it had, the continents would have toppled into each other and the earth would have imploded. If God only created Adam and Eve, and then they "begat" Cain and Abel where did Mrs. Cain come from? If God created light on the fourth day, how do we know that the first day was twenty-four hours long? Don't we need light to tell time? Could the first day have been maybe twenty-five hours long, a week, a year, ten million years? Drummond doesn't attempt to dismiss the Bible, but to find spaces between a fundamentalist's either/or oppositions. A theory of evolution can coexist within a theory of creationism. Of course, Brady has no middle ground in his thinking. And that eventually costs him his life (he dies of a heart attack trying to browbeat the Bible back into the departing courthouse crowd; in terms of historical reality, Bryan died five days after the Scopes trial). Drummond, on the other hand, is open, allowing his intellect to be informed by differing knowledges. He leaves the courtroom carrying both Bible and Darwin, unafraid of a variety of truths.

Further Reading

Brod, Donald F. "The Scopes Trial: A Look at Press Coverage After Forty Years." *Journalism Quarterly* 42.2 (1965): 219–226.

Fenberg, Matilda. "I Remember Clarence Darrow." *Chicago History* 2.4 (1973): 216–223.

Fleming, Thomas J. "Take the Hatred Away and You Have Nothing Left." *American Heritage* 20.1 (1968): 74–80, 104–105.

Hartung, Philip T. "That Old Time Religion." Review of *Inherit the Wind*. *Commonweal* 73 (November 4, 1960): 151.

Kauffmann, Stanley. "O Come, All Ye Faithful." Review of *Inherit the Wind*. *The New Republic* 143 (October 31, 1960): 29–30.

Lawrence, Jerome and Robert E. Lee. *Inherit the Wind*. New York: Random House, 1955.

DOUBLE BILL: DIRECTOR JOHN SAYLES FOREGROUNDS THE LABOR STRUGGLE, ON AND OFF THE FIELD

Eight Men Out (1988) (PG)

Setting: Chicago, New York, 1919–1920

Director: John Sayles

Screenplay: John Sayles

Director of Photography: Robert Richardson

Cast: John Cusack (Buck Weaver), John Mahoney (Kid Gleason), James Read ("Lefty" Williams), Michael Rooker (Chick Gandil), Charlie Sheen (Hap Felsch), David Strathairn (Eddie Cicotte), D. B. Sweeney ("Shoeless" Joe Jackson), and Clifton James (Charles Comiskey)

Availability: Orion Home Video

Matewan (1987) (PG-13) (M)

Setting: Matewan, West Virginia, 1920–1921

Director: John Sayles

Screenplay: John Sayles

Director of Photography: Haskell Wexler

Cast: Chris Cooper (Joe Kenehan), James Earl Jones ("Few Clothes" Johnson), Mary McDonnell (Elma Radnor), Will Oldham (Danny Radnor), and David Strathairn (Sid Hatfield)

Availability: Evergreen Entertainment

John Sayles is a small independent director who makes hard-hitting political films that are free of the backing of major studios and their compromising influences. In the Reagan/Bush era, a time when the federal government was unfriendly towards organized unions, Sayles' *Eight Men Out* and *Matewan* championed workers' rights. In *Eight Men Out*, Sayles brilliantly weaves a complex tale about the Black Sox scandal of 1919. Eight Chicago White Sox players, because they are grossly underpaid by owner Charlie Comiskey, decide to throw the World Series for a bigger payday. Sayles presents each man in differing shades of humanity. First baseman Chick Gandil has a screw loose and seems to like the idea of the fix just to see if it can be done. Right-handed pitcher Eddie Cicotte is angry that Comiskey won't give him a $10,000 bonus. He won twenty-nine games that year, and he would have won thirty (which is what he needed to reach the bonus) if Comiskey hadn't insisted that manager Kid Gleason "rest" the star player for five starts in mid-August. Country boy and free swinging outfielder Joe Jackson goes along with the fix because he wants to be loyal to his friends. And third baseman Buck Weaver, opposed to the fix, plays like a dynamo in the World Series, hoping that his love of baseball and the purity of the game will eventually win over his teammates and make them recommit. All of these elements darken the usually mythical and nostalgic turns that baseball films take. Sayles sets up the dark mood in an opening that follows four lines of action (4:13–13:23). While the White Sox are playing, Sayles highlights on-field turmoil. In the stands are the kids who admire and follow the ball players. Also in the stands are the dark forces, the gamblers, plotting how to fix the World Series and ruin America's national pastime. Away from the field, in the offices of Comiskey, the owner talks to the media about his "horses." For him, the players are animals, commodities that he owns. He treats the press better than his own players, offering the media fine champagne and expensive catered foods. By contrast, he gives the pennant-winning players flat champagne and reneges on his promised "pennant" bonuses. If the players were treated fairly, they probably wouldn't have been tempted to throw the Series. Kid Gleason, on the witness stand, defends them, saying that he would never be bought, but "maybe if a guy feel's he underpaid . . . people are human" (1:46:38–1:47:49). Sayles complicates these dark figures of baseball lore, but he does not exonerate them. If anything, as the film unfolds and Buck Weaver fails to make them play fair, it's ponderously painful to watch them deliberately lose, and to let down the entire city. By the summer of 1920, all eight were banished from baseball for life by Judge Kennesaw Mountain Landis. A tough measure for players, but one that failed to address the owners' unfair labor practices. *Matewan*, set in 1920–1921, is a stunning film about union organizing. The film's hero, Joe Kenehan, a fictional construct by Sayles to hammer home his approach to unionizing, is a martyr who teaches the miners to form a brotherhood of workers. First, the white miners beat up the black and Italian scabs brought in by the coal company (5:57–8:33). But with Kenehan's help, the three sides come together to see a commonality in all people working under one union (21:39–24:30). He encourages the scabs to walk out, to strike with the workers, and they do, reaching a kind of interracial cooperation. Moreover, Kenehan, who had a stay in Kansas' Leavenworth prison for protesting the U.S. involvement in World War One, learned the gospel of nonviolent protest from the Mennonites. He watched them get tortured for refusing to wear buttoned clothes and pants, but he learned from their silent strength a force greater than guns and fists (1:31:57–1:34:04). He tries to teach the merits of nonviolence in combating justice to the people of Matewan, but when two miners are killed by company gun thugs, and the operators send in agents to evict everyone (all of the property is owned by the Stone Mountain Coal Company), Sheriff Sid Hatfield and the community fight back and a massacre erupts. Seven company men are killed, and Kenehan is an accidental victim of stray gunfire. His martyred body lies on the train tracks, his message of social justice unheeded. Sadly, the film's violent apotheosis (although cathartically pleasing) was really just the horrid beginning of a series of real-life, tragic events to follow: Hatfield would be assassinated by gun thugs, and the Great Coalfield war would erupt in 1921 when 10,000 miners clashed with company agents. With the miners gaining the advantage, President Warren Harding declared West Virginia under martial law, setting back the cause of reform in the state for years. Not until the 1930s would a union be ratified in Matewan.

Further Reading

Asinof, Eliot. *Eight Men Out*. New York: Holt, Rinehart, and Winston, 1963.

Corbin, David A. *Life, Work, and Rebellion in the Coal Fields: The Southern West Virginia Miners, 1880–1922*. Urbana: University of Illinois Press, 1981.

Margaronis, Maria. Review of *Matewan*. *The Nation* 245 (October 17, 1987): 427–428.

O'Brien, Tom. Review of *Eight Men Out*. *Commonweal* 115 (October 7, 1988): 529–530.

Sayles, John. *Thinking in Pictures: The Making of the Movie Matewan*. New York: Houghton Mifflin, 1987.

DOUBLE BILL: REPRESENTATIONS OF A SMALL TOWN

Our Town (1940) (W)

Setting: Grover's Corner, New Hampshire, 1901, 1904, and 1913

Director: Sam Wood

Screenplay: Harry Chandlee, Frank Craven, and Thornton Wilder

Director of Photography: Bert Glennon

Cast: William Holden (George Gibbs), Martha Scott (Emily Webb), Fay Bainter (Mrs. Gibbs), Beulah Bondi (Mrs. Webb), Thomas Mitchell (Dr. Gibbs), Frank Craven (Mr. Morgan, the narrator), and Philip Wood (Simon Stimson)

Availability: FOCUSfilm Entertainment

Shadow of a Doubt (1943) (W)

Setting: Philadelphia and Santa Rosa, California, 1942

Director: Alfred Hitchcock

Screenplay: Thornton Wilder, Sally Benson, and Alma Reville

Director of Photography: Joseph Valentine

Cast: Teresa Wright (Young Charlie Newton), Joseph Cotten (Charlie Oakley), and Macdonald Carey (Jack Graham)

Availability: MCA/Universal Home Video

Sam Wood's *Our Town,* adapted from Thornton Wilder's play (which in turn is really a kind of poem to America's hinterland), celebrates the quiet closeness of a small community. The Albany train rides past the town every morning at 5:45 A.M. The milk man walks freely into the homes of Mrs. Webb and Mrs. Gibbs delivering milk (nobody is afraid of burglaries because there just aren't any). A young couple, George and Emily, fall in love as children, their houses and bedrooms just windows apart. Their love blooms in high school and they eventually marry. One of the film's warmest scenes displays the young lovers' coming to terms with their mutual attraction over sodas at the drugstore (50:56–1:01:19). When George asks Emily to be his girl, she responds with a boisterous, "I am now. I always have been" (1:00:07). But this slice of Americana has some dark underpinnings. The drunken church organist, Simon Stimson, is depressed and nobody can help. The townspeople keep their distance, letting him solve matters his own way, which he does, hanging himself in an attic in 1910 (1:11:56). Emily almost dies during childbirth in 1913 and learns a valuable lesson: we need to "look at each other" and "love life to have life" (1:25:33–1:28:22). But not everyone is looked at or talked to in this film. The town of 2,200 is 86 percent Republican, 85 percent Protestant, and largely composed of English ancestry. The foreign-born Poles, alluded to occasionally by our folky narrator, are relegated to "Polish Town" and are never seen. Alfred Hitchcock's *Shadow of a Doubt,* also co-scripted by Wilder, brings the darkness of the city (symbolized by a train spitting thick black smoke) to the country (17:01–17:44). Philadelphia's the "Merry Widow Murderer," Uncle Charlie, intrudes upon Santa Clara, and Wilder's peaceful community is now exposed as blindly ignorant. Unaware of any lurking evil, the small town blithely carries on, reading murder mysteries and planning guest lectures. Only young Charlie (the killer's double figure), a former high school debate champion, can penetrate this evil. A series of clues make her ascertain Uncle Charlie's guilt. First she is puzzled by how his confident swagger had started as a shuffling limp from the train: "Why Uncle Charlie, you're not sick. That was the funniest thing" (17:01–18:59). Then when he gives her an emerald ring (taken from one of his victims), she notices that it's engraved with someone else's initials (25:26–25:56). Later at the bank, she is appalled at his gauche behavior and how he embarrasses her father (a banker) by discussing embezzlement and tossing it all off with a casual "the whole world's a joke to me" (40:48). Young Charlie acts upon her knowledge. At the library, she finds an article that implicates her uncle (58:24–1:02:14). She also discovers that the initials on the ring match those of one of the murder victims. Upon her return home, she finds Charlie coldly discussing widows, labeling them "silly wives" and "useless women" who are "smelling of money . . . fat greedy women." She interjects and says they're human, and he responds with a cold, "Are they?" (1:08:18–1:09:04). Of course, Charlie eventually learns that she knows the truth, and he tries to kill her. He doesn't succeed, but the film ends with a harsh comment against small towns and the instability of the American family. Charlie died (after a botched murder attempt), and at his funeral the preacher sermonizes on all the good he's done and how the community has "gained and lost a son." Young Charlie, unable to stand the ignorance, stands outside of the church, apart from the town. Next to her leans a federal agent, Graham, who was also working on the case. Despondently Charlie flatly states, "I couldn't face it without somebody who knew."

Further Reading

Farber, Manny. "Hitchcock in Stride." Review of *Shadow of a Doubt. The New Republic* 108 (February 8, 1943): 182.

Ferguson, Otis. "Hollywood Town." Review of *Our Town. The New Republic* 102 (June 17, 1940): 824.

Hartung, Philip T. "Your Town and My Town." Review of *Our Town. The Commonweal* 32 (June 7, 1940): 160.

Rothman, William. *"Shadow of a Doubt." Hitchcock: The Murderous Gaze.* Cambridge: Harvard University Press, 1982. 173–244.

FURTHER VIEWING

America 1900 (1999) (Doc.)

Butch Cassidy and the Sundance Kid (1968) (PG)

Days of Heaven (1978) (PG)

Great Gatsby (2001) (TV)

Greed (1924)

East of Eden (1955)

Influenza 1918 (1998) (Doc.)
Inherit the Wind (1999) (PG)
Magnificent Ambersons (1942)
Miracle Worker (1962) (W)
Music Man (1962)
My Antonia (1994) (PG-13)(W)
Road to Wellville (1994) (R)
Singin' in the Rain (1952)
Some Like It Hot (1959)
Titanic (1997) (PG-13) (W)
Wild Bunch (1969) (R)
Wizard of Oz (1939) (W)

5

Immigration and the Challenge to Anglo–Conformity, 1885–1961

Angels with Dirty Faces ◆ *Baseball* ◆ *Eat a Bowl of Tea* ◆ *Ellis Island*
Hester Street ◆ *The Irish in America: From the Emerald Isle to the*
Promised Land ◆ *Mayor of Hell* ◆ *The Rat Pack* ◆ *A Tree Grows in*
Brooklyn ◆ Double Bill: *The Godfather* and *The Godfather II*

Angels with Dirty Faces (1938) (M)

Setting: New York City, 1920s and 1938

Director: Michael Curtiz

Screenplay: John Wexley and Warren Duff

Director of Photography: Sol Polito

Cast: James Cagney (Rocky Sullivan), Pat O'Brien (Father Jerry Connelly), Humphrey Bogart (James Frazier), George Bancroft (Mac Keefer)

Availability: MGM/UA Home Video

This romantic gangster film concerns the battle of two father figures for the wills, allegiances, and souls of a group of Lower East Side juvenile delinquents, the Dead End Kids. Energetic bad boy Rocky Sullivan, played by James Cagney, returns after a prison stretch to his old neighborhood, and the Kids admire and look up to him. They help him hide stolen money, learn to never rob anyone in their own neighborhood, and decide that the quickest way to make it in America is, as Father Jerry Connelly sadly says, with a "racket or a gun." Father Connelly, the parish priest and a boyhood pal of Rocky's, wants to get the kids off the streets and under the socializing influence of the church. But he can't do it by himself, and in the end he'll need the help of the outlaw hero, Sullivan, to assimilate the boys into the American dream. Contextually, the film captures some of the issues in James Cagney's star image. In the early 1930s, educators and sociologists were concerned that stars like James Cagney and Edward G. Robinson falsely Americanized the children of immigrants to the American dream. One pop sociologist, Henry James Forman, believed that by watching gangster films, second-generation immigrants adopted criminal behaviors. According to Forman, Cagney was a hero to these kids. In a way *Angels* addresses those concerns by shifting the boys' belief systems from Rocky to the priest in the film's final moments. Yet *Angels* also affirms the gangster as hero. After saving the priest from the guns of Mac Keefer and Jim Frazier, Sullivan is on death row. Back home in New York, the boys look forward to Rocky dying "in a big way." The priest visits Rocky and asks him, as a favor, to act the coward. Rocky doesn't want to give away his reputation, but the priest pleads, "I want you to let them down. See, you've been a hero to these kids and hundreds of others all throughout your life. . . . They've gotta despise your memory" (1:30:00). Sullivan/Cagney refuses to deconstruct his star image, but in the final moments Rocky does scream for his life. Cagney's acting prior to and during the death scene is very ambiguous and could be read as either a performance or an actual meltdown in bravado (1:25:25–1:33:35). He tries to act cool, but nervously taps a cigarette and with anguish attacks a sadistic prison guard (1:27:05–1:27:20). Afterwards, the priest returns to the downcast boys and answers their questions: "It's true boys. Every word of it. He died like they said" (1:35:38). The semantics of the priest's language is also ambiguous. That he died "like they said," like a yellow rat, doesn't mean he actually was a rat, but that he could have been playacting one. Disconsolate, the boys follow the father up the cellar steps and head back to the church, the gym, and the legal way to the American dream. Connelly has won the battle of two fathers, and yet for the immigrant boys in the movie theater, if Rocky Sullivan play-acted the coward, then he is the film's true hero, reaching sainthood through death.

Further Reading

Forman, Henry James. *Our Movie Made Children*. New York: Macmillan, 1933.

Keyser, Les and Barbara Keyser. "Crime Movie: Immigration, Gangsters and Guns." *Hollywood and the Catholic Church: The Image of Roman Catholicism in American Movies*. Chicago: Loyola University Press, 1984. 41–76.

Naremore, James. "James Cagney in *Angels with Dirty Faces* (1938)." *Acting in the Cinema*. Berkeley: University of California Press, 1988. 157–173.

Ray, Robert B. *A Certain Tendency of the Hollywood Cinema, 1930–1980*. Princeton, NJ: Princeton University Press, 1985.

Baseball 9 vols. (1994) (Doc.) (M)

Setting: America, 1846 to the present

Director: Ken Burns

Writers: Ken Burns and Geoffrey C. Ward

Directors of Photography: Ken Burns, Allen Moore, and Buddy Squires

Narrator: John Chancellor

Editors: Paul Barnes, Rikk Desgres, Yaffa Lerea, Michael Levine, and Tricia Reidy

Availability: PBS Home Video

Ken Burns' nine-volume, eighteen-and-a-half-hour tribute to the national pastime celebrates America's inclusivity and how baseball promoted a vision of diversity. The stars of the game represent America's melting pot and foster emotional identifications across all of America's peoples. The game had its origins in England and was a favorite among Anglo-Saxon Americans until its borders were expanded by the influx of immigrants from Ireland (John McGraw [vol. 1, 1:40:35–1:44:00]) and later Italy (Joe DiMaggio [vol. 5, 1:26:44–1:29:32] and Yogi Berra [vol. 7, 24:45–28:46]). Jews, such as Hank Greenberg (vol. 5, 1:40:41–1:44:44) and Sandy Koufax (vol. 8, 29: 00–34:11), also expanded the game's appeal. Greenberg, who faced anti-Semitic abuse, earned the grudging respect of the fans and players and in 1938 said that every time he hit a homerun, "I was hitting one against Hitler" (vol. 5, 1:43:10). In 1947, seven years before the Supreme Court ruled segregation unconstitutional, baseball led the way for civil rights. Jackie Roosevelt Robinson broke the color barrier and changed the game forever. And in the 1960s, Hispanics such as Roberto Clemente further added to the game's diversity (vol. 9, 14:47–19:32). In volume three, "The Faith of Fifty Million People," Burns details how baseball was a bridge to assimilation, as factories encouraged immigrant employees to play on company teams in order to learn how to be "real Americans" (1:02:20–1:03: 07). In volume five, "Shadow Ball," Burns tells the story of segregation and how African Americans were unjustly kept out of the game. In all, black players played barnstorming games 430 times against white teams. The whites won only 129 of these interleague affairs (6:40). In volume six, "National Pastime," Burns expands the history of baseball to include women as he covers the exciting All-American Girls Professional Baseball League, which operated from 1943 to 1952 (54:20–1:00:42). In the same volume, he also tells the wonderfully inspiring story of Jackie Robinson. Robinson, part of Branch Rickey's inspired vision of integration, said on the eve of his first game with the Brooklyn Dodgers: "I'm ready to take a chance. Maybe I'm doing something for a race" (1:33:15). And he did. At first he experienced prejudice from his own teammates (1:38:10–1:41:00), and then hate letters and death threats from the fans of other teams (2:01:20). But his daring base running controlled the tempo of the game (1:56:48) and his courage and dignity earned him admirers. In a late 1940s national poll, Robinson was the second most popular man in America behind Bing Crosby (2:04:42). Jackie Robinson was social justice in action.

Further Reading

Blount, Rachel. "Burns' Series Has Hits, Errors; Filmmaker Takes a Long, Long
    Look at the National Pastime's History." *Minneapolis Star Tribune* (September 18, 1994): 8C.
Burns, Ken and Geoffrey C. Ward *Baseball: An Illustrated History.* New York: Alfred
    A. Knopf, 1994.
———. "Baseball: The Way It Was." *U.S. News and World Report* 117 (August 29/
    September 5, 1994): 54–100.
Hunter, Bob. "It's Hard to Fathom *Baseball's* Racist Past." *The Columbus Dispatch*
    (September 27, 1994): 1E.

Eat a Bowl of Tea (1989) (PG-13) (M) (W)

Setting: Chinatown, New York, 1948–1949

Director: Wayne Wang

Screenplay: Judith Rascoe

Director of Photography: Amir Mokri

Cast: Victor Wong (Wah Gay), Russell Wong (Ben Loy), Cora Miao (Mei Oi), Lau
Siu Ming (Lee Gong), and Eric Tsang Chi Wai (Ah Song)

Availability: Columbia Tristar Home Video

Wayne Wang's *Eat a Bowl of Tea* is a story of crosscultural and generational
dislocation. Set in Chinatown, New York, in 1949, the story concerns Wah
Gay's desire to have his son Ben Loy accept social responsibility and maturity
by marrying a Chinese bride, a daughter of a best friend, Lee Gong. To
achieve those ends, Wah Gay arranges a marriage for his son and sends him
to China. He hopes that the couple will have children and bring back a
degree of domestic normalcy to Chinatown's predominantly bachelor society. Wah Gay is a victim of American exclusionary laws against Chinese
Laborers that date back to 1882 when the government declared that Chinese men couldn't become American citizens, nor could their brides come
to this country. But during World War Two as Asian Americans fought and
died overseas, this was changed with the lifting of 1924's National Origins
Law, and two years later, in 1945, the War Brides Act allowed Chinese
spouses and children to come to the United States. Wah Gay's son, a World
War Two veteran, benefits from the changes. In China, the young impressionable Loy falls in love with the charming and vivacious Mei Oi (18:28–
28:17). They return to America and the proud community sets him up in
business but the marriage suffers. First Ben Loy gives up on his own plans
for a future (35:37–36:43) because of his father's desires, and later while
making love to his wife, Ben Loy stops, glances over at his father's smiling
portrait on the night table and turns it face down. "I just feel everyone's
watching us," he says exasperated (41:35–43:05). And in a way they are.
The community's desire for Loy to conform to his father's vision creates a

rift in his marriage and an eventual bout with sexual impotency. For Mei Oi too, Ben Loy's sexual dysfunction, combined with her crosscultural dislocation, creates an added pressure to their marriage. She tells her husband that she's homesick (41:07), that she wants him to admit that they have a problem (53:50–54:40), and she gets angry when he brings home a television set: "A machine is not the same thing as a husband" (57:34–59:49). Ignored by her busy husband and trapped in a world of sterile machines and American domesticity (fruitlessly she cleans the apartment [51:26]), Mei Oi has an affair with one of Ben Loy's seedy "uncles," Ah Song, a gambler. Eventually the young couple do reconcile: Ben Loy's impotence is cured by medicinal tea from China, and together they reject the demands of their fathers to seek their own futures. The couple can't restore or normalize the bachelor society of New York, but they can generate a new Chinese-American community centered around family life and children in San Francisco.

Further Reading

Chan, Sucheng. "The Exclusion of Chinese Women, 1870–1943." *Entry Denied: Exclusion and the Chinese Community in America.* Philadelphia: Temple University Press, 1990. 94–146.

Chu, Louis H. *Eat a Bowl of Tea.* 1961. Seattle: University of Washington Press, 1979.

Li, Shu-yan. "Otherness and Transformation in *Eat a Bowl of Tea* and *Crossings.*" *Melus* 18.4 (Winter 1993): 99–110.

Ling, Jingi. "Reading for Historical Specificities: Gender Negotiations in Louis Chu's *Eat a Bowl of Tea.*" *Melus* 20.1 (Spring 1995): 35–52.

Ellis Island 3 vols. (1997) (Doc.) (M)

Setting: Ellis Island, New York, 1892–present

Director: Lisa Bourgoujian

Writer: Rannveig Krokdal

Director of Photography: B. C. Callahan

Narrator: Mandy Patinkin

Editor: Stephen Pomerantz

Availability: A&E/History Channel Home Video

This three-part series beautifully captures immigration into the United States from Eastern and Southern Europe. Producer Lisa Bourgoujian and editor Stephen Pomerantz adroitly select archival footage and still photographs to capture the journey from homelands, to steerage ships, to detention centers, to exiting through the island's golden doors into America. Volume one follows a fourteen-day journey on steerage ships. These immigrants, escap-

ing their origins because of war, economic hardship, and persecution, came
to America as low-cost labor where they fueled the expanding industrial
revolution. On the ships they were classified as cargo. A thousand at a time
were crowded in steerage; they had no separate quarters (37:30–38:08). The
ocean was rough, but the resiliency of the people shined as they danced on
the ship's decks (40:51). Once they arrived at New York, they saw the Statue
of Liberty and it became a stirring emblem of new hope (42:40–44:52).
Volume two, perhaps the best in the series, details what happened once the
immigrants arrived at the island. Even though the goal was always to admit,
two out of ten immigrants would be branded with a chalk mark on their
jacket lapels (11:28–17:30), which required them to undergo further in-
spection. An "X" implied suspected mental defect; an X with a circle around
it meant definite signs of mental illness; a "C" suggested conjunctivitis; a
"T," trachoma. In just seconds a family member could be whisked from
loved ones. The medical examination, too, was humiliating. Men were asked
to take out their penises; women were asked to open their bras. The immigration administration's fixation on diseases suggested a sort of eugenics
obsession, a belief that somehow these non-Anglo Saxons were inferior to
the "nativist" norm and might bring contagion and ruin to the United
States (24:00). Furthermore, nine out of one hundred immigrants received
a mental test (26:33). Women without escorts were very vulnerable (36:30–
36:48). It was feared that they would become prostitutes, so they were often
labeled "L.P.C." (likely to become a public charge). Thus, because of society's sexism, women were detained until an escort, or sponsor, arrived (37:
30). By 1917, foreigners also had to prove that they were literate (38:52).
Volume three covers the post-1924 period when the doors to immigration
closed and new quotas were enforced (20:00–22:52). These quotas, based
on annually letting in only 3 percent of the total American population of a
specific ethnic group, suggested that all whites weren't equal and that some
—Irish, English, and German—were more equal than others. Boatloads of
people were sent back. By 1954, Ellis Island was officially closed. In 1990,
it reopened as a museum. Today, over one hundred million Americans can
trace their ancestral origins back to this historic port (37:10).

Further Reading

Kraut, Alan M. *The Huddled Masses: The Immigrant in American Society, 1880–1921.*
    Arlington Heights, IL: Harlan Davidson, 1982.
Shenton, James P., Editor. *Ethnic Groups in American Life.* New York: Arno Press,
    1978.
Yans-McLaughlin, Virginia. *Family and Community: Italian Immigrants in Buffalo:
    1880–1930.* Ithaca, NY: Cornell University Press, 1977.
———, Editor. *Immigration Reconsidered: History, Sociology, and Politics.* New York:
    Oxford University Press, 1990.

Hester Street (1974) (PG) (M) (W)

Setting: Lower East Side, New York, 1896

Director: Joan Micklin Silver

Screenplay: Joan Micklin Silver

Director of Photography: Kenneth Van Sickle

Cast: Carol Kane (Gitl), Steven Keats (Jake), Mel Howard (Bernstein), Dorrie Kavanaugh (Mamie Fein), Doris Roberts (Mrs. Kavarsky), and Paul Freedman (Joey)

Availability: First Run Features Home Video

Immigration stories usually involve generational conflicts such as parents versus children or grandparents versus grandchildren but Joan Micklin Silver's small independent film, based on a novel by Abraham Cahan, explores the conflict between an estranged husband (the Americanized Jake) and his orthodox Jewish wife (Gitl). Jake has become acculturated. He works in a sweatshop, drops his Jewish name, Yankel, in favor of a more rugged American one, follows baseball, and enjoys dance halls and cavorting with Mamie, a Jewish woman who has also lost her accent in the seven years she has lived in the United States. Jake has thrown off the old world in his desire to become a "Yankee." But following the death of his father in the old country, Jake's wife and nine-year-old son come to America. Jake, because of the gap in their rates of acculturation, can't relate to Gitl. She wears wigs and kerchiefs because according to orthodox Jewish law women aren't supposed to show their hair to gentiles, but America is an "educated land" and Jake worries that this practice makes his wife look like "a greenhorn." Gitl also struggles with the English language (she often speaks Yiddish), and this embarrasses Jake because it reminds him of the ethnicity that he is escaping. Jake relates better with his son and is a responsible father. He shows his child the Lower East Side's fruit carts and vendors (30:22–33:45) and teaches him the fundamentals of baseball (1:06:27–1:07:27). But his neglect of Gitl forces her to develop a silent resiliency, as she endures his growing distance. At first she wants to win back his love; she replaces her old world dresses with corsets and American fashions (53:17), but he remains disinterested. In a final attempt to win his approval, Gitl doffs her wig and has her hair beautifully coiffed. But when Jake returns home, he inexplicably attacks her, shouting "take it off" (1:08:22–1:09:22). She screams that it is her own hair, but his irrational violence grows from a repressed realization that no matter how she changes appearances their marriage no longer works and he cannot love her. Gitl will always be a greenhorn. At this point, Gitl too realizes their incompatibility, as she quietly tells Mrs. Kavarsky, "I don't want him back;" she's had "enough." (1:11:27–1:11:35). Ultimately, she exacts a measure of revenge and comes out ahead in the New World as she negotiates for enough money to open a grocery store with her new husband (the proudly Jewish Talmudic scholar Bernstein). This beautifully quiet film thoughtfully recreates the stresses of Americanization and how it profoundly pressured immigrant marriages.

Further Reading

Antler, Joyce. *"Hester Street." Past Imperfect: History According to the Movies*, ed. Mark C. Carnes. New York: Henry Holt and Co., Inc., 1996. 178–181.

Cahan, Abraham. *Yekl: The Imported Bridegroom and Other Stories of the New York Ghetto*. New York: Dover, 1970.

Michel, Sonya. "*Yekl* and *Hester Street*: Was Assimilation Really Good for the Jews?" *Literature-Film Quarterly* 5 (1977): 142–146.

Sorin, Gerald. *A Time for Building: The Third Migration, 1880–1920*. Baltimore: Johns Hopkins University Press, 1992.

Weinberg, Sydney Stahl. *The World of Our Mothers: The Lives of Jewish Immigrant Women*. Chapel Hill: University of North Carolina Press, 1998.

The Irish in America: From the Emerald Isle to the Promised Land 2 vols. (1996) (Doc.) (M)

Setting: Ireland and America, 1700 to the present

Director: Kevin Browne

Writer: Steve Smith

Director of Photography: John Sorapure

Narrator: Aidan Quinn

Editor: Kevin Browne

Availability: A&E/History Channel Home Video

The Irish immigrated to a WASP-dominated United States in two waves, the first arriving from Northern Ireland in the eighteenth century. The first group was comprised of people who were largely protestant, of Scot-Irish descent, and skilled workers, and they settled in the major cities. Their nickname "Fighting Irish" was not at first a stereotype but an earned badge of honor. George Washington's revolutionary army was one third Irish and contained 1,492 officers and 26 generals of Irish birth or descent. Because they had suffered under English colonialism they despised the monarchy and the British Empire. Among their most noted descendants were President Andrew Jackson (vol. 1, 15:13–26:38), who embodied the image of the common man rising from the bottom of the immigrant ladder. Following the influx of the Ulster Irish, a new group of nineteenth-century Irish immigrants hailed from the south. From 1845 to 1854, two million of these "dirt poor" Irish Catholics fled the potato famine and emigrated to America (vol. 1, 34:27). Here they experienced a host of prejudices. Protestant America feared that there would be a Catholic conspiracy to topple democracy. Convents were burned. Priests and nuns were murdered (vol. 1,

28:04–28:52). Advertisements in newspapers often ended with "No Irish Need Apply," and the Ulster group decided to distance themselves from their Catholic relations (vol. 1, 47:46). Stereotypes branded the new immigrants as lazy and profligate, and cartoon illustrations depicted them as monkeys (vol. 1, 47:46). But these hard working people helped build the railroads, the Erie Canal, and the cities where they largely settled. The second volume documents a series of immigrant success stories: the Silver Kings who hit upon the Comstock Lode in Virginia City (6:19–8:00); Mother Jones who dedicated her life to the labor movement (27:40–30:20); and John L. Sullivan, legendary boxer and ten-year holder of the heavyweight crown (31:53–34:21). In a wonderfully apocryphal and patriotic story, Smith tells about the 1908 Olympic games in England, and how it was customary to dip your nation's flag before the king. As the American flag approached, Matthew McGrath ran up to the flag bearer and told him, "Dip that flag and you're in a hospital tonight." The flag wasn't dipped and the United States set a precedent that carries through to this day (vol. 2, 38:38–39:40). Ultimately, this documentary celebrates Irish ancestral heritage (five million immigrants, forty million descendants) and accurately captures the diversity and competing alliances and struggles within white ethnicity, but the series smooths over the Irish's tension with black Americans. Volume two mentions the Draft Day riots of 1863 in which the Irish in northern cities lynched forty-three African Americans (12:19–13:49), but the series doesn't explore, as does Noel Igantiev in his fine scholarly work, how the Irish became "white" in America by positioning themselves against blacks (in economics and politics). The Irish felt the prejudices of the Anglo-conformists and deflected them onto a group with which they should have been aligned. This disturbing history ought to be more fully addressed.

Further Reading

Griffin, William D. *A Portrait of the Irish in America*. New York: Scribners, 1981.
Ignatiev, Noel. *How the Irish Became White*. New York: Routledge, 1995.
Miller, Kerby. *Emigrants and Exiles: Ireland and the Irish Exiles to North America*. New York: Oxford University Press, 1985.

Mayor of Hell (1933) (M)

Setting: New York City and upstate New York, 1933

Director: Archie Mayo

Screenplay: Edward Chodorov

Director of Photography: Barney "Chick" McGill

Cast: James Cagney (Patsy Gargan), Madge Evans (Dorothy Griffith), Dudley Digges (Mr. Thompson), Frankie Darro (Jimmy Smith), Farina (Smoke), Mickey Bennett

(Butch Kilgore), Arthur Byron (Judge Gilbert), Sidney Miller (Izzy Horowitz), Raymond Borzage (Johnny "Skinny" Stone)

Availability: None

In 1949, sociologist Milton Barron concluded that Irish Americans inhabited an intermediate space in America. They rested between the powerful Anglo-Saxons and the new immigrants from Eastern and Southern Europe who filled the lower rungs of the success ladder. The third migration from Europe (1880–1920) identified with the Irish. Many new immigrants (Italians and Poles) shared their Catholic religion and suffered similar persecutions. Moreover, it was the Irish that the third migration saw in positions of power: running the police and fire departments, the parishes, and city politics. *Mayor of Hell*, in its immigration allegory, presents one Irish American, James Cagney's Patsy Gargan, as the bridge to assimilation. Patsy is an inside/outside figure, simultaneously legitimate and criminal. A ward heeler, Patsy is a shadowy figure guaranteeing votes to a corrupt city machine, but once he attends an unjust reformatory he becomes politicized. The wayward boys locked in the reformatory are Jews, Italians, African Americans, Scots, and Irish, and thus represent an immigrant polyglot in need of guidance. Unfortunately that guidance cannot come from their parents. A courtroom scene in juvenile hall with Judge Gilbert makes it clear that their immigrant fathers lack the controlling discipline to deal with their second-generation children (5:35–16:00). After Patsy's arrival at the school, he becomes their role model. With the help of nurse Dorothy Griffith, Patsy installs a juvenile republic in which the boys will govern themselves. The "Mayor of Hell" scene in which the boys nominate and elect officers reflects Patsy's Irish American intermediacy (42:25–46:36). On the one hand, he is the leader, forcing the boys to play ball with the new experiment, "to be regular," but every now and then he leans over to Griffith for advice. She represents patriarchal order and a full understanding of the republic's principles. Patsy represents the Irish ability to get things done within a predominantly Anglo-Saxon culture. Eventually, Patsy's insider/outsider dialectic brings ruin to the school. When he goes back to New York to take care of a gangland problem, the evil Thompson regains control of the school and returns it to his reign of tyranny. Without their Irish leader, the boys riot, seize munitions, and brandish torches while trying Thompson in their own court (1:24:25–1:26:58). Patsy returns to find Thompson dead (he fell from a rooftop while fleeing the angry mob) and asks the boys to put out the fire. They do so, and the film ends with Patsy and the boys achieving a degree of assimilation and acceptance. Judge Gilbert, convinced that Thompson's death "was his own fault," approves of the job Patsy has done and apologizes for not heeding his earlier warnings about corruption. Patsy waves it off, but he has been accepted professionally (Judge Gilbert asks him to stay on at the school) and personally (he is going to marry Dorothy). The boys too are accepted. They are given a second chance to follow Patsy into the promises of America.

Further Reading

Barron, Milton L. "Intermediacy: Conceptualization of Irish Status in America." *Social Forces* 27 (March 1949): 256–263.

Jowett, Garth S., Ian C. Jarvie, and Kathryn H. Fuller. *Children and the Movies: Media Influence and the Payne Fund Controversy.* New York: Cambridge University Press, 1996.

Tracey, Grant. " 'Let's Go Places with Jimmy': James Cagney as 1930's Immigrant Icon." *Journal of Film and Video* 50.4 (Winter 1998–1999): 3–17.

The Rat Pack (1998) (R) (M)

Setting: Los Angeles, Las Vegas, and Washington, DC, 1959–1961

Director: Rob Cohen

Screenplay: Kario Salem

Director of Photography: Shane Hurlbut

Cast: Ray Liotta (Frank Sinatra), Don Cheadle (Sammy Davis, Jr.), Joe Mantegna (Dean Martin), Angus MacFadden (Peter Lawford), Zeliko Ivanek (Robert F. Kennedy), William Petersen (John F. Kennedy), Megan Dodds (May Britt), and Robert Miranda (Momo Giancana)

Availability: HBO Home Video

In the 1950s, Frank Sinatra lived the American Dream. He was a star in movies and nightclubs, and his swingin' Capitol records were artistic high points of the decade. With his fellow Rat Packers (two Jews, one of them black; two Italians; and a Brit connected to America's premiere Irish-Catholic family), Sinatra embodied America's new success ethic. Three of the Rat Packers, including Sinatra, were second-generation immigrants, and they signified what the war had done to America's class system. Those who held power were no longer the WASPs, but a new multiethnic polyglot. Sinatra was active in the Civil Rights Movement; he supported Sammy Davis, Jr., getting him gigs in segregated clubs and standing up at his wedding when the entertainer married May Britt, a white woman. For Sinatra, the Rat Pack was a gang of street kids, teaching America about the possibilities open to all its peoples. Rob Cohen's fine HBO production captures this spirit, including Sinatra's support of Davis. Behind the glamour, the playboy style, and ring-a-ding-ding attitude stands a man who wanted to "shake things up" in order to change America and gain his own acceptance within it. Sinatra felt that if he could help elect John F. Kennedy to the presidency, all of those people who claimed he was not a real American could no longer say so (40:30–40:40). John F. Kennedy's story, too, is that of the immigrant seeking acceptance. In 1928, Alfred Smith, an Irish Catholic, ran for the presidency and was defeated soundly by Herbert Hoover: 447 to 87 electoral votes. In 1960, there is still a fear that an Irish Catholic could not be president. But the Kennedys ally themselves with Sinatra who in turn asks mobster Sam Giancana and the Teamsters to support Kennedy (first in the West Virginia primary and later in the national election). Kennedy wins, and Sinatra gets his respect, as the president-elect tells a radio audience, "I know we're all indebted to a great friend, Frank Sinatra" (1:21:21–1:21:50). But that respect is short lived. Following the election, Attorney General Robert Kennedy prosecutes organized crime, in particular Giancana, the man who helped put his brother into office. Because of Sinatra's affiliation with Giancana, Robert suggests that John not stay at Sinatra's house during his West Coast visit. For Sammy Davis, Jr., respect and acceptance are even harder to attain. America may be willing to accept the multiethnicity of the Rat Pack polyglot (Italians, Jews, and Irish) but Davis' blackness is never fully accepted. Prior to marrying Britt, Davis receives numerous death threats; he postpones his wedding in order not to affect Kennedy's presidential aspirations; and, despite his support for Kennedy, he is not invited to the celebratory postnomination party. Instead, Davis sits alone in a hotel room watching it on television, and Cohen wonderfully diffuses the *mise-en-scène* with a bright, all-pervasive whiteness (from bed sheets to the walls [50:00–50:59]), suggesting both Davis' captivity and America's blindness.

Further Reading

MacLaine, Shirley. "One for the Road." *Newsweek* 131 (May 25, 1998): 64d–64g.
Rudin, Max. "Fly Me to the Moon: Reflections on the Rat Pack." *American Heritage* 49.8 (December 1998): 52–65.
Talese, Gay. "Frank Sinatra Has a Cold." *Frank Sinatra: His Life in Words and Pictures* (special newsstand edition of *TV Guide*, 1998): 76–80.

A Tree Grows in Brooklyn (1945) (M) (W)

Setting: Brooklyn, 1915

Director: Elia Kazan

Screenplay: Tess Slesinger and Frank Davis

Director of Photography: Leon Shamroy

Cast: Peggy Ann Garner (Francie Nolan), James Dunn (Johnny Nolan), Dorothy McGuire (Katie Nolan)

Availability: Family Home Entertainment Video

A Tree Grows in Brooklyn details the plight of second- and third-generation Irish immigrants in the city tenements and their fight to make it. Johnny Nolan, a charming alcoholic, is a pipe dreamer, and as a part-time singer he brings little money into the home. His wife, Katie, hardened by their lower-class status, has become disillusioned about his charm. In one of the film's haunting moments, Johnny spins colorful tales about a wedding reception at which he performed. Katie is initially enchanted, as she had been during their courting days (47:00–50:19). And Johnny, smitten by his wife's beauty, promises to quit drinking, but before he can say more, Katie explodes and shouts, "Stop!" Separated from him in the *mise-en-scène* (she stands by the door, he in the background, as neither look at each other), she coldly says, "You ain't got a chance. Who are we trying to kid" (49:23). Later Johnny, saddened by their move to a cheaper room and the death of a neighbor girl, Flossy, sings "Annie Laurie" at the piano (1:07:30–1:09:54). His voice is surprisingly elegiac. Katie, moved by the music, approaches her husband. "It's pretty," she says, but Johnny doesn't respond; instead, he keeps singing, "Gave me her promise true," and the wedge is driven further between them. But, the film suggests, it is the children of immigrants who have the chance to get ahead. Grandma Nolan tells the story of coming to this "new land," and how "A child can be better than the parent" (38:39–40:24). Francie Nolan will go far. She combines the best attributes of both her parents: her mom's dogged determination and responsibility and her father's idealism and imagination. Francie learns love and an appreciation of beauty from her father. At the local school Francie is not appreciated. She tries to explain the meaning of beauty in a poem by describing her father, but the teacher isn't interested in meaning. She's more interested in the students' ability to identify the poem's meter (52:32–53:46). Misunderstood and unwelcomed by her peers, Francie wants to go to a school outside her neighborhood, and her father devises a scheme to get her into one (55:40–59:36). Later, during Christmas Eve, a thankful Francie tells her father that she wants to become a writer, and she sadly wonders why people can't be friendly and nice all the time. Her father, moved, asks her to stick out her tongue and says that she's got "a very bad case of growing up" (1:23:37–1:29:04). This moment is the last time she'll see her father alive. He has just learned from Katie that they will be having another baby and that Francie will have to quit school to help support the family. Johnny, unable to disappoint Francie, and perhaps worried that his daughter will also become disillusioned and see her father as an impractical dreamer, leaves in the cold to find work. He dies a few days later from pneumonia. The love between Francie and her father is the most touching aspect of this film, and twelve-year-old Peggy Ann Garner is marvelous with her combination of wonderstruck eyes and withdrawn presence. Director Elia Kazan said of her performance, "She was not pretty at all, or cute or picturesque—only true."

Further Reading

Agee, James. Review of *A Tree Grows in Brooklyn*. *The Nation* 160 (February 17, 1945): 192–93.

Crowther, Bosley. Review of *A Tree Grows in Brooklyn*. *New York Times* (March 1,
        1945): 25.
Hartung, Philip T. "It Grows." *The Commonweal* 41 (March 9, 1945): 517–518.
Smith, Betty. *A Tree Grows in Brooklyn*. New York: Harper, 1943.

DOUBLE BILL: ANCESTRY AND CONFORMITY: COME FROM OR BECOME?

The Godfather (1972) (R) (M)

Setting: New York, New Jersey, Las Vegas, and Sicily, 1945–1955

Director: Francis Ford Coppola

Screenplay: Mario Puzo and Francis Ford Coppola

Director of Photography: Gordon Willis

Cast: Marlon Brando (Don Vito Corleone), Al Pacino (Michael Corleone), James Caan (Sonny Corleone), Sterling Hayden (McCluskey), Diane Keaton (Kay Adams), Al Lettieri (Soliozzo), and Al Martino (Johnny Fontane)

Availability: Paramount Home Video

The Godfather II (1974) (R) (M)

Setting: Las Vegas, Miami, Havana, Cuba, and Washington, DC, 1955–1960; Sicily, 1901 and 1917; Ellis Island, 1901; New York City, 1917

Director: Francis Ford Coppola

Screenplay: Mario Puzo and Francis Ford Coppola

Director of Photography: Gordon Willis

Cast: Al Pacino (Michael Corleone), Diane Keaton (Kay Adams), Robert De Niro (Don Vito Corleone), and John Cazale (Fredo)

Availability: Paramount Home Video

Francis Ford Coppola's adaptations of the Mario Puzo novel deal primarily with crime and family, but are also stories about immigration and Italian Americans' desire for acceptance. The first film opens in oppressive darkness as an undertaker asks the Godfather for justice. His daughter was brutally beaten by two WASP boys who didn't respect her ancestry. "I understand, you found a paradise in America," the Godfather says, but now that paradise isn't working, and the American justice system is unfair to Italians—the two youths had received only a suspended sentence for their brutality. Anglo-conformity doesn't work, and the Godfather promises to right the wrong (vol. 1, 00:00–6:18). Later, the Godfather helps an Italian boy who loves an Italian American girl stay in America and avoid repatriation (vol. 1, 11:32–12:23). He also helps Johnny Fontane, his godson and a figure loosely modeled on Italian American Frank Sinatra, get a key role in a war film that will help resuscitate his career (vol. 1, 22:07–23:52; 30:00–33:55). The Don's youngest son, Michael Corleone, doesn't want anything to do with the family business. He tells Kay, his WASPish girlfriend, "That's my family Kay. It's not me." Michael believes in assimilation, in leaving behind the family you come from for the family you are about to become. He honorably fought in the Marines during World War Two and came home a decorated hero. His relationship with Kay also suggests his desire to "marry up." But after Soliozzo's attempt on his father's life, Michael sits in a chair, the camera slowly tracking in as he commits to the family's way of life, promising to kill both the crooked cop McCluskey and the drug runner Soliozzo (vol. 1, 1:13:30–1:15:00). Following the murders, Michael eventually becomes the leader of the Corleone empire. His father sadly says, "I never wanted this for you." He had bigger dreams: "Senator Corleone . . . Governor . . . something" (vol. 2, 39:27–43:15). Near the end of *The Godfather*, Coppola hauntingly suggests how far Michael has fallen from his original ideals. During the baptism of Michael's godson, Coppola crosscuts to a series of murders organized and brutally executed. As Michael renounces Satan in the eyes of the church, Coppola shows him responsible for satanic acts as his men murder the heads of the five families (vol. 2, 49:44–54:46). *The Godfather II* further develops Michael's moral disintegration through its epic structure of parallel storytelling. Coppola, in a D. W. Griffith–like *tour de force*, cuts between the story of Michael's fall from power and prestige with the story of Vito Corleone's coming to America and accompanying rise in stature and respect. The parallel editing creates a rich moral contrast. Vito's story begins with the murders of his father, mother, and brother and details his arrival at Ellis Island, where he's marked with an "X" and placed in quarantine for three months (7:14–11:00). Later, in 1917, Vito loses his grocery clerk job because the neighborhood extortionist, Fanucci, demands it be given to his nephew. When Fanucci also demands kickback money from the sale of dresses Corleone's gang has stolen, Vito refuses and stalks and kills the heavyset gangster (vol. 2, 11:41–19:22). This makes him a hero in the community and he becomes their Godfather. Vito's story also presents him as a caring family man. In a beautifully quiet scene, he stands back helplessly at the door watching baby Fredo battle pneumonia (vol. 2, 2:49–3:35). Michael lacks his father's loyalty to family. Eventually, he coldly orders the murder of Fredo because of his brother's deception and betrayal (vol. 2, 1:21:30–1:24:01). Also, his marriage falls apart. Kay, while breaking up with him, confesses that her miscarriage wasn't a miscarriage but an abortion (vol. 2, 50:47–56:30). In the public realm, Michael's reputation suffers as a Senate investigation into organized crime strips him of his dignity before both family and country (vol. 2, 32:47–38:40; 47:05–50:08). Finally, the film's ending eerily echoes Michael's lost dreams and idealism. As he sits alienated, the ghosts of the past harken to 1941 when Michael chooses country over family and enlists in the Marines. Older brother Sonny, angry at "Mikey," tells him, "Your country aren't your blood. You remember that." Michael disagrees, and says, what will later become sadly ironic, "I have my own plans for my future" (vol. 2, 1:28:20).

Further Reading

Canby, Vincent. Review of *The Godfather*. *New York Times* (March 16, 1972): 56.

Clarens, Carlos. "All in the Family." *Crime Movies: An Illustrated History of the Gangster Genre from D. W. Griffith to Pulp Fiction*. New York: De Capo, 1997. 270–292.

Lourdeaux, Lee. "Francis Coppola and Ethnic Double Vision." *Italian and Irish Filmmakers in America: Ford, Capra, Coppola, and Scorsese*. Philadelphia: Temple University Press, 1990. 172–215.

Westerbeck, Colin L., Jr. Review of *The Godfather, Part II*. *Commonweal* 102 (May 23, 1975): 146–147.

FURTHER VIEWING

Avalon (1990) (PG) (M)

Far and Away (1992) (PG-13) (M)

The Girl Who Spelled Freedom (1985) (TV) (M) (W)

Green Card (1990) (PG-13)

Jazz Singer (1927) (M)

Misplaced (1990) (TV) (M)

Teresa (1951)

West Is West (1987) (TV) (M)

6

World War One and Goodbye
to All That, 1916–1933

The Big Parade ◆ *Heroes for Sale* ◆ *Johnny Got His Gun* ◆ *Paths of Glory* ◆ *Sergeant York* ◆ *Soldier's Home* ◆ *Wings* ◆ Double Bill: *All Quiet on the Western Front* and *Hell's Angels*

The Big Parade (1925)

Setting: France, 1917–1919

Director: King Vidor

Screenplay: Laurence Stallings and Harry Behn

Director of Photography: John Arnold

Cast: John Gilbert (Jim Apperson), Renée Adorée (Melisande), Karl Dane (Slim), and Tom O'Brien (Bull)

Availability: MGM/UA (Turner)

In the 1920s, World War One was regarded by literary and cultural elites (Ernest Hemingway, T. S. Eliot, Gertrude Stein) as a nightmare of horror and mechanized death dealt by technology. It was a nightmare. The allies (France, England, and the United States) lost a reported 2.3 million men, while the Central Powers (Germany, Austria-Hungary) reported 2.7 million battle deaths. However, responses to the war were not all the same. During 1917–1919, the popular press touted the war's participants as heroes, infused with the spirit of democracy, self-sacrifice, and national idealism. King Vidor's *The Big Parade* (1925) falls somewhere between these two responses. On one level, Vidor and story writer Laurence Stallings (who lost his right leg at Belleau Wood) capture the nightmare of war. After Jim Apperson helplessly watches his friend Slim heroically die on the front lines, he screams "Cheers when we left and when we get back, but who the hell cares after this" (1:49:50). Angry, he charges a German pillbox, destroys it, and falls into a shell hole after being shot in the leg. There, Apperson comes face to face with a wounded German soldier, but he can't bayonet an enemy he can see. They're too much alike in their humanity. Instead Apperson and the soldier smoke together until the German dies (1:54:20–1:56:23). Vidor and Stallings present the war realistically. The battle scenes in the woods and trenches capture the grit and grime of war, and yet, the overall mood of the film is painted with an aura of romanticism and the spirit of adventure. During a parade, Jim, a product of the upper classes, stands in his car and taps his foot to the marching beat. Caught up in the spirit of patriotism, he enlists (7:13–8:51). Moreover, the film is as much a love story as a war story. Many of the film's most memorable moments center around the dashing John Gilbert and the earthy Renée Adorée. In a gentle romantic scene, Jim shows Melisande how to chew American bubble gum (43:06–47:50). When the war is over, Jim returns to France looking for his lost love in the peasant fields. In extreme long shot, he limps along a hill, and she immediately knows who he is. They run to each other and embrace. Years later, Vidor was displeased with the romanticism of the film and his failure to make an antiwar statement. But *The Big Parade* does succeed in providing a window into America's conflicted feelings about the Great War during the 1920s.

Further Reading

Isenberg, Michael T. "The Great War Viewed from the Twenties: *The Big Parade*." *Hollywood's World War One: Motion Picture Images*, ed. Peter C. Rollins and John E. O'Connor. Bowling Green; OH: Popular Press, 1997. 39–58.
Seldes, Gilbert. "The Two Parades." *New Republic* 45 (December 16, 1925): 111–112.
Stallings, Laurence. *The Doughboys: The Story of the AEF, 1917–1918*. New York: Harper, 1963.

Heroes for Sale (1933)

Setting: Western Front, 1918; Milford, Midwest, 1918–1922; Chicago, 1922–1933

Director: William A. Wellman

Screenplay: Robert Lord and Wilson Mizner

Director of Photography: James Van Trees

Cast: Richard Barthelmess (Tom Holmes), Aline MacMahon (Mary), Loretta Young (Ruth), and Grant Mitchell (Mr. Gibson)

Availability: MGM/UA (Turner)

In the summer of 1932, a group of 25,000 World War One veterans and their families marched on Washington and formed a shanty town by the

Acostia River. During the heat of the Depression, they asked the government for their military bonus money granted by the Compensation Act of 1924. Rather than receive it in 1945, when they were eligible, they wanted it now. Five hundred dollars would tide them over a lot of their worries. But the White House refused to respond, and President Hoover dispatched General MacArthur to break up the "red agitators." On July 28, MacArthur led a search-and-destroy attack on the "Bonus Expeditionary Force." With sabres, bayonets, tanks, and gas, the encampment was destroyed and two babies died from military gassing. Warner Bros.' *Heroes for Sale* doesn't directly portray this event, but the studio's story about the nation's forgotten heroes is a sympathetic look at the plight of the veteran in a postwar world. Richard Barthelmess, the all-American kid of the 1920s, plays Tom Holmes, a downtrodden man of the 1930s. During the Great War he is a hero, braving no-man's land and capturing a German officer, but he is wounded by a shell and left for dead (3:30–6:23). In a German prison camp, Tom is given morphine to take care of his back pain, and when he returns home, he is a drug addict and struggles to hold his job (13:02–20:57). The folks at home don't understand his plight. Sanctimoniously his boss condemns him: "The war's over. . . . It's time to quit beating the drum and waving the flag" (17:48). The boss turns Tom in, and he is sent to a narcotics farm (21:26–22:10). Jobless, Tom leaves the rural Midwest for Chicago where he meets Ruth, gets a job, and with the help of a German Marxist inventor convinces his boss to use a mechanical device to increase productivity of the work force and give the workers more leisure time. But the boss dies, and greedy new management increases the efficiency of the invention and squeezes the workers out. A riot ensues. Tom tries to break up the riot, his wife dies in the melee, and the veteran is accused of being a "red agitator" (47:48–51:05). Tom is sentenced to two years, and when he returns home again, he is sent packing by a group from the District Attorney's office who deport "undesirable aliens" and run out of town those who are seen as sympathetic to their cause. Holmes is no red, but he identifies with America's downtrodden, all heroes for sale. In the end, he rides trains looking for work, but Tom Holmes can never find home. In Pennsylvania "detectives" round up Holmes and a bunch of other transients. Harassed and shoved, Holmes shouts with dignity, "Who you calling reds and hoboes? We're ex-servicemen" (1:05:47). The film is brutally honest and it seems America listened to such critiques. During World War Two, Congress passed the G.I. Bill to ensure that the Holmes's and the "Bonus Expeditionary Forces" had a future in this country and that past injustices would not be repeated.

Further Reading

Bergman, Andrew. *We're in the Money: Depression America and Its Films.* New York: NYU Press, 1971.

Manchester, William. "Rock Bottom." *The Glory and the Dream: A Narrative History of America, 1932–1972*. Boston: Little, Brown & Co., 1973. 1–32.
Thompson, Frank T. *William A. Wellman*. Metuchen, NJ: Scarecrow Press, 1983.

Johnny Got His Gun (1971) (PG)

Setting: France, 1917–1918

Director: Dalton Trumbo

Screenplay: Dalton Trumbo

Director of Photography: Robert Touyabot

Cast: Timothy Bottoms (Joseph Bonham), Jason Robards (Mr. Bonham), Diane Varsi (Nurse), Kathy Fields (Kareen), and Donald Sutherland (Christ)

Availability: None (previously available from Media Home Video)

In 1971, Dalton Trumbo's *Johnny Got His Gun* was much maligned by the critical establishment for putting propaganda ahead of art. But Trumbo is a message director, and his film deserves reappraisal. Trumbo's strong antiwar film, speaking in a double voice about the past and the present (World War One versus Viet Nam), sees war as unnatural and ungodly. His hero, Joseph Bonham, has lost all four limbs, his mouth, and most of his brain. He can't scream or, it initially appears, communicate, and the French medical doctors treat him as a scientific experiment. They grant him no dignity and lock him away in a utility closet. But while locked away, we discover that Bonham not only feels things, but that this is a film about memory. Bonham, to understand himself and keep sane, recalls past experiences, such as the only time he made love to his girlfriend Kareen (12:01–15:55). Other reminders of lost innocence include Bonham's reflections on his father and his boyhood in a small town. A second set of memories deals with the dream world transcending the real for the surreal, the imagined, and the absurd. In those memories Bonham converses with dead soldiers (27:11–29:48) and a Christ-like figure (Donald Sutherland) about what to do with his "life" (46:50–49:31). In these dreams, he sees his father as a freak show carny promising to display Joseph's mutilated body (58:58–1:00:56). Eventually, a kind nurse communicates with Joseph (1:15:31). She responds to his erotic dreams, and later touches his chest and writes words across it (1:22:35). Joseph nods his head to the words, and she runs for the authorities who discover that he can communicate in morse code. In code, Joseph asks the American doctors to put him on display for all the world to see. He wants to be an unnamed soldier (fittingly, he refuses to tell them his name), an objective correlative to the evils of war. But they won't allow it, and he asks them to kill him. They won't allow that either, and they leave him in the dark, an experiment to be studied. Trumbo concludes with two epitaphs: "War Dead Since 1914: Over 60,000,000," and "Missing or Mutilated: Over 150,000,000." His message is shattering, and while the establishment disapproved of his propaganda, this film met with the approval of college students and antiwar demonstrators who in 1971 knew about the 40,000 American dead and counting in Viet Nam.

Further Reading

Alpert, Hollis. "Poor Johnny." *Saturday Review* 54 (August 28, 1971): 48.
Gilliatt, Penelope. "Tell Me When I Can Look." *The New Yorker* 47 (August 7, 1971): 65.
"Johnny Got His Gun." Filmfacts 14:22 (1971): 582–585.
Trumbo, Dalton. *Johnny Got His Gun.* New York: Bantam, 1939, 1982.

Paths of Glory (1957)

Setting: France, 1916

Director: Stanley Kubrick

Screenplay: Stanley Kubrick, Calder Willingham, Jim Thompson

Director of Photography: George Krause

Cast: Kirk Douglas (Colonel Dax) and George Macready (General Paul Mireau)

Availability: MGM/UA (Turner)

In several accounts of the Great War, including Robert Graves' novel *Goodbye to All That*, generals are portrayed as arrogant distant leaders who foolishly demand the impossible from their downtrodden doughboys. Safely ensconced behind the lines, the generals have no understanding of the harsh conditions in the trenches, and they are unimaginative and guilty of perpetrating a great amount of human ruin. Such a portrait Stanley Kubrick weaves in his pacifist film *Paths of Glory.* French General Mireau, bucking for a promotion, orders his men to take the enemy "ant hill" in forty-eight hours. Kubrick shows Mireau's inhumanity during a long reverse tracking shot as the general tours the trenches (6:13–7:43). "Ready to kill Germans?" he asks repeatedly in a cold, affected way. When Colonel Dax questions the mission, asking about possible casualties, the general rattles off numbers as if individual lives aren't important: 5 percent will die from friendly fire, 10 percent will die getting to no man's land; 20 percent will die getting to the wire; and an additional 25 percent will die taking the hill (12:39). Dax disapproves of the mission's objectives—his men are spent—but he follows orders. They attack the hill but don't make it half way. An angry Mireau orders shells dropped on his own "cowardly" men. Fortunately, the order is disobeyed, but in the dour aftermath, symbolic charges of cowardice are brought against three randomly chosen men. The film is uncompromising in its portrait of stupidity and military bloodlust. Kirk Douglas brings humanity to the Western Front as he fights for the lives of the three martyrs at the court-martial. But the trial is rigged against them and the men are executed as examples for all.

Further Reading

Burgess, J. "The 'Anti-Militarism' of Stanley Kubrick." *Film Quarterly* 18.1 (1964): 4–11.

Graves, Robert. *Goodbye to All That.* New York: Doubleday, 1929, 1957.

Kelly, Andrew. "Military Incompetence and the Cinema of the First World War: *Paths of Glory.*" *Hollywood's World War I: Motion Picture Images*, ed. Peter C. Rollins and John E. O'Connor. Bowling Green, OH: Popular Press, 1997. 143–159.

Sergeant York (1941)

Setting: Rural Tennessee, 1916–1919; the Western Front, 1918

Director: Howard Hawks

Screenplay: Abem Finkel, Harry Chandlee, Howard Koch, and John Huston

Directors of Photography: Sol Polito and Arthur Edeson

Cast: Gary Cooper (Sergeant York), Walter Brennan (Pastor Rosier Pile), Joan Leslie (Gracie Williams), Margaret Wycherly (Mom/Mrs. York), and Stanley Ridges (Major Buxton)

Availability: MGM/UA (Turner)

Sergeant York, which premiered in July of 1941, was a biopic about World War One hero Alvin York who in the battle of the Meuse-Argonne killed 25 German machine gunners and captured 132 others. The film (made in close consultation with York) faithfully rendered the Tennessean's conversion from drunken carouser to fundamentalist Christian, from conscientious objector to fighting soldier. But as much as it spoke to the past, it spoke to the future: the new war in Europe and America's encroaching involvement. By 1940, Germany had overrun Denmark, Norway, Holland, Belgium, and France, and Adolf Hitler had sent divisions into the Soviet Union. In the South Pacific, the Japanese had marched into China and were threatening to move into Indo-China. Within this cultural context, *Sergeant York* was good inspiration for a country moving from isolationism to interventionism. The film's story provided justification for such a rationale. York, a conscientious objector, reads a history of the United States, learns that fighting for freedom is noble and moral, and while asking for God's guidance on a mountaintop experiences an epiphany. A gust of wind flips his open Bible pages to a quote on rendering to Caesar what is Caesar's, and York thus compartmentalizes his responsibilities between his faith and his country (1: 31:21–1:33:58). He commits to the cause and the reluctant hero becomes a powerful metaphor for America's transformation. Gary Cooper, as York, turns in a strong, sincere performance, and brings dignity and grace to the soldier's life. Writer Harry Chandlee, in typical Hollywood fashion, fictionalizes several events. York never participated in a turkey shoot to win land (46:12–51:49); there was no double-crossing in the sale of the farm to a

Nate Watson (52:22); York didn't shock his military officers by hitting bull's-eye after bull's-eye on the rifle range (1:19:12–1:23:35); York never had a long discussion with his superiors (Major Buxton) about the Bible and American history (1:26:33–1:29:50); and York wasn't converted to fundamentalism by a bolt of lightning (55:03). However, the film does accurately portray the spirit of York's conversion to faith, and how Pastor Rosier Pile helped bring about York's maturation. Moreover, the war-time heroics are truthfully portrayed (they were taken from congressional records and the affidavits of York's fellow soldiers). The film was a smash with the public. To those remaining isolationists who harangued Warner Bros. for producing a patriotic film, Harry Warner said, "it is the factual portrait of the life of one of the heroes of the last war." He unabashedly concluded, "If that is propaganda, we plead guilty."

Further Reading

Cowan, Sam K. *Sergeant York and His People*. New York: Funk & Wagnalls, 1922.
Lee, David D. *Sergeant York: An American Hero*. Lexington: University of Kentucky Press, 1985.
Toplin, Robert Brent. "*Sergeant York*: 'If That Is Propaganda, We Plead Guilty.' " *History by Hollywood: The Use and Abuse of the American Past*. Urbana: University of Illinois Press, 1996. 81–101.

Soldier's Home (1976) (TV)

Setting: Rural Kansas, 1920

Director: Robert Young

Screenplay: Robert Geller

Director of Photography: Peter Sova

Cast: Richard Backus (Harold Krebs), Nancy Marchand (Mrs. Krebs), Robert Mc-Ilwaine (Mr. Krebs), Lane Binkley (Roselle Simmons), Lisa Essary (Marge), and Mark LaMura (Bill Kenner)

Availability: Monterey Home Video

In Ernest Hemingway's short story "Soldier's Home," Harold Krebs returns from the war a year late. The parades are over, nobody wants to listen to him share his experiences, and his mother insists that he reintegrate into civilian life. She pressures him to marry, find a job, and return to God. But Krebs can't forget the war and return to a world of thrift and industry. Disoriented, he seeks "patterns" to control and ritualize his life. By turning inward and studying the town girls' collars Krebs finds a momentary respite from reintegration and a world fraught with hypocrisy. But his mother's urgings break his patterns, forcing him to say that he loves no one, and then when she cries, forcing him to lie. To avoid a second lie, Krebs decides to leave Kansas without paying a last visit to his father. Director Robert Geller captures Krebs' disorientation and disillusionment. There are several scenes of Krebs smoking because he is bored with the conversation around him (5: 42). He also looks away when he talks to others, and he can't commit to social functions or a job in insurance. Through counterpointed scenes, Krebs is often paired off with someone else, and his pain and distance is strongly evident. In one scene, a town local tells Krebs to join his father in the banking business, and Young cuts to Krebs' perspective via a handheld point-of-view shot. The reverse tracking that accompanies the shot mirrors Krebs' retreat from such ideas and his refusal to conform to what people want him to be (11:34). He needs time to sift through his war experiences. But the major difference in the two texts rests in how Young and writer Robert Geller shift Krebs' narrative to one of remembrance. Their Krebs is not merely disillusioned and trying to find order, but he's a soldier who feels proud of how he served his country, and that is the pattern that he values. Later, Krebs meets up with Bill Kenner (a Young/Geller addition to the original source), a troubled veteran who lost part of a knee on a mine. During a drinking session, the bitter Kenner tells how he was always scared on the Western Front, and sometimes slept with a towel in his mouth to stop the screaming. Krebs doesn't share Kenner's experiences and refuses to believe his version of the truth: "I wasn't scared. Not the way you tell it." Krebs wants to remember "Being a good soldier. Doing what you had to do" (30:19). Kenner, too, rejects Krebs' memory of the war, and the two lose their friendship. Following a final scene with his mother, Krebs is left separated from family and friends, and still searching for a home.

Further Reading

DeFalco, Joseph. *The Hero in Hemingway's Short Stories.* Pittsburgh: University of Pittsburgh Press, 1963.

Hemingway, Ernest. "Soldier's Home." *In Our Time.* New York: Scribners', 1925. 69–77.

Roberts, John J. "In Defense of Krebs." *Studies in Short Fiction* 13 (Fall 1976): 515–518.

Smith, Paul. "Soldier's Home." *A Reader's Guide to the Short Stories of Ernest Hemingway.* Boston: G. K. Hall & Co., 1989. 68–74.

Wings (1927) (W)

Setting: the Midwest, 1917–1918; the Western Front, 1917–1918

Director: William A. Wellman

Screenplay: John Monk Saunders, Hope Loring, and Louis D. Lighton

Director of Photography: Harry Perry

Cast: Clara Bow (Mary Preston), Charles "Buddy" Rogers (Jack Powell), and Richard Arlen (David Armstrong)

Availability: Paramount Home Video

World War One offered women the chance to work, and they gained economic strength on the home front. In England, for example, over 500,000 women were gainfully employed because of the war. And in America, during the 1920s, there was a conservative backlash to this shift in sex roles. The "new working woman" was critiqued in the popular magazines as a frivolous flapper who earned money only to have fun and seek sexual pleasure. This notion of the flapper as bad girl was showcased by Jean Harlow in Howard Hughes' *Hell's Angels* (1930). But *Wings*, a powerful war film that also explored the grim glory of flying, differed from *Hell's Angels* in its desire to preserve a Victorian notion of womanly innocence. Ironically, *Wings* converts Clara Bow, the 1920s embodiment of the "It" girl and hedonistic sexuality, into a chaste girl-next-door Mary Preston, loyal to the war effort and her boyfriend, Jack Powell. When Bow makes her first appearance, she plays with her earlier star image of hedonism. She peaks behind a pair of bloomers hanging on a clothesline, and smiles (2:56). In this brightly lit shot, she appears sexy but wholesome. Later, Mary travels overseas as a Red Cross driver. Here, the film unfairly pokes fun at her driving—no doubt this was a conservative attempt to deny her legitimacy in the working world and to suggest that she and all women should return home (56:20). Her main function overseas is an extension of a domestic role: to save her boyfriend from ruin (1:07:20–1:17:43). All of the flyers are to report back to the base for a mission, but Jack, inebriated, is in a house of ill repute. Mary finds him and, saddened by what she sees, cries in a washroom. A washer woman sees her anguish and gives her a chance to win back her man by dressing Mary in a bold and beautiful glittery dress. But Mary, in a reworking of the Cinderella myth, uses the glitter not for sexual conquest but to lure Jack away from the prostitutes and return him to his flying duties. Thus, Bow in glitter references her earlier "It" girl image, but *Wings* transforms "Itness" into passion smoldered by patriotic loyalty. In the end, Mary gets her man. Jack returns home, aged from his experiences, and as they huddle under a dark sky, he confesses to having had one affair: "There was a girl, and I forgot myself." Mary doesn't tell him that she was that woman. Instead, as an allegorical angel of healing, Mary/Clara Bow compassionately speaks to the transgressions committed by all Americans during a dark time: "It's the war."

Further Reading

Gilbert, Sandra M. "Soldier's Heart: Literary Men, Literary Women, and the Great War." *Speaking of Gender*, ed. Elaine Showalter. New York: Routledge, 1991. 282–309.

Leed, Eric. *No Man's Land: Combat and Identity in World War One*. New York: Cambridge University Press, 1979.

Mitchell, David. *Women on the Warpath: The Story of the Women of the First World War*. London: Jonathan Cape, 1966.

DOUBLE BILL: WAR: ABOVE AND ON THE WESTERN FRONT

All Quiet on the Western Front (1930)

Setting: Western Front, 1917–1918

Director: Lewis Milestone

Screenplay: Maxwell Anderson and George Abbott

Director of Photography: Arthur Edeson

Cast: Lew Ayres (Paul Baumner) and Louis Wolheim (Kat Katczinsky)

Availability: MCA/Universal Home Video

Hell's Angels (1930)

Setting: England and Germany, 1917–1918

Directors: Howard Hughes and James Whale

Screenplay: Howard Estabrooks, Harry Behn, and Joseph Moncure

Directors of Photography: Antonio Gaudio, Harry Zech, Devey Wrigley, Harry Perry, E. Burton Stone, and Elmer Dyer

Cast: James Hall (Roy Rutledge), Ben Lyon (Monte Rutledge), John Darrow (Karl Arnstedt), and Jean Harlow (Helen)

Availability: MCA/Universal Home Video

Released months apart in 1930, these films present opposite perspectives on the war from above and on the Western Front. *Hell's Angels*, about England's Royal Flying Corps, grows out of America's fascination with Charles Lindbergh and the romanticism of flying and presents a world of noble courage, heroism, and men who are agents of history acting out their wills against an enemy. *All Quiet on the Western Front*, about a doomed German regiment fighting in the trenches, presents a mechanized horror in which men have no agency but instead are victims buffeted by forces beyond their control. *Hell's Angels* features several moments of noble self-sacrifice. Following a Zeppelin attack on England, the Germans retreat as British Sopwiths gain on them. Nine German men jump to their deaths so that the Zeppelin can gain speed and altitude (56:23–57:27). Moments later, a British flyer outdoes the German heroism. His guns jammed, the Brit soars above the Zeppelin and makes a suicide run into its center, destroying himself and the enemy's death machine (1:00:11–1:01:32). The Rutledge brothers are granted the film's final self-sacrifice. *All Quiet* contains no such moments of grandeur. Instead, Lewis Milestone's camera (his sweeping pan shots and rapid lateral tracks during battle scenes) captures the disorientation of war, the senselessness of it (44:00–49:20). In one harrowing moment,

Milestone photographs a British soldier running toward a barbed wire fence. A shell drops, and all that remains of the soldier are severed hands, clutching the wire he never scaled (44:59). The image of a whole body obliterated in an instant undermines any concept of heroism. Moreover, in *All Quiet*, the real enemy is portrayed as the people back home, filling up boys with false patriotism. Paul Baumner was one such victim. Early on, Paul and his classmates are goaded to war by an overzealous professor (3:25–9:39). Milestone's use of wide-angle close-ups suggests the professor is untrustworthy. Later, when on leave, Paul returns to the school and tells the students that there is no glory in war. "We live in the trenches . . . we try not to be killed . . . some times we are. That's all" (1:54:58). The war, contrary to the teacher's rhetoric, is about survival and nothing more. But the students accuse Paul of being a coward and refuse to believe him (1:56:50). Sadly, they'll have to find out for themselves.

Further Reading

Baird, Robert. *"Hell's Angels* above *The Western Front." Hollywood's World War I: Motion Picture Images,* ed. Peter C. Rollins and John E. O'Connor. Bowling Green, OH: Popular Press, 1997. 79–100.

Fussell, Paul. *The Great War in Modern Memory.* New York: Oxford University Press, 1975.

Leed, Eric J. *No Man's Land: Combat and Identity in World War I.* New York: Cambridge University Press, 1979.

FURTHER VIEWING

Dawn Patrol (1938)

Fighting 69th (1940)

The Great War (1996) (Doc.)

Guns of August (1964) (Doc.)

Unknown Soldier (1998) (TV)

7

The Great Depression, Documentary Expression, and Representing the Previously Unrepresented, 1929–1967

Bonnie and Clyde ◆ *Bound for Glory* ◆ *Bringing Up Baby*
Devil in a Blue Dress ◆ *The Grapes of Wrath* ◆ *It Happened One Night*
Marked Woman ◆ *Marty* ◆ *Meet John Doe* ◆ *On the Waterfront*
Raging Bull ◆ *The Shawshank Redemption* ◆ *Surviving the Dust Bowl*
To Kill a Mockingbird ◆ *Wild Boys of the Road* ◆ Double Bill: *Dance,*
Girl, Dance and *Outrage* ◆ Double Bill: *Gold Diggers of 1933* and
Footlight Parade ◆ Power and the Land: Four Documentary Portraits
of the Great Depression

Bonnie and Clyde (1967) (W)

Setting: Rowena, Texas; Joplin, Missouri; and Platte, Iowa, 1931–1934

Director: Arthur Penn

Screenplay: Robert Benton, David Newman, and Robert Towne (uncredited)

Director of Photography: Burnett Guffey

Cast: Warren Beatty (Clyde Barrow), Faye Dunaway (Bonnie Parker), Estelle Parsons (Blanche), and Denver Pyle (Frank Hamer)

Availability: Warner Bros. Home Video

Arthur Penn's breakout movie of love on the run appealed to counterculture audiences of the 1960s. A kind of American version of a French New Wave film, *Bonnie and Clyde* simultaneously looks back on the 1930s as it exudes a 1960s sensibility. In reality, Bonnie Parker and Clyde Barrow were two violent outlaws who from the spring of 1932 to May 1934 robbed banks, filling stations, and grocery stores across ten states, and they killed at least a dozen people along the way. But Penn's film glamorizes and sympathizes with the outlaws, making them counterculture rebels and 1960s symbols of women's liberation. In the opening sequence, a nude Bonnie Parker moves about restlessly in her bedroom (2:17–3:55). She collapses on the bed, and turns her face, waiting for something to take her from her bored life. Outside Bonnie's window, Clyde Barrow attempts to steal her mother's car. Bonnie runs down the stairs, and eggs him on to commit a robbery (8:33–9:12). After the robbery, Clyde sizes up Bonnie, telling her how she doesn't want to live the boring life of a domesticated woman (11:11–13:03). He even suggests that she get rid of a spit curl on her cheek so that she won't look like a waitress. Bonnie agrees, redesigning her hair in the booth. Her pliability suggests that she's a follower, but as the film evolves she transforms into a gun-toting leader who encourages Clyde in his life of crime. Because of Clyde's sexual problems (he is impotent and afraid of women), her power over him doesn't seem to be grounded in the usual "feminine wiles." The two outlaws are also made sympathetic because of their disrespect for law, a popular theme with college students during the turbulent Viet Nam era. In one telling scene, Clyde helps a farmer whose land has been repossessed rattle bullets into his old home, shattering panes of glass (15:22–17:21). This is a moment of catharsis for the dislocated farmer, and a feeling of comradeship develops between the two, when Clyde gleefully confesses, "We rob banks" (17:10). In reality, the Barrow gang had no sympathies for the dispossessed. Barrow was a remorseless killer after small stakes. He drove his V-8 cars with ruthless and dangerous abandon (he even once wrote a letter to Henry Ford, thanking him for the fine craftsmanship), and fired bullets randomly into crowds. But in the film, Clyde is shaken up after he has to ward off a cleaver-wielding butcher. "I didn't want to hurt him" (20:32–21:06), and later he's saddened when during a robbery he has to kill a teller who hitches on to his running board (37:43). The real villain in this film is Frank Hamer, the Texas Ranger who wants them dead. Ruthlessly, Hamer wheedles information out of the captured Blanche Barrow (Clyde's sister-in-law) by feigning kindness (1:34:43–1:37:37). In the film's violent apogee, Hamer's men bushwhack the two outlaws, firing over 150 rounds of ammunition into their bodies. But the deaths of Bonnie and Clyde have a transcendent glory. Just prior to being destroyed by the establishment, the two outlaws look at each other without regret or remorse, but with kind affirmation and love.

Further Reading

Cott, Nancy F. *"Bonnie and Clyde." Past Imperfect: History According to the Movies,* ed. Mark C. Carnes. New York: Henry Holt, 1996. 220–223.

Crowdus, Gary and Richard Porton. "The Importance of a Singular Guiding Vision: An Interview with Arthur Penn." *Cineaste* 20 (Spring 1993): 4–16.

MacNab, Geoffrey. "Song of the Open Road." *Sight and Sound* 9 (August 1999): 58–59.

Prym, John. "Black Hat, Yellow Hat (From *Bonnie and Clyde* to *Dick Tracy*)." *Sight and Sound* 59 (Autumn): 264–265.

Treherne, John. *The Strange History of Bonnie and Clyde*. New York: Jonathan Cape, 1984.

Bound for Glory (1976) (PG)

Setting: East Palma, Texas; Los Angeles, 1936–1940

Director: Hal Ashby

Screenplay: Robert Getchell

Director of Photography: Haskell Wexler

Cast: David Carradine (Woody Guthrie), Ronny Cox (Ozark Bob), Melinda Dillon (Woody's wife, Mary), and John Lehne (Locke)

Availability: MGM/UA

In 1985, Bruce Springsteen said that Woody Guthrie's "This Land Is Your Land" should become America's new national anthem. Springsteen's working-class music, along with the farm-angst of John Mellencamp, and the word play and rootlessness of Bob Dylan all owe a debt of gratitude to Guthrie, a leftist Okie who in his memoir, *Bound for Glory*, became a living incarnation of John Steinbeck's fictional Tom Joad. Guthrie so loved *The Grapes of Wrath* that he named one of his sons Joady. Recently British rocker Billy Bragg with the help of backing band Wilco recorded two *Mermaid Ave.* albums in which they put music to several of Woody's unrecorded song lyrics. What is it about this man that has so touched the history of popular music? Hal Ashby's *Bound for Glory* attempts some answers. In the film, Woody is portrayed as a rootless, rambling, and talented musician who comes to political consciousness during the turbulent 1930s. Living in Dust-Bowl-ravaged Texas, Woody tries to make a living painting signs. But his heart is in creative energies, not commercial ones. When he is hired to paint, he does things his way. An owner wants a store sign painted black, but Woody stubbornly does it in red and white, claiming that it picks up better from a distance (15:01–15:32). This refusal to conform has lasting appeal for romantic rock musicians. Also appealing is Guthrie's desire to explore. During his travels by car and train Guthrie sees and "lives" a series of injustices. He sees fruit pickers exploited by greedy landowners (1:04:04–1:04:45). He sees 300 people waiting in a fruit-picking camp for jobs that will only accommodate thirty of them (1:10:45–1:12:48). He sees railroad police beating up and killing "tramps" or "bums" (41:36–46:17; 57:00–57:13). He sees the church doing nothing to help the needy (48:08–48:40). When Woody approaches a preacher to work for food, the preacher tells him he has no work to be done, and if he gave him a free meal that would be "charity," and charity does nothing but harm in the long run. All of these experiences make him want to sing the people's music, to sing songs for the needy, songs to help organize the masses to unionize. Woody is further appealing because he cared so deeply about the everyday men and women that he saw and shared stories with that he would never abandon them. He never compromised his artistic vision for commercial success. While playing a live weekly show on Los Angeles's KTNS, Woody refuses to kow-tow to the sponsors. Station manager Locke asks Woody to "clean up" his politics. He even forces him to make a list in advance of "safe" songs to sing (1:44:50–1:45:48). But like the earlier scene with the red/white versus black sign, Woody does things his way. During a live musical number, Woody changes the song list, saying, "I just decided to sing something else," and he goes into a stomping version of "Do-Re-Mi" (1:49:33–1:50:48). The song indicts the California police for turning back migrants at the state line for not having at least $50 in their pockets. Needless to say, Woody eventually loses his gig on KTNS, but his spirit is undeterred: "I don't need this place. . . . I don't need you. I can sing while I'm walking," he tells the station manager (2:13:22–2:13:44). As a family man, Woody was insufferable. He abandoned his wife and children whenever he got the urge to ramble or get in touch with the "people." Because he lived for his art, his rootlessness, womanizing, and nonconformity ruined his marriage. Perhaps it was this desire to be forever free, to work and hone his craft to its greatest potential at the expense of domestic happiness that some rock musicians find strangely appealing. No doubt, it is the most complicated aspect of his persona.

Further Reading

Guthrie, Woody. *Bound for Glory*. New York: E. P. Dutton, 1943.
Kael, Pauline. "Affirmation." Review of *Bound for Glory*. *The New Yorker* 52 (December 13, 1976): 148–152.
McBride, Joseph. "Sneak Preview: On the Set of *Bound for Glory*." *Film Comment* 12.6 (November/December 1976): 26–28.

Bringing Up Baby (1938) (W)

Setting: New York City and Westlake, Connecticut, 1937

Director: Howard Hawks

Screenplay: Dudley Nichols and Hagar Wilde

Director of Photography: Russell Metty

Cast: Katherine Hepburn (Susan Vance), Cary Grant (Dr. David Huxley), Virginia Walker (Alice Swallow), Fritz Feld (Dr. Fritz Lehman), and Walter Catlett (Constable Slocum)

Availability: RKO/Turner Home Video

In the 1930s audiences escaped the Depression by enjoying gangster stories, musicals, and screwball comedies. *Bringing Up Baby* was released near the end of this escapist cycle, but it thrilled audiences with its gender inversions and commentary on intellectual life. Dr. David Huxley is a paleontologist, but his academic work keeps him sequestered from having fun. In the opening shots, Howard Hawks features Huxley high atop scaffolding, musing over the missing bone to his brontosaurus. The dinosaur, by implication, represents Huxley's dead-end life. Even his bride-to-be, Alice Swallow, dressed in a restricting black tailored suit, represses him. "Nothing must interfere with your work," she says about his desire to have a honeymoon (2:47). Alice also feels that the brontosaurus will "be our child" (3:06). But David wants more. Behind his professorial glasses is a fun-loving man bursting to get out. David enjoys using slang ("Gee whiz," and "I'll knock him for a loop"), and he definitely wants an old-fashioned honeymoon. Shortly after Hawks' opening exposition, David meets the carefree and charming Susan Vance on a posh golf course. Susan, unlike Alice, is impetuous. When she first appears on screen, Susan is dressed in white flowing clothes, and she moves briskly in the open space of the golf course (5:06–8:49). She's alive and energized. She plays David's golf ball as if the lie were hers and then says, by way of apology, "What does it matter. It's only a game, anyway" (6:09). Moments later she's driving off in his car. Through a series of plot machinations (one involving a leopard, Baby), David ends up partnered with Susan. Some of the film's great comedy is watching these two opposites actually connect. Together they run around the Westlake, Connecticut, grounds chasing the Vances' dog, George, who has run off with David's dinosaur bone, an intercostal clavicle (44:34–47:23). They also sing to Baby in order to calm her down, and catch her so that she cannot eat George who still hasn't retrieved the buried clavicle (1:17:38–1:19:58). David too, during the quest in Westlake, comes to find Susan's madcap antics attractive. Twice he watches out for her safety (1:04:29–1:08:40;1:34:58–1:36:22). Susan also directly tells him that he looks so much better without his glasses (43:05–43:07; 43:33), suggesting that fun lies under the surface. Susan, played by Katherine Hepburn in one of her early strong-woman roles, is nothing like the stuffy Connecticut family that she hails from. She refuses to fall into boring conformity, and she is splendidly transgressive. Although her objective—to keep David from marrying Miss Swallow—seems sexist and degrading, it is justified in the film because Swallow, as her last name implies, would literally devour David. Moreover, Susan is refreshingly disrespectful towards the law and psychiatry. When, late in the film, the constable, his men, and a crazed psychiatrist refuse to believe the truth, she spins a wonderful yarn, telling them she's "Swing Door Suzy," a member of the dreaded "Leopard Gang" (1:27:46–1:31:31). Her fanciful tale highlights the amount of disdain she holds for them. In the end, David doesn't marry Alice. Instead, he confesses that with Susan he had "the best day I ever had in my whole life" (1:39:30). Susan teaches him to balance academia with fun. In the rousing final scene, David stands atop his scaffolding as Susan, swinging back and forth on a ladder, excitedly confesses her love for him. During the exchange, she loses her balance, jumps on the dinosaur exhibit, and it all crashes underneath as David grabs her arm. The barrier between them is broken and so is David's sheltered way of life.

Further Reading

Cavell, Stanley. "Leopards in Connecticut." *Pursuits of Happiness: The Hollywood Comedy of Remarriage*. Cambridge, MA: Harvard University Press, 1981. 113–132.

Mast, Gerald. "Comedies of Youth and Age: *Bringing Up Baby* and *Monkey Business*." *Howard Hawks: Storyteller*. New York: Oxford University Press, 1982. 133–161.

McCarthy, Todd. "Big Spender: RKO, *Gunga Din*, and *Bringing Up Baby*." *Howard Hawks: The Grey Fox of Hollywood*. New York: Grove Press, 1997. 243–258.

Devil in a Blue Dress (1995) (R) (M)

Setting: Los Angeles, 1948

Director: Carl Franklin

Screenplay: Carl Franklin

Director of Photography: Tak Fujimoto

Cast: Denzel Washington (Easy Rawlins), Tom Sizemore (DeWitt Albright), Don Cheadle (Mouse), Jennifer Beals (Daphne Monet), Terry Kinney (Todd Carter), Maury Chaykin (Matthew Terrell), and Joseph Latimore (Frank Green)

Availability: Columbia Tri-Star Home Video

Carl Franklin's African American–themed Film Noir, based on the novel by Walter Mosley, tells the story of one man's attempt to live the American Dream and of his descent into cynicism. Easy Rawlins is a war vet living in post–World War Two Los Angeles. The city thrives with blacks from Texas and Louisiana (who came to find work) and has become a dynamic cultural landscape with the emergence of such unique forms as Jump Blues (an early incarnation of rock 'n' roll). Easy owns a house, drives a 1946 Pontiac, and envisions becoming a part of the American success myth. But he's black, and thus a victim of racism. First he loses his job. The foreman refuses to explain the firing and calls Easy, "Fella." Easy, as played by Denzel Washington with a Sidney Poitier–type of intensity and integrity, snaps, "My name's not 'fella.' It's Ezekiel Rawlins" (4:23–4:38). He demands to be looked on as a human being. But as an unemployed machinist, he needs work, and thus becomes a hard-boiled detective. Desperate to pay bills, Easy falls into a demi-monde of murder and double-cross and eventually discovers a harder lesson on race. Easy is hired by Dewitt Albright to find mayoral hopeful Todd Carter's missing girlfriend, Daphne. But the plot is full of twists. Easy gets false information on Daphne, the missing white girl, from an old lover, Coretta. But when Coretta is murdered, Easy is implicated.

The police lack enough evidence to convict, but they do flex their power by giving Easy a brutal "race-motivated" beating in the precinct (29:13–30:49). Later, Easy crosses paths with the oily Mr. Terrel, the other mayoral hopeful. Terrel, too, wants to find Daphne. Easy, feeling overwhelmed by the violent threats of Albright and the police, calls for backup from an old childhood friend, the dangerous Mouse (played with a mixture of innocent malevolence and chaotic charm by Don Cheadle). Mouse, a figure further outside the mainstream than Easy, helps the detective defeat the dark forces lurking in Film Noir. With Mouse, Easy learns that Daphne is hooked up with the black gangster Tony Green. He also discovers that Albright wasn't hired by Carter to find Daphne, but is actually working for Terrell who wants to destroy Carter. Nonetheless, there's one final plot twist in this cynical world. Easy discovers that Daphne isn't Green's lover, but his sister. She's black, passing for white in a segregated society (1:17:20–1:18:09). Carter loves her, but he can't cross the "color line" and lose the election (1:31:04–1:32:45). Easy also learns that Terrell, the other candidate, has a fetish for young boys, and Daphne has pictures that prove it. Carter uses the pictures to keep the race-mixing love affair under wraps and wins the election. In the end, Easy becomes a Philip Marlowe–type of detective: world-weary from all he's learned while traveling down the sun-drenched mean streets of L.A.

Further Reading

Arthur, Paul. "Los Angeles as Scene of the Crime." *Film Comment* 32 (July/August 1996):20–27.

Cripps, Thomas. Review of *Devil in a Blue Dress. American Historical Review* 102 (February 1997): 250–251.

Mosley, Walter. *Devil in a Blue Dress.* New York: W. W. Norton, 1990.

Rich, Ruby B. "Dumb Lugs and Femmes Fatales: Film Noir Is Back with a Vengeance from *The Last Seduction* and *Devil in a Blue Dress*. But It's Noir with a Difference." *Sight and Sound* 5 (November 1995): 6–11.

The Grapes of Wrath (1940)

Setting: Oklahoma, Route 66, and California

Director: John Ford

Screenplay: Nunnally Johnson

Director of Photography: Gregg Toland

Cast: Henry Fonda (Tom Joad), Jane Darwell (Ma Joad), John Carradine (Reverend Casey), Charley Grapewin (Grampa Joad), John Qualen (Muley), Russell Simpson (Old Tom "Pa" Joad), Seffie Tilbury (Gramma), Frank Darien (Uncle John), Charles Tannen (Joe), and Paul Guilfoyle (Floyd)

Availability: 20th Century Fox Video

In 1938 *Life Magazine* sent novelist John Steinbeck and photographer Horace Bristol on assignment to write a series of articles on sharecroppers who had migrated from Oklahoma to California in the wake of the Dust Bowl. Steinbeck never completed the assignment. Instead, inundated with a wealth of information and bristling humanity, Steinbeck wrote the Pulitzer Prize–winning novel *The Grapes of Wrath*. In 1939, when director John Ford and photographer Gregg Toland brought Steinbeck's rich novel to the screen, the film's look was indebted to the grit of Farm Security Administration photographers Dorothea Lange (her famous "Migrant Mother" photograph became a 32-cent stamp in 1999), Walker Evans, and Arthur Rothstein. Under President Roosevelt's FSA, photographers documented the previously unrepresented in America. Sharecroppers, with their dignity and indomitable human spirit, became the subjects of many trenchant photographs of suffering. When the Joads arrive at an internment camp full of displaced sharecroppers, the images—captured in a Toland tracking shot—jump from the pages of *Life Magazine*. The worn shirts, muslin dresses, overbundled trucks full of family possessions, the shanty wood shacks, and threadbare tents are FSA images brought to the screen (1:04:03–1:08:54). The story of the Joads, torn from the land by the "dusters" and the banks foreclosing on their mortgage, captures a mood of dislocation and the ultimate triumph of the downtrodden. Everywhere the Joads travel on their odyssey to California they are pushed around. First, in a blistering scene, tractors come and demolish the homes of Muley Graves and other sharecroppers who won't get off the land (15:41–18:20). Tom Joad, who has just been released from prison for manslaughter, finds his parents gone, pushed off the land, and when the police arrive at the homestead, he ducks into the bushes. In closeup he comments, "Anybody ever told me I'd be hiding out on my own place," and then he spits. Lured by handbills that falsely promise work in California, the Joads head west. But the older members of their family, Grandpa and Gramma, die during the road trip (37:19–40:48; 59:21–1:01: 09). They cannot take the strain of being pushed off of a way of the life that they have embraced. After the Joads' misadventures at the internment camp—a man is attacked for being an "agitator," and an innocent woman is shot by an overzealous cop—a despondent Tom tells Ma that he is getting angry: "They working on our spirit" (1:16:10–1:16:38). Their spirit is worn down by a series of injustices. During the journey, the Joads are unwittingly made into scabs for the Keene ranch (1:18:50–1:21:17). They make very little money picking fruit—the company store charges more than what they earn—and when Tom tries to uncover the context behind the Keene ranch, he and his good friend Casey—who is organizing a strike—are attacked by camp police. Casey is killed, and Tom, in retaliation, kills Casey's murderer. The killing makes Tom a fugitive and eventually he abandons his family and lights out. In one of cinema's great moments of the triumph of resistance, Tom, with a Walt Whitmanesque edge, tells Ma what he'll remember: "Our people living like pigs and good rich land laying fallow, or maybe one guy with millions and 100,000 farmers starving." But he is the land, he is the people, and Henry Fonda, in perhaps his greatest role, concludes with some stirring words that suggest that he won't go away and the trouble won't be forgotten: "I'll be around in the dark. I'll be everywhere, wherever you can look. Wherever there's a fight so hungry people can eat, I'll be there. Wherever there's a cop beating on a guy, I'll be there. I'll be there in the way guys yell when they're mad" (1:59:37–2:02:24).

Further Reading

Farm Security Administration Collection, lcweb.loc.gov/spcoll/

Gregory, James N. *American Exodus: The Dust Bowl Migration and Okie Culture in California.* New York: Oxford University Press, 1989.

Sanderson, Jim. "American Romanticism in John Ford's *The Grapes of Wrath*: Horizontalness, Darkness, Christ, and F.D.R." *Literature/Film Quarterly* 17 (1989): 231–246.

Sobchack, Vivian C. "*The Grapes of Wrath* (1940): Thematic Emphasis through Visual Style." *American Quarterly* 31 (1979): 596–615.

"Speaking of Pictures: These by *Life* Prove Facts of *Grapes of Wrath*." *Life* 4 (February 19, 1940): 10–11.

It Happened One Night (1934) (W)

Setting: Miami, Florida; the South; the East Coast; and New York City

Director: Frank Capra

Screenplay: Robert Riskin

Director of Photography: Joseph Walker

Cast: Clark Gable (Peter Warne), Claudette Colbert (Ellie Andrews), Walter Connolly (Alexander Andrews), and Jameson Thomas (King Westley)

Availability: Columbia Tri-Star Home Video

Frank Capra's screwball comedy is a wonderful story of a young debutante's coming to age during the Great Depression. Ellie Andrews is a spoiled rich kid who defies her father by jumping off his yacht and trying to find the man she wants to elope with (and her father strongly disapproves of), King Westley. But by escaping the benign dictates of one patriarch she falls into the arms of another: out-of-work reporter Peter Warne. With Peter she begins an odyssey across the country in which she matures and learns about the Depression firsthand. Peter needs her help to lick his own version of the Depression: with Ellie as his traveling companion, he'll have an engaging story to sell to the newspapers and get back in the business (he was fired for unreliability and drunkenness). Together the two make a wonderful team: she's sassy and caring; he's full of bluster and overconfident bravado, but they are compatible. The key scene that illustrates their compatibility occurs when detectives try to find the lost heiress, and Ellie and Peter feign an argument in their cabin in order to convince the authorities that they are married (39:11–41:46). Ellie is good at taking Peter's lead and expanding the performance: "Well you don't have to lose your temper," she says, in the throes of anguish. After the authorities leave, the two travelers laugh with conspiratorial glee (41:20). On a dark note, this screwball comedy is painted in shades of the Great Depression. On the bus ride, an immigrant city boy cries because his mother is sick. She hasn't eaten "since yesterday," and she has spent all of her money on a bus ticket so that she can try to find work in New York. Ellie is moved by her story and without thinking about herself (a real sign of her newfound maturity) gives the woman the last of her own money, $10. Peter shows Ellie how to dunk a donut (donuts and coffee were standard food for drifters) (36:16–38–46). On their travels, the couple abandons the bus, sleeps in a farmer's field, and eats carrots for breakfast (54:47–59:27). They also hitchhike (a marvelous scene in which Ellie trumps the all-knowing Peter by proving that the "limb is mightier than the thumb" [59:34–1:04:20]). These were all common experiences for Depression-era drifters. As Peter rides back to Ellie to propose (he has been rehired by the paper), he stops at a railroad crossing and smiles at several "tramps" who are riding the train and waving (1:25:45–1:25:52). Of course, the two heroes transcend the shades of Depression surrounding this film and conquer the division between their social classes. Warne wins the approval of Ellie's father by not asking for the $10,000 reward offered for her safe return, and only asking to be compensated $39.60 for expenses. He also confesses his love for her: "Yeah, but don't hold that against me. I'm a little bit screwy myself!" (1:38:17). In the end, Ellie accepts the advice of her father. Earlier she had rejected his advice and ran. Now she runs away with his blessing.

Further Reading

Capra, Frank. "Winning the Grail." *The Name above the Title*. New York: Macmillan, 1971. 159–172.

Gottlieb, Sidney. "From Heroine to Brat: Frank Capra's Adaptation of 'Night Bus' (*It Happened One Night*)." *Literature/Film Quarterly* 16.2 (1988): 129–136.

Maltby, Richard. "*It Happened One Night*: The Recreation of the Patriarch." *Frank Capra: Authorship and the Studio System*, ed. Robert Sklar and Vito Zaggarrio. Philadelphia: Temple University Press, 1998. 130–163.

Scherle, Victor and William Turner Levy. "*It Happened One Night*." *The Films of Frank Capra*. Secaucus, NJ: Citadel Press, 1977. 122–129.

Troy, William. "Picaresque." *The Nation* 138 (March 14, 1934): 314.

Marked Woman (1937) (W)

Setting: New York City, 1936

Director: Lloyd Bacon

Screenplay: Abem Finkel and Robert Rossen

Director of Photography: George Barnes

Cast: Bette Davis (Mary Dwight), Humphrey Bogart (David Graham), Lola Lane (Dorothy "Gabby" Marvin), Isabel Jewell (Emmy Lou Eagan), Eduardo Ciannelli (Johnny Vanning), and Jane Bryan (Betty Strauber)

Availability: MGM/UA Home Video

In the spring of 1936, New York District Attorney Thomas E. Dewey (later a presidential candidate) sent the notorious "Vice Czar" Charles "Lucky" Luciano to prison for a thirty- to fifty-year stretch. Luciano, an heir to "Dutch" Schultz, made his money from kickbacks on prostitution ($10 a week from over 1,000 prostitutes). Dewey was able to indict Luciano through the helpful testimony of prostitutes such as Cokey Flo, Dixie, and Jenny the Factory. *Marked Woman* is based on this tawdry story, but its emphasis is not on the Dewey character, David Graham, but on the five women who testify. Mary Dwight, played by Bette Davis with a rat-a-tat-tat all-knowing energy, is a "clip joint hostess." She works in mobster Johnny Vanning's plush nightclub, entertains men, gets them drunk, and hopes they lose a bundle gambling and drinking. She apparently has no moral compunction about her work. When Vanning first approaches her about the job, she asks, "What's in it for us?" (4:31), and later, when one of the girls complains about their lifestyle, Mary says, "We've all tried the twelve-and-a-half a week stuff. It's no good." She likes her comfort. But under the hard-boiled surface is a sentimentalist: Mary is helping put her upright sister, Betty Strauber, through college. When Betty comes to visit, Mary's four clip-joint companions pretend to be models for a rich clothing store. But the charade doesn't work long. When a young man is murdered by Vanning's thugs for not paying up on his drinking/gambling tab, Mary is indicted as an accessory to murder by Graham (her name and address were written down in a matchbook). Prior to and during the trial, Mary play-acts, pretending to be a cooperative witness but actually setting Graham up for a false testimony (40:00–42:47; 43:35–45:57). Her exploits get Vanning off the hook, but her actions alienate her sister who discovers just how tawdry Mary's lifestyle really is (46:23–46:26). Back at the apartment, Betty confesses that she is not returning to college because she is ashamed. Director Lloyd Bacon photographs the scene with Betty higher in the composition than Mary, suggesting Betty's moral superiority over her "fallen" sister (51:52–53:58). Later, through the insistence of Emmy Lou, Betty attends a Vanning party. Afterwards, Mary calls her a "little fool," and this time she stands higher in the composition, set atop the stairs outside the apartment. Now she's the one with superior knowledge. Angry at Mary's disapproval, Betty leaves and returns to Vanning's. There, she refuses to have sex with a high-powered client, Calhoun, and Vanning, outraged, slaps her down a long winding staircase. Betty is killed (1:02:08–1:03:04). When

Mary finds out, she wants revenge on Vanning and she goes to Graham for help. Vanning tries to strong-arm Mary's silence. He has his thugs violently beat her and cut a cross into her cheek (1:13:01–1:13:57). But Vanning's overzealousness seals his fate. When he tries to murder Emmy Lou, a witness to the Strauber killing, she escapes and agrees to help Mary. Ultimately, the five sisters of the night defeat the vicious mobster because of their collectivist energies. At the trial, they sit strongly together. Afterward, as David Graham is being congratulated on his stunning victory, the five women, all of them "marked" by societal prejudices, walk the street in unison, disappearing into the fog, separate from David's success, but strong in their friendship.

Further Reading

Eckert, Charles. "The Anatomy of a Proletarian Film: Warner's *Marked Woman*." *Movies and Methods*, vol. 2, ed. Bill Nichols. Berkeley: University of California Press, 1985. 418–425.

Haralovich, Mary Beth. "The Proletarian Woman's Film of the 1930s: Contending with Censorship and Entertainment." *Screen* 31 (Summer 1990): 172–187.

Kay, Karen. "Sisters of the Night." *Movies and Methods*, vol. 1, ed. Bill Nichols. Berkeley: University of California Press, 1976. 185–193.

"Movie of the Week." *Life* 2 (April 19, 1937): 49–51.

Marty (1955)

Setting: New York City, 1955

Director: Delbert Mann

Screenplay: Paddy Chayefsky

Director of Photography: Joseph LaShelle

Cast: Ernest Borgnine (Marty Pilletti), Betsy Blair (Clara Snyder), Esther Minciotti (Mrs. Pilletti), and Joe Mantell (Angie)

Availability: MGM/UA Home Video

"When you gonna get married?" a customer asks Marty, the butcher. "What's a matter with you?" (2:04–2:42). Marty, pained by the questions, rolls his eyes in self-defense. At thirty-four he regards himself as a "fat ugly man" who has passed the marrying age. He has felt too much "heartache" and has gone into retreat. Later that night, Marty calls a girl on the telephone, and closes his eyes in pain as she rejects him (16:05–16:29). During dinner, his mother encourages him to go dating and dancing at the ballroom. Marty replies, "Whatever it is women like I ain't got. . . . I got hurt enough. I don't want to get hurt no more. . . . I got feelings, you know?" (17:04–19:20). Paddy Chayefsky's script, from an original teleplay, is one of cinema's most heartfelt stories. Instead of presenting us with the problems of beautiful people (as does the majority of television programming and movies), Chayefsky gives audiences an authentic glimpse into the working class and the lives of the lonely. Later that night, Marty does go to the ballroom, and meets a plain-looking chemistry teacher, Clara, who has been stood up by her date. He identifies with her rejection, and follows her outside. Poignantly he asks, "Excuse me, Miss, would you care to dance?" and she turns and cries on his shoulder (27:33–28:12). Next, they're dancing on the floor and the infectious Marty amuses Clara with his happy chatter. Later, they go to a little restaurant, and he tells her about his army experiences and how he felt lost after the war and had contemplated suicide (42:05–42:20). She responds with a "Yes. I know," implying that she understands his pain, because she too has had similar thoughts. During the evening the couple shows a striking compatibility by offering each other advice. Clara says that Marty should go ahead and buy the butcher shop because he has "so much warmth, so much capacity," that he'll be successful (45:12–45:42). He later tells her that she'll be a little girl forever if she doesn't move away from her Dad (50:24–51:40). But Marty's friends and mother don't approve of Clara (secretly they are afraid of losing him), and the next day he fails to telephone her as he had promised to do. With tears in her eyes, Clara watches "Ed Sullivan" (1:25:43–1:26:11). Marty, back at Michael's bar, hears his buddies talking as always about having nothing to do, and closes his eyes. This gesture repeats a motif used earlier in the film, but this time Marty opens his eyes not to the same old pain of loneliness, but to a future (1:27:07–1:28:21). He no longer wants to be "miserable" and "stupid," and he decides to live free from the opinions of others: "You don't like her? That's too bad." He telephones Clara.

Further Reading

Clum, John M. "The Oscar Winner." *Paddy Chayefsky*. Boston: Twayne Publishers, 1976. 91–99.

Crowther, Bosley. Review of *Marty*. *New York Times* (April 23, 1955): II:1.

Osborne, Robert. "Best Actor, 1955: Ernest Borgnine in *Marty*." *Academy Awards Illustrated: A Complete History of Hollywood's Academy Awards with Words and Pictures*. La Habra: ESE California, 1969. 213.

Meet John Doe (1941)

Setting: A major American metropolitan area, 1941

Director: Frank Capra

Screenplay: Robert Riskin

Director of Photography: George Barnes

Cast: Gary Cooper (Long John Willoughby), Barbara Stanwyck (Ann Mitchell), Edward Arnold (D. B. Norton), Regis Toomey (Bert Hansen), and J. Farrell MacDonald ("Sourpuss" Smithers)

Availability: Good Times Home Video

Frank Capra was not enamored of the New Deal. Despite championing the little guys (down-on-their-luck reporters, novice politicians, and out-of-work farmers) in a series of 1930s films, Capra was a populist and he was opposed to using government intervention to make the economy work. The New Deal had sought to regulate a faltering economy by balancing the power of big business with an increase in the power bases of labor, consumer spending, and the government itself. Capra's philosophy, down home and naïve, was best expressed by Bert Hansen, the soda jerk in *Meet John Doe* (58:44–1:04:48). "Long" John Willoughby, losing his own identity in the fabricated John Doe concocted by reporter Ann Mitchell, had sought asylum in a small town. But while resting in a diner, he is discovered and eventually meets Hansen and fellow members of the John Doe club. Hansen, in a superb near-soliloquy delivered with halting pauses and sincerity by character actor Regis Toomey, tells how he became friends with his neighbor "Sourpuss" Smithers because of what Doe had said during a radio address. Doe has transformed the whole community. Hansen tells how everyone chipped in to help Grubel, an out of work senior citizen, who didn't want any charity. The community supported Grubel by giving him odd jobs such as cutting lawns and making furniture. Hansen's words are coated with an anti–welfare state sentiment. His populist agenda, people should help each other, relies on philanthropy and goodwill, not government intervention. It champions individualism but seems unrealistic during harsh economic times. Nonetheless, after hearing this moving testament to what John Doe represents, Willoughby returns to the cause. He and Ann begin to believe in the character they have created and in the power of the John Doe movement. But as much as Capra distrusts big government, he distrusts big business and fascism even more. Once D. B. Norton, the brutal newspaper publisher who had taken over the *Bulletin* and fired forty workers, sees the strength of the John Doe movement, he decides to use it for his own ends: to create out of the John Doe Club a third political party with himself nominated for president of the United States (1:17:28–1:19:08). In his opinion, the American people need an "iron hand" and "discipline" (1:32:02). Ann is shocked when she hears of his plans, and Doe, who busts in on a meeting of Norton and a host of business executives, refuses to fall in line. His refusal temporarily destroys him. At a John Doe rally, Willoughby tries to inform his fellow Does of Norton's plans, but the editor seizes the moment, accuses Doe of being a phony, and shuts off the power to the microphones before Doe can clear himself (1:39:04–1:48:08). Lost, confused, and somewhat crucified, Doe contemplates suicide. In order to resurrect the John Doe movement, Willoughby stands atop City Hall ready to jump. But Ann, sick with fever, arrives, and in one of cinema's great avowals of love, throws herself into John's arms, and rapidly says "If it's worth dying for, it's worth living for. . . . Oh, please, John, help me. . . . If you die, I want to die too. . . . Oh, I love you," before collapsing in his arms. Together, they leave, ready once again to take up the people's fight.

Further Reading

Phelps, Glenn Alan. "The Populist Films of Frank Capra." *Journal of American Studies* 13.3 (1979): 377–392.

Scherle, Victor and Turner Levy. *"Meet John Doe." The Films of Frank Capra*. Secaucus, NJ: Citadel Press, 1977. 174–185.

Stricker, Frank. "Repressing the Working Class: Individualism and the Masses in Frank Capra's Films." *Labor History* 31.4 (1990): 454–467.

Willis, Donald. "Meet John Doe." *The Films of Frank Capra*. Metuchen, NJ: Scarecrow Press, 1974. 38–57.

On the Waterfront (1954)

Setting: New York City, 1954

Director: Elia Kazan

Screenplay: Malcolm Johnson (articles), Budd Schulberg

Director of Photography: Boris Kaufman

Cast: Marlon Brando (Terry Malloy), Eva Marie Saint (Edie Doyle), Karl Malden (Father Barry), Rod Steiger (Charley Malloy), and Lee J. Cobb (Johnny Friendly)

Availability: Columbia Tri-Star Home Video

On the Waterfront is an exposé of underworld involvement in New York's waterfront local. The longshoremen are exploited by the vicious union organizer Johnny Friendly, who forces workers to take small loans with a high return rate in order to work. The conditions and wages are also bad. In a disturbing scene, waterfront foreman Mac tosses several numbered tags into a mass of workers. They fight and scrape with each other for the tags—a ticket to work in the "hole" (17:37–18:06). Working under Friendly is Terry Malloy, a former prizefighter now pushing thirty. Terry is oblivious to the corruption around him. All he cares about is having some loose change "jangling" in his pocket. But after he unwittingly sets up Joey Doyle to be killed, Terry starts questioning things. Outside the saloon he shakes his head and says, "He wasn't a bad kid, that Joey" (3:49). He thought Friendly's goons were going to "lean on him a little bit," not kill him. Inside the bar, he tries to express his feelings to Friendly, but he can't. Instead, he observes Friendly's viciousness as he brutally smacks around Skin, who is $50 short in his "collections" (9:36–10:23). Terry leaves confused, open to change. The next day, Terry is asked to spy on Joey's sister Edie and Father Barry, people who are organizing resistance to the corruption. At the church, Terry's awakening continues (21:06–24:11). As Father Barry concludes his talk on "fighting back," a group of Friendly's goons, holding truncheon sticks and baseball bats, attack the parishioners. Terry grabs

Edie's hand and leads her to safety through a backdoor fire escape. At the park, Terry opens up to Edie in one of cinema's great love scenes (25:58–30:47). Somewhat inarticulate, Terry tries to hold Edie's attention by teasing her and picking up a glove she dropped and placing it on his own hand. The gesture shows both tenderness and an inability to say directly what he feels. She in turn expresses her tenderness toward him by saying that if he were one of her students (and if she were a parochial school teacher) she would have used a "little more patience and kindness." Edie's love, Father Barry's two-fisted preaching, and Terry's witnessing of Friendly's continued cruelty (the waterfront death of state witness Dugan) make Terry speak out against the corruption: "For years I've been ratting on myself and I didn't even know it" (1:39:39). For several critics, the film's plot of testifying seemed to be director Elia Kazan's apologia and rationalization for naming names before the House Un-American Activities Committee (HUAC) and helping to ferret out communists in the movie industry. No doubt, the parallels between film story and Kazan's life are a little too conveniently allegorical, and blurring communists with mobsters is grossly unfair, but *On the Waterfront*, in its story of one man's redemption and discovery of lost dignity, still packs a real emotional punch. When Terry realizes that "I ain't a bum, Edie," that he was right, the screen glows with his epiphany (1:34:27–1:34:41). That moment occurs because of a prior scene in back of a cab between Terry and his big-brother Charley (1:10:57–1:15:02). Charley tries to stop Terry from testifying by offering him a cushy job, but Terry is no longer concerned about his own comforts. The rights of the workers are now a greater responsibility. Charley, nervous, knowing that if Terry doesn't come around, one or both of them will be killed, pulls a gun on his brother, demanding that he take the job. An incredulous Terry pushes the gun away, and mumbles, "Wow." Charley tries to change the subject by bringing up Terry's prize-fighting past and saying how it was a shame that the manager brought him along too fast. But Terry won't allow Charley to delude himself anymore. "It wasn't him Charley, it was you." Terry goes on to express how his own brother and Friendly asked him to throw the fight against Wilson for some "short end money." Terry was ready that night and could have beat Wilson, but because of a "favor" he threw away his "shot" at the title and his career. The action made him "a bum. Which is what I am. Let's face it." Charley recognizes his own guilt in Terry's fallen dignity and lets him go, sacrificing himself. And Terry, by testifying, proves that he can stand up against the man who ruined him and is ruining the lives of hundreds along the waterfront daily.

Further Reading

Hey, Kenneth R. "Ambivalence in a Theme in *On the Waterfront* (1954): An Interdisciplinary Approach to Film Study." *Hollywood as Historian: American Film in a Cultural Context*, ed. Peter C. Rollins and Ray B. Browne, Lexington: University Press of Kentucky, 1983. 159–189.

Murray, Edward. *"On the Waterfront." Ten Film Classics: A Reviewing*. New York: Frederick Ungar Publishing Co., 1978. 86–101.

Naremore, James. "Marlon Brando in *On the Waterfront*." *Acting in the Cinema*. Berkeley: University of California Press, 1988. 193–212.

Neve, Brian. "The 1950's: the Case of Elia Kazan and *On the Waterfront*." *Cinema, Politics, and Society in America*, ed. Philip Davies and Brian Neve. New York: St. Martin's Press, 1981. 97–118.

———. "*On the Waterfront* (Film in Context)." *History Today* 45 (June 1995): 19–24.

Raging Bull (1980) (R)

Setting: New York City, Detroit, and Miami, 1941–1964

Director: Martin Scorsese

Screenplay: Paul Schrader and Mardik Martin

Director of Photography: Michael Chapman

Cast: Robert De Niro (Jake LaMotta), Cathy Moriarty (Vicki LaMotta), Joe Pesci (Joey LaMotta), and Nicholas Colasanto (Tommy Como)

Availability: MGM/UA Home Video

Sports films are rarely great works of art (the situations tend to be too grandiose and clichéd, or the film can't replicate the reality of the sports-watching television experience), but Martin Scorsese's biopic, *Raging Bull*, succeeds because it is not romanticized and it exposes the underbelly of boxing and one man's personal obsessions and demons. Jake LaMotta is a middleweight contender, but because he refuses to strike a deal with mobster Tommy Como, he will never get a shot at the title. His drive to rise above his Bronx background is thwarted by powers beyond him. In the ring, he's a dynamo, but outside of it, his frustrations and insecurities spill into his domestic life. Robert De Niro plays the part with improvisational brilliance, often repeating snatches of dialogue to give the character more menace, and to portray a man, who through repetition, feels he can control his universe. But LaMotta is frequently out of control. After losing a fight, he gets into a needless argument with his first wife over a steak. "Don't overcook it. You overcook it, it's no good," he says. And the argument escalates until she's violently dropping the steak on the table, and he's turning the table over (8:14–9:34). Later with the second wife, Vicki, a similar pattern emerges. When she comments that boxer Tony Janiro is "handsome," he wakes her up in the middle of the night and asks, "Why'd you say he had a pretty face?" (56:14–58:06). Later in the ring, LaMotta decimates Janiro's face. And in 1949 prior to his championship bout with Marcel Cerdan,

LaMotta brutalizes Vicki. After mobster Tommy Como, the man who arranged the fight, leaves, Jake goes ballistic. Como had kissed Vicki on his way out of the apartment. Jake takes Vicki aside. "What's that all about?" he asks. She doesn't answer to his satisfaction and he slaps her hard. "You hear what I said?" he rages. "You don't ever have any disrespect for me. You hear what I said? You hear what I said!" (1:16:02–1:18:02). And months after winning the title, as he fears holding onto it, Jake's suspicions of his wife's infidelity loom. He asks his brother, "You fuck my wife?" (1:26:46), and then he confronts Vicki with similar questions. He eventually brutally beats them both (1:30:28–1:31:24). Jake's obsessions eventually destroy his two closest relationships. And in the end, he's doing stand-up comedy, and ironically quoting Marlon Brando in *On the Waterfront*. Sadly, perhaps Jake was only happy for a brief period from 1944 to 1946 (41:06–43:33). During a montage sequence, Scorsese mixes black-and-white still photographs of LaMotta's matches with colorful home-style movies of Jake and Vicki playing by a swimming pool, Joey getting married atop a brownstone roof, and the brothers' kids playing in a backyard. The home movies break the black-and-white continuity and present a brief moment when warm-hued colors had entered the starkness surrounding LaMotta.

Further Reading

Bromwich, David. Review of *Raging Bull*. *The New Leader* 76 (December 13, 1993): 21.

Hemmeter, Gail Carnicelli and Thomas Hemmeter. "The Word Made Flesh: Language in *Raging Bull*." *Literature/Film Quarterly* 14.2 (1986): 101–105.

Librach, Ronald S. "The Last Temptation in *Mean Streets* and *Raging Bull*." *Literature/Film Quarterly* 20.1 (1992): 14–24.

Thomson, David. "The Director as Raging Bull: Why Can a Woman Be More Like a Photograph?" *Film Comment* 34 (May/June 1998): 52–59.

The Shawshank Redemption (1994) (R) (M)

Setting: Shawshank Prison, Maine, 1947–1967

Director: Frank Darabont

Screenplay: Frank Darabont

Director of Photography: Roger Deakins

Cast: Tim Robbins (Andy Dufresne), Morgan Freeman (Ellis Boyd "Red" Redding), Bob Gunton (Warden Samuel Norton), Clancy Brown (Captain Brian Hadley), and James Whitmore (Brooks Hatlen)

Availability: Warner Bros. Home Video

Set in Shawshank Prison, Maine, from 1947 to 1967, this hard-hitting exposé based on a short story by Stephen King tells of dehumanizing conditions in prisons and one man's redemption. In Shawshank, the men have been brutalized to disrespect each other. As new inmates are brought in, lifers stand along the fences catcalling and hollering (10:37–12:35). They even place bets on who will be the first to crack. That night a heavy-set guy breaks down and is beaten to death by Hadley, a twisted guard (15:41–19:47). The next morning, newcomer Andy Dufresne asks what the dead man's name is and nobody cares. Life has become cheapened. In prison, Andy also discovers the horrors of personal trauma. He is raped repeatedly by the "sisters." He tells Red, his best friend and an expert in procuring contraband, "I'm not a homosexual." "Neither are they. You have to be human first," Red replies, suggesting that prison strips a man of his sexual identity and decency (26:40). Ultimately rehabilitation is a joke in prison. Instead of being socialized for reentry into society, the men are made dependent on the institution. Brooks, a lifer since 1912, is released in the mid-1950s. He has a job sacking groceries, but the world is too fast. He lacks survival skills. As a result, he hangs himself, leaving knife scratches in his boarding room wall, sadly reminding people that he did exist (1:00:51–1:05:15). Red too is brutalized by the system. Every ten years he goes before the parole board, apologetically saying what he thinks they want to hear, and every time he's rejected (6:42–7:32; 1:13:01–1:13:42). Andy differs from his fellow prisoners. He's an intellectual, askew in his thinking, and somewhat withdrawn. But while working prison detail, he shows Hadley how to keep a $35,000 windfall out of the hands of the federal government. A tax accountant, Andy promises to do the paperwork for Hadley if he'll give each of the work detail three cold beers (34:01–38:38). Red, sipping on his beer, states in voice-over, "I think he did it just to feel normal again" (38:37). Later, in 1955, Andy, who has been promoted to library detail, acquires a bundle of books from his letter writing campaign. And when he discovers some classical opera records in the bundle, he places it on the turntable and broadcasts it over the entire compound. Defying the warden's orders, Andy brings redemption to Shawshank (1:07:32–1:10:51). For a brief moment time stops, the prisoners look over the grounds and into the skies, and Red rhapsodizes, "I tell you those voices soared . . . for the briefest of moments every last man in Shawshank felt free." Andy can see the humanity of others, but because those in power (Warden Norton and Hadley) can't, Andy is able, through subterfuge, to set up his own escape. He digs a hole in his wall behind posters of Rita Hayworth, then Marilyn Monroe, and finally Raquel Welch. But because he helps the guards with their income tax forms and aids the warden in his kickback schemes, nobody looks under the surface of Andy's room and what he's really up to. Narratively, the film positions the audience to also falsely assess Andy. Through the opening trial sequence, we are made to believe that Andy coldly and with premeditated calculation murdered his wife and her golf-pro lover. A series of coincidences stack the evidence against Andy, and his apparent aloofness at the trial is taken as a lack of remorse. But, like the prison guards, we discover that we aren't looking deep enough into his humanity, as later Andy's innocence is established. Andy's compassion for others, however, has a profound effect on Red. Through Andy's love and example, Red quits play-acting before the authorities. In his final visit before the parole board, in 1967, Red scoffs at the word "rehabilitated" (2:05:42–2:08:11). "I don't have any idea what that means." He says that the kid who committed murder is "long gone" and "I gotta live with that." Red's honesty shows his rediscovered humanity and independence. The parole board approves his release.

Further Reading

Alleva, Richard. Review of *The Shawshank Redemption*. *Commonweal* 121 (November 4, 1994): 16–17.

Francke, Lizze. Review of *The Shawshank Redemption*. *Sight and Sound* 5 (February 1995): 52.

Schickel, Richard. Review of *The Shawshank Redemption*. *Time* 144 (September 26, 1994): 78.

Surviving the Dust Bowl (1998) (Doc.)

Setting: Eastern New Mexico, Eastern Colorado, Kansas, Oklahoma, and Texas, 1931–1939

Director: Chana Gazit

Writer: Chana Gazit

Director of Photography: Allan Palmer

Sound Recording: Michael Haines

Narrator: Liev Schreiber

Editor: David Steward

Availability: PBS Home Video

Whereas John Steinbeck's novel *The Grapes of Wrath* follows the lives of South Plains farmers who leave destitute Oklahoma for what turn out to be false promises in California, this film documents the lives of the majority, those who stayed on the land and fought the "black blizzards" of the Dust Bowl. Only one-fourth of all farmers actually migrated west during the Dust Bowl, and this documentary relives with stunning clarity those bleak years from 1931 to late 1939. Prior to 1931 the South Plains was a land of abundance. State agencies showed pictures of watermelons the size of automobiles in order to lure settlers to their region. With the advent of the steel plow, the tractor, and Turkey Red wheat, the land was fertile from the turn of the century until 1931 (6:04–12:13). But because of bad conservation practices, "suitcase farming," and a cycle of droughts, 100 million acres of land became a wasteland. Director Chana Gazit brings the hardship to life with images of children in dust masks (13:10–13:22), homes buried in dirt up to their doors, and people having to climb through windows to get outside (15:52–16:08). Liev Schreiber's narration, combined with the oral histories of several farmers, punctuates the images with added edges: "It seemed as if the whole surface of the world would be blown away" (12:44); "It always felt like you had grit between your teeth" (16:43). April 14, 1935, "Black Sunday," was the worst day of all. For twenty-seven straight nights dust and wind blew, and there are unbelievable images of blackened skies, and cars dotted against an almost apocalyptic landscape (28:12–32:12). The dust also brought death. In 1935, one-third of all deaths in Ford County, Kansas, were from "dust pneumonia." Relief for the farmers came from President Roosevelt's New Deal. Farmers were given food, but for many it was humiliating (22:40–24:48). By 1936, Hugh Bennett argued that better conservation practices could restore farming (43:42–47:54). Following Bennett's lead, Washington made a documentary, *The Plow that Broke the Plains*, promoting conservation, and the government paid farmers $1 an acre to practice at least one of several methods to preserve the soil (47:54–49:30). In 1938, with farmers following the government's conservation policy, blowing sod was curtailed by 65 percent (49:34). But the drought continued and so did the hardship, until the skies finally opened with rain in 1939.

Further Reading

Bonnefield, Mathew Paul. *The Dust Bowl: Men, Dirt and Depression*. Albuquerque: University of New Mexico Press, 1979.

Hurt, Douglas R. *The Dust Bowl: An Agricultural and Social History*. Chicago: Nelson-Hall, 1981.

Low, Ann Marie. *Dust Bowl Diary*. Lincoln: University of Nebraska Press, 1984.

Shindo, Charles J. *Dust Bowl Migrants in the American Imagination*. Lawrence: University of Kansas Press, 1997.

Worster, Donald. *Dust Bowl: The Southern Plains in the 1930s*. New York: Oxford University Press, 1979.

To Kill a Mockingbird (1962) (W)

Setting: Maycomb, Alabama, 1932–1933

Director: Robert Mulligan

Screenplay: Horton Foote

Director of Photography: Russell Harlan

Cast: Gregory Peck (Atticus Finch), Mary Badham (Jean Louise "Scout" Finch), Phillip Alford (Jem Finch), Kim Stanley (voice of the older Scout), Brock Peters (Tom Robinson), and Robert Duvall (Boo Radley)

Availability: Universal Home Video

Robert Mulligan's *To Kill a Mockingbird*, based on the novel by Harper Lee, wonderfully blends the imaginative wonder of childhood, Southern

Gothic traditions, and social commentary to weave a marvelous coming-of-age story. Scout, a six-year-old girl growing up in the Deep South, watches and slowly learns to appreciate her quiet, reserved father, Atticus Finch. Finch is appointed by the court to defend a black man, Tom Robinson, falsely accused of raping a white woman, and as the case evolves Scout's appreciation deepens. Prior to the case, Scout and her older brother, Jem, have fanciful games in which they spy on neighbors. One night, they crawl through backyards to see what Boo Radley (a reclusive young man) is doing (24:21–32:37). As they squirm along the ground, the scene becomes shrouded with Southern Gothicism (the wind blows, gnarled branches bend, and a ragged shadow of Boo appears on the back porch). The children escape, convinced that their lives were in danger. But the real danger occurs much later as Jem and Scout again wander outside, and this time follow their father to the county jail (1:00:55–1:06:40). There Atticus sits, a book in his hand, waiting to turn back a lynch mob that demands to hang Robinson. Scout arrives. Jem knows that Dad's in trouble, and he refuses to leave. Scout agrees with Jem, and she breaks the lynch mob's mood by striking up a conversation with Mr. Cunningham, "Tell Walter I said 'Hey.' " Her naiveté and earnestness shame the lynch mob and they leave. But what she eventually comes to learn from this encounter is that there's an edgy, blistering violence smoldering in her community when the "color line" is crossed. Earlier, Jem and Scout had thought of their dad as unathletic. But as a rabid dog approached their home, Atticus' actions surprise them. He takes the sheriff's rifle, and in one shot fells the dog (41:17–44:17). The sequence, containing five cutaway reaction shots of Jem and two of Scout (unfortunately, here the film seems to violate the novel's point of view, privileging Jem's coming of age over the narrator's), highlights the children seeing their father in a new light. And later during Tom's trial, in which the children sit in the balcony with the segregated "Negroes," Scout and Jem earn an even greater admiration for Atticus. In his final summation, Atticus uses logic and emotion, demanding that the jury let Tom go free. He asks them to overcome the fear "that all Negro men are not to be trusted with our women." That assumption is "a lie," he says (1:36:00). It's an impassioned appeal, and even though he loses the trial, all of the African Americans stay and wait for Atticus to collect his briefcase and pass by (1:42:08–1:43:23). This is the ultimate sign of respect and one that resonates strongly with the children.

Further Reading

Kael, Pauline. "Mostly Children." *New Yorker* 39 (February 23, 1963): 127–128.

Lee, Harper. *To Kill a Mockingbird*. New York: Popular Library, 1962.

Sarris, Andrew. *"To Kill a Mockingbird." On the Cinema, 1955–1966*. New York: Simon and Schuster, 1970. 75–77.

Shackelford, Dean. "The Female Voice in *To Kill a Mockingbird*: Narrative Strategies in Film and Novel." *The Mississippi Quarterly* 50.1 (Winter 1996): 101–113.

Wild Boys of the Road (1933)

Setting: Los Angeles, Columbus, Cleveland, and New York City, 1933

Director: William Wellman

Screenplay: Daniel Ahern and Earl Baldwin

Director of Photography: Arthur L. Todd

Cast: Frankie Darro (Eddie Smith), Edwin Phillips (Tommy Gordon), Dorothy Coonan (Sally), Rochelle Hudson (Grace), and Robert Barrat (Judge R. H. White)

Availability: None

In the 1930s, Warner Bros. was somewhat of an exploitation studio, borrowing from the newspaper headlines of the day to tell sensational stories of cultural relevance. In the gritty *Wild Boys of the Road*, the Studio highlighted the troubles faced by "tramps" traveling the railroads and looking for jobs during the Great Depression. But these "tramps" weren't World War One veterans or out-of-work farmers; these tramps were just fifteen- and sixteen-year-olds. Set in an affluent neighborhood of Los Angeles, the film begins with sophomores Eddie and Tommy going to a high-school social dance. They seem to be living the good life, but on the way home from the party, Tommy confesses that "For the past week we've been getting our eats from the community chest" (9:04). Suddenly the Depression seems more real to Eddie. Later at home, Eddie's connection to the Depression deepens. Dad sits in the living room, slumped in a chair, and mom has been crying (10:17–11:14). Eddie discovers that Dad has been laid off. When his dad continues to be unable to find work (14:20–17:27), Eddie sadly sells his old jalopy, and when his Dad remains unemployed, Eddie and Tommy hit the rails. "Why should I stick in school and have a good time when he has to stand in the bread line" (20:28), Eddie reasons. On the road they meet up with a female "wild boy," Sally, and together the three face a series of realistic hardships. A railroad brakeman throws rocks at them (26:26–26:38); in Chicago, all of the tramps are rounded up, sent home, or sent to detention centers. Eddie, Tommy, and Sally are allowed to stay in the city because Sally's aunt has promised to take her in. But just after arriving at Aunt Carrie's, the trio witnesses her being arrested for prostitution (32:10–34:33). Back on the rails, the three get drenched in the rain, a fellow female traveler is raped by another brakeman (35:17–40:13), and all of the kids are hounded off the rails by railroad "dicks." While fleeing, Tommy bangs into a brake sign, is knocked semi-conscious, and loses a leg in a brutal railroad accident (41:10–42:01). Following this misadventure, the kids travel from Columbus to Cleveland, where they live in makeshift shantytowns. Unfortunately, the city doesn't approve and, in a harrowing scene, the police arrive and douse all the shanty kids with fire hoses (52:28–55:42), busting up their homes and "Republic." But this is a Warner Bros. film, and it ends with hope. A "New Deal" studio, Warner Bros. openly supported Franklin Delano Roosevelt's fight against the Depression (they were the only studio to do so). Thus, even though the Warners portrayed the dark side of the Great Depression, the studio believed that under Roosevelt things would get better, and for these kids, they do. Following a weird plot turn, in which Eddie gets innocently mixed up with some gangsters, a patriarchal Juvenile Hall judge decides to help the three find work and eventually return home.

Further Reading

Bergman, Andrew. "Warner Brothers Presents Social Consciousness." *We're in the Money: Depression America and Its Films.* New York: NYU Press, 1971. 100–103.

Kromer, Tom. *Waiting for Nothing.* New York: Hill and Wang, 1935.

Minehan, Thomas. *Boy and Girl Tramps of America.* New York: Farrar and Rinehart, 1934.

Nugent, Frank S. Review of *Wild Boys of the Road. New York Times* (September 22, 1933): 14.

Troy, William. Review of *Wild Boys of the Road. The Nation* 137 (October 18, 1933): 458.

DOUBLE BILL: TWO WOMEN DIRECTORS REPRESENTING THE PREVIOUSLY UNREPRESENTED, 1930–1960

Dance, Girl, Dance (1940) (W)

Setting: Akron, Ohio; New York City, 1940

Director: Dorothy Arzner

Screenplay: Frank Davis and Tess Slesinger

Director of Photography: Russell Metty

Cast: Maureen O'Hara (Judy "Irish" O'Brien), Lucille Ball (Bubbles, aka Tiger Lily White), Louis Hayward (Jimmy Harris), Ralph Bellamy (Steve Adams), Maria Ouspenskaya (Madame Lydia Basilova), and Harold Huber (Mr. Kajulian, Hoboken Gent)

Availability: None

Outrage (1950) (W)

Setting: Southern California, 1950

Director: Ida Lupino

Screenplay: Ida Lupino, Malvin Wald, and Collier Young

Director of Photography: Archie Stout

Cast: Mala Powers (Ann Walton), Tod Andrews (Dr. Ferguson), Robert Clarke (Jim Owens), Jerry Paris (Frank Marini), and Raymond Bond (Mr. Walton)

Availability: None

In the classical Hollywood period of 1930–1960 there were very few women directors. Dorothy Arzner and Ida Lupino were two of the best. Both women represented issues that were largely ignored by their male counterparts. In *Dance, Girl, Dance*, Arzner tackles the "male gaze," the male prerogative to look at and eroticize women's bodies. In *Outrage*, Lupino takes on the usually repressed topic of rape and the aftereffects rape-trauma has on a young woman's life. *Dance, Girl, Dance* looks at the lives of a dance troupe led by Bubbles and Judy. The girls provide lowbrow entertainment for men. Judy's teacher, Madame Basilova, knows that her prize student should be doing highbrow ballet, but instead the teacher is "a flesh peddler" selling her students to the "smoker" circuit. In a troubling scene, Madame Basilova disapprovingly stands in the wings as Mr. Kajulian, a Hoboken club owner, watches Judy dance and decides that she has no "oomph," no sex appeal. But when Bubbles arrives and dances, Kajulian finds what he and his clientele are looking for. Bubbles dances erotically for Kajulian, slapping her hips as she sashays to an Hawaiian boogie. Arzner shows her contempt for Kajulian and his crowd by photographing his leering looks in an unflattering closeup: face sweating, eyes glazed, and a cigar chomped in his mouth. It's her subtle way of challenging the male gaze and troubling male spectators from identifying with Kajulian as he enjoys watching Bubbles. Later, Arzner further challenges the gaze with a stunning break in the film's narrative for an almost editorial aside. After Bubbles dances for Kajulian she lands a posh gig in New York's higher-end burlesque circuit. Dancing brassily to coyly sexual material she wows her audience. As an added comical highlight, Bubbles, now known as "Tiger" Lily, hires Judy as her "stooge." Judy's job is to present an absurd foil—a high-class ballet dancer—that the audience can ridicule, and thereby justify their pleasure in gazing. But one night (after Bubbles has stolen Judy's boyfriend, Jimmy Harris, and married him), Judy snaps and stops in the middle of her routine. Proudly, she walks to the center arch of the stage and with arms folded tells off the gazing men: "Go ahead and stare. I'm not ashamed. . . . Fifty cents for the privilege to stare at a girl the way your wives won't let you . . . and play at being the stronger sex for the minute. I'm sure that they see through you just like we do" (1:17:14–1:18:22). Unfortunately, this strong moment of women's rights is quickly undercut. Judy's editorial aside is followed with Bubbles and Judy mixing it up in a violent "cat fight" (they scratch at each other and the film is sped up to create a herky-jerky comical effect) (1:19:14–1: 19:43). Nevertheless, Judy's speech does, momentarily, challenge cinema's built-in voyeurism and makes the men in the story's burlesque theater, and those of us watching, somewhat uncomfortable and self-conscious. The opening credits to *Outrage* set the tone: a woman desperately wanders down a darkly lit street, looking for exits, for people, and finding neither. Lupino's credit scene foreshadows the violent rape that occurs nine minutes into the film and establishes a pervasive mood of horror that will linger through and after the viewing. Ann Walton works in an accounting office and looks forward to marrying her boyfriend, Jim Owens. But one day, after working late at the office, she is raped by a concessions stand operator (9:06–14:14). Days later as she tries to return to work, Ann feels that everyone is watching and judging her (21:39–24:21). Unnerved, she explodes at her colleagues and leaves. Later, with Jim, Ann expresses a distaste for sex and a desire to never marry: "I don't want you to touch me. . . . Everything's dirty, filthy and dirty" (28:38–28:44). Traumatized and confused, she runs from her community. Out in the country, she meets kind Dr. Ferguson (a former Navy chaplain and a doctor of divinity). He senses that she's lost her faith and tells her of his troubles, how he too had doubted himself and God after having lost a lung in the war and being unable to practice where he had wanted to. But suddenly he found himself and his faith (47:21–48:52). He offers to help her, finding Ann work in the office of a fruit-packing company. But the past haunts her. During a picnic, Frank Marini makes advances on Ann, and she conflates his desires to kiss her with the wanton actions of the rapist (54:20–58:57). She brands him with a monkey wrench, nearly killing him. Interestingly, Lupino shoots Marini's desire to kiss Ann in strongly ambiguous hues. The story text assumes that he is an innocent victim. Ann lashed out at him for what someone else, the rapist, had done. But a closer look at the scene shows that Marini's actions, too, were unwarranted. Although not a form of rape, Marini's overtures were a form of sexual harassment. Marini tells Ann that her hair is beautiful and twice he gropes it without her permission. And when she refuses his advances (because of her anxiety) he tries to force a kiss. In a subtle way, Lupino, in the second "attack" scene, questions the sexual politics of the times and argues that it is always a woman's right to say no.

Further Reading

Houston, Beverle. "Missing in Action: Notes on Dorothy Arzner." *Multiple Voices in Feminist Film Criticism,* ed. Diane Carson, Linda Dittmar, and Janice R. Welsch. Minneapolis: University of Minnesota Press, 1994. 271–279.

Kort, Melissa Sue. " 'Spectacular Spinelessness': The Men in Dorothy Arzner's Films." *Women and Literature* 2 (1982): 189–205.

Nerenberg, Ellen. "Overlooking and Looking Over Ida Lupino." *Voices in Italian Americana* 7.2 (1996): 69–81.

DOUBLE BILL: JOAN BLONDELL HELPS LICK THE DEPRESSION

Gold Diggers of 1933 (1933) (W)

Setting: Broadway, New York City, 1933

Director: Mervyn LeRoy, Busby Berkeley (musical numbers)

Screenplay: David Boehm, Erwin S. Gelsey, Ben Markson, and James Seymour

Director of Photography: Sol Polito

Cast: Joan Blondell (Carol King), Dick Powell (Brad Roberts), Ruby Keeler (Polly Parker), Ned Sparks (Barney Hopkins), and Warren William (J. Lawrence Bradford)

Availability: Warner Bros. Home Video

Footlight Parade (1933) (W)

Setting: New York City, 1933

Director: Lloyd Bacon, Busby Berkeley (musical numbers)

Screenplay: Manuel Seff and James Seymour

Director of Photography: George Barnes

Cast: Joan Blondell (Nan Prescott), James Cagney (Chester Kent), Claire Dodd (Vivian Rich), Guy Kibbee (Silas "Si" Gould), and Arthur Hohl (Al Frazer)

Availability: Warner Bros. Home Video

In the 1930s, Joan Blondell embodied a "can do" spirit in the face of the Depression. She was a sassy, hands-on-hips, strong-striding woman in a series of Warner Bros. backstage musicals. In *Gold Diggers*, Blondell plays a hard-working girl who knows the Depression firsthand. "We won't have to rehearse that," she says about doing a musical on the subject (14:33). The film opens with an opulent "We're in the Money" number, with chorines decked in glittering coins, but the escapism is undercut by the reality (1:01–4:16). The play's rehearsal is closed down right after the number because of no funding. The play's director Barney wants to bring the Depression to the masses, but he needs a Sugar Daddy. And he finds one in Brad, a rich kid who rejects his blue-blooded background and sponsors the show. Brad is also an accomplished composer, and his music drives the film's Depression theme, including his rousing "Forgotten Man" number. But Brad is also in love with dancer Polly Parker of whom his rich family disapproves. In order to keep the show running smoothly, and all of the girls happy, Carol, one of the show's main headliners, poses as Parker. She woos Brad's older brother, stops him from meddling with the play, brings him around to appreciate "low" art, and the show goes on. The final number is a pungent attack on the Herbert Hoover administration. Carol, dressed like a street-walker, laments the forgotten World War One veterans (just a year before the film's release, the Bonus Expeditionary Marchers were attacked by the U.S. military outside of Washington when asking for help and money [see *Heroes for Sale* for more on this]). The final number is full of stirring images (1:30:28–1:37:06). In one sequence, a cop roughs up a street tramp. Carol, hands on hips, steps between the two men and pulls back the tramp's lapel to reveal a war medal. The cop backs away. Overall, the film's final number suggests a need for the nation to return to a wartime spirit of collectivism to beat the Depression. Such shocking imagery challenges any notion that musicals are mere escapism. In *Footlight Parade*, Blondell plays Nan, the loyal secretary to the energetic Chester Kent (played with robust enthusiasm and big-city verve by James Cagney). Chester is so busy creating prologues to put on before films that he doesn't see the corruption around him, but Nan does. She protects him from Thompson who has been stealing his ideas (12:08), and she barges into the offices of producers Frazer and Gould demanding the $25,000 they have been cheating him out of (1:00:29–1:00:46). She also protects him from marrying the supposedly "cultured" Miss Rich (1:05:36–1:06:29). Together, Blondell and Cagney are a dynamic team (they both move quickly through rooms, talk with a rapid patter, and are shot in symmetrical compositions that emphasize their equality). Without Nan watching over him Chester would fail, but more importantly, without Nan watching over Chester his production numbers would fail and all of those hard-working Depression-era dancers would be out of work. In a way, Chester is an allegorical Roosevelt figure. He's the man with the energy and ideas, the man who rallies the collective around him. "We're giving you a new deal," Frazer says at one point, his words echoing the language of Roosevelt's promise to the American people (1:05:32). Chester responds, "Yeah. And I'm the dealer." But his New Deal (balancing his own anarchic energies with the larger goals of the collective) isn't possible without Nan. As in *Gold Diggers*, she saves the show, and in her own way does her part to lick the Depression.

Further Reading

Bergman, Andrew. "A Musical Interlude." *We're in the Money: Depression America and Its Films.* New York: NYU Press, 1971. 62–65.

Haskell, Molly. "The Thirties." *From Reverence to Rape: The Treatment of Women in the Movies.* Chicago: University of Chicago Press, 1974, 1987. 90–152.

Rubin, Martin. "The Crowd, the Collective, and the Chorus: Busby Berkeley and the New Deal." *Movies and Mass Culture*, ed. John Belton. New Brunswick, NJ: Rutgers University Press, 1996. 59–92.

POWER AND THE LAND: FOUR DOCUMENTARY PORTRAITS OF THE GREAT DEPRESSION (1934–1940)

The New Frontier (1934) (Doc.)

Director: H. B. McClure
Writer: John H. Caulfield
Director of Photography: W. R. McCarthy
Narrator: Morse Salisbury

The Plow that Broke the Plains (1936) (Doc.)

Director: Pare Lorentz
Writer: Pare Lorentz
Directors of Photography: Ralph Steiner, Paul Ivano, Paul Strand, and Leo T. Hurwitz
Narrator: Thomas Chalmers

The River (1937) (PG) (Doc.)

Director: Pare Lorentz
Writer: Pare Lorentz
Directors of Photography: Floyd Crosby, Stacy Woodard, Willard Van Dyke
Narrator: Thomas Chalmers

Power and the Land (1940) (Doc.)

Director: Joris Ivens
Writer: Edwin Locke
Directors of Photography: Floyd Crosby and Arthur Ornitz
Narrator: William P. Adams
Availability: Kino Video (all four documentaries on one two-hour tape)

In the 1930s, President Roosevelt sought new avenues to communicate the ideals of the New Deal to the American people. This was an especially vexing problem as the newspapers and radio were controlled by conservative Republicans who despised his "government intervention" programs. Roosevelt's "fireside chats" helped convey the ideas of the New Deal. Also, under the Farm Security Administration an extensive photographic survey of rural conditions was taken to educate the city dweller on the needs of the rural population. The New Deal documentaries were an extension of this policy. The first one, *The New Frontier*, looks at life in an experimental "Rural Community" sponsored by the Federal Emergency Relief Administration.

Out-of-work laborers migrate to this East Texas commune where they build homes. Instead of huddling in poor pup tents, they live decently, and a social worker helps the women manage the family diet (1:04:47). The narrator concludes: "The New Deal has given these people what they wanted more than anything else in the round world. A chance to exchange their work for home, food, clothing, and education for their children" (1:07:11–1:07:28). The story is a metaphorical tale of the New Deal (something is wrong, something needs to be done, and government intervention is the necessary solution to return people to self-sufficiency.) Pare Lorentz's *The Plow that Broke the Plains*, divided into seven sections, looks at an exciting section of the country and the effects of the Great Drought. After the cattle herders, farm settlers arrived in the Grain Plains and grew wheat, transforming the land into a golden harvest. And with the tractor, their yield grew. World War One, with its demand for wheat, created a boom period. Lorentz captures this boom with a montage of a ticker-tape machine spooling out rounds of tape, and then tilting, and breaking on the floor. The broken tape machine is then juxtaposed with an image of a cattle's skull on dry parched earth, connecting the two (48:56–49:00). Lorentz contends that the demand for wheat was met, but at the tremendous cost of failed conservation practices. These failures created the Dust Bowl, and Lorentz has several gripping images of a farmer looking up at the sky, horses and children running in the black blizzard, and homes covered in Sahara-type sand dunes (50:49–53:48). The film concludes bleakly with farmers migrating west. Lorentz did shoot a "solution" section, detailing government intervention (aid and soil conservation strategies) for the farmers, but this sequence was excised—probably by conservative factions—from most prints upon the film's initial release. *The River* is Lorentz's masterpiece. Combining Walt Whitmanesque narration ("We built a hundred cities and a thousand towns. St. Paul and Minneapolis. Davenport and Keokuk. Moline and Quincy. Cincinnati and St. Louis. Omaha and Kansas City . . . we built a new continent" [13:08–13:38]) and montage, Lorentz puts forward a rhetorical argument that asserts that humanity needs tools and technology despite our previous excesses (we caused the floods of 1936 by depleting the Mississippi valley of its forests; we eroded the topsoil, and the rootless earth was unable to hold back the mighty river [19:53–26:00]). There are several striking aerial shots of towns flooded under, rooftops barely visible (20:50–21:05). What's needed is intelligent guidance (provided by Roosevelt's Tennessee Valley Authority) to coordinate the application of technology and humanity in order to control the delta (27:00–31:39). Once such coordination takes place, life will be better for all. *Power and the Land* is an interesting piece of Americana. The film follows the hard-working Parkinsons, dairy farmers who live without electricity. The big power companies don't come to the country because there's not as much profit in it as lighting up a city (1:28:

00–1:28:38). But under Roosevelt's Rural Electrification Act, the government provides for the deserving: "hard-working people deserve the best tools man can make" (1:25:30). In 1935, 95 percent of all farms lacked electricity. By 1940, over 500,000 homes, including the Parkinsons', had light.

Further Reading

Allan, Blaine. "Canada's *Heritage* (1939) and America's *The Plow that Broke the Plains* (1936)." *Historical Journal of Film, Radio and Television* 19 (October 1999): 439–452.

Keil, Charlie. "American Documentary Finds Its Voice: Persuasion and Expression in *The Plow that Broke the Plains* and *The City*." *Documenting the Documentary: Close Readings of Documentary Film and Video*, ed. Barry Keith Grant and Jeanette Sloniowski. Detroit: Wayne State University Press, 1998. 119–135.

Leab, Daniel J. "Pare Lorentz and American Government Film Production." *Midcontinent American Studies Journal* 6.1 (1965): 41–49.

Rollins, Peter C. "Ideology and Film Rhetoric: Three Documentaries of the New Deal Era (1936–41)." *Hollywood as Historian*, ed. Peter C. Rollins. Lexington: University Press of Kentucky, 1983. 32–48.

Stott, William. *Documentary Expression and Thirties America*. New York: Oxford University Press, 1973.

FURTHER VIEWING

Black Legion (1937)

Chinatown (1974) (R)

The Cider House Rules (1999) (PG-13)

Fried Green Tomatoes (1991) (PG-13) (W)

Glass Menagerie (1987) (PG)

"G" Men (1935)

Hallelujah, I'm a Bum (1933)

His Girl Friday (1940) (W)

The Lady Eve (1941) (W)

A League of Their Own (1992) (PG) (W)

Lost Weekend (1945)

Mr. Smith Goes to Washington (1939)

Now Voyager (1942) (W)

Of Mice and Men (1992) (PG-13)

Our Daily Bread (1934)

Sounder (1972) (G) (M)

Stand Up and Cheer (1934)
Street Scene (1931)
Sullivan's Travels (1941)
Tucker: The Man and His Dream (1988) (PG)

8

World War Two and the Individual versus the Collective, 1933–1950s

Air Force ◆ America and the Holocaust: Deceit and Indifference
Attack ◆ Casablanca ◆ Fat Man and Little Boy ◆ Fly Girls
From Here to Eternity ◆ The GI Bill: The Law that Changed America
Let There Be Light ◆ The Life and Times of Rosie the Riveter
Saving Private Ryan ◆ So Proudly We Hail ◆ They Were Expendable

Air Force (1943) (M)

Setting: San Francisco, Maui, Wake Island, Manilla, December 6–11, 1941

Director: Howard Hawks

Screenplay: William Faulkner (uncredited) and Dudley Nichols

Directors of Photography: Elmer Dyer, James Wong Howe, and Charles A. Marshall

Cast: John Ridgely (Capt. Mike "Irish" Quincannon, pilot), John Garfield (Sgt. Joe Winocki, aerial gunner), Harry Carey (Sgt. Robby White, crew chief), Arthur Kennedy (Lt. Tommy McMartin, bombardier), Charles Drake (Lt. Hauser, navigator), George Tobias (Cpl. Weinberg, assistant crew chief), Ward Wood (Cpl. Peterson, radio operator), and James Brown (Lt. "Tex" Rader, pursuit pilot)

Availability: Warner Bros. Home Video

In the 1941 film *Sergeant York*, legendary director Howard Hawks recreated the Congressional Medal of Honor–winning assault on German soldiers during World War One. There, York's heroism helped capture 132 Germans. But two years later, when Hawks filmed *Air Force*, York's brand of heroism—the strong rugged, individualist—had given way to a new World War Two brand of heroism: a melting-pot America, a collective of men fighting together for the greater good. In *Air Force*, no superstar actor such as Gary Cooper is the main headliner. Instead, the opening credits suggest that the film's B-17, "the Mary-Ann," number 05564, is the star. The rest of the cast is listed not by character names, but by the positions the men fill aboard the Mary Ann: pilot, co-pilot, bombadier, navigator, crew chief, aerial gunner, etc. And the crew is a diverse cross-section of America: Weinberg, a Jewish cabbie from New York City; Peterson, a farm kid from Minnesota; Lt. Rader, a Southern pursuit flyer; Sergeant White, a lifer from Chicago; Gunner Winocki, an Eastern European descendent; and Captain Quincannon, an Irish American. Set in the moments just prior to and after the bombing of Pearl Harbor, the film follows this crew through several harrowing encounters in the South Pacific as they blend into an elite fighting force. Winocki, an embittered washout from flight school, has a Sergeant York–type of transformation. Instead of hearing God's word in the mountaintops of Tennessee, Winocki's "Road to Damascus" happens as he flies over Pearl Harbor and sees the wreckage. There he recommits to the air force, apologizes to Captain Quincannon, and becomes a team player. He even rigs up a "stinger," a gun in the plane's tail, to help shoot down enemy aircraft. Like Winocki, each member of the B-17 gets to have a shining moment placed within the context of helping the entire crew. Captain Quincannon flies for seventy-two hours without sleep, bonding the crew with his positive outlook. Modestly, he defers the praise he receives from the higher ups: "I've got a good crew, Sir" (1:13:42). Crew chief Sergeant White holds the bomber together by orchestrating its repairs and sustaining the ship. Navigator Hauser, who lives in the shadow of his famous World War One fighter pilot father, heroically finds Wake Island in the dark of night, allowing the bomber to refuel. Peterson, the radioman, communicates the location of the Japanese task force and helps set up an all-out aerial assault. McMartin, the bombardier, hones in on and hits several of the Task Force targets. And the gunners, led by Weinberg and Winocki, defend the ship from Japanese Zeroes. Even when Captain Quincannon dies from wounds received in battle, the Mary Ann soars on, replacing him with the able-minded Lieutenant Rader (a former P-40 fighter pilot, and now a part of the larger collective).

Further Reading

Agee, James. Review of *Air Force*. *The Nation* 156 (February 20, 1943): 283.

Doherty, Thomas. "Genre Work." *Projections of War: Hollywood, American Culture, and World War II*. New York: Columbia University Press, 1993. 85–121.

Farber, Manny. "The Heroes of the Mary Ann." Review of *Air Force*. *The New Republic* 108 (February 22, 1943): 254–255.

Hartung, Philip T. Review of *Air Force*. *The Commonweal* 37 (February 12, 1943): 423–424.

McCarthy, Todd. "*Air Force*." *Howard Hawks*. New York: Grove Press, 1997. 331–344.

America and the Holocaust: Deceit and Indifference (1994) (Doc.) (M)

Setting: Europe and the United States, 1936–1945 and 1994

Director: Martin Ostrow

Writer: Martin Ostrow

Directors of Photography: Richard Chisolm, Peter Hoving, Dan Duncan, Edward Marritz, Doug Shaffer, Joel Shapiro, Martin Smok, Mark Trottenberg, Joseph Vitagliana, Jason Zacharias

Narrator: Hal Linden

Editor: Stephanie Munroe

Availability: Schanachie Home Video

"We can delay and effectively stop for a temporary period of indefinite length the number of immigrants into the United States . . . by simply advising our consuls to postpone and postpone and postpone the granting of visas." Secretary of State Breckenridge Long wrote these apocryphal words in a June 1940 memo in which he was advising consuls at U.S. embassies around the world to deny Jews entry into America (30:40–31:30). By then the world knew of some of the atrocities being perpetrated by the Nazis against the Jews, but America was indifferent and mired in its own pervasive anti-Semitism. In a U.S. public opinion poll, Jews were listed third behind the Germans and the Japanese as the group that "menaced America the most" (1:22–3:24). Senators and large chunks of the public felt that Europe was "dumping" its Jewish problem on the United States. In response 100 "patriotic" societies formed insisting that "charity begins at home" (15:37–15:58). Silver Shirts ran an Aryan bookstore in Los Angeles. Jews were blamed for communism. Father Coughlin, a radio personality, railed against them. Hotel reservation agents in the 1920s and 1930s asked if "there were any Hebrews in your party," and in many areas of the country restricted beaches posted signs, "No Jews or Dogs Allowed." Economically, Jews were also thwarted. Insurance companies, the telephone company, the big three in the auto industry, and even medical schools excluded Jews from positions of power (18:35–22:57). These pervasive prejudices allowed for visas to be blocked and for thousands more European Jews to be rounded up and sent to German concentration camps. And by 1941 because of U.S. indifference and the State Department's collusion, over half a million Jews who could have been saved were murdered (42:43). This documentary is extremely haunting because it takes the horror of the Holocaust and doesn't just leave the blame at the feet of Germany, but turns it towards ourselves and our complicity. In November of 1942, stories of mass exodus, murders, and the Nazi plan to exterminate all Jews were finally leaked to the newspapers, but the story did not appear on page one (47:01–48:58). A group of Jews decided to galvanize the public and inform them of the horrors. Screenwriter Ben Hecht wrote a series of ads to wake people up. "For Sale to Humanity: 70,000 Jews" (55:20–56:03); actor Paul Muni appeared in the political play "The Pageant" (56:04–57:45); and Henry Morgenthau, a long-time friend of FDR and a member of the Treasury Department, discovered a communique in which the state department tried to repress the extent of the Holocaust (1:07:00–1:14:13). This clearly made the government an accomplice to what the Nazis were doing. Outraged, Morgenthau approached the president and together they created the War Refugee Board, which granted immediate visas to those German Jews in need. In all, 200,000 were saved. But of the 6 million killed, how many lives would have been spared had the United States acted sooner?

Further Reading

Elson, John. Review of *America and the Holocaust: Deceit and Indifference. Time* 143 (April 18, 1994): 83.
Feingold, Henry L. Review of *America and the Holocaust: Deceit and Indifference. Journal of American History* 81 (December 1994): 1409–1410.
Kaplan, Paul. Review of *America and the Holocaust: Deceit and Indifference. Library Journal* 120 (June 1, 1995): 186–187.
"Libel and Indifference." *National Review* 46 (May 2, 1994): 19–20.

Attack (1956)

Setting: Europe, 1944

Director: Robert Aldrich

Screenplay: James Poe

Director of Photography: Joseph Biroc

Cast: Jack Palance (Lt. Joe Costa), Eddie Albert (Captain Cooney), William Smithers (Lt. Harold Woodruff), Buddy Ebsen (Sergeant Tolliver), and Lee Marvin (Lieutenant Colonel Bartlett)

Availability: MGM/UA Home Video

Robert Aldrich's sturdy war film studies the failure of command. Made during a period of glamorized World War Two films, Aldrich's vision is less romantic. His film explores what happens to fighting men when they are led by an incompetent captain. Captain Cooney is overly cautious and downright cowardly. The film begins with Cooney's back to the camera, his hand twitching as he speaks into the radio and promises Lieutenant Costa's men support. Costa, on the flank of the battle, ducks behind a brick wall, and looks on disgustedly as support doesn't come and fourteen men from an adjoining squad to his platoon are killed. An empty helmet rolls down the hill symbolizing the attack's futility and Cooney's inability to lead (00:00–3:58). Later, Costa confronts Cooney during a poker game (15:47–20:02).

Lieutenant Colonel Bartlett, sitting in on the games, hears the complaints from Costa and Lieutenant Woodruff, but because his connection with fellow Southerner Cooney will provide a cushy postwar job, he refuses to act on the evidence of incompetence. When the next dangerous assignment comes up, the occupying of LaNell, Costa confronts Cooney directly, "You play the gutless wonder just once more, I'll come back and get you, Cooney" (33:47–35:40). And that's just what happens. Costa's men move toward the town, are fired upon, take up positions in an abandoned house, and aren't given support. Back at headquarters, Woodruff tells Cooney, "It's our turn now," and the captain refuses: "Maybe there's more to this than we can handle," he falsely reasons (50:43). Costa, meanwhile, holed up in a house with five men and waiting for reinforcements, breaks down. Angry and frazzled from the pressures of serving under a failed leader, he pushes a captured German officer into a hail of his own company's bullets (59:01–1:00:02). Eventually, Cooney, given an order by Colonel Bartlett to hold the line against the advancing Germans, hides out with his squad in an abandoned basement. As Germans march outside, he suggests that his men surrender. Woodruff refuses, worrying what the SS might do to a Jew in their unit (Bernstein). Cooney, unable to stand the pressure, moves to the stairs. He expects to greet an SS officer, but it's Costa, dying from mortal wounds. Costa, slithering down the stairs, tries to kill the coward but he hasn't the strength. He falls and as he reaches for his thrown .45, Cooney sadistically kicks it away, laughing at and torturing the brave lieutenant. After Costa dies, Cooney grabs a machine gun and gives the surrender order. Woodruff and the rest of the squad, appalled by Cooney's cowardice and cruelty, refuse. Woodruff threatens, "You take one more step up those stairs and I'll kill you" (1:34:04). Cooney does and he's killed. Woodruff asks Sergeant Tolliver to place himself under arrest after the battle's over, but the Sergeant refuses: "If any man needed killing, it's that no good putrid piece of trash" (1:36:52). All of the other men agree, firing bullets into Cooney's corpse. But Woodruff, a much more by-the-book soldier than Costa, decides to tell General Parsons what happened—or does he? Aldrich ends the film with Woodruff on the radio, talking to the general, but the angle is an extremely high one and the audience can't hear what's being said as the closing credits roll.

Further Reading

Arnold, Edwin T. and Eugene L. Miller. "Le Gros Robert." *The Films and Career of Robert Aldrich.* Knoxville: University of Tennessee Press, 1986. 60–75.

Hartung, Philip T. Review of *Attack. The Commonweal* 65 (October 5, 1956): 15–16.

Hatch, Robert. Review of *Attack. The Nation* 183 (October 6, 1956): 294.

Knight, Arthur. "Aldrich Against the Army." Review of *Attack. Saturday Review* 39 (September 1, 1956): 25–26.

Robinson, George. "Three by Aldrich." *The Velvet Light Trap* 11 (Winter 1974): 46–49.

Casablanca (1942)

Setting: Casablanca, 1941; Paris, 1939

Director: Michael Curtiz

Screenplay: Julius J. Epstein, Philip G. Epstein, and Howard Koch

Director of Photography: Arthur Edeson

Cast: Humphrey Bogart (Rick Blaine), Ingrid Bergman (Ilsa Lund), Paul Henried (Victor Laszlo), Claude Rains (Capt. Louis Renault), and Conrad Veidt (Major Strasser)

Availability: MGM/UA Home Video

Casablanca, one of America's most popular and enduring films, centers on a bitter man conquering his own individualism for the greater collective good. Set just prior to the bombing of Pearl Harbor, Rick Blaine, a former American adventurer, has settled down as a saloonkeeper in French-occupied North Africa. But when his old Paris lover, Ilsa, reenters his life, Blaine becomes unsettled. She's traveling with Victor Laszlo, a Czech freedom fighter/activist who is also her husband (she had kept that a secret from Rick during their affair in Paris). At first, Rick vents anger at Ilsa for abandoning him, and then he tries to win her from her husband, and, confused, she returns his love while yet admiring her husband's patriotism and ideals. During an uplifting scene, Ilsa watches with admiration as Victor rallies the French people to the war effort (1:12:15–1:14:08). A group of boorish German officers sing "The Fatherland" at Rick's Café, when Laszlo, angered, briskly strides to the band and demands that they play "The Marseillaise." Together the French banish the voices of the enemy. Even though she greatly admires her husband's commitment to freedom, she has greater passion for Rick. Much like F. Scott Fitzgerald's dashing Jay Gatsby, Rick is a romantic trying to win back the love of his lost Daisy Buchanan, Ilsa. Moreover, like Gatsby, he's a mysterious figure. Captain Renault speculates on Rick's past, and like a party-goer in Fitzgerald's novel, jokingly suggests, "I'd like to think you killed a man. It's the romantic in me" (16:58). But even though Blaine wins back his girl, he discovers at the airport—in part through observing Laszlo's commitment to the cause and the evil machinations of Strasser—that the "problems of three little people don't amount to a hill of beans in this crazy world" (1:36:26–1:39:39). In one of cinema's grand gestures of self-sacrifice, he gives up his relationship with Ilsa for the greater collective good: "You're part of his work, the thing that keeps him going." Laszlo's beliefs help keep the world free. Ultimately, Blaine loses in love, but in a sense he rediscovers his own lost humanity. In the end, as he and Louis walk across the wet airport runway, and acknowledge their friendship, Rick is no longer an isolationist, but a superpatriot ready to take up the fight.

Further Reading

Crowther, Bosley. Review of *Casablanca*. *The New York Times* (November 27, 1942): 27.
Farber, Manny. "The Warner Boys in Africa." Review of *Casablanca*. *The New Republic* 107 (December 14, 1942): 993–994.
Ray, Robert B. "The Culmination of Classic Hollywood: *Casablanca*." *A Certain Tendency of the Hollywood Cinema, 1930–1980*. Princeton, NJ: Princeton University Press, 1985. 89–111.

Fat Man and Little Boy (1989) (PG-13)

Setting: Chicago; northern California; Los Alamos, New Mexico; San Francisco; and Washington, DC, 1942–1945

Director: Roland Joffe

Screenplay: Bruce Robinson and Roland Joffe

Director of Photography: Vilmos Zsigmond

Cast: Paul Newman (Gen. Leslie R. Groves), Dwight Schultz (J. Robert Oppenheimer), and Natasha Richardson (Jean Tatlock)

Availability: Paramount Home Video

Roland Joffe's *Fat Man and Little Boy* recounts the nineteen-month buildup to the testing of an atomic bomb in New Mexico. Made during the Reagan administration—a period in which there was a lot of talk about a *Star Wars* defense plan and the president had increased the American nuclear output to exceed 12,000 bombs and missiles—*Fat Man and Little Boy* argues persuasively that the nuclear age had been driven from the outset by bullying militarists who wanted to play with the toys they had created. The film charts the Manhattan Project, a gathering of superstar scientists and engineers who forged an uneasy alliance with Gen. Leslie R. Groves. Groves seeks both personal and military gain. He wants to create the atomic bomb before the Germans do, and once the Nazi empire falls, Groves wants to turn the atomic bomb on Japan in order to end the war against a "kamikaze" country (1:25:36–1:26:38). But he also has ulterior motives. Groves seeks personal glory, and he wants to give President Truman a foreign policy weapon with which the president can supposedly divide up and hold power over a postwar world. What makes Groves admirable is his ability to work with head scientist J. Robert Oppenheimer, a former communist, who the general labels a "bohemian" and an "eight ball" egghead. Despite these prejudices, General Groves has "a weakness for good men," and he can set aside his differences to work with the best. Oppenheimer, with his conflicting moral dilemmas, is also an ambiguous figure. He desires to be a part of the project, in order to end the war with Germany and to beat them to the atomic bomb, but he also desires to be a part of the team because of his own drive for fame and notoriety. When Germany is on the verge of defeat, Oppenheimer wants to pull his scientists off the project. Japan "hasn't the technology. If we don't need it, why make it?" (1:12:23). The general, wanting to detonate the toys his team creates, viciously forces Oppenheimer to play ball by informing the FBI of his past communist ties and his involvement with Jean Tatlock (a card-carrying communist who committed suicide after her affair with Oppenheimer ended). Fearing reprisals, and needing to prove his loyalty to America, Oppenheimer forces the project through to the end. He abandons his "crisis of conscience" and tells his group of scientists who want to pull out on moral grounds that "the dropping of the device has always been implicit in this project" (1:30:24). Ultimately, he's a weak man who is bullied into setting the world on edge. The film ends with the Trinity Test at Alamogordo, New Mexico, as television cameras, and Oppenheimer in infrared goggles, look on in eager anticipation. During the test's final countdown, Tchaikovsky's "Dance of the Reed Flutes" bleeds into the army's sound system. It can't be silenced, and as the screen fills with the red of the blast, Tchaikovsky's music seems to be Joffe's ironic jest, dancing around the horror and snickering at men, in 1945 and again during the Reagan years, who insist on playing with fire.

Further Reading

Carnes, Mark C. *"Fat Man and Little Boy." Past Imperfect: History According to the Movies,* ed. Mark C. Carnes. New York: Henry Holt & Co., 1996. 246–249.
Groves, Leslie R. *Now It Can Be Told.* New York: Harper & Row, 1962.
Kauffmann, Stanley. Review of *Fat Man and Little Boy. The New Republic* 201 (November 20, 1989): 28–29.
Novak, Ralph. Review of *Fat Man and Little Boy. People Weekly* 32 (November 6, 1989): 19.
Rhodes, Richard. *The Making of the Atomic Bomb.* New York: Simon & Schuster, 1986.

Fly Girls (1999) (DOC.) (W)

Setting: U.S. Air Force bases, 1942–1944

Director: Laurel Ladevich

Writer: Laurel Ladevich

Directors of Photography: Mitch Wilson and Jack Tankard

Narrator: Mary McDonnell

Editor: Kathleen North

Availability: PBS Home Video

From 1942 to 1944 a group of just over a thousand women, the Women's Air Force Service Pilots, flew every type of plane designed under the auspices of the military. Founded by Jacqueline Cochran, a pilot who captured seventeen world records in ten years, and in 1938 won the most prestigious air race in the world, the Transcontinental Bendix (6:40–11:07), the WASP were the equals of male pilots. They had 200 hours of flight instruction, 400 hours of ground training, and they ferried aircraft across the country for male pilots to fly in battle. The film details their successes through a combination of interviews with six former pilots, and exciting 8mm and 16mm color footage. With their successes, the women's roles broadened to include test flying. Ann Baumgartner first flew the Bell YP59A, an experimental jet plane, in 1943 (31:22–31:59). Dora Dougherty convinced male pilots that the new B-29 was a safe bomber (32:46–35:12). Despite being the equals to their male counterparts, however, the female pilots weren't treated equally (36:38–41:24). At Camp Davis, two WASP died in one month, and foul play was suspected. Cochran did find sugar in the gas line of one downed plane, but she feared adverse publicity and didn't seek an investigation. Moreover, the women weren't granted veteran status. When they died, they received no benefits, no flag, no gold star to hang in their family's window. By mid-1944, public opinion was turned against the WASP (43:46–47:49). With war approaching its end, the public and the military wanted the women back in the home, and no longer in the cockpits. Prejudices, however, did not deter these women. By contrast, in *The Life and Times of Rosie the Riveter*, director Connie Field suggests that the postwar push to return women to the home adversely affected the riveters. They lost the economic gain they had during the war, and they also lost any concept of self-worth. But these Fly Girls, despite the breakup of the WASP in 1944, were able to stay in the world of their dreams and achieve personal satisfaction. Dora Dougherty earned a Ph.D. in aviation education and became a helicopter pilot, setting two world records. Barbara Erickson sells aircraft for a living, and her oldest daughter is a commercial airline pilot. Ann Baumgartner is a science writer, mother, and flight instructor. Moreover, these female pioneers set the standard, proving that women could serve in the military and compete equally with male pilots. In 1977, President Jimmy Carter honored their accomplishments and contributions to history by passing a law that officially recognized them as veterans.

Further Reading

Douglas, Deborah G. *United States Women in Aviation, 1940–1985*. Washington, DC: Smithsonian Institution Press, 1990.

Finnigan, David. "Fly Girls." *Daily Variety* (May 24, 1999): 10.

Hartmann, Susan M. "Women in the Military Service." *Clio Was a Woman: Studies in the History of American Women*. Washington, DC: Howard University Press, 1980. 195–205.

From Here to Eternity (1953)

Setting: Hawaii, fall 1941–December 8, 1941

Director: Fred Zinnemann

Screenplay: Daniel Taradash

Director of Photography: Burnett Guffey

Cast: Montgomery Clift (Robert E. Lee Prewitt), Donna Reed (Alma [Lorene]), Philip Ober (Capt. Dana Holmes), Burt Lancaster (Sgt. Milton Warden), Deborah Kerr (Karen Holmes), and Frank Sinatra (Angelo Maggio)

Availability: Columbia Pictures Home Video

Most war-era films express the need for everyone to pull together, to sacrifice individual goals and energies for the larger communal good. *From Here to Eternity*, based on the novel by James Jones, does not. Private Robert E. Lee Prewitt insists on being an individual. When Prewitt first appears on the screen, director Fred Zinnemann clearly marks his antihero's difference from the mainstream. Prewitt walks loose-limbed, a kit bag tossed over his shoulder, as a group of soldiers in the frame's foreground march in rigid military lines. Rebellious and full of unlimited determination, Prewitt demanded a transfer from his previous outfit because he was "a better bugler" and when a less talented man was given the top spot, Prew wanted out on principle (5:02), and in this film, the army lacks principles. Prewitt's new commanding officer, the insecure Capt. Dana Holmes, insists that Prewitt join the company boxing team. But Prewitt refuses because in a past match he had blinded Dixie Wells. Holmes chastises the reluctant fighter: "You should know that in the army it's not the individual that counts" (6:17). But Holmes' call for collective sacrifice is selfish, and not really within the bounds of military duty. Because Prew refuses to fight, he's given "the treatment" by Holmes and his coterie of boxers in an attempt to break his resistance. Prew is forced to excessively march, run extra laps (16:02–19:00), dig and refill holes and crawl through mud (44:17–48:57). His need to be seen as an individual leads him to an affair with Lorene, a prostitute at the New Congress Club. When Lorene first meets him, she talks warmly and then bounces to other men, claiming that "all the boys" are "alike." Prew gets indignant. "We're not," he says (34:48–35:03). She is attracted to his desire to be unique, but their relationship is doomed. Prew, despite the brutal "treatment" he receives, is dedicated to the army; Lorene, in love with Prew, initially refuses to marry him. She wants to marry up, and "nobody's gonna stop me from my plan" (1:14:44–1:16:40). By the time she fully commits to Prew, it's too late. His base is attacked by the Japanese, and the AWOL Prewitt (who had left to avenge the death of a friend) attempts to make it back. He dies, a victim of the army's cruelty and his own hard-headed individualism. In the early glimmers of dawn, Prewitt refuses the "Halt" warnings of the U.S. Army, and is shot attempting to outrun their bullets.

Further Reading

Hartung, Philip T. Review of *From Here to Eternity. Commonweal* 58 (August 21, 1953): 488–489.
Jones, James. *From Here to Eternity.* New York: Dell 1951, 1985.
McCann, Graham. "Montgomery Clift." *Rebel Males: Clift, Brando, and Dean.* New Brunswick, NJ: Rutgers, 1993. 31–78.

The GI Bill: The Law that Changed America (1998) (Doc.) (M)

Setting: United States, 1943–present

Director: Karen Thomas

Writer: Karen Thomas

Director of Photography: Foster Wiley

Narrator: Cliff Robertson

Editor: Mark Muheim

Availability: PBS Home Video

No veterans experienced such good postwar benefits as those who served during World War Two. As the war raged in Europe and the South Pacific, President Roosevelt, members of Congress, and the American Legion feared what might happen when the sixteen million men and women serving returned home. They didn't want to see a repeat of the appalling treatment experienced by World War One veterans (3:33–6:23). Thus in 1943, a bill was drawn up to help returning vets. Roosevelt promised that there would be no environment of inflation or unemployment—no returning veteran would be reduced to selling apples on a street corner (11:57–12:45). Roosevelt's plan was a first step, but the American Legion wanted much more, and with the help of William Randolph Hearst's chain of newspapers they lobbied for a comprehensive set of benefits: education, job training, unemployment insurance, and business and housing loans (12:46–14:11). They got thirty-second spots on radio and in movie theaters, and they pressured Congress for real promises. Congressman Rankin, a racist Democrat from Mississippi who was virulently opposed to the New Deal and disliked the idea of black soldiers getting the same benefits as white ones, tried to line up votes against the sweeping legislation, but when Congressman Gibson heard of soldiers dying on the beaches of Normandy he ratified the bill (15:44–18:22). Ultimately, the GI Bill changed the cultural landscape of America. Before the war, immigrants worked in low level civil service jobs, teaching, nursing, or labor. But with the bill's promise of higher education, six million went into vocational training and 1.6 million attended public and private universities. In 1942, there were 10,000 students at the University of Michigan. By 1946–1947, there were over 40,000 attending. These vets changed the course of higher education, making it less elitist, less ivory-tower centered, and less of an Anglo-Saxon domain (33:27–37: 54). For African Americans, the GI Bill became a great leveler, or as recipient Harry Belafonte acknowledges, "a subsidy that helped us go to school" (26:34–26:51). Prior to the GI Bill, Belafonte had no "thirst for knowledge." The bill gave him that thirst and ability to compete (29:20–29:27). This education boom also shifted America from a blue collar to a white collar economy. Also, prior to the war, two-thirds of Americans were renters. After the war, two-thirds were home owners (48:11–51:42). The bill's housing provisions (federally backed loans) upgraded the GI's standard of living and created the spread of Levittown-style suburbs. The bill was truly democratic and was perhaps America's greatest piece of social legislation.

Further Reading

Goulden, Joseph C. *The Best Years, 1945–1960.* New York: Continuum, 1976.
Ringle, Ken. "The GI Bill: America's Peacetime Revolution." *The Washington Post* (October 22, 1997): D1.
Severo, Richard and Milford Lewis. *The Wages of War: When America's Soldiers Came Home from Valley Forge to Vietnam.* New York: Simon and Schuster, 1989.
Willenz, June A. *Women Veterans: America's Forgotten Heroes.* New York: Continuum, 1983.

Let There Be Light (1946) (Doc.)

Setting: Mason General Hospital, United States, 1945–1946

Director: John Huston

Writer: John Huston

Directors of Photography: Stanley Cortez, John Doran, Lloyd Fromm, Joseph Jackman, and George Smith

Narrator: Walter Huston

Editor: None Listed

Availability: Hollywood's Attic

This gripping documentary, made for the Office of War Information in 1946 by the brilliant John Huston, details soldiers fighting "battle neuroses." Huston's ultimate purpose was to show soldiers who had been "damaged emotionally" conquering their fears through the help of a dedicated team of doctors who use hypnosis and "narcosynthesis." Sadly however the OWI found the film so disturbing that they refused to sponsor it, and it was never released for public viewing. But Huston's point wasn't to embarrass soldiers or to denigrate them; instead, Huston sought for viewers to understand and admire the soldiers he filmed. The film's God-like voiceover empathizes with the soldiers' illnesses, telling us that "these are men who cannot sleep . . . cannot remember," their paralysis is "dictated by the mind" and a fear of "impending disaster" (2:04–3:30). Compassionately, Huston follows several veterans into their sessions with doctors. One man, upset about a buddy who was killed, keeps his head down while he talks (5:50–7:30). "I feel all right," he says with a lethargic shrug. Another man, a black soldier, has constant headaches, misses his girlfriend, and starts to cry. "I'm not doing this deliberate," he says ashamedly. The doctor assures him that it's okay to let go of his emotions—crying is an important step towards recovery (7:29–9:37). Following the interviews, Huston and chief cinematographer Stanley Cortez feature a series of small miracles brought about through sodium ambatol and hypnotic suggestion. One young soldier is so shook up by what he had experienced that he can no longer walk. His limbs are physically fine, but his mind won't let his feet move. While under hypnosis, the doctor tells him, "You love walking. Now you're going to get right up and walk. . . . When you wake up, you'll be all right" (17:27–24:33)—and he walks. Another soldier, suffering amnesia from a shell that nearly killed him, claims back his battle history and family under hypnosis (31:30–38:34). A third soldier, who developed a stuttering pattern around "S" sounds because of the stresses of war, suddenly finds the answer under hypnosis. The "S" sounds replicate the hissing noises of German 88 shells. The fear of those shells transposed itself into the enunciation of words such as "flying *fishes*." Cured of his stuttering, the soldier suddenly shouts joyously, "I can talk! I can talk! I can talk! Oh, God, listen, I can talk!" (38:52–43:33). Of course these successes are just the beginning to recovery, not the end. There are still a lot of dimensions to their "battle neuroses" to be dealt with. But Huston sought to provide viewers with the understanding to help these men reintegrate into a postwar booming society. The reasons the military banned the film are somewhat sketchy. They objected that the veterans portrayed in the film might sue the army (but Huston had acquired releases from them all). They also objected that some families of those veterans who weren't healed might find the film misleading. But probably the real reason the film was banned was because of its honest depiction of battle trauma and how that might damage future recruiting. Fortunately, because of the tireless efforts of Jack Valenti (president of the Motion Picture Association), Ray Stark (producer of the film) who lobbied the government to liberate the film, and Joseph McBride, whose barrage of articles in *Variety* detailed the film's sorry history, *Let There Be Light* was finally released by the defense department in 1981.

Further Reading

Corliss, Richard. Review of "Let There Be Light." *Time* 117 (January 19, 1981): 80.

Hammen, Scott. "At War with the Army: John Huston Made a Great War Trilogy. Now If We Could Just See It." *Film Comment* 16 (March/April 1980): 19–23.

The Life and Times of Rosie the Riveter (1980) (Doc.) (M) (W)

Setting: United States, 1941–1945, 1980

Director: Connie Field

Research: Jane Scantlebury, Rebecca Wilson, and Bill Bryce

Photography: Cathy Zhetlin, Bonnie Friedman, Robert Handley, Emiko Omori

Sound: Marilyn Mulford, Chat Gunter, Clyde Stringer

Cast: Lola Weixel (Brooklyn, New York), Margaret Wright (Los Angeles), Lyn Childs (San Francisco), Gladys Belcher (Richmond, California), and Wanita Allen (Detroit)

Availability: Direct Cinema Limited

This marvelous documentary looks at five riveters from the war years—three black women, two white—and tells a tripartite story: life before riveting, life on the job, and life after riveting. Around their stunning stories and interviews, director Connie Field adds a troubling historical context: newsreels and media images that represent the riveters as all-white, buffed babes and a government propaganda campaign that seeks to preserve their femininity—welding is compared to sewing; lathe work compared to running an electric washing machine (10:30–11:40)—and eventually forces them back into the home, or more accurately back to low-paying menial jobs, after the men return from war (42:57–48:06). Prior to becoming riveters, these women held demeaning jobs. Lola worked on a boring assembly line, making party favors (2:04–2:40). Wanita's husband worked at Oldsmobile, but she and her mother cooked in restaurants or did domestic work for upper middle class whites (3:42–4:25). Gladys labored dully on a farm (4:26–6:11). But when workers were needed in the factories because of the wartime manpower shortage, these woman found true fulfillment. Margaret found factory work a monetary and self-actualizing godsend. She proudly remembers her social security number: 366–24–9339 (8:03–9:02). Lola found artistry in her craft: being a welder was "a very beautiful kind of work" (9:03–9:15). But the eighteen million women working in a man's world didn't find the going easy. They were treated poorly by their male co-workers, and earned less money. Among the women, there were rifts between blacks and whites. Wanita, an African American, tells how white women were permitted showers at work, but black women weren't (28:26–30:03). Thankfully the union stepped in and corrected that injustice. Outside of the workplace, the women also suffered. Lola says her extended family expected her to do household chores when she came home—the men, by contrast, relaxed in the living room (31:06–31:26). Lyn tells how the demands of the job made her lose contact with her infant daughter—a rift that still exists to this day (31:27–32:21). After the war, the government instituted the GI Bill, but to assure that veterans weren't underemployed or selling apples on street corners, a propaganda campaign was instituted to send the women home. One government newsreel showcases a welding woman who promises to return home and raise children now that the men are back. The narrator strongly encourages her with a "good for you" (42:57–44:30). But what about the women who didn't want to voluntarily return? Lyn says that the women were laid off first, then the black men (47:52–48:06). "We can't have you, you're a woman," Gladys was told by several plant foremen (51:57). They were forced out, discriminated against, and the loss of their earning power was shocking. After the war, Gladys worked seventeen years in a hot kitchen (55:59), Margaret returned to domestic work (56:23), Lyn wound up in a department store (56:44), Wanita washed dishes in an airport cafeteria (56: 50–57:06), and Lola learned mimeography and dark room technology. As of 1980, she still misses welding, often wistfully dreaming of making "a beautiful, ornamental gate. Is that too much to want?" No, it isn't and it's a shame that these women—once knowing the pleasures of satisfying work—weren't allowed to continue seeking self-fulfillment.

Further Reading

Dowling, John. Review of *The Life and Times of Rosie the Riveter*. *The Bulletin of Atomic Scientists* 37 (October 1981): 41.

Haskell, Molly. Review of *The Life and Times of Rosie the Riveter*. *Ms.* 9 (January 1981): 23.

Kauffmann, Stanley. Review of *The Life and Times of Rosie the Riveter*. *The New Republic* 184 (May 23, 1981): 24.

Skold, Karen Beck. "The Job Left Behind: American Women in the Shipyards During World War II." *Women, War and Revolution*. New York: Holman and Meier, 1980. 55–75.

White, Mimi. "Rehearsing Feminism: Women/History in *The Life and Times of Rosie the Riveter* and *Swing Shift*." *Wide Angle* 7 (1985): 34–43.

Saving Private Ryan (1998) (R)

Setting: Normandy and Europe, June 6–June 15, 1944; Arlington, 1998

Director: Steven Spielberg

Screenplay: Robert Rodat

Director of Photography: Janusz Kaminski

Cast: Tom Hanks (Capt. John Miller), Tom Sizemore (Sgt. Michael Horvath), Edward Burns (Pvt. Richard Reiben), and Matt Damon (Pvt. James Francis Ryan)

Availability: DreamWorks Home Video

Steven Spielberg's *Saving Private Ryan* is a 1990s return to the combat film of World War Two. Part antiwar, part prowar, the film's three-act structure is a mishmash of agendas, trying to please all points of view. The first act, the D-Day landing at Omaha Beach, Normandy, contains some of the most graphic and gripping war footage ever filmed. As Captain Miller waits to hit the beach from the landing barge, he tries to instill confidence in his men: "I'll see you on the beach" (5:28). But that confidence is short lived. Once the barge doors lower, bullets tear through the helmets and heads of several of Miller's men. On the beach, Miller watches in slow motion, his face bathed in blood, as intestines spill out of soldiers, a man with a severed limb picks up his lost arm and walks dumbfoundedly, and other men are set ablaze. Spielberg films a lot of the footage in a herky-jerky newsreel style that disorients and engages us (4:05–28:06). After the beach is taken, Captain Miller is given a seemingly insane and absurd mission. He and a crack squad of seven men are to comb the countryside, dropping behind enemy lines, to find a missing paratrooper, Pvt. James Francis Ryan. Three of Ryan's brothers have died in combat in the past few days, and the army, feeling compassion for his mother, wants Miller and his fellow Rangers to rescue Ryan from meeting a similar fate and from having his family become a sort of second wave of Sullivans (five brothers from Waterloo, Iowa, who lost their lives while serving on the same battleship in the South Pacific). Miller's men resent the mission and the privileged status of Ryan. On the way, one man is killed trying to help a young Italian girl. Later a medic is killed as Miller insists on taking out a German sandbag bunker. The men had wanted to avoid the bunker—it wasn't part of their mission. But Miller refused: "Our objective is to win the war." Following the death of the medic, and Miller's subsequent release of a German POW, Brooklyn street-kid Private Reiben wants out of the patrol. Miller's friend, Sergeant Horvath, a burly tough guy, holds a gun to Reiben's head, threatening to kill him if he doesn't "fall back in." As all collapses around him, Captain Miller acts heroically by redirecting the built-up anxiety. "What's the pool on me up to?" he asks. Everyone in the patrol had wondered about Miller's background, but, a private person, he refuses to divulge personal history. Now, to deflect the drama, he does. Miller tells his men that he's an English teacher at Thomas Elva Edison High School. Then eloquently, like an earlier Henry Fonda in *The Grapes of Wrath* and *The Ox-Bow Incident*, Tom Hanks delivers a speech filled with dignity and purpose: "I don't know anything about Ryan. I don't care. . . . If getting him home earns me the right to get back to my wife then that's my mission." Reiben and Sergeant Horvath are moved by his words, and the unrest ceases (1:40:04–1:42:28). Following this moment of combat patrol loyalty, Rodat's act three transforms the film into *Dirty Dozen* rah-rah. After finding private Ryan, the men discover that he's a well-meaning kid, dedicated to his airborne buddies. Ryan refuses to leave, to take advantage of his privileged status. Miller and his men are

moved by Ryan's loyalty, and together, with old-fashioned Hollywood hokum, they decide to hold a bridge against a Nazi advance. Rodat's motivation in act three is just too unbelievable. Almost any soldier given the
chance to get out of a harrowing situation will take it. Ryan may feel guilty
about the opportunity to go home, but he would leave. In this fantasy film,
he stays with his "new brothers," writing his name into history with a phony
"Remember the Alamo" pyrotechnical flourish.

Further Reading

Alleva, Richard. "A Brutal Masterpiece." Review of *Saving Private Ryan. Common-
    weal* 125 (September 11, 1998): 29–30.
Ambrose, Stephen E. *D-Day, June 6, 1944: The Climactic Battle of World War II.*
    New York: Simon and Schuster, 1995.
Caldwell, Christopher. "Spielberg at War." *Commentary* 106 (October 1998): 48–
    51.
Kaufman, Gerald. Review of *Saving Private Ryan. New Statesmen* 127 (September
    11, 1998): 38.
McDonald, Neil. "Revitalising the Combat Movie." *Quadrant* 43 (March 1999):
    71.

So Proudly We Hail (1943) (W)

Setting: San Francisco, Honolulu, Bataan, and Corregidor, 1941–1942

Director: Mark Sandrich

Screenplay: Allan Scott

Director of Photography: Charles Lang

Cast: Claudette Colbert (Lt. Janet Davidson), Paulette Goddard (Lt. Joan O'Doul),
Veronica Lake (Lt. Olivia D'Arcy), George Reeves (Lt. John Summers), and Sonny
Tufts (Kansas)

Availability: Paramount Home Video

This female-centered combat film, set in the Philippines during the dark
days of World War Two, does not share *Air Force*'s vision of absorbing
ethnic differences. Instead, it centers on unifying divergent female stereotypes—the cynical, world-weary dame, the boy-crazy gal, the Midwestern
sweetheart, and the old mother hen army lifer. Whereas John Garfield in
Air Force and Humphrey Bogart in *Casablanca* were torn between their
own concepts of rugged individualism and sacrifice to the collective good,
this film's central protagonist, Lieutenant Janet Davidson, wrestles with the
conflicting pulls of duty and romance. She's a good leader and holds nurses
together in the most dangerous times. In one harrowing scene, the nurses
are being evacuated from Bataan when the driver of the truck and the remaining forces protecting the women are killed by the Japanese (1:03:00–
1:07:30). Davey and her nursing corps retreat back into the barracks. As

shots are fired and bombs burst overhead, the women fear being raped at the hands of Japan's imperial army. Davey tells them to knock it off, and she crawls out into the darkness, grabs the keys from a dead GI and starts the truck. Davey is aided by Olivia D'Arcy, the world-weary nurse who lost her fiancé the day Pearl Harbor was attacked. Thanking Davey for "everything," and saying "It's one of us or all of us," Lieutenant D'Arcy recommits to the collective, sacrificing herself for their good. As she surrenders and walks into the hands of the Japanese, D'Arcy pulls the pin on a grenade and blows up herself and a handful of the enemy. Davey, shocked by D'Arcy's actions, maintains her composure and during the distraction of the explosion helps the nurses escape. Later as the Japanese bomb a mobile army hospital, Davey again shows her heroism, diving over and protecting the bodies of the wounded while shaking a fist and shouting to the heavens, "Slimy beasts!" (1:25:14–1:29:09). But despite these moments of action and heroism, the film insists on undercutting her, positioning Davidson as a love-pining woman. *So Proudly We Hail* opens with Davidson in a semi-comatose state. Fearing that her husband (Lt. John Summers) is dead, she's immobile and inarticulate, lying despondently on a stretcher as she and her crew are bound for rest and relaxation in Australia. Her fellow nurses can't bring her around, and Davey's condition becomes the frame from which to provide a series of flashbacks to explain the nurses' adventure and the how and why of Davey's condition. Glam-actress Paulette Goddard is another nurse presented in a contradictory light. As Lt. Joan O'Doul, Goddard plays the boy-crazy gal, working long vigorous hours watching over the sick and dying, while insisting on maintaining her femininity. Unable to find a dress, O'Doul attends a camp party wearing a black night gown (28:03–32:18). She also flirts with many of the men, including the rugged ex-football player "Kansas." And during her heart-rending departure from the men on Corregidor, O'Doul, sad to be pulling out, hands one man a fountain pen, another a watch, and to the rest, her collection of love letters. Choked up, she quietly waves as she departs, and they wave back, her letters staying behind, permanently positioning her as an object of interest for the men (1:56:33–1:57:16). The film ends with Davidson, at the hands of a male doctor, recovering her consciousness as a letter from her husband is read aloud. "This is our war now, and this time it will be our peace," the letter says, and Davey finding hope in her life suddenly looks into the sun and exclaims, "John!" The moment is pure Hollywood hokum and reinforces the film's thinly veiled sexism: women cannot live without men.

Further Reading

Crowther, Bosley. Review of *So Proudly We Hail*. *The New York Times* (September 10, 1943): 29.
Doherty, Thomas. "Women Without Men." *Projections of War: Hollywood, American*

Culture, and World War II. New York: Columbia University Press, 1993. 149–179.

Farber, Manny. "Love in the Foxholes." Review of *So Proudly We Hail*. *The New Republic* 109 (September 27, 1943): 426.

Kurtzleben, Jeri. " 'Accentuate the Positive' and Ignore the Real: Representations of W.W. II Nurses in Movietone Newsreels." *Images* #3, www.imagesjournal.com

They Were Expendable (1945)

Setting: South Pacific, 1941–1942

Director: John Ford

Screenplay: William L. White and Frank Wead

Director of Photography: Joseph H. August

Cast: Robert Montgomery (Lt. John Brickley), John Wayne (Lt. Rusty Ryan), Donna Reed (2nd Lt. Sandy Davyss), and Charles Trowbridge (Admiral Blackwell)

Availability: Warner Bros. Home Video

This gutsy story follows Captain Brickley, a commander of a PT boat, after America's disastrous defeat in the Philippines during the early days of World War Two. Similar to Howard Hawks' *Air Force* and Michael Curtiz's *Casablanca*, the emphasis here is on the collective. An admiral tells Captain Brickley that he and his men are to lay down a bunt, to provide a sacrifice for the team (24:59–25:46). During their skirmishes with the Japanese, Brickley's crew, a self-sufficient all-male unit, holds their own, but, for John Ford, sacrifice doesn't only mean to bravely face the threat of wartime death, but entails the disruption and loss of rituals: dances, phone calls with loved ones, romance, and funerals. Brickley's second in command, Rusty Ryan, falls in love with a nurse, Lt. Sandy Davyss, but the war keeps them apart. She's a no-nonsense woman who joins the all-male enclave by snapping back at them. Playfully, she teases Rusty about needing some relaxation, and he comments tersely, "Listen sister I don't dance. . . . All I want to do is get out of here" (48:04–48:11). But eventually Rusty also understands her need to reconnect with civilian life, to throw off her potato bag uniform and feel womanly. Rusty joins her at a party, dances with her, and they have an enjoyable talk in a makeshift front porch swing (an army hammock), sharing their backgrounds (50:19–54:44). Later Rusty invites Sandy to his group's compound and she enjoys a candlelit dinner (1:00:15–1:05:00). The men in attendance equally enjoy her company, as they too, through her presence, feel like they're back home. But such transformations are short-lived. A series of battles ensues, and Rusty tries to talk to Sandy by telephone, but the conversation is interrupted by generals who need the line. Rusty never gets to say goodbye, and the film ends with the two lovers separated and unable to find each other. Along with lost rituals, the film represents the disintegration of the team through no fault of their own. Bases are bombed and then deserted. Brickley is separated from the men through battle, and then later by company orders: he and Rusty are to return to the United States and teach navy men how to man the PT boats. "You older men . . . take care of the kids," Brickley says sadly, because ultimately in war, coaches are asked not only to lay down the sacrifice bunt, but also to desert their own team.

Further Reading

Crowther, Bosley. Review of *They Were Expendable*. *New York Times* (December 21, 1945): 25.

Davis, Ronald L. "War." *John Ford: Hollywood's Old Master*. Norman: University of Oklahoma Press, 1995. 154–178.

Gallagher, Tag. "*They Were Expendable*." *John Ford: The Man and His Films*. Berkeley: University of California Press, 1986. 221–224.

Hartung, Philip T. Review of *They Were Expendable*. *The Commonweal* 43 (December 28, 1945): 288.

FURTHER VIEWING

Big Red One (1980) (PG)

Caine Mutiny (1954)

Catch-22 (1970) (R)

Go for Broke! (1951) (M)

The Greatest Generation (1999) (Doc.)

Midnight Clear (1998) (R)

Mister Roberts (1955)

Objective, Burma! (1945)

Patton (1970) (PG)

Sands of Iwo Jima (1949)

Sophie's Choice (1982) (R) (W)

Story of G.I. Joe (1945)

The Thin Red Line (1998) (R)

To Hell and Back (1955)

Tuskegee Airmen (1996) (PG-13) (M)

A Walk in the Sun (1945)

9

Postwar Alienation and Despair, 1946–1962

Anatomy of a Murder (1959)

Setting: Upper Peninsula, Michigan, 1959

Director: Otto Preminger

Screenplay: Wendell Mayes

Director of Photography: Sam Leavitt

Cast: James Stewart (Paul Biegler), Lee Remick (Laura Manion), Ben Gazzara (Lt. Frederick Manion), and Arthur O'Connell (Parnell McCarthy)

Availability: Columbia Home Video

From 1957 to 1966 Raymond Burr's Perry Mason fought for those falsely accused by the legal system. On CBS, Mason was always the noble idealist and his clients forever innocent. The series had a repetitive formula, one that was confident in the lawyer/hero making sure the scales of justice were righted. By contrast, Otto Preminger's cynical 1959 film *Anatomy of a Murder* challenges the safe security of the Perry Mason mythos. Preminger's defense attorney (James Stewart as Paul Biegler) isn't an ideal man, but a sly trickster, playing the homespun populist to manipulate the jury's emotions and sway them to his side. In one memorable scene, Biegler shouts at an unfriendly witness, "What are you trying to do, railroad this soldier into the clink!" (1:27:00). The plot concerns Biegler defending Lieutenant Manion for the murder of Barney Quill, a tavern owner who beat and raped

Manion's wife. The wife, Laura, supports Manion's story, but the medical examiner finds no evidence of rape. Moreover, Laura is a striking southern belle who flirts and flaunts her beauty in tight-fitting slacks and sweaters. Her husband, a veteran of the Korean War and an officer trained to kill, has a bad reputation as a hothead, and may even be guilty of domestic violence. Ultimately, Biegler is not concerned with truth. Whereas Mason wouldn't defend anyone unless he believed his client was falsely accused, Biegler seems to relish finding a way to free a possibly justly accused man. When Biegler first visits Manion, he finds the lieutenant a little too cocksure. Manion assumes that the killing was justified because he has the "unwritten law" on his side. Biegler says that that law is a myth, and in a second visit (20:17–23:52) informs him on the four ways to defend murder. He tells Manion that his case doesn't fit under the first three defenses, but encourages him to find a reason under number four: "the killing was excusable." At this point, Manion's defense becomes a game, a performance. "What's your legal excuse, lieutenant?" Manion stands, paces, ponders. "Well, I, I, must have been mad. I mean, I uh, must have been crazy." Seconds later he asks, "Am I getting warmer?" Biegler smiles, having planted the seed for the entire defense, and bright-thinking Manion concocts a dissociative reaction plea to go along with it. Thus the film darkly suggests that Manion's legal defense doesn't hinge on questions of right and wrong but on an "irresistible impulse." Biegler and his assistant Parnell McCarthy find a Michigan precedent dating back to 1866 which says that even if a person is aware that his action was wrong, he will be excused from punishment if he was forced to commit the crime by an impulse that he was powerless to control (1:04:49). They use that defense and they win. The film has several other darkly cynical moments, including two that comment on gender. In one scene, Biegler takes the drunk Mrs. Manion aside at a juke joint, and tells her to conform to the public's notions of a supportive wife and rape victim: "Until this trial is over you're going to be a meek little housewife with horn-rimmed spectacles." He also insists that she stay away from other men and wear a girdle: "save that jiggle for your husband to look at" (55:00). The film's final image, a shot of Laura Manion's broken high-heeled shoe clamped on a trash can rim, signifies a woman victimized by a rapist, a violent husband, and a lawyer who can manipulate the scales of justice.

Further Reading

Bingham, Dennis. "Remembering Stewart." *Acting Male: Masculinities in the Films of James Stewart, Jack Nicholson, and Clint Eastwood.* New Brunswick, NJ: Rutgers University Press, 1994. 84–96.

Stark, John. *"Perry Mason* and the Criminal Lawyer as Brief Television Hero." *The 60 Television Shows and Events That Made Us Who We Are Today.* New York: Free Press, 1997. 96–100.

Zinman, David. *"Anatomy of a Murder* (1959)." *50 from the 50s: Vintage Films from*

America's Mid-Century. New Rochelle, NY: Arlington House Publishers, 1979. 9–16.

The Apartment (1960) (W)

Setting: New York, 1959

Director: Billy Wilder

Screenplay: Billy Wilder and I.A.L. Diamond

Director of Photography: Joseph LaShelle

Cast: Jack Lemmon (C. C. "Bud" Baxter), Shirley MacLaine (Fran Kubelik), and Fred MacMurray (J. D. Sheldrake)

Availability: MGM/UA (Turner)

Billy Wilder's bittersweet comedy for the Anacin-taking age deals with C. C. Baxter, an IBM operator at Consolidated Life Insurance who gets ahead in the business world—employmentwise—by lending out his apartment key to a group of randy executives who are having extramarital affairs. Cynically, the film suggests that the only way to "make it" in the competitive world of business (Baxter works for a corporation with 3,100 employees) isn't through personal initiative, drive, or talent, but through some sort of "racket." The complication arises when Baxter discovers that the company director, J. D. Sheldrake, is having an affair with Fran Kubelik, a sweet and downtrodden elevator operator with whom Baxter is in love. Once he learns of their tryst, he can no longer remain detached from the goings on at his apartment, and thus becomes morally culpable. Moreover, after Fran attempts suicide there, Baxter is fully involved, helping nurse her back to health and healing her psyche. Their scenes together—his unrequited love and yearning for her as they play gin rummy or talk about past histories combined with her elfin innocence and anguish over falling for a heartless married man—give the film its beauty. Wilder wonderfully inverts traditional gender roles: Baxter nurtures the wounded, vulnerable female, and Fran represents the complexity of adult sexual relationships. She's the urban, single girl, whose life contains neither career nor marriage. She sleeps with a married man because she loves him and winds up an unfortunate victim of loneliness and naiveté. But she and C. C. eventually escape Sheldrake and the amoral business world. Sheldrake feels nothing for Fran. Following her suicide attempt, he initially refuses to talk to her on the phone (78:11), and later he inappropriately chides her, "Why'd you do it, Fran? It's so childish and never solves anything" (1:39:38–1:39:45). Fran finally realizes Sheldrake's shallowness and her love for Baxter after Sheldrake complains about not being able to get the apartment key from "the punk." Baxter's epiphany is even more dramatic. In the previous scene (1:58:16), he hands over the key to the executive washroom instead of the key to his apartment, choosing human values over monetary ones. His actions win the girl, and together Fran and Baxter celebrate the new year—happy and jobless, but free.

Further Reading

Baltake, Joe. *The Films of Jack Lemmon. "The Apartment."* Secaucus, NJ: The Citadel Press, 1977. 106–112.

Dick, Bernard F. "The Human Comedies: *Some Like It Hot, The Apartment*, and *Avanti!" Billy Wilder.* Boston: Twayne Publishers, 1980. 86–98.

Erens, Patricia. *"The Apartment." The Films of Shirley MacLaine.* New York: A. S. Barnes & Company, 1978. 83–87.

The Best Years of Our Lives (1946)

Setting: Boone City, 1945

Director: William Wyler

Screenplay: Robert E. Sherwood

Director of Photography: Gregg Toland

Cast: Dana Andrews (Fred Derry), Frederic March (Al Stephenson), Myrna Loy (Milly Stephenson), Teresa Wright (Peggy Stephenson), Virginia Mayo (Marie Derry), Harold Russell (Homer Parrish), and Cathy O'Donnell (Wilma Cameron)

Availability: Samuel Goldwyn Presents

This splendid film captures the dilemmas faced by three veterans returning to a postwar economy. Capt. Fred Derry, an Air Force hero, can't prosper in the prosperous Boone City. He finds himself trapped in his old job as a soda jerk, and his quickie wartime marriage with Marie falls apart as she disparages his lack of success. Derry's lack of postwar success is an ironic contrast to his wartime heroics. Sgt. Al Stephenson can't communicate with his children (their adolescence seems to have passed while he was away). He also finds the conservative ideas of banking, especially with respect to giving loans to returning vets, closed-minded and heartless. He wants to judge men by their "guts," not their collateral, and he later tells off the board of governors in an inebriated, yet insightful, dinner speech (1:53:38). Ensign Homer Parrish lost his hands in combat and has to adjust to his family, and his girl Wilma, whom he loves but feels inadequate around because he can't hold her. William Wyler's direction and Gregg Toland's deep focus photography wonderfully capture the dislocation of these men in several brilliant scenes. Derry wakes in the middle of the night, screaming "Gadowski," a pilot who died in combat, and Al's daughter, Peggy, runs into his room, covers his eyes and soothes him back to sleep (50:56–53:55). Her nurturing love and kindness is something painfully missing in his relationship with his wife. Later, Derry wanders around a salvage site of old war planes, hops into a B-17, and experiences a traumatic flashback. The plane, its engines absent from the wings, mirrors his lost manhood (2:35:58). Homer shows

Wilma how his "hooks" work and confesses that when his "hands" are cast aside on the bed, he's as "dependent as a baby." If the door to the room should shut, he couldn't get out. Wilma says little, but compassionately takes charge of the scene, doing up his pajamas and kissing him. Homer, tears in his eyes and now somewhat reintegrated into society, finally throws his arms around her (2:20:52–2:28:53). Al Stephenson feels dislocated from his children and job, and in one of the film's most candid scenes he and wife Milly tell daughter Peggy how often they've fallen out of love, and have had to find a way to fall back in (2:04:38). The film deservedly won several Academy Awards, and its graceful depiction of the returning veteran is one of the most enduring ever filmed.

Further Reading

Beidler, Philip D. "Remembering *The Best Years of Our Lives*." *Virginia Quarterly Review* 72.4 (Fall 1996): 589–604.

Jackson, Martin A. "The Uncertain Peace: *The Best Years of Our Lives* (1946)." *American History/American Film: Interpreting the Hollywood Image*, ed. John E. O'Connor and Martin A. Jackson. New York: Continuum, 1988. 147–165.

The Big Sleep (1946) (W)

Setting: Los Angeles, 1946

Director: Howard Hawks

Screenplay: William Faulkner, Leigh Brackett, and Jules Furthman

Director of Photography: Sid Hickox

Cast: Humphrey Bogart (Philip Marlowe), Lauren Bacall (Vivian Rutledge), John Ridgely (Eddie Mars), Martha Vickers (Carmen Sternwood), Elisha Cook, Jr. (Harry Jones), Bob Steele (Lash Canino), Louis-John Heydt (Sam Brody), and Charles Waldron (General Sternwood)

Availability: MGM/UA (Turner)

The Big Sleep, based on the novel by Raymond Chandler, captures a mood of foreboding violence, of a world on the edge of the atomic precipice. Down these mean streets of film noir walks private-eye Philip Marlowe, a tarnished knight hired by General Sternwood to take care of a blackmailing scheme and to find the old man's lost drinking buddy, Sean Regan. But the journey leads Marlowe through more murder, gay revenge killings, and several acts of sudden violence (Marlowe is beaten in a back alley, helplessly crouches by an office doorway as a witness is murdered, gets viciously clobbered by Lash Canino, and in the film's waning moments, somewhat unnerved, sends the master villain out of Geiger's house and into a hail of bullets from his own gang). The incomprehensible plot only adds to the film's mood of disorientation. Women, as in Chandler's novel, are femme fatales, causing several "big sleeps": Agnes is directly responsible for the murders of Brody and Jones. Carmen is indirectly linked to the deaths of Taylor and Regan. But for director Howard Hawks, the question of why is meaningless because all that counts under his Hemingwayesque code is action (doing) and personal authenticity. Marlowe might be working for General Sternwood, but his real quest is to find out if he and Vivian Rutledge are compatible and can trust each other. This journey of self-discovery poses the film's central question: Will Marlowe and Vivian catch each other when the race is over? Their world is a nightmare landscape, and only those who are quick-witted and lucky survive. Within this Hawksian code, Vivian is Marlowe's equal. She joins him in several moments of verbal sparring, and in a splendid Abbott and Costello routine, they telephone the police and convince the officer that he was calling them (35:47–36:40). Moreover, in one of Hollywood's most daring scenes, Vivian engages Marlowe in some sexualized horse-racing innuendo: "Well speaking of horses . . . see if they're front runners or come from behind." "You got a touch of class," Marlowe responds to her lead, "But I don't know how far you can go." "It depends on who's in the saddle," she smartly says (1:01:41–1:05:46). Together, the two leads, husband and wife offscreen, sparkle with sexual chemistry. They bring hope and redemptive love to a cynical genre (contrast Hawks' film with John Huston's *The Maltese Falcon* [1941]), and an even darker world gripped in the violent specter of the atomic age.

Further Reading

Chandler, Raymond. *The Big Sleep*. Boston: Houghton Mifflin, 1939.
Mast, Gerald. "Hemingway and Chandler into Bogart-Bacall and Hawks: *To Have and Have Not* and *The Big Sleep*." *Howard Hawks, Storyteller*. New York: Oxford University Press, 1982. 243–296.
Walker, Michael. "*The Big Sleep*: Howard Hawks and Film Noir." *The Book of Film Noir*, ed. Ian Cameron. New York: Continuum, 1993. 191–202.
Wood, Robin. "Appendix: Failures and Marginal Works." *Howard Hawks*. London: BFI, 1968. 163–172.

Blackboard Jungle (1955)

Setting: New York, 1955

Director: Richard Brooks

Screenplay: Richard Brooks

Director of Photography: Charles Wolcott

Cast: Glenn Ford (Richard Dadier), Sidney Poitier (Gregory Miller), Vic Morrow (Artie West), and Anne Francis (Anne Dadier)

Availability: MGM/UA (Turner)

When Richard Brooks' social problem film, based on an Evan Hunter novel, was released in 1955, it sent sharp surges along the spines of educators for it revealed an inner city school system that was uncontrollable. At North Manual High, the teenage boys have no future aspirations for higher education or high-level jobs. Once they come of age, they'll wind up in menial labor, on welfare, or drafted by the army. Within this cycle of hopelessness, they form gangs in order to feel powerful. Richard Dadier is a soft-spoken veteran who as an English teacher attempts to make a difference, but he quickly finds himself outnumbered in the classroom. When he tries to instill discipline, Artie West warns him, "You ever try to fight thirty-five guys at one time, teach?" (19:10). Brooks suggests that government is uncommitted to solving the problem (late in the film, Glenn Ford gives an impassioned speech about how little public school teachers make [$2 an hour], versus congressmen [$9 an hour]; "Why a household cook gets more money than we do. And they get board" [1:27:00]). The solution for Brooks seems to be committed teachers who can somehow rise above an indifferent system. Dadier tries to reach the kids by appealing to one of the leaders of the gang (Greg Miller), but that takes time, as Miller, afraid of peer pressure, initially refuses to cross over and help. Dadier's eventual friendship with Miller is also clouded by the teacher's own hidden prejudices, which he must honestly confront and conquer. After being falsely accused by the school principal of bigotry in the classroom, Dadier believes that Miller was the accuser (it was actually West), and he confronts him on the stairs. Higher up in the composition, Dadier seems to take on a position of power and authority, but his words belie the appearance. Agitated and angry, he yells, "Why you black . . . ," and then he apologizes for thinking a racial slur (54:40). Eventually, Dadier's commitment to the tough kids wins over Miller and most of his classmates. The breakthrough scene is a splendid triumph for media education. Dadier shows a short animated film, "Jack and the Beanstalk" (this type of pedagogy was revolutionary in the 1950s, when film texts were deemed inherently less worthy than the written word), and the students become engaged in critical viewing, raising a series of complicated questions about Jack's motivation and the ethics of the storyline (1:11:14–1:15:34). Despite this victory, Brooks ultimately believes that Dadier's complete respect and leadership can only be achieved through force, as he disarms the knife-wielding West in a scary final confrontation.

Further Reading

Considine, David M. "From Mentors to Murderers." *The Cinema of Adolescence.* Jefferson, NC: McFarland & Co., 1985. 111–143.

Doherty, Thomas. "Teenagers and Teenpics, 1955–57: A Study of Exploitation Film-making." *The Studio System*, ed. Janet Staiger. New Brunswick, NJ: Rutgers University Press, 1995. 298–316.

McLean, Mari Margaret. "It's a *Blackboard Jungle* Out There—or Is It?" *The Education Digest* 61 (January 1996): 4–7.

Breaking Point (1950)

Setting: Southern California, 1950

Director: Michael Curtiz

Screenplay: Ranald MacDougall

Director of Photography: Ted McCord

Cast: John Garfield (Harry Morgan), Phyllis Thaxter (Lucy Morgan), Patricia Neal (Leona Charles), Juano Hernandez (Wesley Park), and Juan Hernandez (Joe)

Availability: None

Director Michael Curtiz and screenwriter Ranald MacDougall trouble Ernest Hemingway's masculine codes of conduct in *Breaking Point*. In Warner Bros.' adaptation of Hemingway's *To Have and Have Not*, John Garfield plays Harry Morgan, a World War Two veteran who struggles to pay his bills. He has a devoted wife and two daughters, but his livelihood (driving a schooner, and taking people offshore to fish) is threatened when a rich client abandons Harry and his sidekick Wes in Mexico, and he hasn't got enough money to reenter the United States. Stranded, he agrees to smuggle eight Chinese into California. The operation backfires and Morgan kills a man. Back home, the dislocated vet drinks to shade his guilt. Eventually, he confesses and admits to his wife a fear of not living up to a masculine code: "I can't take it anymore. A lot of things I can't take anymore. I used to think I was a pretty tough guy" (47:08). During the war in the Philippines, Morgan felt successful and courageous. In the postwar world, he longs to return to that earlier jazzed moment of manliness. Following an aborted affair with Lucy, Morgan tells her why he's throwing in with some gangsters: "I've got no choice. All I've got left to pedal is guts. I'm not sure I got any. I have to find out" (1:08:40). But to find out is costly. Because of a second economic crisis, Morgan agrees to ferry a group of gangsters to a rendezvous ship. But just prior to their departure, the gangsters kill Wes in front of Morgan. In a later shipboard shootout, Morgan may have reclaimed his lost masculinity by conquering the gangsters, but his need for such a ritualized test indirectly killed his best friend. Curtiz further troubles Hemingway's aesthetics in a disturbing final image. Wes' son, Joe, in a high-angle, extreme long shot, stands along the pier waiting for his father to return. Morgan is carted off in an ambulance, the congregation breaks away, and nobody seems concerned about the African American kid who remains alone, invisible. As the scene fades to black, Curtiz renders a powerful social statement about the consequences of tough guy codes and America's insensitivity to race.

Further Reading

Comley, Nancy R. and Robert Scholes. *Hemingway's Genders: Rereading the Hemingway Text.* New Haven: Yale University Press, 1994.

Flinn, Tom, and John Davis. *"The Breaking Point." The Velvet Light Trap* 14 (Winter 1975): 17–20.

Review of *Breaking Point. Time* 56 (September 25, 1950): 96.

Death of a Salesman (1985) (PG)

Setting: New York, 1947

Director: Volker Schlondorff

Screenplay: Arthur Miller

Director of Photography: Michael Ballhaus

Cast: Dustin Hoffman (Willy Loman), John Malkovich (Biff Loman), Kate Reid (Linda Loman), Stephen Lang (Hap Loman), and Louis Zorich (Uncle Ben)

Availability: Anchor Bay Video

Arthur Miller's 1949 indictment of business radically changed how Americans perceive jobs in sales and forced us to reconsider the American myth of success. By 1964, only one in seventeen American college students were willing to try sales as a career. This change from the false optimism contained in Andrew Carnegie's 1936 self-help book, *How to Win Friends and Influence People,* can be partly attributed to Miller whose play struck a chord with the post–World War Two mood of alienation. His Willy Loman is a man divorced from his work, himself, and reality; he's a "lost drummer," trapped, as Joseph Hirsch's cover drawing of Willy (back to us, shoulders hunched, hands gripping his sample bags as he trudges toward a bleak horizon) sadly illustrates. Willy's true identity is swamped in a world of businessese; he adopts the jargon: "Gee, kid," "knock 'em dead," "I could swing it," and the desire to be liked at the expense, as his son Biff tells us, of finding out who and what he really is. His wife, Linda, and younger son, Happy, further his alienation by co-enabling him to live a series of lies and Carnegieesque fantasies. By contrast, Uncle Ben—the Panama'd specter of success—represents Miller's debunking of the salesman dream. The myth of success for Miller means to aggressively dominate others through colonialism and interpersonal relations. Success is based on greed and punishment. In a shocking moment from the Schlondorff production, young Biff playfully roughhouses Uncle Ben (who made his success in Africa) and learns a hard lesson. After the sparring match ends, Ben offers to shake hands, and then suddenly trips Biff and nudges the tip of his umbrella under the teenager's neck. "Never fight fair with a stranger, boy. You'll never get out of the jungle that way," he coldly advises (36:00), reaffirming a policy of aggression. All of the actors, especially John Malkovich who plays Biff with a quiet restraint and subdued anger, are marvelous. There are some memorable scenes: Willy gets fired by Howard and discovers that company loyalty and personal history mean nothing (1:04:20–1:14:00); and Biff's final conversation with his father testifies to his love for him, as well as his intense desire to have his father let the "phony" dream go (1:57:00–2:04:50).

Further Reading

Carnegie, Dale. *How to Win Friends and Influence People*. New York: Pocket Books, 1936.
Miller, Arthur. *Death of a Salesman*. New York: Viking, 1949.
Murphy, Brenda. "Willy Loman: Icon of Business Culture." *Michigan Quarterly Review* 37.4 (Fall 1998): 755–766.

Force of Evil (1948)

Setting: New York, 1948

Director: Abraham Polonsky

Screenplay: Abraham Polonsky and Ira Wolfert

Director of Photography: George Barnes

Cast: John Garfield (Joe Morse), Thomas Gomez (Leo Morse), Beatrice Pearson (Doris Lowry), Howland Chamberlain (Freddy Bauer), and Roy Roberts (Ben Tucker)

Availability: Republic Home Video

Whereas Arthur Miller's Willy Loman is a victim of capitalism's undercurrents of greed and aggression (the worker is an orange that management eats and then throws the remaining peel away), Abraham Polonsky's Joe Morse knows that the world of business is corrupt and alienating but he's tough and cynical enough to "fight for a piece of it." Yet his cynicism is a mask, alienating himself from his conscience. As "a crooked little lawyer," Morse has reason to feel guilty. He's in league with Ben Tucker, a former beer runner, who is planning to take over the numbers racket by fixing the old liberty number, 776, to fall on July 4th. After 776 hits, the big Tucker corporation will move in and consolidate the small numbers banks that can't pay off their debts and form a monopoly. John Garfield's opening voiceover suggests his guilt-free, matter-of-fact involvement in the enterprise: "Tomorrow, July 4th, I intended to make my first million," but Polonsky's *mise-en-scène* troubles the confidence. A quick tilt down and bird's eye swish pan shows spots of people moving along Wall Street. Polonsky's visuals suggest that Morse and Tucker's success in business is contingent upon their ability to aggressively crush others (2:14). Joe seems unconcerned about this, but when he fears that his brother Leo, a small numbers banker, will also get destroyed in the scheme, he jeopardizes his success in order to bring him in on the deal. Following Leo's initial rejection, Joe emotes one of cinema's great meditations on guilt. In a two shot, he stops his playful conversation with girlfriend Doris Lowry to say, "To reach out, to take it, that's human, that's natural. But to get your pleasure from not taking. From cheating yourself deliberately like my brother did today, from not getting, from not taking. Don't you see what a black thing that is for a man to do? How it is to hate yourself, your brother, to make him feel that he's guilty, that I'm guilty. Just to live and be guilty" (29:20). Joe's trailing words mirror his central dilemma. He may be willing to take risks in Tucker's enterprise, but as his last name suggests, (re)Morse, and his self-absorbed repetition of "guilty," he's a man of conscience who vainly tries to hide behind a street-smart sense of social Darwinism. Ultimately, Doris, who is also tempted by money and greed, speaks the film's noirish fatalism: "Oh, you'll make him [Leo] rich, in his death," she yells at Joe angrily, from inside a phone booth (54:36). As the film's moral center, she's right. Unlike other noirs, *Force of Evil* blames institutions (Wall Street) and the pursuit of monopoly capital for dehumanizing and destroying people.

Further Reading

Peary, Danny. *"Force of Evil." Cult Movies: The Classics, the Sleepers, the Weird and the Wonderful.* New York: Delacorte Press, 1981. 99–102.
Schultheiss, John and Mark Schaubert, Editors. *Force of Evil: The Critical Edition.* Northridge: Center for Telecommunication Studies, California State University, 1996.
Shadoian, Jack. *"Force of Evil (1948)." Dreams and Dead Ends.* Cambridge, MA: MIT Press, 1977. 134–147.

The Hudsucker Proxy (1994) (PG) (W)

Setting: New York City, 1958–1959

Director: Joel Coen

Screenplay: Ethan Coen, Joel Coen, and Sam Raimi

Director of Photography: Roger Deakins

Cast: Tim Robbins (Norville Barnes), Jennifer Jason Leigh (Amy Archer), Paul Newman (Sidney J. Mussburger), and Charles Durning (Waring Hudsucker)

Availability: Warner Bros. Home Video

The Coen brothers are experts at taking old Hollywood formulas and infusing them with modern, edgy irony. In *Hudsucker Proxy* they transpose the films of Frank Capra to create a screwball dramedy. Part comedy, part serious social statement, *Hudsucker* features a naive character who's thought to be an imbecile or insane (in *Mr. Deeds Goes to Town* Gary Cooper was thought to be pixillated), falls in love with a reporter (Jennifer Jason Leigh) who had initially tried to destroy him but now loves him too (Jean Arthur and Barbara Stanwyck played these roles in *Mr. Deeds* and *Meet John Doe*, respectively), and eventually contemplates suicide when all other avenues of hope seem dashed (*It's a Wonderful Life* opens with this hook and *Meet John Doe* closes with it). But whereas the Capra films had a rural, populist sentiment, the Coen brothers uncover a harsh world of Wall Street and the rat race, circa 1958–1959. Norville Barnes is a bright young man from Muncie, Indiana, full of dreams. He has visions. On a piece of paper he has drawn a circle and says it's his big idea, "for the kids" (15:29). Most people glance at the paper and assume that he's touched. After seeing the circle, Sidney Mussburger takes Barnes for an imbecile and hires him as the VP in the wake of Waring Hudsucker's suicide. Mussburger, cognizant of the by-laws which insist that Hudsucker stock be made public after the president's death, wants to create a panic among the investors in order to undersell the open stock. But Mussburger's greedy plan backfires, as Barnes exceeds expectations, invents the hula-hoop, and Hudsucker stock soars. Barnes' love life soars, too. Reporter Amy Archer, who had been assigned to uncover his imbecility, finds herself moved by Barnes' sincerity and kindness. Leigh's scenes with Tim Robbins are also howlingly funny. The highlight occurs when Barnes sings his alma mater, and Amy, a resident New Yorker posing as a "Muncie gal," hesitatingly sings along, guessing at the unknown words and often falling a note behind (37:33–38:23). The scene's strange synergy—Amy's ability to sing what she had never heard before—suggests that these characters are compatible and meant for each other. Their love is nearly thwarted as the ruthless Mussburger almost destroys Barnes by suggesting that he's insane to the board and the press. In the wake of discovering that Amy is the reporter writing bad stories about Hudsucker, Barnes sinks into depression and appears headed for death. In interviews over *Meet John Doe*, Capra always felt the film's ending boxed him in. He wanted a happy ending, but the logical conclusion should have featured John Doe jumping from the tower to his death on New Year's Eve. In *Hudsucker*, the Coen brothers take Capra's idea and have it both ways. Barnes does fall from the forty-fourth floor of the Hudsucker building, but in a splendid moment of ironic absurdism, the Hudsucker clock stops ticking through the help of a watchful custodian, and Barnes death flight halts, midair. Waring, now a Clarence-type of angel, descends from heaven, offers advice, and grants Barnes power against Mussburger. The clock ticks again, and Barnes lands safely. The little guy, in this business fantasy, conquers the evil corporate machine, and wins back Amy. And on a corporate level, Barnes will be an ideal king, treating employees fairly and continuing to create gems for children, such as the Frisbee, his next invention.

Further Reading

Alleva, Richard. Review of *The Hudsucker Proxy*. *Commonweal* 121 (May 20, 1994): 24.

Romney, Jonathan. Review of *The Hudsucker Proxy*. *New Statesmen & Society* 7 (August 26, 1994): 31.
Schickel, Richard. Review of *The Hudsucker Proxy*. *Time* 143 (March 14, 1994): 103.

It's Always Fair Weather (1955)

Setting: New York, 1945 and 1955

Directors: Gene Kelly and Stanley Donen

Screenplay: Betty Comden and Adolph Green

Director of Photography: Robert J. Bronner

Cast: Gene Kelly (Ted Riley), Dan Dailey (Douglas Hallerton), Michael Kidd (Angelo Valentine), Cyd Charisse (Jackie Leighton), and Dolores Gray (Madeline)

Availability: MGM/UA (Turner)

Gene Kelly's *It's Always Fair Weather* is in marked contrast to the upbeat utopias of most musicals. Kelly's film concerns three dislocated vets who return stateside in 1945, visit a New York bar, and vow to remain friends forever. To prove their loyalty they promise to reunite in 1955. They do, but much has changed. They hardly know each other and in the supposed glow of the postwar economic boom, these men are bitterly disappointed with themselves and their friends. In the intervening years, Angelo Valentine married, raised four kids, and flipped burgers at a Midwest diner. Douglas Hallerton, once an aspiring painter along the lines of Picasso, has become a man in a grey flannel suit, working in graphic advertising and creating such infantile cartoon characters as "Little Miss Mop Up." And Ted Riley, a loser in love, hides behind a cynical front, having given up on his political aspirations to become a racketeer and fight promoter. Their displeasure with each other is comically rendered in a restaurant scene in which Kelly reveals each character's inner monologue and judgments to the tune of the "Blue Danube Waltz" (24:36–29:00). Although most of the other songs aren't very memorable, the film has several great scenes. A wonderful montage (15:00–16:53) shows how each character's life progressed in ten years, and it highlights several 1950s obsessions: a desire to keep up with the Joneses, the baby boom, and the *Playboy* philosophy of guiltless sexual pleasure. In the montage, Kelly divides the Cinemascope screen into a triptych with Dailey on the left, Kidd on the right, and himself in the center, and the collisions among the three frames are hilarious—in one segment Doug and his bride are poised in a living room portrait, and quickly possessions pop up around and engulf them; on the right, Angelo and his wife, seated for a similar portrait, suddenly have four children pop into the scene, and then in the middle, Ted, surrounded by *Playboy*-type models, plays cards at a swank night club. He holds up his arms and looks directly at us, as if to say, "oh well," and then one by one the women pop away, suggesting a lack of lasting relationships in his life. Cyd Charisse is also on hand to enliven the film. She plays a surprising pre–Title IX feminist woman who knows all about boxing, and in the "You Knock Me Out" number dances with a bunch of pug-uglies and rattles off all the heavyweight champs, in order, from Sullivan to Marciano (43:53–48:43). Ideologically, the film critiques pre–Jerry Springer television, especially live shows that cash in and commodify the real lives of people. In the "Midnight with Madeline" scene, the dignity of the three vets is sacrificed for television ratings (1:25:00–1:36:20). During the "surprisingly candid" moment, in which the boys are presented with certificates before a live audience, Angelo refuses to be pitied, Doug ironically accepts his recognition with a downbeat "I deserve every bit of it . . . a fitting climax to ten years of self-degradation," and Ted simply describes himself as a "bum." Their refusal to conform to a programming format of complaint victims allows them to regain their dignity and emerge victorious. Of course the ending is also happy (this is a musical after all): Ted gets the girl, and in a battle with gangsters the three vets reclaim their troubled friendships. But despite the afterglow of such reconciliations, the vestiges of 1950s disappointment and dislocation remain.

Further Reading

Altman, Rick. *The American Film Musical*. Bloomington: University of Indiana Press, 1986.
Feuer, Jane. "The Self-Reflexive Musical and the Myth of Entertainment." *Film Theory and Criticism*, ed. Gerald Mast, Marshall Cohen, and Leo Braudy. Fourth Edition. New York: Oxford University Press, 1992. 486–497.
Halberstam, David. *The Fifties*. New York: Villard Books, 1993.

It's a Wonderful Life (1946)

Setting: Bedford Falls, 1919–1945

Director: Frank Capra

Screenplay: Frances Goodrich, Albert Hackett, Frank Capra, and Jo Swerling

Directors of Photography: Joseph Walker and Joseph Biroc

Cast: James Stewart (George Bailey), Donna Reed (Mary Hatch), Lionel Barrymore (Mr. Potter), Henry Travers (Clarence), Beulah Bondi (Mrs. Bailey), Frank Faylen (Ernie Bishop), H. B. Warner (Mr. Gower), Todd Karns (Harry Bailey), and Samuel S. Hinds (Pa Bailey)

Availability: Republic Home Video

Frank Capra's greatest film explores the struggle between worldly success and communal values. George Bailey would rather build bridges and see the world than stay in Bedford Falls. But in Bedford, he helps hard-working people earn loans so that they can live decently and, as his father puts it, "not have to go crawling to Potter," a mean banker who covets monopolizing the town. But George stands at a crossroads. As an embodiment of

James Stewart's prewar and postwar personae, Bailey represents both the naive, rural man of dignity (the Stewart of *Mr. Smith Goes to Washington* and *The Philadelphia Story*) and the angry, disillusioned postwar heroes of the Alfred Hitchcock thrillers and Anthony Mann westerns. George resents having settled down and surrendered his dreams for the ordinary life. But he never could get away. On the eve of his trip to Europe, his father died. Three months later, on his way to catch a train to college, he was asked to stay on at the Building and Loan to keep it out of Potter's clutching hands. As George ponders his choices, Capra uses an intense wide angle closeup to capture his anxiousness. Capra also leaves the background in shallow focus, suggesting a lack of future (35:10). Later, after his brother marries and has a promising job in Buffalo, George, trapped, finally opts for marriage. His proposal to Mary Hatch is one of the most bizarre and conflicted in cinema. While he violently grabs her, he yells in a harsh whisper, "I don't want to get married to anyone. . . . I want to do what I want to do," and then he hugs her, almost in a hurtful way, "Oh, Mary, Mary" (49:43–50:14). George's conflict reflects a struggle in American thought. By 1946, Americans were far more impressed with men of adventure (go-getters in business, war heroes like brother Harry Bailey, sports figures like Babe Ruth and Joe Louis) who had won in the world of competition. But Capra's Bailey represents the quiet triumph of Americans who do the necessary work at home to build their communities. Bailey may be ordinary, but he ultimately learns, through an angel (second class) and a film noirish nightmare, that he's had a wonderful life. The film begins with George contemplating suicide over $8,000 in missing funds. Following a long series of flashbacks, we find him at the height of his disillusionment, ready to jump from a bridge to his death. At this moment, Clarence the angel arrives, and in a pre-*Twilight Zone*-type episode shows George what life would be like in Bedford Falls without him (1:44:27–2:01:57). Through the dark world of Clarence's noir, George and all of us everyday types discover that ordinariness can be quite extraordinary.

Further Reading

Maland, Charles J. "*It's a Wonderful Life*: The Masterpiece (1945–46)." *Frank Capra*. Boston: Twayne Publishers, 1980. 131–152.

Ray, Robert B. "*It's a Wonderful Life* and *The Man Who Shot Liberty Valance*." *A Certain Tendency of the Hollywood Cinema, 1930–1980*. Princeton, NJ: Princeton University Press, 1985. 175–246.

Roffman, Peter and Jim Purdy. "The Individual and Society: Darker Views of the Postwar World." *The Hollywood Social Problem Film: Madness, Despair, and Politics from the Depression to the Fifties*. Bloomington: Indiana University Press, 1981. 268–283.

Wolfe, Charles. "The Return of Jimmy Stewart: The Publicity Photograph as Text." *Stardom: Industry of Desire*, ed. Christine Gledhill. New York: Routledge, 1981. 92–106.

The Last Picture Show (1971) (R) (W)

Setting: Rural Texas, 1951–1952

Director: Peter Bogdanovich

Screenplay: Peter Bogdanovich and Larry McMurtry

Director of Photography: Robert Surtees

Cast: Timothy Bottoms (Sonny Crawford), Jeff Bridges (Duane Jackson), Cybill Shepherd (Jacy Farrow), Ellen Burstyn (Mrs. Farrow), Cloris Leachman (Ruth Popper), Ben Johnson (Sam the Lion), Sam Bottoms (Billy), and Sharon Taggart (Charlene)

Availability: Columbia Home Video

In *The Last Picture Show* director Peter Bogdanovich and cinematographer Robert Surtees created a film that looks like John Ford's *The Grapes of Wrath*, but with a different mood of depression—one capturing 1950s sexual discontent and repression. Sex in this film is full of misconceptions and is largely dehumanizing. Duane, Sonny, and a group of boys traumatize Billy, the retarded kid, by initiating him into sex with a fat prostitute. Excited and unfamiliar with the moment, he ejaculates too soon and the woman castigates him (40:42–42:00). Similarly, Duane is unable to perform during his first sexual encounter with Jacy, and later when he does perform and feels triumphant, she snaps, "Oh quit prissing. I don't think you did it right, anyway" (1:09:38–1:10:00). Unfulfilled by the experience, Jacy transforms herself into a different kind of victim, one who uses sex as a weapon. Earlier, Jacy had attended Bobby Sheen's party, at which all of the guests cavorted around a pool naked. Standing atop a diving board, Jacy stripped for the group below, her body objectified (36:07–39:26). She passes this rite of passage, but at what expense? Recognizing the power of sex, Jacy breaks up with Duane and then breaks up Sonny's relationship with Ruth Popper by offering herself to him. In a complicated act of triumphant vindictiveness she marries Sonny, but arranges for her mother to annul it prior to consummation (1:32:47). Jacy's mother is a much more sympathetic character. A fiery woman, more at home in the 1960s than the socially repressive 1950s, she's married to a sexless man, and seeks relations with others. Years ago she and Sam used to swim naked at the old pond and race horses. "It's terrible to only meet one man in your life who knows what you're worth," she sadly confesses to Sonny (1:36:37). Sonny is sexually frustrated by Jacy, and earlier by his first girlfriend, Charlene. He was allowed to feel her breasts, but the relationship could go no further, and their "petting" rendezvous in a pickup truck was as sexy as a visit to the doctor's office (11:11–13:02). After their breakup, Sonny becomes involved with the neglected Ruth Popper, the wife of the school's football coach. But with Sonny, Ruth finds sexual pleasure. At first their lovemaking is hurried and somewhat mechanical, but later she combs her hair in a less severe manner, wears brighter clothes, and refurbishes the room with blue wallpaper, awaiting his visits. Painfully, Sonny leaves her for his dream girl, Jacy (Larry McMurtry's version of F. Scott Fitzgerald's Daisy Buchanan), but returns to Ruth in the end, because that's all he has left. Alfred Kinsey's sex reports on the human male (1948) and human female (1953) may have shown how we engage in sex for pleasure and not just procreation, but this film shows how messed up sex was for many in the repressive 1950s.

Further Reading

Kael, Pauline. "Movies in Movies." *Deeper into Movies*. Boston: Atlantic Monthly Press Book, 1973. 293–299.

Silver, Isadore. "The Last Picture Show: A Concurring Opinion." *Commonweal* 95 (January 14, 1972): 348–350.

Westerbeck, Colin L. "Remembrance of Things Past." Review of *The Last Picture Show. Commonweal* 95 (November 5, 1971): 132–133.

Mildred Pierce (1945) (W)

Setting: Los Angeles, 1945

Director: Michael Curtiz

Screenplay: Ranald MacDougall

Director of Photography: Ernest Haller

Cast: Joan Crawford (Mildred Pierce), Jack Carson (Wally Fay), Zacharay Scott (Monte Beragon), Eve Arden (Ida), Ann Blyth (Veda Pierce), Bruce Bennett (Bert Pierce), and Lee Patrick (Maggie Binderhof)

Availability: MGM/UA (Turner)

Michael Curtiz's *Mildred Pierce* seeks to return women to the realm of domesticity. After the nation had been through the Depression and World War Two, American middle classes moved to the suburbs, downsized from extended families to nuclear families, and strongly sought "normalcy." Normalcy demanded that "Rosie the Riveter" leave the work force, return home, and raise children. Mildred is punished for bucking that paradigm. She rises in business from waitress to entrepreneur of a chain of restaurants. While Mildred is pursuing material and personal success, her younger daughter is struck with pneumonia. When the absent mother returns, she is scolded by Bert, her estranged husband ("Where have you been. . . . It's Kay. She's sick. . . . She's at Mrs. Binderhof's" [53:10]). Bert's scolding suggests that Mrs. Binderhof is more of a mother than Mildred. Moments later, Kay dies, and Mildred vows not to let anything ever happen to her older daughter, Veda. But this desire is also mistaken. Mildred's yearning for material success converts her daughter into a monster of consumption, coveting more and more possessions. Veda even fakes a pregnancy to blackmail money from a rich suitor. Mildred, angry at her daughter's emotional games, tears up a check from the boy's family and tells her "you're cheap and horrible" (1:21:40). Curtiz's *mise-en-scène*, however, has both women dressed in identical black dresses, shoes, and high hairstyles, suggesting an inextricable doubling between them. Somehow each woman is equally cheap and horrible, guilty for the behavior of the other (Veda's desire to transcend her class origins, to get away from everything that "smells of grease," forces her mother to strive in business to please her; Mildred's success in business and motherly neglect gives Veda the insatiable need for more, which includes having an affair with her mother's second husband, Monte; the story eventually ends in murder). The film's conservative ideology seems to tell women to stay at home, and yet at the time of the film's release the opposite was true. Women age twenty to twenty-four were returning to their suburb homes, but now the majority of married women with children were heading into the work force, on their own choice, looking for fulfillment. There is one additional element to consider: the filmic structure criticizes Mildred, but an alternative reading might be suggested; perhaps the ideological issue shouldn't be solely Mildred's absence as a mother, but the need for Bert to take on a greater fatherly presence.

Further Reading

Boozer, Jack, Jr. "Entrepreneurs and 'Family Values' in the Postwar Film." *Authority and Transgression in Literature and Film*, ed. Bonnie Braendlin and Hans Braendlin. Gainesville: University of Florida Press, 1996. 89–102.

Fox-Genovese, Elizabeth. "Mixed Messages: Women and the Impact of World War II." *Southern Humanities Review* 27.3 (Summer 1993): 235–245.

Haralovich, Mary Beth. "Too Much Guilt Is Never Enough for Working Mothers: Joan Crawford, *Mildred Pierce*, and *Mommie Dearest*." *The Velvet Light Trap* 29 (Spring 1992): 43–52.

Net Worth (1995) (TV) (docudrama)

Setting: Detroit, 1956–1957

Director: Jerry Ciccorritti

Screenplay: Dan Truckey, Phil Savath, David Cruise, and Alison Griffiths

Director of Photography: Barry Stone

Cast: Aidan Devine (Ted Lindsay), Kevin Conway (Gordie Howe), and Al Waxman (Jack Adams)

Availability: Quality Home Video

From 1942 to 1967 the National Hockey League was a six-team league run by three owners and a president, Clarence Campbell, who had convinced the league's 120 players that their game was in jeopardy, and the league could not afford the salaries, benefits, and working conditions they demanded. If they persisted, the players would kill the sport. But in 1956, the Detroit Red Wings made $1 million in profits, twice the margin of baseball's most successful franchise, the New York Yankees. In 1956–1957, Detroit left winger "Terrible" Ted Lindsay formed a players association to earn the players a real pension and to get them the salaries they deserved. This CBC docudrama explores those early days of working-class struggles when most NHL players made under $10,000 a year and were told it was a privilege to play the game. Fired up by the death of Larry Saharchuk (a former player who died homeless because he was unable to collect his pension from the league), Lindsay unionizes his fellow Red Wings. Lindsay's legendary right-winger on the famed "Production Line," Gordie Howe, is reluctant at first—he believes in the paternalistic assurances of general manager Jack Adams. Howe, portrayed as naive at best, is a simpleton wide open to manipulation. When the organizing spreads to other teams, the owners plot against the ringleaders, accusing them of being "communists" and "agitators," and Adams banishes Lindsay to the lowly Chicago Blackhawks, and then plants false stories in the press, destroying Lindsay's credibility with his old teammates. They decide to vote against the union, and the hopes and aspirations of equality are crushed. *Net Worth* is one-sided in its rhetoric (the owners are Runyonesque robber barons), but the film's mood and feeling accurately capture an era in which owners grabbed as much as they could from their players. Aidan Devine as Ted Lindsay resonates, with his sincerity and quiet intensity, the full humanity and integrity of the Hall-of-Famer. There are several powerful moments in the film. In the contract scene (12:42–16:21), Howe is given a blank space by Adams and pencils in a paltry $13,000. Because he believed in hockey's fragility, the game's greatest player had acted as an unwitting salary cap for years. By contrast, Lindsay refuses to sign for $10,000. "Nope," he says defiantly, and a rebel is born. Later a brief scene of exploitation (33:52–34:27) shows players posing for their hockey cards, and being compensated with a mere box of bubble gum. Finally, Lindsay's speech to the Toronto Maple Leafs, as they first vote on ratifying a union in Canada, is one of the most powerful statements of athletic rights and personal dignity captured on film (1:08:34–1:10:02). Lindsay tells his fellow workers to look at former Leaf legend and future Hall-of-Famer Harvey "Busher" Jackson, who sells broken hockey sticks outside the hallowed Gardens for a quarter apiece. He doesn't need a plaque in the Hall, but a place to sleep. The owners did nothing for Jackson, and they aren't "going to help us guys. . . . They're making millions of dollars off us. . . . We do love this game, [but we also love ourselves and our rights]." The Leafs ratify. Unfortunately, weeks later, Detroit, in the United States, does not. This production won several Gemini Awards (the Emmy of Canada), including best dramatic program, direction, supporting actor (Waxman), and actor (Devine). *Net Worth* reminds us that despite false-hoods promoted by an ascendent right wing mythos that somehow unions hamper productivity and threaten prosperity, workers' associations *do* protect the vulnerable against the predatory.

Further Reading

Atherton, Tony. "Us Against Them." *The Ottawa Citizen* (November 26, 1995): C7.

Boone, Mike. "Players Take on Icy-Hearted NHL Brass." *The Montreal Gazette* (November 26, 1995): F2.

Cruise, David and Alison Griffiths. *Net Worth: Exploding the Myths of Pro Hockey.* New York: Viking, 1991.

Dowbiggin, Bruce. "Unmasking 75 Years of NHL Duplicity." *The Toronto Star* (October 5, 1991): F16.

Quiz Show (1994) (PG-13) (M)

Setting: New York, 1957–1958

Director: Robert Redford

Screenplay: Paul Attanasio

Director of Photography: Michael Ballhaus

Cast: Ralph Fiennes (Charles Van Doren), John Turturro (Herbie Stempel), Rob Morrow (Dick Goodwin), Paul Scofield (Mark Van Doren), and David Paymer (Dan Enright)

Availability: Hollywood Pictures Home Video

In 1957 Charles Van Doren, the reigning quiz show champ on *Twenty One,* graced the cover of *Time.* In the era of Sputnik and unruly rock 'n' roll, Van Doren became an intellectual hero, counteracting America's perceived lack of technological prowess, and with his charm made elitism fashionable. But two years later the euphoria ended. Van Doren testified before a Senate hearing that he had been given answers to the questions ahead of time. The show was rigged. Van Doren's testimony shocked the public. While recounting the story, Dave Garroway openly cried on the *Today Show.* Van Doren and NBC's greedy pursuit of material gain undermined the public's trust of television. This central conflict of public trust versus personal greed is accurately captured by director Robert Redford. But in Redford's film, Van Doren is a tragic hero caught by the legacy of his parents. A struggling, underpaid teaching adjunct at Columbia University, Van Doren wants to emerge from his father's long shadow, and thus allows himself to be deceived. In a moment of hazy rationale, Van Doren decides it is okay to cheat on television because somehow his winnings will enhance the image of education (20:07). Ralph Fiennes plays Van Doren as a charming, polite man, who is tempted, falls, and eventually finds redemption. Redford also dramatizes the story's central conflict (Herbert Stempel versus Van Doren) into a narrative on ethnicity and anti-Semitism. During a time of the whitening of America, when Eisenhowerese and the mainstreaming of television programming emphasized a WASP culture, the Jewish Stempel couldn't sell Geritol as well as Van Doren, a fair-haired Nordic aristocrat, could. The sponsors forced Stempel off the show because he was too Jewish. Stempel, in a telling scene with investigator Richard Goodwin, argues, "a Jew is always followed by a gentile, and the gentile always wins more" (55:53–58: 23). This charge Goodwin later confirms (1:09:14). Goodwin, who is also Jewish, represents a kind of ethnic in-between, at ease in both Stempel's and Van Doren's realms, while pondering his own identity. When Goodwin refuses to hound Van Doren, claiming his investigation won't repeat the errors of McCarthyism, his wife accuses him of being "the Uncle Tom of the Jews" (1:46:37). The Harvard-educated Goodwin hesitates because he shares Van Doren's desire for success and acceptance. Redford uses several balanced shot/reverse-shots in Fiennes and Morrow's scenes together to suggest a doubling between gentile and Jew. Following the quiz show scandal, President Eisenhower said it was "a terrible thing to do to the American people." But the lies the shows were founded upon, their misuse of television and their manipulation of public trust only became a sad portent of things to come in the political realm. In the 1950s, President Eisenhower lied to the American public about a CIA-sponsored war in Guatemala; and in the 1960s and 1970s, Presidents Johnson and Nixon lied about the war in Viet Nam.

Further Reading

Doherty, Thomas. Review of *Quiz Show*. *Cineaste* 21.1+2 (1995): 85.
Goodwin, Richard N. *Remembering America: A Voice from the Sixties*. Boston: Little, Brown and Co., 1988.
Stark, Steven D. "*Twenty One*, The Quiz Scandal, and the Decline of Public Trust." *Glued to the Set: The 60 Television Shows and Events That Made Us Who We Are Today*. New York: The Free Press, 1997. 73–80.
"The Wizard of Quiz." *Time* 69 (February 11, 1957): 44–46+.

Raw Deal (1948) (W)

Setting: San Francisco, 1948

Director: Anthony Mann

Screenplay: Leopold Atlas and John C. Higgins

Director of Photography: John Alton

Cast: Dennis O'Keefe (Joe Sullivan), Claire Trevor (Pat), Marsha Hunt (Ann Martin), and Raymond Burr (Rick Coyle)

Availability: Kino Video

In 1940s film noir, sex was fatal and women were often portrayed as black widow figures transgressing societal norms and killing men. In order to contain the threat of women, many noir narratives centered around ascertaining women's guilt. *Raw Deal* differs from this noir norm. It's not a film about female guilt, but about male redemption and female loss, and its uniqueness rests in its point of view. *Raw Deal* relies on an eerie voiceover, hailing not from a male, but a doomed female protagonist. Pat loves Joe, a convict she helps to escape from prison. Joe feels beholden to Pat, but seems to love Ann, a good girl who struggled the hard way to make it. Sadly for Pat and Joe there's no dream to achieve, let alone keep. They are noir's fatalistic losers, and John Alton's darkly haunting photography mirrors their future unhappiness. Late in *Raw Deal*, Joe stands on a ship, ready to leave the United States and make a different life for himself. He tells Pat his desires, to have a "good place . . . new place . . . get a little ranch . . . business or something . . . have a house . . . kids maybe . . . bring 'em up right" (1:09:40). His words evoke the post-war dreams of stability and normalcy aspired to by many veterans, but Alton's visuals belie their attainability. Joe, engulfed in darkness, speaks alone in the frame, looking out a porthole. Pat, in separate shots, looks off in a different direction, their eyes never meeting, their faces and bodies separate, alienated. In voiceover Trevor confesses: "The lyrics were his all right but the music Ann's. Suddenly I saw every time he'd be kissing me, he'd be kissing Ann" (1:10:57). Overcome, she tells Joe that Rick is holding Ann captive. Joe rushes ashore, rescues Ann from Rick and a burning building, and dies in her arms, redeemed. For Joe there's peace, for Pat, loneliness. "There's my Joe . . . with a kind of happiness on his face," she says in a disconnected voiceover. "In my heart, I know that this is right for Joe. This is what he wanted." But what did she want, and could she or any of us ever attain it?

Further Reading

Alton, John. *Painting with Light*. Los Angeles: University of California Press, 1997.
Place, Janey. "Women in Film Noir." *Women in Film Noir*, ed. E. Ann Kaplan. London: B.F.I., 1978. 35–67.

Rebel Without a Cause (1955)

Setting: Los Angeles, 1955

Director: Nicholas Ray

Screenplay: Stewart Stern

Director of Photography: Ernest Haller

Cast: James Dean (Jim Stark), Natalie Wood (Judy), Sal Mineo (Plato), Jim Backus (Jim's father), and Edward Platt (Ray Frammic)

Availability: Warner Home Video

Nobody protrayed teenage angst better than James Dean. His Jim Stark wasn't so much a portrait as a lived, shared experience with his audience.

He was the inarticulately troubled, rebel figure that parents feared and teens adored, for he accurately captured teenage confusion and restlessness. In *Rebel Without a Cause*, Dean plays the new kid in town who can't fit in and through tragic circumstances is led on a series of ritualized tests (a knife fight [31:35–38:15] and a "chickie run" [45:24–55:05]) to authenticate his life. The film has a strong sense of existential absurdity: the planetarium scene, in which the world is destroyed, suggests that, contrary to the narrative arc of most social problem films, these kids' problems are somewhat insignificant and meaningless in the vast configuration of the universe (24: 46–28:12). Therefore meaning can't come from corrective reforms, but must come from action and from within, and Jim is driven to prove himself honorable, courageous, and manly. The latter is especially important to him since he finds his apron-wearing father a disappointment. All three main characters (Jim, Judy, and Plato) have problems with their fathers and all are looking for understanding. Together they briefly form a family until the tragic ending. In *Blackboard Jungle* the juvenile delinquency problem seemed a product of inner city life, but this film showed that even "nice kids" with economic means were troubled too. *Rebel* has many brilliant moments. Jim's revelations with Ray Frammic marvelously capture teenage angst and guilt: "If I just had one day when, when I didn't have to be all confused and didn't have to feel ashamed of everything, and felt that I belonged some place, you know?" (17:01). Jim's discussion with his parents in the aftermath of the "chickie-run" (58:06–1:05:39) is a shocking reversal of the *Father Knows Best* 1950s norm. Director Nicholas Ray used canted framing to suggest a weird instability as Dean's moral arguments—"We are all involved"—convert him into the parental figure and his parents, who wish him to say nothing to the police and to tell a little "white lie," are converted into children. Jim and Judy's late romantic rendezvous in the run-down mansion (1:25:25–1:27:40) is one of cinema's gentlest expressions of love. Judy explains what girls want in a man: someone who "can be gentle and sweet . . . like you are . . . and someone who doesn't run away when you want him. Like being Plato's friend when nobody else liked him. That's being strong." Jim, moved, inarticulately mumbles, "oh, wow," and then they kiss. Her affirmation, "I love you Jim. I really mean it," is heart-felt, sincere, and a bright moment of adolescent truth that counteracts the film's existential nothingness.

Further Reading

Perkins, V. F. "The Cinema of Nicholas Ray." *Movies and Methods*, vol. 1, ed. Bill Nichols. Berkeley: University of California Press, 1976. 251–262.

Wilson, George M. "Nicholas Ray's *Rebel Without a Cause*." *Narration in Light: Studies in Cinematic Point of View*. Baltimore: Johns Hopkins University Press, 1986. 166–190.

Zinman, David. "*Rebel Without a Cause* (1955)." *Fifty from the Fifties: Vintage Films from America's Mid-Century.* New York: Arlington House Publishers, 1979. 269–276.

12 Angry Men (1957) (PG-13)

Setting: New York, 1957

Director: Sidney Lumet

Screenplay: Reginald Rose

Director of Photography: Boris Kaufman

Cast: Martin Balsam (Juror #1), John Fielder (Juror #2), Lee J. Cobb (Juror #3), E. G. Marshall (Juror #4), Jack Klugman (Juror #5), Edward Binns (Juror #6), Jack Warden (Juror #7), Henry Fonda (Juror #8), Joseph Sweeney (Juror #9), Ed Begley, Sr. (Juror #10), George Voskovec (Juror #11), and Robert Webber (Juror #12)

Availability: MGM/UA (Turner)

In the 1950s, white middle-class America might have been a little too self-satisfied. With the booming postwar economy, the movement to the suburbs, and the expansion of leisure time, many were comfortable with the status quo. But in *12 Angry Men* scriptwriter Reginald Rose, who also wrote the stage play, suggests that we were too complacent, too self-assured that all was right with the world. In this film, Rose argues that the legal system doesn't always work, and it is our duty as citizens to question evidence and to think critically. The trial judge, brow-beaten from the heat, seems bored and dismisses the jury in a "death penalty" case with little concern or vigor. The court-appointed defense lawyer lacks expertise and commitment to his client. The defendant, a Puerto Rican slum kid, is tried not by his peers but by a predominantly white, all-male jury. The jurors are a mix of 1950s types all confident that the kid is guilty. Juror Three, the boss of a messenger service, would rather bully a juvenile delinquent than deal with the troubled relationship he has with his own son. Juror Five, a former slum kid, has climbed America's ladder to success. Juror Seven, a salesman, is more interested in getting to a ball game than weighing the facts of the case. Juror Ten, a racist who runs a group of garages, assumes any immigrant accused of crime must be guilty. And Juror Twelve, an ad-man, can not distinguish truth from a slogan. All of these men have their prejudices and biases, but among that mix stands one man, Juror Eight (Henry Fonda), an architect, who dissents from the popular vote because he has a reasonable doubt. That's what our system of justice is founded upon, and Fonda's body becomes that system incarnated. Fonda's honest face, the smooth lines around his eyes, the even cadence to his voice, and his friendly Midwest manner represent a man of dignity and a triumph of individualism. He contends that the defense counsel "let too much go by" (1:23:22), and he methodically, with rational logic, pokes holes in the evidence (23:03–24:40; 55:18–55:

55). Fonda's clear thinking wins over the rest of the jurors, including a climactic episode in which they discover that one of the key witnesses wasn't wearing glasses during the time of her supposed witness of the killing (1: 21:00–1:25:02). Rose's script encourages us to question authority and our preconceived biases. But Rose also leaves us troubled about our legal system: What if Juror Eight hadn't been on that jury?

Further Reading

Alpert, Hollis. "Gentlemen of the Jury." 40 *Saturday Review* (April 20, 1957): 29–30.
Cowie, Peter. "Fonda." *Films and Filming* 8.7 (April 1962): 22–23, 41.
Review of *Twelve Angry Men. Time* 69 (April 29, 1957): 94, 96.

DOUBLE BILL: DISILLUSIONED YOUTH

American Graffiti (1973) (PG)

Setting: Modesto, California, 1962

Director: George Lucas

Screenplay: George Lucas, Gloria Huyck, and Gloria Katz

Director of Photography: Ron Everslage and Jan D'Alquen

Cast: Richard Dreyfuss (Curt), Ron Howard (Steve), Paul LeMat (John), Charles Martin Smith (Toad), Cindy Williams (Laurie), Candy Clark (Debbie), and Mackenzie Phillips (Carol)

Availability: Universal Home Video

Diner (1982) (R)

Setting: Baltimore, 1959

Director: Barry Levinson

Screenplay: Barry Levinson

Director of Photography: Peter Sova

Cast: Steve Guttenberg (Eddie), Daniel Stern (Shrevie), Mickey Rourke (Boogie), Kevin Bacon (Fenwick), Timothy Daly (Billy), and Ellen Barkin (Beth)

Availability: MGM/UA

America has always been fascinated by troubled youth, and *American Graffiti* and *Diner* capture the disillusionment of high school seniors contemplating their uncertain futures or twenty-something men struggling with women and finding comfort in a diner, talking sports, music, and sex. The two films, both about restless youth in transition, are bookended by history. *American Graffiti* is set in 1962, when America was on the cusp of the Kennedy assassination, the escalation of troops in Viet Nam, and the protest

movement. The film's characters are innocents on the edge. *Diner* is set in
Baltimore in 1959 just prior to the Kennedy inauguration, when America
was supposedly contented and on the brink of a new frontier, but in both
films the innocents are disconnected. The characters are, like Holden Caulfield, stuck in their youth. In *American Graffiti,* Toad is trapped in his white
buck shoes and nerdy image. He has to pretend to be someone else in order
to woo the sluttish Debbie. Steve reaches a false maturity and breaks up
with his girlfriend, Laurie, in order to play the college field, but after watching her crash in a drag race, he decides to stay behind and forego his college
education. Milner, a twenty-something over-the-hill James Dean, is stuck
with twelve-year-old Carol and spends much of the night trying to return
her home. Milner is an aging gunfighter, always anticipating that the
younger hot-rodder will take away his fame. Only Curt shows the promise
of truly growing up. Initially, Curt isn't sure that he wants to go to an East
Coast college, and he spends his night hanging with a street gang and pursuing his metaphoric dream, the unattainable angel in a '56 T-Bird. But
only following two encounters—one with Mr. Wolfe, a teacher who got
away only for a semester and now teaches high school and has affairs with
students (24:22–26:04), and a second with Wolfman Jack, the legendary
dee-jay who tells him to "Get your ass in gear" and denies being the Wolfman because he's too embarrassed about being trapped in Modesto (1:37:
01–1:40:50)—does Curt heed their advice and leave. In *Diner,* the
characters are also trapped but the film offers hope. Shrevie struggles with
his marriage, and yells at his wife when she miscatalogues his record collection. He gets mad at her for never asking him what's on the flip sides of
his 45s (52:44–56:22). In essence, he's angry because she isn't one of the
guys. Eddie the sports nut forces his fiancé to take a football quiz on the
Baltimore Colts. If she fails, the marriage is off. But the quiz only masks his
real fear: losing his virginity and growing up. The ultrasmart Fenwick drinks
too much and always appears on edge—he's a combustible fluid waiting for
the ignition of the 1960s. Billy is involved with a protofeminist woman
who's not sure she wants to marry him just because their one sexual encounter led to a pregnancy. And Boogie, the dreamer, works at a salon and
always has one foot in the shady underworld of gambling and point shaving.
He also treats women as sex objects, placing bets on who he can "Ball."
But in the end, most of the characters in *Diner* appear to be moving ahead.
Shrevie promises to spend more time with Beth and take her on a vacation.
Eddie decides to get married, even though Elyse failed the quiz. And Boo-
gie, in a complicated subplot of gambling debts and male prowess, tells Beth
she's beautiful but that he respects her too much to have an affair with her.
In the end, these films about disillusionment and a fearful future explore
America's perverse fascination with youth, and our troubled desire for some
kind of adolescent permanence.

Further Reading

Dempsey, Michael. Review of *American Graffiti*. *Film Quarterly* 27 (Fall 1973): 58–60.

Kael, Pauline. Review of *American Graffiti*. *The New Yorker* 49 (October 29, 1973): 153–159.

———. Review of *Diner*. *The New Yorker* 58 (April 5, 1982): 180–188.

Kauffmann, Stanley. "In Baltimore, for Instance." *The New Republic* 186 (April 28, 1982): 24–26.

Westerbeck, Colin L., Jr. "The American Dream." *Commonweal* 99 (October 5, 1973): 12–13.

DOUBLE BILL: AMERICA'S CORPORATE EXPANSION AND THE LOSS OF INDIVIDUALISM

The Man in the Gray Flannel Suit (1956)

Setting: New York and Connecticut, 1956

Director: Nunnally Johnson

Screenplay: Nunnally Johnson

Director of Photography: Charles G. Clarke

Cast: Gregory Peck (Tom Rath), Jennifer Jones (Betsy Rath), and Frederic March (Ralph Hopkins)

Availability: 20th Century Fox Home Video

Patterns (1956)

Setting: New York, 1956

Director: Fielder Cook

Screenplay: Rod Serling

Director of Photography: Boris Kaufman

Cast: Van Heflin (Fred Staples), Everett Sloane (Mr. Ramsey), Ed Begley, Sr. (Bill Briggs), Elizabeth Wilson (Marge Fleming), and Beatrice Straight (Nancy Staples)

Availability: MGM/UA (Turner)

In the 1930s, the human spirit was threatened by poverty and the Great Depression. By the 1950s, the human spirit may have been corrupted by America's new found affluence and a perceived corporate indifference. As men filled the ranks of white collar work they felt less in control of their lives, and the material benefits of their success seemed overshadowed by the loss of freedom and individuality. *The Man in the Gray Flannel Suit* concerns Tom Rath, a World War II veteran who is faced with the challenges of white collar workers: whether to be frank with his boss at the risk of losing his job; whether to be honest with his wife over a wartime affair; and whether to allow his work to usurp his family life. In the course of the narrative, Rath makes the right choices and regains his respect, dignity, and autonomy. During the war, Tom Rath felt alive, exhilarated. Back home, he has joined a new army of grey-suited yes men and has "lost his guts" (12:10). In an attempt to no longer play it "safe" and to regain his wartime prowess, Rath joins the liberal-minded United Broadcasting Corporation to make more money. During his initial interview, he's asked to type his biography in an hour, beginning with the phrase: "The most significant thing about me is . . ." (41:01–52:45). Rath retreats into an adjoining office, looks out the window, and flashes back to the war and death of his best friend. But he refuses to explore these experiences with his superiors. Instead, he writes a rather limited bio: "After a reasonable period of learning, I believe I could do a good job." Rath can't commodify his war experiences for the business world, and this is the first sign of his growing independence. Later, he tells his boss, Mr. Hopkins, the truth about a speech: "I don't think that it's the right approach at all" (1:57:14). Hopkins appreciates Tom's honesty and subsequently asks him to accompany him on a trip, but Rath refuses, saying he's a family man. Hopkins, a tragic figure who has sacrificed family and personal happiness for the greater good of the company, approves of Rath's choice. In Rod Serling's brilliant *Patterns* the corporate state seems an even more immensely powerful machine, ordered and rational and yet indifferent to human values. Ramsey is the heartless president of a Wall Street corporation who in order to increase future productivity shuts down a plant that employs 600 men for six months. Ramsey's inhumanity also extends to his close personal circle. He seeks to discard Bill Briggs because he now lacks efficiency, although he is a kind executive who has given forty years to the corporation. Ramsey calls in industrial relations expert Fred Staples from a satellite office in Ohio, places him in Briggs' old office, teams him with Briggs' former secretary, and situates him in Briggs' seat at board meetings. Staples slowly learns that he is to be Briggs' replacement, and even though he likes Briggs and disapproves of Ramsey's hard-hearted ethics, he really wants Briggs' job. Moreover, Ramsey won't fire Briggs, but he humiliates him and drives him to a fatal heart attack. Serling's conclusion is wonderfully ambiguous. Following Briggs' death, Staples decides to stay on at the corporation, vowing to right some of the wrongs done in the name of Ramsey's business. But Staples appears trapped in the vicious pattern of competition as he shouts at Ramsey, "I'll do everything in my power to push you out and take your place, myself" (1:20:37), and we are left wondering if he is still his own man or if Ramsey has successfully molded him into a heartless, business executive like himself.

Further Reading

Halberstam, David. "Thirty-five." *The Fifties*. New York: Villard Books, 1993. 521–536.

Hartung, Philip T. "What Are Patterns For?" Review of *Patterns*. *Commonweal* 63 (March 16, 1956): 617.

Hatch, Robert. Review of *Patterns*. *The Nation* 182 (March 24, 1956): 246.

Review of *The Man in the Gray Flannel Suit*. *Look* 20 (May 1, 1956): 104+.

DOUBLE BILL: WOMEN AND THE "MISTAKEN CHOICE"

My Reputation (1946) (W)

Setting: the Northeast, 1946

Director: Curtis Bernhardt

Screenplay: Catherine Turney

Director of Photography: James Wong Howe

Cast: Barbara Stanwyck (Jessica Drummond), George Brent (Maj. Scott Landis), Eve Arden (Gina Abott), Lucile Watson (Mrs. Kimball), Scotty Beckett (Kim Drummond), and Bobby Cooper (Keith Drummond)

Availability: None

All That Heaven Allows (1955) (W)

Setting: the Northeast, 1955

Director: Douglas Sirk

Screenplay: Peg Fenwick

Director of Photography: Russell Metty

Cast: Jane Wyman (Carrie Scott), Rock Hudson (Ron Kirby), Conrad Nagel (Harvey), Gloria Talbott (Kay), and William Reynolds (Ned)

Availability: Universal Home Video

According to Betty Friedan, the postwar years presented upper and middle class women with a "mistaken choice." Just as America shrugged off the Holocaust, the atomic bomb, Alger Hiss, and McCarthyism, women returned to the supposedly safe conformity of the home. Locked within a world of convention and limited mobility women felt unfulfilled. *My Reputation* (1946) and *All That Heaven Allows* (1955) capture those frustrations. In *My Reputation*, Jessica Drummond is a widow who is trapped in upper class conventions. Her mother insists that a widow always ought to wear black (12:40). She never allows Jessica to break free from her servitude of mourning and remembrance. Director Curtis Bernhardt's opening panning shot evokes Jessica's isolation, despair, and loneliness. Half-lit in shadow, Stanwyck lies on a bed, her eyes blank. She rises and mumbles, "Nothing to do at all." Later she moans to her best friend Gina: "This house is closing down on me" (26:49). All of her life, her decisions had been made by her husband, but now Jessica must find her own way and Gina helps. During a skiing trip with Gina, Jessica meets an officer, Scott Landis, and he with his roguish charm breaks through some of her icy conventionality. Stanwyck, in their scenes together, no longer wears black, and her hair often radiates with backlighting (35:40). She confesses to Landis that "I've never had much chance to express me" (35:52), but she's also finding independence. Around him she opens up, but her mother disapproves of Landis' class standing, and her adolescent sons, hearing vicious rumors from society's upper crust who want Jessica to remain trapped in black, also disapprove (1:22:41–1:27:58). The children are too young to understand how their mother can love a second man and still be loyal to the memory of their father. In a gut-wrenching scene, Jessica tells her sons how terribly lonely she's been, but for the sake of her family she decides not to follow Scott to New York. At the train station, Scott and Jessica promise to get back together after his stint in the service ends, and director Curtis Bernhardt concludes with an image of triumph. Jessica waves to the departing Scott, bites the back of her hand, and looks worried. A group of sailors whistle, and she smiles, and then her facial expression pauses with an internal gaze, and quickly moves from doubt to strength. Stanwyck throws her shoulders back, turns, and in long shot leaves the depot, a woman who can make it now, on her own. *All That Heaven Allows* also tackles conventionality and conformity. Widow Cary Scot feels trapped by her home and the attitudes of her children and the upper-middle-class community she lives in. An early scene establishes the film's central theme. Cary's college-age daughter discusses how society has advanced from the days in which Egyptians buried wives alive with their dead husbands. "And the community saw to it that she died. Of course, that doesn't happen anymore," the daughter says. The camera cuts to a strained looking Jane Wyman. "Doesn't it? Well, perhaps not in Egypt" (7:50–8:10). Everyone else assumes what Cary wants and when she falls in love with Ron, a much younger man from a lower social class (he's a gardener and a follower of the teachings of Henry David Thoreau), her children object. They feel he's inappropriate: what would others think? They contend that she ought to marry Harvey, an aging, impotent suitor. Harvey's proposal to Cary is passionless: "I realize that I'm not very romantic or impetuous. But then you hardly want that sort of thing" (14:26–15:10). But director Douglas Sirk's closeup of Wyman (her eyes worried, her glance downward), illustrates that passion is indeed something she seeks. However, because of her own conventionality and fears of change, Cary gives in to the conformist pressures of her children and friends, and stops her love affair with Ron. Thus, Cary makes the "mistaken choice" twice. Her husband had trapped her with his bourgeois values, and now her children also confine her to the home. They give her a television set for Christmas, the object becoming Cary's substitute for companionship and passion. In a chilling Christmas morning scene, Sirk photographs Cary looking into the blank abyss of the grey television screen and seeing only herself (1:17:01). All seems bleak, but an accident rekindles Cary and Ron's romance, and the film concludes with some optimism: Cary is not as free or independent as Jessica Drummond, but she does move out of a harsh system of patriarchy into a compromised relationship with a more gentle patriarch.

Further Reading

Friedan, Betty. "The Mistaken Choice." *The Feminine Mystique*. New York: Laurel, 1963. 182–205.

Halliday, Jon. "America II: 1950–59." *Sirk on Sirk*. New York: Viking Press, 1972. 82–135.

Kawin, Bruce. "Distribution." *How Movies Work*. Berkeley: University of California Press, 1992. 481–521.

Schatz, Thomas. "The Family Melodrama." *Hollywood Genres: Formulas, Filmmaking and the Studio System*. New York: Random House, 1981. 221–260.

"A Widow in Love." Review of *My Reputation*. *Newsweek* 27 (January 26, 1946): 93–94.

FURTHER VIEWING

All About Eve (1950) (W)

The Bad and the Beautiful (1952)

Cat on a Hot Tin Roof (1958) (W)

Gentlemen's Agreement (1947) (M)

I Want to Live (1958) (W)

Last Exit to Brooklyn (1990) (R)

The Little Fugitive (1953)

Man with a Golden Arm (1955)

Out of the Past (1947)

Phantom Lady (1944) (W)

Picnic (1955)

A Streetcar Named Desire (1951)

This Boy's Life (1993) (R)

Touch of Evil (1958)

12 Angry Men (1997) (PG-13)

10

Civil Rights and the Battle for Inclusion into the American Dream, 1949–Present

The Autobiography of Miss Jane Pittman ◆ *Boyz 'N' the Hood*
Corrina, Corrina ◆ *The Crimson Kimono* ◆ *The Defiant Ones*
Do the Right Thing ◆ *Eyes on the Prize* ◆ *Intruder in the Dust*
Mississippi Burning ◆ *Pleasantville* ◆ *Smoke Signals* ◆ *Zoot Suit*
Double Bill: *Incident at Oglala* and *Thunderheart* ◆ Double Bill:
Lilies of the Field and *In the Heat of the Night* ◆ Double Bill:
Malcolm X and *Malcolm X: Make It Plain*

The Autobiography of Miss Jane Pittman (1974) (TV) (M) (W)

Setting: Bayonne, Mississippi, 1962; the South, 1863–1865, 1880s, 1901, 1927

Director: John Korty

Screenplay: Tracy Keenan Wynn

Director of Photography: James Crabe

Cast: Cicely Tyson (Jane Pittman), Michael Murphy (Quentin), Valeria Odell (Ticey), Thalmus Rasulala (Ned, 42), Rod Perry (Joe Pittman), Vaughn Taylor (Dyer), Arnold Wilson (Jimmy)

Availability: UAV Home Video/Broadway Home Video

The winner of several Emmys, *The Autobiography of Miss Jane Pittman* was a striking television achievement in 1974. Based on a novel by Ernest J. Gaines, it was one of the first dramatic specials to historicize the African American experience, and it did so with breadth (moving from slavery and Civil War to marches and Civil Rights). Structured as a series of four flashbacks and oral histories, the 110-year-old Miss Jane tells a well-meaning white reporter, Quentin, about her and her peoples' troubles and triumphs. By contrast, Jan's story in Ernest J. Gaines' novel is told to a black historian. The replacing of a black observer with a white one switches the novel's emphasis from appreciating black pride and the ongoing march for freedom to educating white people about the black experience. Jane's first flashback tells of the Civil War and how as young Ticey she was whipped by her owner (15:45–18:06). Young Ticey is renamed Jane by a kind Union trooper from Ohio who had stopped at the plantation for water (17:42). Following the Civil War and the Emancipation Proclamation of 1863 Jane decides to head to the North to freedom in Ohio. But she and the other former slaves find freedom difficult to attain. Several are attacked and murdered by rednecks during the harsh period of Reconstruction (26:09–26:59). When Jane and young Ned arrive at a Mississippi barge, they can't cross because she doesn't have any nickels (36:32). Lacking options, they return to the South and become sharecroppers chopping sugarcane on the Dyer plantation. The second flashback, set in the 1880s, concerns the men in her life: her love Joe Pittman and her surrogate brother Ned Douglass. Ned is a proud man; he politicizes African Americans about their rights, but his life is threatened by the KKK and he has to leave his home (47:11–47:41). Joe Pittman, her husband, desires their freedom from Dyer. They raise the necessary $55 to leave the plantation, including interest (56:06), and take up life on the rodeo circuit until his tragic death. The third flashback is set at the turn of the century, as Ned returns from exile to tell his people to be proud of their blackness. By a river he preaches, "A 'nigger' cares about nothing. He'll never be a citizen. A black American cares" (1:16:43). Ned wants his people to eschew labels like "nigger," to not let whites define them and to strive to be "men" (1:17:50). For speaking his message of black pride, Ned is murdered. When yet another black man, young civil rights leader Jimmy, is killed in 1962 for supposedly trying to escape from prison, Miss Jane becomes politicized. Throughout the story, the white establishment has kept blacks down by either killing their leaders or forcing them into economic dependence. In the film's final moments, Miss Jane defies the laws of segregation. In a pulsing series of edits—low-angled medium shots, closeups, and high-angled long shots—director John Korty dramatizes Miss Jane's agonized walk to a segregated public fountain. Her struggle to get there mirrors the struggle of her people, and when she arrives and drinks, she metaphorically sets her people free. This moment is powerful television, but it wasn't in Ernest J. Gaines' original novel. Whereas Gaines' novel contends that the struggle for freedom is always ongoing, Tracy Keenan Wynn's adaptation creates a safe lie for a sentimental audience: The Civil Rights movement works, and the problem has now been solved. But the problem isn't solved: issues of economic justice remain unanswered.

Further Reading

Callahan, John. "Image-Making: Tradition and the Two Versions of *The Autobiography of Miss Jane Pittman*." *Chicago Review* 29.2 (Autumn 1977): 45–62.
Gaines, Ernest J. *The Autobiography of Miss Jane Pittman*. New York: Bantam, 1971.
Gaudet, Marcia. "Miss Jane and Personal Experience Narrative: Ernest Gaines' *The*

Autobiography of Miss Jane Pittman." *Western Folklore* 51 (January 1992): 23–32.

Potter, Vilma Raskin. "*The Autobiography of Miss Jane Pittman*: How to Make a White Film from a Black Novel." *Literature/Film Quarterly* 3.4 (Fall 1975): 371–375.

Boyz 'N' the Hood (1991) (R) (M)

Setting: South Central Los Angeles, 1991

Director: John Singleton

Screenplay: John Singleton

Director of Photography: Charles Mills

Cast: Larry Fishburne (Furious Styles), Ice Cube (Doughboy), Cuba Gooding, Jr. (Tre), Morris Chestnut (Ricky Baker), Tyra Ferrell (Mrs. Baker), Angela Bassett (Reva Styles)

Availability: Columbia Pictures Home Video

Filmed three years before the Million Man March, John Singleton's *Boyz 'N' the Hood*, about a triangular friendship of three kids in South Central Los Angeles, concerns the need for black fathers to raise their sons. Tre, who begins the film living with his mother, isn't finding the right influences in her community. On his way to school he crosses yellow police tape, finds blood and bullet marks, and at school, he's taught the white man's history. In a stunning sequence, Singleton has an insensitive teacher prattle on about the pilgrims and Thanksgiving, while he shows us childrens' crayon drawings of circling LAPD helicopters, black-on-black shootings, and death. Her teachings have no applicability to the real-life worlds of these children (2: 52–5:02). Tre's mom realizes this, and sends him to her ex-husband: "I can't teach him how to be a man. . . . That's your job" (8:57). With his father, Furious Styles, a man of Afro pride and compassion, Tre learns to respect himself and his people. When he first arrives, Furious tells him, "You're the prince, I'm the king" (13:22). When their home is burglarized and Furious scares off a thief by shooting at him, Tre is disappointed that his dad didn't kill the criminal. Furious corrects his attitude, by saying that "just would be contributing to killing another brother" (15:37). Later in the film, Furious tells Tre and his friend Ricky about "gentrification," a process by which whites buy homes from blacks, then up the property value and move blacks out. He also states that whites allow crack to flow into the neighborhood, and encourage gun shops on every corner because they want brothers to kill brothers (1:03:22–1:06:22). By contrast, Tre's two friends, half-brothers Doughboy and Ricky, have no strong father figure in their lives. Their mother works hard for her children, but she clearly favors Ricky over Doughboy, and following Ricky's drive-by murder, Doughboy seeks misguided vengeance. However, because of his father's influence and his own inner strength, Tre asks to be let out of the car before the killing, and breaks himself free of the cycle that Singleton alludes to in his opening typescript: "One out of every twenty-one Black American males will be murdered in their lifetime" (0:33).

Further Reading

Dyson, Michael Eric. "Between Apocalypse and Redemption: John Singleton's *Boyz N the Hood.*" *Cultural Critique* (Spring 1992): 121–141.
Little, Benilde. "John Singleton." *Essence* 22.5 (September 1991): 43.
Wood, Joe. "John Singleton and the Impossible Greenback Bind of the Assimilated Black Artist." *Esquire* 120.2 (August): 59–66.

Corrina, Corrina (1994) (PG) (M) (W)

Setting: Los Angeles, 1959

Director: Jessie Nelson

Director of Photography: Bruce Surtees

Screenplay: Jessie Nelson

Cast: Ray Liotta (Manny Singer), Whoopi Goldberg (Corrina Washington), and Tina Majorino (Molly Singer)

Availability: New Line Home Video/Turner Home Entertainment

Corrina, Corrina, set in 1959 Los Angeles, weaves together two deeply felt stories: a child's grief over the death of her mother and the interracial relationship of a Jewish ad-man and an African American nanny. Following the sudden death of her mother, seven-year-old Molly Singer becomes uncommunicative with her father. She feels guilty (she must have done something "bad" for her mother to leave) and angry (Mom left too suddenly). Her father, Manny, works in the homogenized world of 1950s advertising, coming up with inane jingles for Mr. Potato Head and Jell-O pudding. He needs help with his daughter on both a caretaking and spiritual level. After failing with several other nannies, Manny hires Corrina Washington because he sees how well she connects with his daughter (10:50–13:02). Corrina treats Molly like an equal, and the child responds to her nanny's fairness. But life has not been fair to Corrina. She's witty (she gets off some great zingers), appreciates jazz, and has completed four years of college, but in 1959 America she's not going to get much of an opportunity to climb the success ladder. However, her ease and the honesty and respect with which she treats the girl finally get Molly to communicate. Molly, enchanted with her caretaker, converts Corrina into a surrogate mom. But this isn't acceptable in the 1950s. At school, while the white kids draw pictures of their nuclear families, the centerpiece of Molly's portrait is big, black, and proud. The kids pick on her for drawing her maid and not her mom: they're unable to conceptualize a family outside of certain boundaries (49:57). Ostracized,

Molly refuses to return to school, and she spends her days with Corrina, cleaning rich people's homes and learning about life. Manny, too, needs to learn about life. He needs to let go of his wife (there's a touching scene in which he watches home movies of her late at night [24:50–25:26]) and to make his peace with God (he's angry and hides from God behind a veil of atheism). Through Corrina, Manny expands his boundaries, and eventually finds God. While struggling with an ad jingle and simultaneously discovering that Corrina admires jazz, Manny asks, "you ever been blocked?" "All my life," she replies (1:02:08–1:04:30). Manny begins to see the world through her eyes and not just his own, and he begins to feel her sadness. She longs to write liner notes on jazz albums but she'll probably never get the chance in America's segregated society. Later, Corrina even helps Manny through a rough spot with a pudding jingle, suggesting the bridge as the answer to his problem with the ending (1:04:30–1:05:49). Manny is grateful and their relationship, through mutual respect and admiration, blossoms.

Further Reading

Coleman, Beth. Review of *Corrina, Corrina*. *Village Voice* (August 16, 1994): 50.
Medved, Michael. Review of *Corrina, Corrina*. *New York Post* (August 12, 1994): 46.
Rainer, Peter. Review of *Corrina, Corrina*. *Los Angeles Times* (August 12, 1994): Calendar/1.

The Crimson Kimono (1959) (M)

Setting: Los Angeles, 1959

Director: Samuel Fuller

Screenplay: Samuel Fuller

Director of Photography: Sam Leavitt

Cast: Glenn Corbett (Sgt. Charlie Bancroft), James Shigeta (Detective Joe Kojaku), and Victoria Shaw (Chris Downes)

Availability: Columbia Tri-Star Home Video

Samuel Fuller's 1959 potboiler explores racial identity and an interracial love affair. Korean War buddies and Los Angeles cops, Sgt. Charlie Bancroft and Detective Joe Kojaku are investigating the murder of stripper Sugar Torch. Their investigation leads them to Chris Downes, an artist who painted a portrait of Sugar in a kimono. At first Charlie and Chris are interested in each other, but when Chris discovers that Joe appreciates art she finds a kindred spirit, and they fall in love. Their union challenges the buddy-buddy relationship of Charlie and Joe. Joe's burgeoning guilt over loving the woman Charlie wanted to marry, combined with his own guilt over being a Nisei trying to fit into the American melting pot, eventually affects his judgment. Joe visits a sensei (54:26–55:39) and tells him "I've got a problem." He looks at his teacher and painfully asks, "How do I rate a girl like this?" His low self-esteem surprises the sensei but he doesn't realize the weakness in himself. Prior to this scene, Fuller stopped the flow of the murder mystery to present us with images of Evergreen Cemetery and a mini-essay on integration and segregation. Fuller begins the sequence with a long-shot of the cemetery and then cuts to a white column with a soldier standing erect. This image is followed by a huge stone with an Eisenhower quote that salutes "The men who gave for their country." Then he shows us another huge stone and a quote by Mark W. Clark, General, U.S. Army: "The soldiers who lie here symbolize the fealty and courage of Nisei troops . . . may they rest in honored peace." The sequence both separates Nisei soldiers (they have their own monument and burial plot) and links them (through the words of white generals) to the mainstream. Joe desires equality but society's veiled racism, as suggested by the segregated monument, has made him dislike himself. This dislike boils over during the Kendo match, as Joe, contrary to Kendo's rituals of "disciplined assault," beats Charlie into unconsciousness (1:02:25–1:05:36). Later in the dressing room, Joe apologizes and tells Charlie that he wants to marry Chris. "Marry her," Charlie responds with surprise, and Joe accuses his friend of being a racist. "You wouldn't have said it that way if I were white" (1:07:02). He maps onto his friend's face his own self-loathing. This misunderstanding is rectified in the film's ending, as Joe guns down the female killer in Little Tokyo and her story of obsession mirrors his own: "It was all in my mind," she says (1:18:08). Disturbingly, Joe is cured of self-loathing through violent action, but the egalitarian Fuller does end the film with a daring interracial kiss.

Further Reading

Marchetti, Gina. "Tragic and Transcendent Love: *Sayonara* and *Crimson Kimono*." *Romance and the "Yellow Peril": Races, Sex and Discursive Strategies in Hollywood Fiction*. Berkeley: University of California Press, 1993. 125–57.

Tracey, Grant. "Film Noir and Samuel Fuller's Tabloid Cinema: Red (Action), White (Exposition), and Blue (Romance)." *Film Noir Reader 2*, ed. Alain Silver and James Ursini. New York: Limelight Edition, 1999. 158–175.

The Defiant Ones (1958) (M)

Setting: the South, 1958

Director: Stanley Kramer

Screenplay: Nathan E. Douglas and Harold Jacob Smith

Director of Photography: Sam Leavitt

Cast: Tony Curtis (John "Joker" Jackson) and Sidney Poitier (Noah Cullen)

Availability: MGM/UA Home Video

The Defiant Ones, a message film about two chain-gang convict escapees—one black, one white—has a wicked catch: the two men are joined at the wrists by twenty-nine feet of chain, and they hate each other. The journey becomes a metaphor. On one level their flight to freedom takes them through painful struggles: clay pits, swollen rivers, swamps, woodlands, and a turpentine town that wants to lynch them; but on another level, the pain is on the inside as both men, John "Joker" Jackson and Noah Cullen, learn to find the humanity in each other. Initially, the men are separated by their race. John, a roughneck who has worked on cars and dreams of being a big shot, denies Noah's humanity. He repeatedly calls him "boy" and "nigger." When Noah objects, Joker says, "You can call me a honky if you want, I don't mind." But Noah tells him the two terms aren't equal: "You ever hear tell of catch a bohunk by the toe?" (21:50–22:58). Noah, a tenant farmer, has been "mad" all his life. His wife was always telling him to "be nice" to white folks, but she never understood how he felt on the inside (36:10–36:50). When Sidney Poitier delivers these lines, his quiet expressions and breathy pain capture over 300 years of injustice. Surprisingly, Joker understands. That understanding is enriched in the story's structure. During the quest, each man saves the other twice. Joker pulls Noah out of a rushing stream (17:30); and later after the two are separated from their chains, Joker risks his own freedom to rescue Noah from a treacherous swamp (88:23). Noah, during a burglary, drops from a beam, risking certain capture rather than let Joker dangle by his aching, infected arm (46:12). During the film's final scene, Noah leaps aboard the Ohio-bound train, but Joker, bleeding from a gunshot wound, can't stretch, can't run fast enough. Together, they tumble down the hill and await the arrival of the police (93:01). Their shared experiences have changed them. As Noah defiantly sings before the sheriff, he resonates a hard-fought victory of understanding.

Further Reading

Kauffmann, Stanley. "Together and Alone." Review of *The Defiant Ones*. *The New Republic* 139 (September 1, 1958): 22–23.
Review of *The Defiant Ones*. *Newsweek* 77 (August 25, 1958): 77.
Review of *The Defiant Ones*. *Time* 78 (August 25, 1958): 78.
Spoto, Donald. " 'Bowling Green, Sewing Machine!' " *Stanley Kramer: Film Maker*. New York: G. P. Putnam's Sons, 1978. 198–206.

Do the Right Thing (1989) (R) (M)

Setting: Bedford-Stuyvesant, Brooklyn, 1989

Director: Spike Lee

Screenplay: Spike Lee

Director of Photography: Ernest Dickerson

Cast: Spike Lee (Mookie), Danny Aiello (Sal), Ossie Davis (Da Mayor), Giancarlo Esposito (Buggin' Out), and Bill Nunn (Radio Raheem)

Availability: MCA Home Video

Spike Lee's brilliance as a screenwriter and director rests in his uncanny ability to create films that speak to blacks and whites differently. His explosive *Do the Right Thing*, about a hot summer day in Brooklyn's Bed-Stuy neighborhood that erupts in violence following the death of a young black man, Radio Raheem, scared the mainstream white media who feared summer riots upon its release. By contrast, African Americans praised the film for its unrelenting honesty. The film's final riot scene grows out of an ambiguously complex set of circumstances. How responsible is Sal, the pizzeria owner, for Raheem's death? How responsible are Raheem and his cohort in political astuteness, Buggin' Out, for the tragedy that befalls? Sal makes money from the black community and spends it in his own white suburbs. He's proud of having black kids grow up on his food (59:54), but he patronizes them. He treats Da Mayor as a shoeshine boy, throwing him spare bits of change, and he misreads Mookie, his disgruntled worker, absurdly promising him a low income future with the pizzeria: "There's always gonna be a place here" (1:29:08). Moreover, his wall of fame, littered with images of famous Italian Americans, is an affront to his predominantly African American customers. Buggin' Out is bothered by this lack of black representation and plans a boycott of Sal's. On the night of the riot, he and Raheem stroll into the pizzeria, radio boom box blasting, and a heated exchange takes place with Sal. Buggin' Out calls Sal a "guinea bastard," and Sal calls them "niggers." Then Sal displaces his hidden racial animosity onto the boom box, obliterating it with a baseball bat (1:31:01). A fight ensues, the police arrive, Raheem is killed by a deadly police choke hold, and Mookie, caught up in the melee, struggles to do the right thing. Earlier, Buggin' Out, aware of Mookie's compromised position in working "for the man," reminded him to "Stay black" (21:51). And now, following Raheem's death, Mookie heaves a trash can through the pizzeria window, sparking the riot (1:38:18–1:40:08). Mookie's actions are complex. He's avenging the death of a friend and brother. He's also speaking out against years of economic injustice (Sal's Pizzeria represents low-wage opportunities for blacks). But his actions may have also saved Sal and his sons, displacing the crowd's anger onto the pizzeria and not the people running it. Along with the complexities of character motivations, Lee also succeeds in politicizing his film. Midway through the film, in a series of ground-breaking low-angled tracking shots, Lee has various characters speak a slew of racial slurs (blacks against whites, whites against blacks, Hispanics against Koreans, white cops against Hispanics, and Koreans against Jews) (47:50–49:07). This jarring moment, like a descriptive pause or editorial, throws us out of the story world and into our larger social contexts, reminding us of the troubles we still have with racial harmony.

Further Reading

Fenner, Jeffrey L. *"Do the Right Thing." Magill's Cinema Annual 1990.* Pasadena, CA: Salem Press, 1990. 94–98.

McKelly, James C. "The Double Truth, Ruth: *Do the Right Thing* and the Culture of Ambiguity." *African American Review* 32.2 (Summer 1998): 215–227.

Mitchell, W.J.T. "Seeing *Do the Right Thing." Critical Inquiry* 16 (Spring 1991): 596–608.

Eyes on the Prize (1986, 1990) (Doc.) (M)

Setting: United States, 1954–1980s

Directors: Judith Vecchione, James A. DeVinney, Callie Crossley, Orlando Bagwell, Sheila Bernard, Sam Pollard, Louis J. Massiah, Terry Kay Rockefeller, Paul Stekler, Jacqueline Shearer, and Thomas Ott

Writers: Lewanne Jones, David Thaxton, Kevin P. Green, Steve Fayer, James A. DeVinney, Callie Crossley, Madison Davis Lacy, Jr., Sheila Bernard, Sam Pollard, Louis J. Massiah, Terry Kay Rockefeller, Paul Stekler, Jacqueline Shearer, and Thomas Ott

Directors of Photography: Orlando Bagwell, Werner Bandschuh, Michael Chin, Jon Else, Steve Ferrier, John M. Gordon, Tom Kaufman, Christopher Li, Tom McDonough, and Bobby Shephard

Narrator: Julian Bond

Editors: Daniel Eisenberg, Jeanne Jordan, Charles Scott, Betty Ciccarelli, Thomas Ott, and Lillian Benson

Availability: PBS Home Video

This fourteen-hour PBS documentary series covers in great breadth the Civil Rights Movement from the *Brown vs. the Board of Education* decree in 1954 to tensions in northern cities and the issue of affirmative action in the mid-1980s. Volumes 1–3 follow the civil rights struggle in the south and the battle for social equality led by Dr. Martin Luther King, Jr. Dr. King's nonviolent protest required that the federal government respond morally to injustice and facilitate social change. Volumes 4–6 follow the fight in the North and how leaders like Malcolm X, Stokely Carmichael, and the Black Panthers in Chicago demanded economic justice. Their chants for "black power" reflected an increase in black pride, a desire to understand their black history, and a sense that freedom can only come through an infrastructure of black political and entrepreneurial power in their own communities. Volume 1 details early stories of civil rights consciousness raising. First, the brutal murder of Chicago teenager, Emmett Till, in Mississippi and the subsequent acquittal of the killers by an all-white jury (10:10–24:50) made

Americans realize the horrific double standards of our republic. Second, Rosa Parks' refusal to give up her bus seat in Montgomery (26:00–53:26), and the subsequent successful boycott of the bus system, led by Dr. King, galvanized African Americans to organize and fight back. Third, the intervention of federal troops, in 1957, to assist nine black children who wanted to attend an all-white school in Little Rock, Arkansas (1:01:47–1:25:20) and U.S. marshals in 1961 to protect James Meredith in his quest to attend segregated Ole Miss in Oxford sent strong messages that the federal government would aid and abet the movement. Volume 2 explores student organized sit-ins at Nashville lunch counters to defeat "Jim Crowism" (14:07–22:41), and the success of the "Freedom Riders," a mixed group of whites and blacks who brought a message of desegregation. Following the beatings of Freedom Riders in Birmingham, the federal government legislated that bus facilities along the interstate system could not be segregated (27:00–54:58). The volume concludes with Dr. King's stirring march on Washington, attended by over 250,000 people urgently demanding rights, jobs, and freedom (1:39:20–1:46:10). Volume 3 explores the horrors in Mississippi, the most segregated state in the union. In Mississippi, Medgar Evers, a NAACP leader for integration, was murdered in his home (12:09–15:35), and in 1964, during "Freedom Summer," three civil rights leaders (James Chaney, Andrew Goodman, and James Schwermer) disappeared while organizing voter registration drives in the South (18:50–42:10). Their bodies were later found and the murderers, including Deputy Sheriff Price, were acquitted. But the federal government had Price and several others serve three to ten years for violating civil rights. The voter registration drive that these and other activists promoted during Freedom Summer politicized blacks, and the face of politics began to change in the South. Volume 4 switches emphasis from Southern nonviolence to a more angry form of protest: Black Nationalism, Malcolm X and the Nation of Islam, and Black Power. Malcolm X espoused pride in his ancestral past and scared whites when he said, "We're nonviolent with people who are nonviolent with us" (17:21). He believed that blacks should control politics and commerce in their communities, and he wanted the United Nations to bring repatriation charges against the United States for its crimes against black humanity (23:28). This volume also explores the invisible lines of segregation in the north, how blacks were shut out from "white only" neighborhoods in Chicago (1:02:02–1:25:50), and why tensions erupted into the burning of 100 blocks in Detroit as urban renewal left the black community behind (1:27:09–1:47:01). Volume 5 follows the Black Panthers in Oakland, California, and how they challenged the police, labeling them "pigs," and how their radical chic (black berets and displayed guns) emphasized a street-wise black pride. They also politicized the community with their "ten-point program" (19:00–35:22). Volume 5 concludes with Dr. King's critique of the war in Viet

Nam. He felt that "injustice anywhere is a threat to justice everywhere" (1: 04:22) and the federal government should be spending its money on domestic policy and not foreign policy. The government, King said, spent $322,000 for every enemy killed in Viet Nam and only $53 for each person classified as poor in the United States (56:32). Such statements made King unpopular with the LBJ administration, but he boldly demanded more than just social rights; he was now moving in the direction of his radical colleagues and stressing the urgent need for economic change. Unfortunately, in 1968, an assassin's bullet ended King's life and stalled his miraculous vision. The Civil Rights Movement would be in flux for several years following his death. Volume 6 highlights black pride and the abuse of state power. Black pride found a voice in boxer Muhammad Ali. In 1967, he refused induction into the U.S. military on moral and religious grounds: "The real enemies of my people are right here. Not in Viet Nam" (12:01). Ali's conversion to the Muslim faith and his refusal to fight overseas forced white America to recognize him on his own terms (2:01–20:21). Volume 6 also explores a northern lynching. In 1969, Chicago police murdered Black Panther leader Fred Hampton while he was sleeping (58:51–1:25:34). The official word was that Hampton fired first, but although a subsequent investigation stripped the law department of their credibility, there were no arrests in the case. Two years later, black and Latino prisoners at Attica rioted and took over the New York state prison, holding twenty-nine hostages and demanding improved health care and education. Talks stumbled, and Governor Rockefeller sent in helicopters with gas pellets. Thirty-nine men died, including ten hostages (eight of them killed by Rockefeller's "liberators"). The surrendering prisoners were stripped, ordered to crawl through mud, and those selectively marked with an "X" were brutally beaten. Volume 7 analyzes affirmative action (36:44–52:33) and white rage against Judge W. Arthur Garrity's busing plan to help desegregate and equalize schools in Boston (15:27–30:24). Overall, this series is richly nuanced and provides a crucial context to viewing any Hollywood films that represent this time period.

Further Reading

Broderick, Francis, and August Meier. *Black Protest Thought in the Twentieth Century.* Indianapolis: Bobbs-Merrill, 1971.

Bush, Rod. *We Are Not What We Seem: Black Nationalism and Class Struggle in the American Century.* New York: NYU Press, 1999.

Rhea, Joseph Tilden. *Race Pride and the American Identity.* Cambridge, MA: Harvard University Press, 1997.

Sitkoff, Harvard. *The Struggle for Black Equality, 1954–1992.* New York: Hill & Wang, 1993.

Zinn, Howard. "Or Does It Explode?" *A People's History of the United States, 1492–Present.* New York: Harper Perennial, 1980, 1995. 435–459.

Intruder in the Dust (1949) (M)

Setting: Oxford, Mississippi, 1949

Director: Clarence Brown

Screenplay: Ben Maddow

Director of Photography: Robert Surtees

Cast: Juano Hernandez (Lucas Beauchamp), David Brian (John Gavin Stevens), Claude Jarman, Jr. (Chick Mallison), Porter Hall (Nub Gowrie), Elizabeth Pattersón (Miss Eunice Habersham), and David Clarke (Vinson Gowrie)

Availability: MGM/UA Home Video

Intruder in the Dust, based on the novel by William Faulkner, is a tough-minded film about an African American, Lucas Beauchamp, awaiting trial for murder in segregated Oxford, Mississippi. This bleak piece of Americana suggests that he has little chance for justice in this country. Even his lawyer, John Gavin Stevens, who can barely rise above his own regional prejudices to defend him, says, "Has it even occurred to you, if you just said 'Mr.' to white folks and said it like you meant it, you might not be sitting here now?" (26:58). Stevens finds Lucas "proud" and "insufferable," but for African Americans Juano Hernandez is a strong role model. He refuses to feel inferior to whites, and he carries himself with dignity and strength. Director Clarence Brown's camera reflects Hernandez's powerful presence: he's often photographed from low angles that emphasize his massive shoulders, steady, peering eyes, and commanding gait (4:22–5:21). He's an independent landowner, somewhat withdrawn, and a proud individualist. But when Lucas is accused of killing a white lumberjack, Vinson Gowrie, and the town is set to lynch him (and even his lawyer seems resigned to that fate), Lucas needs help from whites who have not been socialized into segregationist hatred. Chick, an adolescent, and Eunice Habersham, an older genteel woman, come to his aid and prove him innocent. Chick's motivation for helping Lucas stems from his own guilt. His parents are racists (7:56), and he's never been taught to respect blacks. During a flashback scene (10:28–19:58), Chick explains to Stevens his conflicted feelings over Lucas. The boy had fallen into an icy pond and was rescued by the accused. Later, at Lucas' house, the boy is treated to a hot meal and fresh clothes. Uncertain as to how to show his gratitude, Chick reaches into his pockets for money. Lucas won't take it, and the boy, offended, drops the change on the floor and demands that Lucas pick it up. Lucas won't. The boy doesn't understand Lucas, but more importantly he also doesn't understand his own anger at Lucas and he feels he owes him. Stevens' guilt comes from realizing his own prejudices. "I was wrong," he apologizes to Lucas for assuming him guilty (1:06:30), and in the end regards him as the "keeper of my conscience" (1:26:40). As for the town folks, those that gathered eating ice cream cones and standing against parked cars eagerly awaiting a lynching (1:01:10–1:05:23; 1:19:49–1:21:47), the film offers little hope. Disappointed by the outcome (Lucas' innocence and the arrest of the real murderer), they disperse. Perhaps they are as Stevens says "running from themselves," but, as a collective, their twisted psychology hasn't changed. Sadly, scenarist Ben Maddow suggests that their hatred lingers, awaiting another lynching.

Further Reading

Bogle, Donald. "The 1940's: The Entertainers, the New Negroes, and the Problem People." *Toms, Coons, Mulattoes, Mammies and Bucks: An Interpretive History of Blacks in Films.* New York: Continuum, 1973, 1989. 117–158.

Crowther, Bosley. Review of *Intruder in the Dust. New York Times* (November 23, 1949): 19.

Faulkner, William. *Intruder in the Dust.* New York: Random House, 1948.

Review of *Intruder in the Dust. Newsweek* 34 (December 5, 1949): 81–82.

Mississippi Burning (1988) (R) (M)

Setting: Jessup County, Mississippi, 1964

Director: Alan Parker

Screenplay: Chris Gerolmo

Director of Photography: Peter Biziou

Cast: Gene Hackman (Anderson), Willem Dafoe (Ward), Frances McDormand (Mrs. Pell), Brad Dourif (Deputy Pell)

Availability: Orion Home Video

Between 1840 and 1960 some 600 African Americans were lynched in Mississippi. None of the murderers were ever jailed. Despite these acts of terror, World War Two veterans such as Medgar Evers and Amzie Moore went to local courthouses to insist on their right to vote. In Freedom Summer, 1964, one thousand volunteers, a third of them white, traveled to Mississippi to register black voters. Because black registration threatened the white power structure, racists violently responded to the movement. Homes and churches were burned; civil rights workers were arrested and beaten. On June 20, 1964, three activists (two Jews and one black) were arrested on trumped-up speeding charges. They disappeared following their release from the Neshoba County jail. Six weeks later the FBI found their bullet-riddled bodies in an earthen dam near Philadelphia, Mississippi. This is the background context for Alan Parker's *Mississippi Burning.* Parker accurately captures the period's terror and fear with his powerful rendering of homes and churches burning and black children being beaten. Unfortunately, although *Mississippi Burning* packs an emotional wallop and contains jarring visuals and a fine performance by Gene Hackman, Parker so distorts history as to be offensive. His story sinks history into genre flair as good white cops (the FBI led by the Kennedyesque Willem Dafoe and the downhome but enlightened southerner, Hackman) fight bad local cops (the Mississippi force led by the quirky twisted smiles of the Deputy Chief Pell). In the spirit of his earlier acting in *The French Connection*, Hackman's gang adopts antihero status and bad boy intimidation tactics (threats of castration and random beatings on racists) to get results. On a larger ideological level, the film's greatest distortion has the heroic FBI rescuing submissive blacks who can't stand on their own. During the 1960s, the FBI was in fact an enemy to the Civil Rights Movement. Chief J. Edgar Hoover didn't provide any protection for Dr. Martin Luther King's March on Washington in 1963, and throughout the decade he wire-tapped King hoping to destroy him by proving that he was a dangerous communist. Second, this film continues a long tradition of films featuring white heroes in films with interracial themes. The Mississippi Freedom Summer could have been the source for a wonderful story about African Americans fighting the battle for civil rights with their lives. Instead, Parker gives us not black heroes but black victims. And to suggest that a group of FBI "untouchables" paved the way for the Civil Rights Movement's success is insulting to thousands of blacks who demonstrated in freedom marches and put their lives in danger for the greater good of Dr. King's nonviolent protest.

Further Reading

Bourgeois, Henry. "Hollywood and the Civil Rights Movement: The Case of *Mississippi Burning*." *The Howard Journal of Communications* 4.1 + 2 (Summer/ Fall 1992): 157–163.

Brinson, Susan L. "The Myth of White Superiority in *Mississippi Burning*." *The Southern Communication Journal* 60.3 (Spring 1995): 211–221.

Chafe, William H. *"Mississippi Burning." Past Imperfect: History According to the Movies*, ed. Mark C. Carnes. New York: Henry Holt & Co., 1996. 274–277.

Doherty, Thomas. Review of *Mississippi Burning*. *Cineaste* 17.2 (1989): 48–50.

Pleasantville (1998) (PG-13) (M)

Setting: 1998 and Pleasantville, 1958

Director: Gary Ross

Screenplay: Gary Ross

Director of Photography: John Lindley

Cast: Toby Maguire (David/Bud Parker), Reese Witherspoon (Jennifer/Mary Sue Parker), Joan Allen (Betty Parker), Jeff Daniels (Bill Johnson), and J. T. Walsh (Big Bob)

Availability: New Line Home Video

This film is an allegory on diversity, difference, and change. David, a nerdy suburb kid, escapes from his dislocation with other students and his mother by watching "Pleasantville," a 1950s sitcom rerun on "T.V. Time." In the fictional black-and-white world of "Pleasantville" everything is "swell." There is no AIDS crisis, no global warming, and no family trauma. But when David and his sister Jennifer, through a cosmic TV clicker, are tossed into that television sitcom of 1958, knowledge comes to the allegorical Eden. Before their arrival, the citizens of Pleasantville didn't question authority. Their thinking was as black and white as the world they lived in. The pages in their library books were blank; and in geography class they learned that the end of Main Street is "just the beginning again" (22:32). They have no idea of a world outside. But Jennifer/Mary Sue deliberately messes with the cosmic order of the syndicated television series by sleeping with Skip, the captain of the basketball team (39:19–39:31), and later, she tells Betty, her mom, about sex and masturbation. That night her mother pleases herself in the bathtub, and the ceiling turns to color (45:44–48:23). With this new knowledge comes danger, as a tree outside her window catches fire (45:44–48:23), and the homogenized pleasantness of Pleasantville becomes a mix of color and black and white. These changes worry Big Bob the mayor and he organizes a citizen's action committee to do something about it. Betty, too, is worried by becoming "colored," and she, with the help of Bud/David, covers up her identity with makeup and "passes" for black and white. Overall, change brings about community divisiveness. Big Bob at a council meeting says "it's a question of values" (1:20:04), and he wants to "separate out the things that are pleasant from the things that are unpleasant" (1:26:11). With these words, Jim Crow segregation besieges Pleasantville. A sign in a window reads "no coloreds." A group of noncolored kids harass Betty because she's colored (1:28:47–1:29:56). Also, the arts are affected by the fear of change. Books are burned, and budding artist Bill Johnson, along with Bud/David, is arrested for painting a revolutionary mural that decries the injustices of the once placid town. At their trial—a visual echo of *To Kill a Mockingbird* with the "coloreds" sitting in the balcony, and the "non-coloreds" sitting below—David defends knowledge, emotion, and difference. "You see those faces up there? They're no different than you are" (1:44:34). The trial ends with David triumphing and the whole world turning to color. Director/writer Gary Ross completes his allegory: diversity brings knowledge, and the differences among the races are very small, indeed.

Further Reading

Corliss, Richard. "Shading the Past." Review of *Pleasantville*. *Time* 118 (October 26, 1998): 91.

Leydon, Joe. Review of *Pleasantville*. *Variety* 372.6 (September 21, 1998): 104–105.

Marcus, Greil. "While the Frank Capra in Hell Award Goes to. . . ." Review of *Pleasantville*. *Esquire* 131.3 (March 1999): 76.

Smoke Signals (1998) (PG-13) (M)

Setting: Coeur d'Alene Indian Reservation, Idaho, 1976–1998; and Phoenix, Arizona

Director: Chris Eyre

Screenplay: Sherman Alexie

Director of Photography: Brian Capener

Cast: Adam Beach (Victor Joseph), Evan Adams (Thomas), Irene Bedard (Suzy Song), Gary Farmer (Arnold Joseph), and Tantoo Cardinal (Arelene Joseph)

Availability: Miramax Home Video

Sherman Alexie's *Smoke Signals* is, in some ways, a very basic story: a buddy/ buddy road trip combined with the quest to find one's father, but within these two narrative archetypes, Alexie presents Native Americans as we've never seen them on film. Instead of filmic stereotypes, Alexie presents fully realized human beings. In this regard, *Smoke Signals* is ground breaking, and the film's title links to previous Hollywood images of Native Americans, but also suggests a deeper psychological underpinning of distress or cries for help. Victor and Thomas, the two protagonists, travel from Coeur d'Alené Indian Reservation in Idaho to Phoenix, Arizona, to claim the remains of Victor's father, Arnold Joseph. Thomas' inner quest is for companionship and to discover himself, not the self he has cobbled together from Hollywood films like *Dances with Wolves*. In a hilarious scene aboard a bus, Victor tells Thomas to quit grinning, lose the suit, unbraid the hair and "get stoic" (35:43–37:44). But Victor's demands for authenticity merely replace one stereotype with another. Eventually through the journey, Thomas learns that Victor's father was responsible for his parents' accidental deaths, and he learns a greater appreciation for him. In the film's final moments, Thomas meditates on the troubles of Native Americans and the desire for scapegoats. His epiphanic voiceover intones: "If we forgive our fathers, what's left?" (83:00). He has come to knowledge. Victor, too, needs to forgive. His father, although a loving man, was often drunk and violent, and he abandoned the young Victor and his mother over ten years ago. Angry, Victor has refused to let go of the past (both personal and communal). In a telling scene, he snaps at a white woman on a bus, "You ain't got nothing to complain about so why doncha just be quiet?" (25:07–25: 14). By contrast, he as a Native American living "on the rez" has a lot to complain about. On his journey, he discovers another side of his father. While visiting with Suzy, his dad's friend, Victor learns how greatly Arnold Joseph loved him. Ultimately, Victor forgives his father, and later, in the offices of a police chief, completes his break with the past. Charged with drunk driving, Victor asserts, "I don't drink" (1:11:40). He is not his father and he will not follow the same destructive path. The future is open.

Further Reading

Alexie, Sherman. *The Lone Ranger and Tonto Fistfight in Heaven*. New York: Atlantic
    Monthly Press, 1993.
Maslin, Janet. "Miles to Go and Worlds Apart." *New York Times* (March 27, 1998):
    E1.
Sterngold, James. "Able to Laugh at Their People, Not Just Cry for Them." *New
    York Times* (June 21, 1998): 13.
West, Dennis and Joan M. West. "Sending Cinematic Smoke Signals: An Interview
    with Sherman Alexie." *Cineaste* 23 (Fall 1998): 28–32.

Zoot Suit (1981) (R) (M)

Setting: Los Angeles, 1942–1943, 1981

Director: Luis Valdez

Screenplay: Luis Valdez

Director of Photography: David Myers

Cast: Daniel Valdez (Henry Reyna), Edward James Olmos (El Pachuco), Tyne Daly
(Alice), and Charles Aidman (George)

Availability: MCA Home Video

Luis Valdez's *Zoot Suit*, a film about racism, injustice, and Chicano identity,
is rooted in Los Angeles of the 1940s but also resonates with the late twentieth century. The opening credit sequence, a blue-tinged vintage photograph that dissolves into 1980s contemporaneity (1:42–2:00), suggests that
Henry Reyna's story is still current. On August 2, 1942, a Chicano boy was
found murdered near the Sleepy Lagoon reservoir in Los Angeles. Nearly
600 Chicanos were initially arrested, and although no substantial evidence
was found, a racist judge who presided over the case sentenced a dozen
men, all members of the 38th Street Gang, to life in San Quentin. A year
after their imprisonment, the zoot suit riots broke out in downtown L.A.
as over 200 sailors brutally, in a racially motivated hate crime, beat up a
group of *pachucos* (Chicano gang members in zoot suits). With this as a
backdrop, Valdez tells the story of Reyna, a member of the 38th Street Gang
who straddles both cultures. On the eve of joining the U.S. Navy, he gets
caught up in the tragedy of Sleepy Lagoon. His father was proud of Henry's
allegiance to his country and his decision to join the navy (18:52), and he
had asked his son to call himself an "Americano" not a "Chicano" (15:56–
16:10). But Henry, as his alter-ego the mythic El Pachuco informs him,
can't leave behind his gang, his racial identity, and his past. El Pachuco,
played with stunning flamboyance by Edward James Olmos, tells Henry,
"Forget the war overseas, carnal. Your war is on the homefront" (8:42).
Throughout the film, El Pachuco advises Henry. El Pachuco's a jutting,
striking figure in red shirts, black pants and wide-brim hats, bopping and
striding with switchblade cool. He represents a hypermasculinity, and a con-

fidence apart from the white mainstream. He advises Henry to pack a switch-blade, to have brutal sex with Della (50:24), and to distrust the whites, such as George and Alice, his public defenders (26:03). Henry eventually realizes that El Pachuco is his darker side: "You're me. My worst enemy. And my best friend" (1:22:53–1:23:14), and he frees himself from self-destruction. During his imprisonment he comes to an understanding with Alice (1:07:42–1:09:31). He appreciates her dedication to justice and admires her strength (as a communist and a Jew, she's also had to fight for her place in America). Eventually with the help of Alice and the gang's attorney, George, the judge's unjust decision is overturned upon appeal. The film ends with several "histories" of Henry's future. The "press" tells the story of Henry's return to prison in 1947 and his death from hard drugs in 1972. For the white conservative media there is no place in the melting pot for Mexican Americans. The military story is one of sacrifice: Henry Reyna was a Korean war hero, decorated with the Congressional Medal of Honor, and he died at Inchon in 1952. This heroic story celebrates the man's patriotism, but also brackets him off through death as having no contemporary future in America. Alice's story, the final one, is much more inclusive and multicul-tural. She says that Henry married Della, had five children, three of whom attended universities and now speak rich Pachuco slang and call themselves "Chicanos" (1:38:08).

Further Reading

Daniels, Douglas Henry. "Los Angeles Zoot: Race 'Riot,' the Pachuco, and Black Music Culture." *The Journal of Negro History* 82.2 (Spring 1997): 201–220.
Pizzato, Mark. "Brechtian and Aztec Violence in Valdez's *Zoot Suit*." *Journal of Popular Film and Television* 26.2 (Summer 1998): 52–61.
Westerbreck, Colin L., Jr. "The Legend Lives: Rootie Zoot Suit." *Commonweal* 109 (February 26, 1982): 111.

DOUBLE BILL: THE AMERICAN INDIAN MOVEMENT

Incident at Oglala (1992) (Doc.) (M)

Setting: Oglala Reservation, 1975, 1991
Director: Michael Apted
Writers: Chip Selby and Stephanie Black
Director of Photography: Maryse Alberti
Narrator: Robert Redford
Editor: Susanne Rostock
Availability: IVE Home Video

Thunderheart (1992) (R) (M)

Setting: Oglala Reservation, 1970s

Director: Michael Apted

Screenplay: John Fusco

Director of Photography: Roger Deakins

Cast: Val Kilmer (Ray Levoi), Sam Shepard (Frank Coutelle), Graham Greene (Walking Crow Horse), Sheila Tousey (Maggie Eagle Bear), Chief Ten Thin Elk (Grandpa Sam Reaches), Fred Ward (Jack Milton), and John Trudell (Jimmy Looks Twice)

Availability: Columbia Tri-Star Home Video

In 1992, British director Michael Apted explored the Native American experience in two stunning films. His documentary *Incident at Oglala* analyzes the miscarriage of justice that has made Leonard Peltier an American political prisoner. *Thunderheart*, a rich paranoid chiller about corruption in the FBI, explores a man's journey home to his Native American ancestry. *Incident at Oglala* is told like a detective story. It begins with the murders of two FBI agents, Coler and Williams, who were killed on June 26, 1975. The agents were in pursuit of a red vehicle when they drove onto the Jumping Bull compound on the Oglala Reservation. There they opened fire and had fire returned by members of the American Indian Movement. Following their deaths, a series of clues led to the arrests of three Native Americans: Dino Butler, Bob Robideau, and Leonard Peltier. From here the film takes a step back to offer a context for the violence (10:42–30:35). In the early 1970s the home of 10,000 Lakota Sioux was a killing ground as civil war ensued between traditionalists (those Natives who were dedicated to the old ways and made up the American Indian Movement) and the nontraditionalists (those Indians on the government side who teamed up with Dick Wilson to harass, intimidate, and murder AIM members). Chillingly, the film reveals how government money was spent by Wilson for guns and ammo to kill his own people (22:40; 23:41–26:10). In part, Apted suggests that the government, following the seventy-one-day siege of Wounded Knee in 1973, felt intimidated by AIM and didn't do anything to check the excesses of Wilson and his goon squads (26:52–27:10). Following the arrests, Robideau and Butler were surprisingly acquitted by an all-white working-class jury in Cedar Rapids, Iowa. Peltier, who had fled to Canada, was later extradited, and this time the government held a trial in a different jurisdiction: Fargo, North Dakota. To ensure a guilty verdict, the case was moved and the FBI doctored evidence. The FBI changed the description of the red pickup agents Coler and Williams had pursued into a red and white van, Peltier's vehicle (1:13:00). They also coerced a witness, Michael Anderson, to tell a story that would fill in the blanks and convict Peltier (1:16:54). Unfortunately, Anderson died in an auto accident in 1978 and his story can't be challenged. Finally, Apted solves the detective mystery by having

Peltier tell us that he knows who the real killer is, but he won't reveal him, because he won't give up a brother. "I've got my self respect" (1:24:21). *Thunderheart* also looks at a mistrial of justice as the government frames a radical AIM-like member, Jimmy Looks Twice (played by real AIM activist John Trudell), on a trumped-up murder charge. The FBI, led by the corrupt Coutelle, wants to run the Indians off the reservation so that the federal government can grab hold of the rich uranium mines hidden in the valley. Thrown into this mix of a revisionist western is a young crackshot agent, Levoi, who is not proud of his Indian past. "I didn't know my father, sir," he tells his superior early on (4:57). And later to Coutelle, Levoi confesses, "These are not my people" (14:29). But as he solves the murder, Levoi becomes disenchanted with the FBI. As he collides with Jack Milton's goon squads and sees children shot at (46:33–50:12), Levoi questions the FBI's supposed allies. His disenchantment grows further when he spots a Colt semiautomatic in the back of Coutelle's car and suspects his superior's complicity in a larger conspiracy (1:13:00–1:13:44). Through the help of two Native Americans—Walking Crow Horse and Grampa Sam Reaches—Levoi finds his true self. With their prodding, he discovers that he's connected to the blood of Thunderheart, a warrior killed at Wounded Knee, and in fine western tradition the film concludes with a triumphant last stand. Chased by a posse of feds, Levoi drives hard and fast into the Red Deer Table. He is surrounded by Coutelle, FBI agents, and Milton's goons, their guns trained on his back (1:49:21). Just as it looks like he and Crow Horse are about to join the list of the murdered, from the edges of the hilly cliffs rise Native Americans. Their guns and vantage point have Coutelle trapped. The Native American cavalry rescues Levoi, and he shouts a line that echoes through the valley and a history of injustice perpetrated by whites: "This land is not for sale" (1:51:21).

Further Reading

Brown, Georgia. Review of *Incident at Oglala*. *Village Voice* (May 19, 1992): 60.
Johnson, Brian D. Review of *Thunderheart*. *Maclean's* 105 (April 13, 1992): 71.
Maslin, Janet. Review of *Thunderheart*. *New York Times* (April 3, 1992): C12.
Schickel, Richard. Review of *Thunderheart*. *Time* 139 (May 4, 1992): 77–78.
Turan, Kenneth. Review of *Incident at Oglala*. *Los Angeles Times* (May 8, 1992): Calendar/1.

DOUBLE BILL: SIDNEY POITIER, AFRICAN-AMERICAN STAR

Lilies of the Field (1963) (M)

Setting: Tuscon, Arizona, 1963
Director: Ralph Nelson

Screenplay: James Poe

Director of Photography: Ernest Haller

Cast: Sidney Poitier (Homer Smith), Lilia Skala (Mother Maria), and Ralph Nelson (Mr. Ashton)

Availability: MGM/UA Home Video

In the Heat of the Night (1967) (M)

Setting: Sparta, Mississippi, 1967

Director: Norman Jewison

Screenplay: Stirling Silliphant

Director of Photography: Haskell Wexler

Cast: Sidney Poitier (Virgil Tibbs), Rod Steiger (Chief Gillespie), and Larry Gates (Endicott)

Availability: MGM/UA Home Video

Sidney Poitier was the first great African American star. Before him, African Americans were consigned to second lead roles or forced to play belittling stereotypes (the stuttering fool, the sambo, the mammy, or the hot mama). There were brilliant black actors—Juano Hernandez, Paul Robeson, Dorothy Dandridge, and Ethel Waters—but Poitier achieved the stardom previously reserved for white males. His stardom began with *No Way Out* (1950), a story about an intern (Poitier) confronted by a bigot (Richard Widmark). In this film, Poitier established his persona: the black man seeking respect and dignity within a white world. His films had an integrationist subtext, and Poitier could carry scenes by his expressive eyes, his powerful silences, and the lilting rhythms of his voice that resonated an Afro pride and a desire to be seen as a man. Poitier reveals such feelings when he shouts to Rod Steiger, "They call me Mr. Tibbs," in *In the Heat of the Night* (35: 50). In 1963, Poitier became the first and so far only African American to win the Academy Award for best actor. *Lilies of the Field*, a small scale story about a drifter who helps a group of catholic nuns from Vienna build a chapel in Arizona, was not initially supported by United Artists or the Hollywood establishment. Director Ralph Nelson had to put up his house as a completion bond against the production cost of $240,000. Poitier did the film for a small fee because he believed in its message. On the surface, Poitier's Homer Smith seemed to be a character that either a black or a white actor could play. This was the claim Bosley Crowther made in the *New York Times* arguing that it was a breakthrough in casting. But Poitier does embue the film with black pride. Homer builds the chapel because of his kindness and a sense of religious calling. But he may also identify with the nuns. They too are outsiders, having traveled 8,000 miles from communist East Germany to America. Furthermore, he also gains respect from the white community. A local contractor, Ashton, who had earlier called him "boy" (41:00), later calls him "Mr. Smith" (1:18:12–1:18:22) after seeing the fine work he's done. In the end, as the drifter leaves the nuns for the open road, there's a sad feeling that a black man still hasn't found his place, his home in America. *In the Heat of the Night* is a film that much more overtly showcases two powerful acting talents—Steiger and Poitier— as strong minded professionals (one a local sheriff in Sparta, Mississippi, the other a homicide detective en route from Philadelphia to Memphis) who find their common humanity and help solve a murder. But before they team up, Tibbs is the prime murder suspect. The first question Police Chief Gillespie asks is "got a name, boy?" Gillespie doesn't see Tibbs as a man; instead because he's a stranger in town and black, Gillespie assumes that he's guilty. But once it's revealed that Tibbs is a police officer, too, and Gillespie has specific orders to work with him, the chief begins to see him as an equal. No longer calling him "boy," he awkwardly asks Tibbs to examine the body of the murdered industrialist Colbert: "I'm not an expert, officer" (20:23). In a wonderful break from stereotypes, Poitier, and not Steiger, is the man of scientific knowledge, of cool rational logic who can piece together clues (chalk dust under fingernails, for example, proves one murder suspect's innocence [43:16]). Later, Tibbs and Gillespie interview a murder suspect, Endicott. The wealthy Endicott, disgusted by Tibbs' charges of racism, slaps the detective in the face. Tibbs slaps him back (1:01:44). Endicott expects the chief to murder the "uppity" Tibbs on the spot for hitting a white man, but Gillespie stands still, saying, "I'm thinking." This is a powerful moment because the racist police chief sees the humanity in his partner and refuses to follow unjust social customs. Eventually, the two lawmen solve the crime, and as Tibbs walks to catch the train for Memphis, Gillespie, in a subtle role reversal, carries Tibbs' bags like a Pullman porter (1:43:50–1:44:17). In the end, each man, in their reserved way, smiles at the other, resonating a small but meaningful breakthrough.

Further Reading

Crowther, Bosley. "The Negro in Films." *The New York Times* (October 6, 1963): II:1.

Morgenstern, Joseph. "Red Neck and Scapegoat." Review of *In the Heat of the Night*. *Newsweek* 70 (August 14, 1967): 83.

Spotnitz, Frank. "Sidney Poitier: Since He's Come to Dinner, He's Helped Change Hollywood's Manners." *American Film* 16 (September/October, 1991): 18–21+.

DOUBLE BILL: BLACK NATIONALISM AND BLACK PRIDE

Malcolm X 2 vols. (1992) (PG-13) (M)

Setting: 1930s–1993
Director: Spike Lee

Screenplay: Spike Lee and Marvin Worth

Director of Photography: Ernest Dickerson

Cast: Denzel Washington (Malcolm X), Angela Bassett (Betty Shabazz), Albert Hall (Baines), Al Freeman, Jr. (Elijah Muhammad), and Spike Lee (Shorty)

Availability: Warner Bros. Home Video

Malcolm X: Make It Plain (1994) (Doc.) (M)

Setting: 1925–1965

Director: Orlando Bagwell

Writers: Steve Fayer and Orlando Bagwell

Narrator: Alfred Woodard

Editor: Jean Tsien

Availability: MPI Home Video

At Malcolm X's funeral, Ossie Davis best explained this fallen leader's importance to African Americans: "He was our shining black prince, our manhood." Malcolm X was a role model: he made blacks proud to be black. Spike Lee's epic tribute to Malcolm X captures his pride and faithfully follows Alex Haley's tripartite structure to *The Autobiography of Malcolm X*: the early gangster days, the conversion to the Nation of Islam, and Malcolm's second conversion and his widening social activism. The hustler days provide an image of Malcolm as victim of white power. His father was murdered by the KKK (vol. 1, 19:02); in the aftermath of his father's death, social workers parceled out his brothers and sisters to different homes (vol. 1, 23:24–24:16). As a child at an all-white school, his teacher told him that he shouldn't aspire to be a lawyer: That's not "a realistic goal for a nigger" (vol. 1, 25:18). Because white power has taught him to dislike himself, Malcolm lives a life of self-abuse, painfully conking his hair with lye (5:17–7:05), and running with white women and gangsters (vol. 1, 31:31–47:51). Eventually he's sent to prison where he meets up with Brother Baines who frees Malcolm from "the prison in your mind" (1:07:36). There he studies religion and history, learns that the "white man is the devil" (vol. 1, 1:17:20), and following a vision dedicates himself to the Nation of Islam and the honorable Elijah Muhammad. With these new teachings, Malcolm discovers new pride: "We didn't land on Plymouth Rock. Plymouth Rock landed on us" (vol. 1, 1:31:11). Following his release from prison, Malcolm becomes Muhammad's main minister, expanding his temples across the United States and preaching the evils of the white power structure: "you've been kid . . . fooled . . . bamboozled" (vol. 2, 19:35–20:05). In part two Lee shows us Malcolm's growing activism. In 1957, following the police beating of Brother Johnson in Harlem, Malcolm and a large group of blacks march to the precinct and demand to see Johnson and insist on an ambulance after seeing how badly he's beaten. Later, as word reaches the street that Johnson will be okay, the crowd remains gathered, violent tension simmering. The police try to break up the crowd but they are powerless. Malcolm steps forward, calmly waves his gloved hand, and the crowd disperses (vol. 2, 4: 08–10:08). This growth in power and popularity will eventually be his downfall as the Black Muslim circle fears that he's becoming more important than Elijah Muhammad. Malcolm's fallout is further precipitated by his own discovery of Muhammad's moral failings. Muhammad lives in a swank home, drives fancy cars, and has fathered several children with his young secretaries (vol. 2, 40:13–41:58). In 1964, Malcolm broke from the Nation of Islam and traveled to Mecca where he had a second conversion (55:10–1:04:58). In Mecca he walks alongside whites during his pilgrimage and learns that some of his generalizations have "caused injuries to some white folks who did not deserve them" (vol. 2, 1:10:22–1:10:36). Malcolm's second conversion came on the heels of his break from Muhammad. No doubt Malcolm was disillusioned by Muhammad's hypocrisy, but he had been moving away from the Nation's focus on spiritual issues for a long time. The documentary, *Malcolm X: Make It Plain* suggests Malcolm's growing disenfranchisement following the killing of Randall Stokes by L.A. police in 1959. In this clear case of police brutality, Malcolm wanted to pursue further charges against the police following their acquittal by an all-white jury, but Muhammad ordered him to back off (1:03:43–1:04:56). Muhammad desired changes within the black communities, focusing on business development and socially conservative behavior. Malcolm traveled to Africa and other nations, seeking a larger connectedness with the world. He even wanted to bring charges before the United Nations against the United States for its cruelties to blacks (vol. 2, 1:05:49). By breaking with Muhammad and denouncing him, Malcolm precipitated his own assassination by members from Temple 23 in Harlem. Overall, Spike Lee's film is a provocative triumph. Denzel Washington as Malcolm is marvelous. He captures the fallen leader's flair for rhetoric, his vocal inflections, and his thoughtful poise (especially the way Malcolm often placed two fingers at the right side of his face during moments of reflection). Lee ends his film with a moment of transcendence. He flashes forward to the present, and in a series of medium closeup shots, ten children stand up from their school desks, shouting "I'm Malcolm X." The legend and symbol of black pride and consciousness is alive.

Further Reading

Haley, Alex. *The Autobiography of Malcolm X*. New York: Bantam, 1965.
Locke, John. "Adapting the Autobiography: The Transformation of Malcolm X." *Cineaste* 19.4 (Fall 1992): 5–7.
Marable, Manning. "Malcolm as Messiah: Cultural Myth vs. Historical Reality in *Malcolm X*." *Cineaste* 19.4 (Fall 1992): 7–9.
Verniere, James. "Doing the Job." *Sight and Sound* 3 (February 1993): 10–11.

FURTHER VIEWING

Assault on Precinct 13 (1977) (R) (M)

Clockers (1999) (R) (M)

Foxy Brown (1974) (R) (M)

George Wallace (1998) (TV) (M)

Higher Learning (1994) (R) (M)

Just Cause (1995) (R) (M)

Lakota Woman: Siege at Wounded Knee (1994) (TV) (M)

Lost Boundaries (1951) (M)

Powwow Highway (1989) (R) (M)

Sweet Sweetback's Bad Ass Song (1973) (R) (M)

11

The Atomic Bomb, Cold War Paranoia, and the Expanding National Security State, 1946– Present

Air Force One ◆ *Atomic Café* ◆ *Courage Under Fire* ◆ *Enemy of the State* ◆ *Executive Decision* ◆ *The Front* ◆ *Invasion of the Body Snatchers* ◆ *JFK* ◆ *Kiss Me Deadly* ◆ *M*A*S*H* ◆ *The Missiles of October* ◆ *North by Northwest* ◆ *October Sky* ◆ *One, Two, Three Pickup on South Street* ◆ *Pork Chop Hill* ◆ Double Bill: *The Big Heat* and *The Big Combo* ◆ Double Bill: *The China Syndrome* and *Meltdown at Three Mile Island* ◆ Double Bill: *Dr. Strangelove* and *Fail Safe* ◆ Double Bill: *The Manchurian Candidate* and *Seven Days in May* ◆ Double Bill: *The Right Stuff* and *Apollo 13* ◆ Double Bill: *The Steel Helmet* and *I Want You* ◆ Double Bill: *The Thing from Another World* and *The Day the Earth Stood Still*

Air Force One (1997) (R)

Setting: Russia and Air Force One, 1997

Director: Wolfgang Petersen

Screenplay: Andrew W. Marlowe

Director of Photography: Michael Ballhaus

Cast: Harrison Ford (President James Marshall), Gary Oldman (Egor Korshunov), Donna Bullock (Press Secretary Melanie Mitchel), Wendy Crewson (Grace Marshall), and Liesel Matthews (Alice Marshall)

Availability: Paramount Home Video

Air Force One is *Die Hard* on a jet. Harrison Ford plays Jim Marshall, a tough U.S. president who uses the powers of his office to protect the world from Cold War dictators. In an opening gambit, Marshall drops a combined paramilitary force of American and Russian paratroopers into Kazakhstan and captures the ruthless Radic (00:00–5:50). Radic had murdered over 200,000 people, and the president at a Moscow news conference justifies his own actions: "Real peace is the presence of justice" (7:54). He further confesses that we've allowed our self-interest to deter us from "acting morally" (8:06). This speech, combined with the film's dramatic opening, reconfigures 1990s Cold War frustrations. Despite our struggle to bring Bosnian war criminals, such as Slobodan Milsoevic, to trial, *Air Force One* provides us with the fantasy scenario to achieve that justice. Shortly after capturing Radic, the president leaves Moscow aboard Air Force One and finds himself besieged by a group of terrorists led by the hyperventilating Gary Oldman as Korshunov. Korshunov seeks Radic's release from prison. He also mouths a lot of platitudes about "Mother Russia" and labels the United States hypocrites for espousing morality when they murdered 100,000 Iraqis just "to save a nickel on a gallon of gas" (1:07:42). Like the cold-blooded killers in the *Die Hard* films, Korshunov ruthlessly executes someone every thirty minutes while awaiting the fulfillment of his demands. In one of the film's most terrifying scenes, the president helplessly listens as Korshunov murders Melanie who watches over the president's adolescent daughter (1:06:41–1:06:49). But no one knows that the president is down below. The terrorists thought he had exited aboard an escape pod. Instead, Marshall stealthily moves in the bowels of the jet, killing terrorists and contacting his cabinet via a cell phone. And in the best *Die Hard* tradition, Marshall, trapped in an enclosed space, converts the jet into his jungle. A veteran of Viet Nam, Marshall knows guerilla fighting, and he wins a guerilla war. The film's portrayal of a virile, potent president belies America's fears of dwindling potency in our quest to police terrorists and crush tyrannical regimes.

Further Reading

Fineman, Howard. "Last Action President." *Newsweek* 75 (July 21, 1997): 66–67.
Kauffmann, Stanley. Review of *Air Force One*. *New Republic* 217 (August 25, 1997): 24.
Schickel, Richard. Review of *Air Force One*. *Time* 150 (July 28, 1997): 69.

Atomic Café (1982) (Doc.)

Setting: United States, 1945–1950s
Directors: Kevin Rafferty, Jayne Loader, and Pierce Rafferty
Research: Pierce Rafferty
Editors: Jayne Loader and Kevin Rafferty
Availability: First Run Video

Atomic Café recreates, through newsreel clips, television footage, and Civilian Defense and military films, U.S. attitudes during the Cold War. The expert editing of Jayne Loader and Kevin Rafferty showcases how misinformed we were about the dangers of atomic radiation. During a military briefing, a group of soldiers prepare to observe an atomic test in the desert.

The officer tells the men that they only have three things to fear: "blast, heat, and radiation." Radiation is the least important of the three, he claims, because if a soldier were to become sterile he'd be dead from the heat and blast anyway (50:47–53:11). The logic is flawed, of course, but the clip reveals one kind of military double-speak inundating the 1950s. One naive soldier, oblivious to the real danger of radioactive fallout, joyously exclaims after observing the atomic blast: "I got a mouthful and face full of dirt!" (54:54–57:36). With the public, the army took a different tack. To alleviate civilian fears of death from radiation, an informative animated film contended that only 15 percent of a population would die from a twenty-megaton bomb. So, why worry? (58:33–1:00:57). Even children's cartoons were used to create a positive spin on nuclear war. The animated Bert the Turtle, in an innocuous looking Civilian Defense short, tells children how to avoid atomic dust by rolling up against walls, under desks, newspapers, and chairs, while a bright chorus chants: "Duck and cover, duck and cover" (1:03:16–1:05:02). The sad truth is if those children were within 2,000 square miles of ground zero, there would be nothing left of them to cover (1:06:00–1:07:11). Along with documenting a wealth of misinformation fed the public during the atomic age, directors Rafferty, Loader, and Rafferty remind Americans of our insensitivity and ignorance about atomic energy. During the 1950s, several atomic tests occurred in the American Southwest and the Pacific. Pigs were radiated to see how they responded (48:30–50:11). The military was so overwhelmed with watching the majestic power of bomb blasts that they failed to consider prevailing winds that carried atomic dust to a fishing boat and poisoned twenty-three men during the Castle-Bravo test on March 1, 1954 (47:00–47:24). Some politicians overzealously wanted to unleash atomic weapons as a foreign policy big stick. In 1952, Representative Lloyd Bentsen suggested that we nuke the North Koreans to force them back across the 38th Parallel (26:00–26:23). Bentsen's threat of contained nuclear strike (when radiation now appears uncontrollable) was naive at best and world-threatening at worst. Perhaps the most shocking moments of insensitivity occurred immediately following the World War Two devastation of Hiroshima and Nagasaki. After the bombing of Hiroshima, radio comic Fred Allen callously joked that the great city "looks like Ebbets Field after a double-header with the Giants" (7:48–8:14). Allen's joke is followed by contrapuntal images of charred bodies and a hollowed-out city that looks nothing like a post-ballgame aftermath. Later, an American scientist declared the atomic "tests" on Japan a "classroom experiment." This sound byte is followed up with medical footage of a topless Japanese adolescent. She has radiation burns that look like continents across her upper body and face (9:02–9:39). Her disfigured nascent sexuality grimly reminds us of the unwieldy and devastating power of atomic weaponry.

Further Reading

Canby, Vincent. "Film: Documentary on Views About Atom Bomb." *New York Times* (March 17, 1982): C16.
Hoberman, J. "White Light, White Heat." *The Village Voice* (March 23, 1982): 52.
Seitz, Michael. "End Games." *The Progressive* 46 (August 1982): 52.
Westerbeck, Colin, Jr. Review of *Atomic Café*. *Commonweal* 109 (July 16, 1982): 405–406.

Courage Under Fire (1996) (R) (W)

Setting: The Gulf War and Washington, DC, 1991

Director: Edward Zwick

Screenplay: Patrick Sheane Duncan

Director of Photography: Roger Deakins

Cast: Denzel Washington (Lt. Col. Nat Serling), Meg Ryan (Capt. Karen Emma Walden), Lou Diamond Phillips (Sergeant Monfriez), and Matt Damon (Specialist Ilario)

Availability: Paramount Home Video

In *Courage Under Fire*, Nat Serling investigates the death of Capt. Karen Emma Walden, a Gulf War Medevac pilot who has been nominated for the Congressional Medal of Honor. Serling has to make out a report to prove that she deserves such an honor, but he discovers a tangled murder mystery. Walden's story revolves around a series of flashbacks from different characters. In each flashback the speaker tries to place himself in a more positive light. Serling muddles through the distortions to ultimately find truth. But the investigation is also taxing on a personal level for Serling as he deals with his own nightmares. During the Gulf War, Serling ordered friendly fire on one of his own tanks and accidentally killed a friend, Boylar. Conflicted, he looks for the truth behind Karen's story while his own story is being covered up by the military hierarchy. What Serling finds, eventually, is inner peace, but he also discovers a heroic woman deserving the medal. Serling first interviews Karen's co-pilot (24:43–28:41) who was knocked unconscious after their helicopter crash-landed. From his limited perspective, he tells Serling two essential components of the larger mystery. First, Sergeant Monfriez wanted to retreat from the area and get secondary support. Second, the copilot's wife betrays a prejudice against Karen: "She was so butch" (25:18). This comment reflects a larger injustice that most military women confront, and hints at tension within the unit. Next, Serling hears another variation from Ilario, the company medic (32:32–45:08). Ilario, played with halting hesitation by Matt Damon, has a sickly appearance: his skin is taut against his bones, as if something is eating away at him. In his story, Karen acted bravely, insisting that the men conserve ammo. She shoots an Iraqi hopping over the ridge of a sand dune, and takes a round in the stomach. Dying, she insists that her men board the rescue helicopter. While giving cover, she's killed by enemy shells. In a third story told by Monfriez, Serling hears a disturbing variation (56:51–1:05:14). Monfriez claims that Karen was a coward. In his telling, he killed the Iraqi hopping over the sand dune, and when the evacuation helicopter arrived, Karen didn't want to leave: "It's not safe," she screamed. His story covers up his own cowardice revealed in the co-pilot's version. Serling doesn't believe Monfriez, and during a second interview uncovers how unnerved the sergeant is. Monfriez, riddled with guilt and complicity, orders Serling at gunpoint from his car, and then drives head on into an approaching train (1:25:37). Karen's mystery closes when Serling interviews the AWOL Ilario a second time (1:27:07–1:35:58). Following these revelations, Serling returns with a full report. At the military briefing, he experiences an epiphany. Unlike Monfriez who could not live with the facts, the truth frees Serling from personal pain. A friend, *Washington Post* reporter Rading, replays a tank transcript from the Gulf War battle, showcasing the friendly fire that killed Boylar, but the tape also reveals Serling's heroic actions (1:40:17–1:40:59). This a moving film about a woman proving her grit in an all-male enclave. But it is also a therapeutic story. Serling understands and conquers his own guilt. In the end, when Serling salutes Karen's grave site at Arlington, he honors both her memory and his own heroic service.

Further Reading

Ansen, David. Review of *Courage Under Fire*. *Newsweek* 128 (July 15, 1996): 59.

Dowell, Pat. "A Gulf War *Rashomon*: An Interview with Edward Zwick." *Cineaste* 22 (Summer 1996): 11–13.

Kauffmann, Stanley. Review of *Courage Under Fire*. *The New Republic* 215 (July 29, 1996): 24–25.

Maslin, Janet. Review of *Courage Under Fire*. *New York Times* (July 12, 1996): C1+.

Enemy of the State (1998) (R) (M)

Setting: Georgetown; Baltimore, MD; Washington, DC, 1998

Director: Tony Scott

Screenplay: David Marconi

Director of Photography: Daniel Mindel

Cast: Will Smith (Robert Clayton Dean), Gene Hackman (Brill), Jon Voight (Thomas Brian Reynolds), Lisa Bonet (Rachel Banks), Regina King (Carla Dean), Jason Robards (Congressman Phillip Hammersley), Jason Lee (Daniel Leon Zavits), and Tom Sizemore (Boss Pintero)

Availability: Buena Vista Home Video

"Fort Mead has 18 acres of mainframe computers—underground. You're talking to your wife on the phone, you use the word bomb, president, Allah, any of a hundred key words, computer recognizes it, automatically records it, and red flags it for analysis. That was 20 years ago," former National Security Op Brill tells runaway lawyer, Robert Clayton Dean, late in Tony Scott's Hitchcockian thriller, *Enemy of the State* (1:30:28–1:30:47). And Brill's mood of paranoia is warranted. With the help of one hundred satellites glowing down at the earth, a group of renegade NSA agents, led by a corrupt politician, Thomas Brian Reynolds, abuse surveillance technology. America has won the Cold War, and now Reynolds seeks to "win the peace." Reynolds believes that "we are at war 24 hours every day" (3:01), and he has Senator Hammersley murdered because he's opposed to his views and won't support the Telecommunications Security and Privacy Act. "Invasion of privacy is more like it," the senator says, and seconds later, an NSA agent immobilizes him with a needle to the neck, and then sends his car into the Occuquan bay (1:22–4:26). This splinter NSA group intends for the senator's death to look like a heart attack, but in one of the films great ironies, the covert murder was captured on a non-NSA surveillance camera. Daniel Zavits was recording the migratory patterns of Canadian geese from a hidden camera across the bay. Upon learning of the camera, the NSA hounds Zavits, rushing him toward an apparent accidental death (22:30–27:23). But just before his murder, Zavits abruptly bumps into his old Georgetown acquaintance, Dean, at a lingerie shop and drops a disk copy of Senator Hammersley's murder into his bag. After the drop, Dean's life—like that of *North by Northwest*'s Roger O. Thornhill—spins out of control. The NSA discredits him with a series of lies planted in the newspapers, including innuendoes of money laundering, mob ties, and an extramarital affair with Rachel Banks. As a result, Dean's marriage becomes turbulent and his job crashes (45:54–48:45). The film's intensity grows out of these situations. Dean is a good man, hard-working, law-abiding. But once renegades in the government seek to discredit him, Dean, and by association all of us, are helpless against their power and technology. Fortunately, the on-the-lam Dean finds help from Brill (the most unlikely of sources), a hardened former NSA agent who agrees to help the young lawyer after he learns of Banks' murder (she was the daughter of Brill's former NSA partner). Together, Brill and Dean tackle Reynolds and company, and like the quick-thinking Thornhill, Dean, caught up in a world of subterfuge and home-front espionage outfoxes the NSA by "acting," convincing them that a mobster, Pintero, has what they want. Marketed with the tagline, "It's not paranoia when they're really after you," *Enemy of State* marvelously critiques society's ever-pervasive feeling of being watched by "Big Brother."

Further Reading

Bownman, James. Review of *Enemy of the State*. *The American Spectator* 32 (January
        1999): 62.

Travers, Peter. Review of *Enemy of the State. Rolling Stone* (December 10, 1998): 133.

"Will Smith Runs for His Life in Action Thriller *Enemy of the State.*" *Jet* 94 (November 23, 1998): 58–61.

Executive Decision (1996) (R)

Setting: Trieste, Italy; Frederick Field, Maryland; London, England; Athens, Greece; and Washington, DC., 1996

Director: Stuart Baird

Screenplay: Jim Thomas and John Thomas

Director of Photography: Alex Thomson

Cast: Kurt Russell (David Grant), Steven Seagal (Lt. Col. Austin Travis), Halle Berry (Jean), John Leguizamo (Rat), Oliver Platt (Cahill), David Suchet (Nagi Hassan)

Availability: Warner Home Video

With the fall of communism in Russia and the reunification of Germany, America declared that it had won the Cold War. But since the American economy is driven by military spending, new enemies, new fears had almost to be invented. By the end of the 1990s, the new threat to national security was perceived to be international terrorists, especially those in the Middle East who might get their hands on an Anthrax virus or concoct their own nerve gas of mass destruction. *Executive Decision*, made in 1996, grows out of these post–Cold War fears. Nagi Hassan, a religious zealot, seizes control of an American aircraft. On the surface, he wants the United States to free his terrorist friend, Jaffa, and then he will release his prisoners. But Hassan's ulterior motives are to land the jet in Washington, DC, and let loose a vast amount of Dz-5 toxin to destroy all of the population along the northeast seaboard (1:23:50). Against this melodramatic peril to our national security is played personal stories of masculinity in crisis. David Grant, played with professorial calm by Kurt Russell, knows the terrorist mind. Lieutenant Colonel Travis, an expert in dealing with terrorists, insists that Grant accompany him and his elite group of special forces agents on a counterterrorist mission. Travis, disappointed in a failed earlier mission, wants to test Grant's manhood. Grant reluctantly agrees, and he and the elite group, through the aid of an experimental jet, the Remora F117x, attach a pressurized sleeve-like tunnel to the belly of the 747 and climb aboard. During the crossover, however, the sleeve begins to break. Grant, aboard the 747, reaches for Travis caught down below in the sleeve. "We're not going to make it," he says. "You are," the ultra-macho Travis responds, closing the hatch, sealing his own fate, and forcing Grant to become the leader of the mission (43:00–43:58). During the course of the film, Grant is transformed from nerdy intellectual into heroic man of action. He gives Cahill, the flabby engineer, the necessary confidence to dismantle the bomb; he works in concert with Jean, a flight attendant, to find the sleeper, the man holding the button to blow up the plane; he also confronts Hassan and safely lands the jet after the two pilots are assassinated. Ultimately, he earns respect from Jean and the special forces.

Further Reading

Arnold, Gary. Review of *Executive Decision*. *Insight on the News* 12 (May 6, 1996): 34.

"Halle Berry/Kurt Russell Star in New Action Film *Executive Decision*." *Jet* 89 (March 11, 1996): 60–63.

Rozen, Leah. Review of *Executive Decision*. *People Weekly* 45 (March 25, 1996): 19.

The Front (1976) (PG)

Setting: New York, early 1950s

Director: Martin Ritt

Screenplay: Walter Bernstein

Director of Photography: Michael Chapman

Cast: Woody Allen (Howard Prince), Zero Mostel (Hecky Brown), Herschel Bernardi (Phil Sussman), Michael Murphy (Alfred Miller), Remak Ramsay (Hennessey), and Andrea Marcovicci (Florence Barrett)

Availability: Key Home Video

Martin Ritt's *The Front* begins with Frank Sinatra's celebratory paean to 1950s innocence, "Young at Heart," but the mood is discordantly ironic. Layered over the song are images of Korea, General MacArthur, fallout shelters, the Rosenbergs, and Senator Joe McCarthy. The images quickly establish a context of fear and insist that we reconsider our feel-good memories of the 1950s. Amid the specter of ferreting out and blacklisting Hollywood communists walks Howard Prince, a well-meaning nebbish who struggles to keep ahead of his gambling debts. Innocent and naive, he agrees to help his friend Alfred Miller sell his scripts to the television networks. Miller, a communist sympathizer, has been blacklisted, and Prince "fronts" his scripts, acting as the writer. Prince's naivete creates a lot of the film's early humor. During a story conference at the television studio, Prince is told that he immediately needs to cut four and a half minutes of the script (12:02–13:45). Prince stalls: "there's a lot of facets here." Prince isn't the writer, and he can not really "pass" as one. Eventually Prince is moved into political consciousness by his love for a TV assistant producer, Florence, and the death of a good friend, Hecky Brown. Hecky's story is one of the film's powerful subplots. Called before Hennessey's committee, he's asked to name names of fellow communists (13:50–14:27). In high angle shots, Hennessey passes judgment: "The question is, Mr. Brown, what have you done?" Banned from the television networks, Hecky agrees to spy on Prince for Hennessey's "Americanism" committee (42:06–42:57). By "cooperating" he hopes to get to work again. But ultimately despondent over his fallen self-esteem, Hecky jumps from the window of a posh New York hotel (1:15:50–1:18:13). Following Hecky's death, Prince is moved to tell Florence the truth about himself. She's shocked that he's not a writer, but he desires to prove himself worthy of her love. Called before Hennessey's committee, Prince has his revenge in a triumphant moment of catharsis (1:31: 00–1:31:19). Rather than slink back in fear, he confronts the committee. When they ask him to name names and to disparage the memory of Hecky Brown, Prince stands from the table, separating himself through a symbolic moral hierarchy (they remain sitting). "Fellas. I don't recognize the right of this committee to ask me these kind of questions. And furthermore, you can all go fuck yourselves." If only more people, during the Cold War 1950s, had challenged fearful hate mongers. But in reality, college campuses, television and news reporters, and citizens were all too quiet about the horrors of the homefront witch hunts.

Further Reading

Crist, Judith. "Cinematic Blacklisting and Censorship." *Saturday Review* 4 (October 2, 1976): 38–39.

Kael, Pauline. Review of *The Front. The New Yorker* 52 (October 4, 1976): 130–133.

Kramer, Hilton. "The Blacklist and the Cold War." *New York Times* (October 3, 1976): II:1, 16.

Sarris, Andrew. "Woody Allen Exorcises the Not-So-Grand Inquisitors." *The Village Voice* (October 4, 1976): 121.

Westerbeck, Colin L., Jr. Review of *The Front. Commonweal* 103 (December 3, 1976): 785–787.

Invasion of the Body Snatchers (1956)

Setting: Santa Mira, California, 1956

Director: Don Siegel

Screenplay: Daniel Mainwaring

Director of Photography: Ellsworth Fredericks

Cast: Kevin McCarthy (Dr. Miles Bennell), Dana Wynter (Becky Driscoll), and Virginia Christine (Wilma Lantz)

Availability: Republic Home Video

"You're next, you're next already," Dr. Miles Bennell shouts into the camera as highway cars cruise past ignoring his warnings (1:18:05). Bennell's hysteria suggests that we might all be losing our humanity and becoming robotic, unemotional pod-like beings. This fast-moving Don Siegel potboiler is an allegory on our loss of individualism through the spread of a communist evil. The plot packs a Cold War punch. Miles returns from a convention to find several patients desperate to see him. A boy says that his mother isn't his mother. A woman says that her uncle isn't her uncle. People look and act the same, but something's missing. Later Miles learns that alien microorganisms have fallen from the sky, and that they can grow into giant sea pods and take humans over cell for cell. But in the transformation people lose their emotions and sense of beauty. As Miles and Becky uncover this insidious takeover, they desire to preserve their love for one another, but it appears that they have no choice. Their emotional identities must be subsumed by a town that seeks sterile conformity (1:00:50). Siegel's film creates fear by making the ordinary strange. Early on, Miles and Becky visit a club for dinner and nobody there dances or drinks (16:54–18:22). Such an absence of leisure-time fun subtly suggests a loss of pleasure in Santa Mira. Later, when Miles visits to convince her that her uncle really is her uncle, the two of them talk by an outside swing chair (10:38–14:10), but the mood of the pastoral idyll is broken by Siegel's long shots of her uncle cutting grass. He's placed on the fringes of the frame and made strange and ominous. Perhaps the most haunting moment occurs early on a Sunday morning (54:37–57:58). As Miles and Becky hide in his office, they look out on the streets of Santa Mira. Everything appears normal, but too many people are out early, and they're organizing. A group of farm trucks arrive, and inside are pods to be systematically spread throughout the town and outlying communities. Along with making the normal abnormal, Siegel masters a suspenseful mood by expertly handling his camera. It is always moving. Siegel's lateral tracking shots suggest a threat lurking off frame. Often he cuts on action, photographing characters moving in and out of the frame during the cut to create a hurried mood. Moreover, when Miles arrives at Becky's to rescue her from her pod-like father, Miles climbs out of the car before it's in park, and it continues to roll, knocking into the curb with a violent shake (30:12). Siegel also uses canted framing during the greenhouse scene where Miles and Becky discover their pod doubles forming (43:00–46:32). These disoriented shots suggest a world off kilter. Much later, as Miles and Becky run through hallways and streets, up and over hills and stairs, Siegel uses high-angle long shots to create a dream-like maze, suggesting that our heroes are doomed. And in the spirit of 1950s Cold War paranoia, perhaps everyone is.

Further Reading

Kaminsky, Stuart M. "*Invasion of the Body Snatchers*: A Classic of Subtle Horror." *Science Fiction Films*, ed. Thomas R. Atkins. New York: Monarch Press, 1976. 63–72.

Peary, Danny. "*Invasion of the Body Snatchers.*" *Cult Movies: The Classics, the Sleepers, the Weird, and the Wonderful.* New York: Delacorte Press, 1981. 154–158.

Samuels, Stuart. "The Age of Conspiracy and Conformity: *The Invasion of the Body Snatchers* (1956)." *American History/American Film*, ed. John E. O'Connor and Martin A. Jackson. New York: Continuum, 1988. 203–217.

JFK (1991) (R)

Setting: Dallas, 1963; New Orleans and Washington, DC, 1963 to the early 1970s

Director: Oliver Stone

Screenplay: Oliver Stone and Zachary Sklar

Director of Photography: Robert Richardson

Cast: Kevin Costner (Jim Garrison), Gary Oldman (Lee Harvey Oswald), Sissy Spacek (Liz Garrison), Tommy Lee Jones (Clay Shaw), and Donald Sutherland (X).

Availability: Warner Bros. Home Video

Oliver Stone's stylishly paced political thriller is one of the great films of the 1990s. An expansion on the paranoid visions of John Frankenheimer's *Seven Days in May*, Stone's film proposes that President Kennedy was assassinated by the vast military industrial complex, a consortium of war generals and businessmen who didn't want to see the United States extricate itself from Viet Nam because billions of dollars were involved. According to Stone, Kennedy was about to remove a thousand advisors from Viet Nam and insist that the South Vietnamese learn to defend themselves (vol. 2, 1:39–17:53). This agenda was outlined in secret memorandum 263. Prior to this memorandum, some generals already felt that Kennedy was soft on the Cold War. He had solved the Cuban Missile Crisis of October 1962 by promising Khrushchev, in part, that the United States would never invade or try to change the political landscape of Cuba. Moreover, Kennedy was also earnest about seeking a nuclear test ban with the Soviets. His softening jeopardized economic prosperity. The conspiracy behind the Kennedy assassination comes to light for the crusading Jim Garrison in a park in Washington, D.C. There, the shadowy Mr. X tells him that "the organizing principle of any society is for war," and Kennedy threatened that principle by wanting to end the Cold War (vol. 2, 12:06). Garrison, a New Orleans district attorney, is a Jefferson Smith, Frank Capraesque man of integrity. And in the film's final thirty-seven minutes, Garrison outlines how Kennedy was assassinated in a 100-billion-dollar *coup d'état* by the Pentagon. Garrison's integrity, his soft-spoken eloquence, and his desire to seek the truth in order to live in an America free from fascism make the final moments of *JFK* great theater. He convinces us that there *was* a conspiracy to kill the president. However, whether or not that conspiracy involved the Pentagon is highly questionable. *JFK* suggests that Kennedy was a great man who was killed before he had a chance to fulfill his greatness. In reality, Kennedy's record on Civil Rights wasn't that strong (Lyndon Johnson's was much more impressive), and if Kennedy had intended to get out of Viet Nam, he had never told Johnson of those plans. And how was Johnson to know? In 1959/1960, Kennedy's anticommunist rhetoric was as strong as Richard Nixon's, and in 1963 he escalated troop commitment to Viet Nam. Even if his intentions were good and he had not been assassinated, could Kennedy have withstood the Cold War pressure, at the time, and still gotten the United States out of Viet Nam? Stone also takes liberties with Garrison's characterization. The person portrayed as a mythic everyman of integrity actually had mob ties, and his case against businessman Clay Shaw on conspiring to kill the president wasn't very well articulated or supported with factual evidence. Moreover, Stone received heavy criticism for freely mixing the famous Zapruder assassination footage with his own recreations. But despite these criticisms, *JFK* is a stunning work of art. Stone's use of MTV-type editing, flash forwards, flash backs, conflating of black and white photography with color, and suspenseful crosscutting makes this an enjoyable ride of the paranoid.

Further Reading

Benoit, William L. and Dawn M. Nill. "Oliver Stone's Defense of *JFK*." *Communication Quarterly* 46 (Spring 1998): 127–136.

Brustein, Robert. Review of *JFK*. *The New Republic* 206 (January 27, 1992): 26–28.

Keller, James R. "Oliver Stone's *JFK* and the 'Circulation of Social Energy' and 'Textuality of History.' " *Journal of Popular Film and Television* 21 (Summer 1993): 72–78.

Steel, Ronald. "Mr. Smith Goes to the Twilight Zone: Oliver Stone's Riveting Offense Against History." *The New Republic* 206 (February 3, 1992): 30–32.

Toplin, Robert Brent. "*JFK*: Fact, Fiction, and Supposition." *History by Hollywood: The Use and Abuse of the American Past.*" Urbana-Champaign: University of Illinois Press, 1996. 45–78.

Kiss Me Deadly (1955)

Setting: Los Angeles, 1955

Director: Robert Aldrich

Screenplay: A. I. Bezzerides

Director of Photography: Ernest Laszlo

Cast: Ralph Meeker (Mike Hammer), Albert Dekker (Dr. Soberin), Paul Stewart (Carl Evello), Maxine Cooper (Velda), Gaby Rodgers (Gabrielle/Lily Carver), Wesley Addy (Pat Murphy), Nick Dennis (Nick), and Fortunio Bonanova (Carmen Trivago)

Availability: MGM/UA Home Video

"Manhattan Project . . . Los Alamos . . . Trinity," Captain Murphy says to Private Eye Mike Hammer, and suddenly the antihero realizes that his quest is impossible to achieve, that the "great whatsit" he's pursuing is an atomic bomb (1:31:47). But in *Kiss Me Deadly*, based on the novel by Mickey Spillane, nobody can mention the bomb by name. Instead Murphy speaks in a code that a 1950s audience would immediately connect to atomic test sites and scientific experiments. Earlier in the film, Christina, too, speaks in guarded language. Wearing nothing but a trench coat, Christina stops Hammer on a lonely highway, passes judgment on his sexism and self-indulgence (6:38–8:40), and utters "remember me" without telling him what he's supposed to remember (8:37). After she's murdered, Hammer wants her killers, but more importantly he wants to find out why she was killed. His quest leads him to truck drivers, science fiction writers, the mafia, double-crossing women, and the quirky Dr. Soberin. Even the evil Soberin, in the throes of death, will not speak directly to his killer, Lily. Instead he hints at the atomic horror buried in the black box she covets. He speaks through allusions to Pandora, Lot, pillars of salt, and Cerebus barking with all his heads (1:41:11–1:41:52). Lily, curious and failing to understand Soberin's coded language, opens the box and unleashes a nuclear explosion. The paranoia of the atomic age permeates this film in a conspiracy of silence. Robert Aldrich's film is an audacious mix of genres: the hardboiled detective story conflated with overtures of science fiction horror and radiated monsters rising from the ocean. The opening credits, running like train tracks into a vanishing point, are listed in reverse order, suggesting a world of disorientation and a mood reminiscent of the introductory episodes in the Flash Gordon serials of the 1930s. Aldrich also uses dark noir shadows to create a world on the edge of apocalypse. In a spirit of misanthropy and distrust, Ralph Meeker's portrayal of Mike Hammer is troubling. The film's hero Hammer is a brute. He gets sadistic pleasure from knocking a knife-wielding punk down a set of stairs (25:37–27:42), breaking a collector's favorite Caruso record (58:13), and slamming a morgue attendant's hand in a drawer (1:26:42–1:27:21). Hammer even offends mobster Carl Evello when the detective's offer to put in with the mob appears too sincere (53:56–55:34). He breaks the rules of protocol. In *Kiss Me Deadly*'s waning minutes, Hammer desperately loses control of his universe, violently slapping and socking everyone on his mad dash to get the bomb and rescue Velda, his trustworthy secretary. Clearly Aldrich doesn't like Mickey Spillane's Mike Hammer. His treatment of Spillane's character verges on contempt, but because Aldrich and screenwriter A. I. Bezzerides created such a distorted, misanthropic world there's no one else for the audience to identify with. The police (1:29:40–1:36:52), the crime commission (12:19–13:50), gangster Evello, and even Christina judge Mike Hammer as a bad man. But in so doing they incriminate themselves and thus move the audience toward the antihero. In the end, Hammer rescues Velda from the exploding house, and as they tumble into the surf to look at the nuclear cloud perhaps we and they reach a kind of redemption.

Further Reading

Arnold, Edwin T. and Eugene L. Miller. "*Kiss Me Deadly.*" *The Films and Career of Robert Aldrich.* Knoxville: University of Tennessee Press, 1986. 36–45.
Silver, Alain. "*Kiss Me Deadly.* Evidence of a Style." *Film Noir Reader.* New York: Limelight Editions, 1996. 209–236.

Spillane, Mickey. *Kiss Me Deadly*. New York: New American Library, 1952.
Telotte, J. P. "Talk and Trouble: *Kiss Me Deadly*'s Apocalyptic Discourse." *Voices in the Dark: the Narrative Patterns of Film Noir*. Urbana-Champaign: University of Illinois Press, 1989. 198–215.
Truffaut, Francois. "Robert Aldrich: *Kiss Me Deadly*." *The Films in My Life*, translated by Leonard Mayhew. New York: Simon and Schuster, 1978. 93–94.

M*A*S*H (1970) (PG)

Setting: Seoul, South Korea, 1951–1952

Director: Robert Altman

Screenplay: Ring Lardner, Jr.

Director of Photography: Harold E. Stine

Cast: Donald Sutherland (Capt. Benjamin Franklin "Hawkeye" Pierce, MD), Elliott Gould (Capt. John Francis Xavier "Trapper John" McIntyre, MD), Tom Skerritt (Capt. Augustus Bedford "Duke" Forrest, MD), Sally Kellerman (Maj. Margaret "Hot Lips" Houlihan, RN), Robert Duvall (Maj. Frank Burns), Rene Auberjonois (Father John Patrick Mulcahy), Fred Williamson (Cap. Oliver Harmon "Spear-chucker" Jones, MD), and John Schuck (Capt. Walter Kosciusko "Painless Pole" Waldowski, DDS)

Availability: CBS/FOX Home Video

In 1962 Robert Altman directed eleven episodes of the television-action series *Combat!* The story lines, detailing the exploits of Sergeant Saunders and his platoon fighting across World War Two Europe, were hard-edged and gritty, but always supportive of the U.S. Army. By decade's end, Altman returned to depicting the military. But *M*A*S*H*, set in Cold War Korea, was filtered through the fractious lens of Viet Nam and 1960s protest. Thus, Altman's portrait of the doctors and nurses of a mobile army surgical hospital was much more rebellious and rich in antiestablishment ethos. Seen apart from Larry Gelbart's award-winning TV series, *M*A*S*H*, the movie, is less mawkishly sentimental and more angry, absurdist, and intolerant. Hawkeye Pierce's anger reveals itself in his disregard for army protocol. He steals a jeep for kicks (6:22). To relax from the harsh rigors of saving lives, he drinks dry martinis, plays golf on helicopter landing pads, and carouses with married women. His partners in misbehavior are Duke Forrest and the renowned chest surgeon, Trapper John. By 1970, the image of the company man was something to disparage. For the triumvirate of Pierce, Forrest, and McIntyre, Frank Burns is one such man. In order to escape the horrors around him, Burns engulfs himself in the Bible. Disapproving of Burns' moralizing, Hawkeye asks the zealous doctor if he was on this kick back home or did he "crack up over here" (16:03). The Bible allows Frank to escape responsibility for making his own decisions. A married man, he has an affair with Hot Lips claiming it is "God's will" (42:20). Frank's cohort in military efficiency and coldness is Margaret "Hot Lips" Houlihan. When she confronts Hawkeye over his informal clothing, he calls her "a regular army clown" (35:40). Dismayed, she wonders aloud how such a man could rise to the rank of doctor in the military. Father Mulcahy answers her: "He was drafted" (35:38). The latter comment reflects a kind of division in the film between regular and draftee army. In order to crush the overly officious types, Hawkeye, Trapper, and Duke humiliate Frank and Margaret. They place a microphone in her tent, broadcasting Frank and Margaret's love-making session to the entire compound (42:22–45:08). This leads to Frank's meltdown and eventual dismissal. Later, Margaret is further humiliated while showering (1:11:43–1:14:21). "This isn't a hospital. This is an insane asylum!" she shouts to Colonel Blake in the embarrassing aftermath. Ultimately, Altman's *M*A*S*H* captures the spirit of an era, but despite its antiestablishment, antiwar bent, the film has a disturbing dose of reactionary conservatism. Strong women like Margaret need to be broken. A talented black neurosurgeon and former San Francisco 49er is nicknamed "Spear-chucker." And in a troubling subplot, Dr. Painless, the camp dentist, is brought back into the bounds of sexual normalcy. Painless fears that he's a latent homosexual. In despair, he plans a ritualized suicide. Pierce "coop-erates" but tricks Painless with tranquilizing pills, tosses a sacrificial nurse into his bed, and the next day Painless is "cured." It is too bad, in its rebelliousness, that *M*A*S*H* couldn't also tolerate differences in sexual orientation.

Further Reading

Hooker, Richard. *M*A*S*H*. New York: Morrow, 1968.
Kael, Pauline. "Blessed Profanity." *The New Yorker* 45 (January 24, 1970): 74–75.
Kauffmann, Stanley. Review of *M*A*S*H*. *The New Republic* 162 (January 31, 1970): 30–31.

The Missiles of October (1974) (TV)

Setting: Washington, DC, Russia, and Cuba, October 16–28, 1962

Director: Anthony Page

Screenplay: Stanley R. Greenberg

Cameras: Jim Angel, Jim Balden, Ron Brooks, and Art LaCombe

Video: Hugo Di Lonardo

Cast: William Devane (President John F. Kennedy), Martin Sheen (Attorney General Robert F. Kennedy), Howard Da Silva (Soviet Premier Nikita Khrushchev), and Andrew Duggan (Gen. Maxwell Taylor)

Availability: MPI Home Video

This rather theatrical looking made-for-TV movie explores the thirteen days in October 1962 in which the world stood on the brink of nuclear war. On

October 16 President Kennedy learns that the Russians are setting up nuclear missiles in Cuba. The threat of attack has to be stopped, and the president has to find a way to send a strong signal, to "remove those missiles without war" (14:00). The diplomatic trick is for Kennedy to act forthrightly but to also allow Khrushchev enough time to give "an appropriate response." Some of Kennedy's cabinet, including General Taylor of the Air Force, fail to recognize the nuances of the situation and want to launch an all-out air strike on Cuba (6:34–9:04). The president's brother, the attorney general, eloquently dissuades most of the cabinet from such action. "This country is supposed to stand for something. It's supposed to be a symbol of morals and values and fair play" (34:16–34:48). An attack on a small Latin country will destroy America's credibility in the world. The cabinet agrees to a naval blockade that stops nuclear weapons flowing into Cuba. Khrushchev refuses to obey, and Kennedy, recognizing a kind of Cold War game in the works, constricts the blockade arc to 500 miles, giving Khrushchev more time for an appropriate response (1:25:50). The air command is placed on maximum alert, and as the world seems headed to nuclear disaster, the Russian ships stop at the arc line (1:34:50–1:35:34). Again more time is bought and Khrushchev works a deal to save his reputation. He insists that the "defensive" weapons will be removed from Cuba, if the United States promises to respect the Latin country's political differences and never to try a second Bay of Pigs (2:23:00–2:23:54). Kennedy agrees to respect Cuba's autonomy and both sides declare a victory. But the indirect dialogue between the countries, the inability to speak plainly, sadly reflects the distrust between political systems during the Cold War. One also ponders the absence of women in the making of these momentous diplomatic decisions. At one point Kennedy wishes he had assigned Barbara Tuckman's *The Guns of August* to all naval officers (1:16:40–1:17:18). Maybe if there were more Tuckmans in his cabinet, Kennedy wouldn't be guilty of subscribing to a gunslinger mentality. He claims that "this is between Khrushchev and myself" (1:16:34). But should he have played *High Noon* with nuclear weapons?

Further Reading

Abel, Elie. *The Missile Crisis.* Philadelphia: Lippincott, 1966.

Beschloss, Michael. *The Crisis Years: Kennedy and Khrushchev, 1960–63.* New York: HarperCollins, 1991.

Blight, James G. and David A. Welch. *On the Brink: Americans and Soviets Reexamine the Missile Crisis.* New York: Farrar, Straus & Giroux, 1989.

North by Northwest (1959)

Setting: New York; Chicago; Rapid City, South Dakota; Cornfields of Illinois, 1959

Director: Alfred Hitchcock

Screenplay: Ernest Lehman

Director of Photography: Robert Burks

Cast: Cary Grant (Roger O. Thornhill/Kaplan), Eva Marie Saint (Eve Kendall), Leo G. Carroll (the professor), and James Mason (Van Dam)

Availability: MGM/UA Home Video

"You lied to me," Roger Thornhill shouts to the professor late in this delightful Alfred Hitchcock thriller (1:50:43). His anger reflects a larger disenfranchisement with the politics and inconveniences of the Cold War. Roger is a slick Madison Avenue businessman who thinks that there are no lies in the world of advertising, only the "expedient exaggeration" (3:14). In the film's whirling opening, Roger briskly walks out of an elevator and through a foyer and tells his secretary to send a box of candy to a girlfriend and sign the card: "For your sweet tooth, baby, and all your sweet parts." Seconds later, he lies to a couple that he has "a very sick woman here," and takes their taxi (2:14–4:23). He's a man who can think quickly, but he's also a man without sincere convictions or a moral center. Moments later, he is mistaken for a government agent, Kaplan, and spun into a world of espionage (5:40). In order to survive in this world, he must take on the identity of a man who doesn't exist. This transformation becomes therapeutic in nature. Roger, to become a caring somebody, must embody a nobody first. Contrary to what he tells Eve on the train, that the "O" of his middle name stands for nothing (50:10–50:18), by the end of the film Roger will stand for something. Aside from the personal growth of Roger O. Thornhill, the world he is thrown into is a thorny one. The United States Intelligence Agency (a combined FBI/CIA surrogate), led by the professor, does nothing to help him. Roger is falsely accused of a United Nations murder, and the USIA, knowing of his innocence, fails to intervene on his behalf. They allow him to fend off the police and Van Dam's killers in order to protect Eve, their own double-agent working under Van Dam (38:25–41:21). This lack of intervention may cost Roger his life. Moreover, Eve, in order to protect herself from Van Dam's growing suspicions, sends Roger to the cornfields and almost certain death (1:06:01–1:15:47). After Roger's surprising return, the professor must intervene because Roger confronts Eve at an art gallery auction and Van Dam's suspicions are reaffirmed. The professor informs Roger of Eve's undercover work, and concocts a crazy scheme to regain Van Dam's confidence. But in order to gain Roger's confidence in the subterfuge, the professor lies to him and plays with his emotions. After a staged shooting, Roger expects Eve to be his. Instead, because she's so valuable to national security, the professor intends for Eve to become Van Dam's lover in order to collect more Cold War information. Roger, outraged, indignant, and in love with Eve, shouts, "I don't like the kind of games you play, professor" (1:50:50). Angry about the Cold War's intervention in his life, he suggests that maybe the professor and his ilk "might want to start learning how to lose a few Cold Wars" (1:51:10). He has changed from a slick man of "expedient exaggeration" to a compassionate human being who no longer believes in lies. Eventually, Roger disobeys orders and rescues Eve from Van Dam who, upon discovering her deception, has planned to dispose of her over water. Again, as in the dynamics of the cornfield sequence, the professor's decisions could have brought about death. The professor, in his commitment to country, is too self-assured and, ultimately, far too careless.

Further Reading

Bordwell, David and Kristin Thompson. *"North by Northwest." Film Art: An Introduction*. 4th Edition. New York: McGraw Hill, 1993. 370–375.

Naremore, James. "Cary Grant in *North by Northwest.*" *Acting in the Cinema*. Berkeley: University of California Press, 1988. 213–235.

Weiler, A. H. Review of *North by Northwest*. *New York Times* (August 7, 1959): L28.

Wilson, George M. "Alfred Hitchcock's *North by Northwest.*" *Narration in Light: Studies in Cinematic Point of View*. Baltimore: Johns Hopkins University Press, 1986. 62–81.

Wood, Robin. *"North by Northwest." Hitchcock's Films*. New York: A. S. Barnes, 1966. 96–105.

October Sky (1999) (PG)

Setting: Coalwood, West Virginia, 1957–1958

Director: Joe Johnston

Screenplay: Lewis Colick, Homer H. Hickam, Jr.

Director of Photography: Fred Murphy

Cast: Jake Gyllenhaal (Homer Hickham), Chris Cooper (John Hickham), Chris Owen (Quentin Wilson), Chad Lindberg (Sherman O'Dell), Laura Dern (Miss Freida Riley), Natalie Canderday (Elsie Hickham), and Chris Ellis (Principal Turner)

Availability: Universal Home Video

This is a wonderful film about an adolescent boy who dreams of leaving the grit and blue hue of a coal-mining town for a future outside of Coalwood, West Virginia. Following the fear and surprise surrounding the Russian launching of the Sputnik satellite in 1957, Homer, a child of the atomic age, aspires to become a rocket man. He is helped in his quest by his community. His high school teacher, the inspirational Freida Riley, encourages his aspirations. Homer also approaches a nerdy outsider, Quentin, in order to learn the physics of rocketry. A welder, a mechanic, and Homer's mother also rally around the boy. Even his two adversaries—the school principal, Mr. Turner, and Homer's coal-mining foreman father—support him in his moments of deepest need. The first moment occurs in a classroom retribution scene. After being accused of setting a forest fire with a scattered rocket, a disconsolate Homer quits school, smashes his rockets, and goes to work in the mines. As he heads underground, he glimpses, through the metal grates of the elevator, Sputnik sputtering across the sky (1:00:41–1:01:19). The contrast between dropping into the earth and striving to reach above it is elegaically haunting. The contrasting images imply a dream that Homer should not let go of. Eventually, he has an epiphany. He turns to the rocketry book Freida gave him as a birthday gift and using mathematical logic and physics discovers that his rocket could not have caused the fire. He, transformed almost into a nuclear scientist, explains his innocence before his class (1:15:24–1:16:32). Mr. Turner, impressed by Homer's reasoned defense, encourages the former student to reenroll so that he can attend the national science fair later that semester in Indiana. Homer does. At the fair, Homer's second moment of crisis arrives when someone steals his display rocket. His father helps, mobilizing people to create a second rocket. Homer's dad is jealous of his son's desire to leave the mining life behind. He is also envious of his son's admiration for the famed rocket scientist Werhner Von Braun. But through the urgings of his wife, he realizes that his son's dreams are separate from his own. Eventually, the two reconcile, as Homer tells Dad that he is his real hero, not Von Braun (1:33:54–1:34:43). Dad, who never showed much interest in Homer's rocketry, arrives at the final public display and pushes the launch button. An American success story, *October Sky* suggests that we need not fear any advances that the Russians have made in Cold War technology because America will always have a collected spirit to pull together, equal, and outdistance such challenges.

Further Reading

Bownman, James. Review of *October Sky*. *The American Spectator* 32 (April 1999): 68.

Denby, David. "Popular Mechanics: A Coal Town's Fifties Poetry, and a Bottled Romance." *The New Yorker* 75 (February 22, 1999): 184–186.

Hickham, Homer H. *Rocket Boys: A True Story*. London: Fourth Estate, 1998.

Leydon, Joe and Todd McCarthy. Review of *October Sky*. *Variety* 373 (February 8, 1999): 75.

Rayner, Richard. Review of *October Sky*. *Harper's Bazaar* 115 (March 1999): 308.

One, Two, Three (1961)

Setting: East and West Berlin, Germany, 1961

Director: Billy Wilder

Screenplay: Billy Wilder and I.A.L. Diamond

Director of Photography: Daniel L. Fapp

Cast: James Cagney (C. R. MacNamara), Horst Buchholz (Otto Ludwig Piffl), Pamela Tiffin (Scarlet Hazeltine), Arlene Francis (Phyllis MacNamara), Howard St. John (Hazeltine), and Hanns Lothar (Schlemmer)

Availability: MGM/UA Home Video

In 1933's *Hard to Handle*, James Cagney plays "Lefty" Merrill, a shady street-hustler who makes a bundle with the help of a grapefruit chiselry racket. By the Cold War Eisenhower and Kennedy eras, Cagney's streetwise shyster had transformed into a quasi-respectable Coca-Cola executive. The dramatic change in Cagney's persona from New Deal leftist to Cold War conservative reflected a larger cultural change in America's sociopolitical landscape. By 1961, Cagney and the country had moved from "lefty" to "righty." Cagney's MacNamara, situated in a divided Germany, is a Cold War colonialist. His wife, Phyllis, frequently calls him "mein fuhrer," satirizing his authority and revealing his baser desires to dominate others. Moreover, Mac is unconcerned about the space race or social justice. He is mainly concerned with profits and protecting the cushy life (flings with secretaries included) that he already has. He also plans to infiltrate the Russian beverage market (12:46). But Mac can't achieve his ultimate dream—a posh desk job in London. Instead, he has to play nursemaid to his boss's swinging daughter, the *tres* "marvy" Scarlet Hazeltine. Once Scarlet arrives in West Germany, Mac's life becomes a mess. Scarlet falls in love and marries an East German communist, Piffl. After Mac has cleverly schemed to have Piffl arrested on charges of treason, he has to negotiate for his release because he discovers that Scarlet is *schwenge*—pregnant. The film's frantic last half becomes a Cold War *Pygmalion*. Before Scarlet's dad arrives from the home office in Atlanta, Mac has to convert her card-carrying husband into a respectable capitalist. The scenes of the conversion create some of the film's greatest moments. In one rapid-fire exchange, Piffl denounces Mac, Coca-Cola, and the United States: "I spit on your money, I spit on Fort Knox. I spit on Wall Street." Mac quickly fires back, "Unsanitary little jerk, isn't he?" (36:08). Moreover, as Hazeltine's arrival approaches, Cagney revitalizes his dynamic 1930s persona. He struts, snaps his fingers, and chatters like a smoking Tommy gun as he orders others and selects Piffl's new, capitalist clothing (1:14:21–1:17:22). Overall, *One, Two, Three* is a delicious farce that works to alleviate Cold War fears. The film portrays the Russians as nonthreatening incompetents who secretly want to be Americans, and the Americans are avuncular colonialists, merely wanting to give the world a Coke.

Further Reading

Gill, Brendan. "Faster, Faster." *The New Yorker* 37 (January 6, 1962): 70–71.
Hartung, Philip T. Review of *One, Two, Three*. *Commonweal* 75 (January 19, 1962): 436.
Review of *One, Two, Three*. *Nation* 194 (January 6, 1962): 20.
Review of *One, Two, Three*. *Newsweek* 58 (December 25, 1961): 72–73.
Sklar, Robert. "Top of the World." *City Boys: Cagney, Bogart, Garfield*. Princeton, NJ: Princeton University Press, 1992. 252–277.

Pickup on South Street (1953)

Setting: New York City, 1953

Director: Samuel Fuller

Screenplay: Samuel Fuller and Dwight Taylor

Director of Photography: Joe Macdonald

Cast: Richard Widmark (Skip McCoy), Jean Peters (Candy), Richard Kiley (Joey), Thelma Ritter (Mo), Murvyn Vye (Capt. Dan Tiger), and Milburn Stone (Winoki)

Availability: CBS/FOX Home Video

In the early 1950s, Julius and Ethel Rosenberg were executed for passing atomic secrets to the Soviets. In 1953, within this context of traitorous spies and possible communist infiltration in America, movie maverick Samuel Fuller directed *Pickup on South Street*, a two-fisted piece of Cold War hysteria. Fuller suggests, as did Nyby and Hawks in *The Thing from Another World*, that we need to be ever vigilant against totalitarianism. Candy, one of the film's two heroes, is not vigilant. Initially, she is oblivious to the communist threat. She believes that her former boyfriend, Joey, is merely mixed up with stealing industrial secrets for a capitalist competitor (6:34–6:48). Fuller illustrates her ignorance during an opening subway ride (00:00–3:44). As she blithely carries government secrets, she is being watched by two police. She doesn't sense their stares, nor does she sense having her purse picked by Skip McCoy. Later, after meeting Skip and being labeled "a commie," Candy returns to Joey and his friends, incredulously tells them of Skip's accusations, and reaches an epiphany of the dangers around her (42:51–44:57). Fuller now photographs her in long shots and closeups, slinking about the room, as she discerns in a series of her own stares that Joey and his sweat-faced associates *are* communists. After learning this, she decides to cooperate with the police. But the right wing police, in Fuller's world, aren't to be trusted either. Too eager for their own success and zealous ends, they place Candy in danger. Earlier, the gung-ho police's patriotic appeals to Skip hadn't worked. Talking with a kink his mouth, Skip shrugged his shoulders and said, "You waving the flag at me?" (17:57–20:11). Candy, on the other hand, gives in to the police's McCarthyesque jingoism. After she recovers the microfilm from Skip, the police ask Candy to hand it back to Joey so that they can capture the entire communist ring. She complies, but when Candy won't give Joey Skip's address, Joey savagely beats and nearly kills her. Skip, a three-time criminal loser who lives in a waterfront shack, is too far outside of society ever to be manipulated by the authorities. Motivation must be personal, not patriotic. Initially, Skip was moved by greed. Upon stumbling upon the "grifted" microfilm, Skip had planned to make "a big score," demanding $50,000 for the secrets. But after Joey murders Skip's friend, Mo, and nearly kills Candy, the ambiguous loner is motivated by vengeance and love, and he eventually confronts and conquers the communists. Politically, Fuller, a fervent Democrat, hates totalitarianists of any ilk (right wing police and sweaty communist infiltrators alike). *Pickup on South Street* blurs the lines between the two, telling a story that is simultaneously reactionary and liberal, as Fuller places freedom's redemption in the hands of a streetwise tough.

Further Reading

Place, Janey. *"Pickup on South Street." Magill's Survey of Cinema*, Series II. Englewood Cliffs, NJ: Salem Press, 1981. 1892–1894.

Review of *Pickup on South Street. Newsweek* 41 (June 22, 1953): 91–92.

Tracey, Grant. "Film Noir and Samuel Fuller's Tabloid Cinema: Red (Action), White (Exposition), and Blue (Romance)." *Film Noir Reader 2*, ed. Alain Silver and James Ursini. New York: Limelight Edition, 1999. 158–75.

Pork Chop Hill (1959)

Setting: A reserve position near Pork Chop Hill, seventy miles from the Peace Conference at Panmunjom, Korea, 1953

Director: Lewis Milestone

Screenplay: James R. Webb

Director of Photography: Sam Leavitt

Cast: Gregory Peck (Lt. Joe Clemons), Woody Strode (Franklin), and George Shibata (Lieutenant O'Hashi)

Availability: MGM/UA Home Video

In 1930, Lewis Milestone directed the harrowing antiwar drama *All Quiet on the Western Front*. In 1959, Milestone again depicts the brutality and carnage of war, but this time the sacrifice of manhood is justified. When Lt. Joe Clemons briefs his men about their counterattack mission on Pork Chop Hill, they question its efficacy. Clemons defends the military's decision. In order for the peace conference at Panmunjom, Korea, to go smoothly, the army has to convince "the reds that we aren't about to give up any more chips" (10:02–10:29). Clemons ascribes to the domino theory popular in the 1950s and 1960s. If one country falls to communist rule, then the advancing spread of communism threatens adjacent countries. Despite these justifications for our "police action" in Korea, Milestone still captures the nightmare quality of war. He uses variable framing during the initial hill attack, and he laterally tracks from right to left as U.S. soldiers are shot and spun into concertina wire (22:00–23:32). As in the World War One films, generals are alienated from the GIs. After Clemons, who has experienced 40 percent casualties among his company of 135 men, takes two trenches and calls the top brass, they expect a lot more. A crosscut sequence reflects the disparity in outlooks. Clemons, photographed in medium closeup, appears exhausted, talking on a radio. By contrast, the faces of the generals are invisible. Milestone's crosscut only shows a bayonet stabbing into a miniature model of a hill, as an offscreen voice insists that they push on and get all the trenches. The disembodiment of voice and action reflects a larger indifference (37:00–37:42). But Clemons differs from the World War One fighting soldier in that he can take control of his environment. He is not dwarfed by it. During the battle, he makes several sound decisions, such as holding his third platoon back in reserve and bucking up his men's morale when they're disgruntled by losses due to friendly fire (47:00–48:46). He is also a moral man who soldiers want to follow. When a black soldier, Franklin, refuses to fight, Clemons motivates him. He tells Franklin that many other guys come from bad homes, and don't care about Korea, either. But there are only twenty-five men left: "That's a pretty exclusive club. You can still join up" (1:17:40–1:20:18). Franklin integrates into the platoon. The film's ending becomes a transcendent moment of American mythology. In a last stand, reminiscent of the Alamo, Clemons' meager forces are surrounded by red Chinese who dwarf their bunker. Holed up inside, Clemons' platoon desperately sandbags cracks and crevices, protecting themselves from enemy flamethrowers. The moment is extremely claustrophobic. Just when it appears that death is imminent, the heroism of the Alamo is converted into a western, as the cavalry in the form of U.S. reinforcements arrives. Strangely, Milestone and screenwriter Webb's conclusion achieves an additional transcendence, conflating America's interests in Korea with nineteenth-century Manifest Destiny.

Further Reading

Kauffmann, Stanley. Review of *Pork Chop Hill. The New Republic* 140 (June 15, 1959): 22.
McCarten, John. Review of *Pork Chop Hill. The New Yorker* 35 (June 13, 1959): 117–118.
Review of *Pork Chop Hill. Time* (June 8, 1959): 91.
Walsh, Moira. Review of *Pork Chop Hill. America* (May 30, 1959): 397.

DOUBLE BILL: GUILT, GANGSTERS, AND SOCIAL ORDER: THE 1950s

The Big Heat (1953) (W)

Setting: New York, 1953

Director: Fritz Lang

Screenplay: Sydney Boehm

Director of Photography: Charles Lang

Cast: Glenn Ford (Dave Bannion), Gloria Grahame (Debby Marsh), Jocelyn Brando (Katie Bannion), Alexander Scourby (Mike Lagana), Lee Marvin (Vince Stone), and Jeanette Nolan (Bertha Duncan)

Availability: Columbia Home Video

The Big Combo (1955) (W)

Setting: Los Angeles, 1955

Director: Joseph Lewis

Screenplay: Philip Yordan

Director of Photography: John Alton

Cast: Cornel Wilde (Leonard Diamond), Jean Wallace (Susan Lowell), Richard Conte (Mr. Brown), Helen Walker (Alicia), and Roy Gordon (Audobon)

Availability: TV Matters/Image Entertainment

In 1930s films, gangsters were victims of social circumstances. By the 1950s, the genre had turned mean, nasty, and conservative. Gangsters had become corporate kingpins, weaving their way into the social fabric. In the light of the Kefauver hearings on organized crime, *The Big Heat* and *The Big Combo* portray the syndicate as gripping the city. In the *Big Heat*, gangster Mike Lagana controls the police force and city commissioner Higgins. In *The Big Combo*, Mr. Brown runs the Bolemac corporation and threatens America's youth with his readily available guns and drugs. But what makes these films fascinating isn't the portrayal of the gangsters but the representations of the women trapped within the fallout of corporate gangsterism. In *The Big Heat* Sgt. Dave Bannion, in his quest to restore social order, destroys the lives of four women. First, he dismisses what Lucy Chapman has to say because she was having an affair with the murdered Tom Duncan. His inability to listen to and respect Lucy indirectly leads to her death. Second, his over-aggressiveness causes his wife's death. Following a lewd, threatening phone call directed at his wife, Bannion barges into Lagana's estate and insults the mobster: "You creeps have no compunction about phoning my home, talking to my wife like she was. . . ." George, Lagana's strong arm, intervenes and Bannion knocks him flying. "You want to pinch hit for your boy, Lagana?" Bannion challenges (27:22–31:17). Lagana, threatened, responds with two pinch hitters, Vince Stone and Larry Gordon. But the hit men inadvertently kill Mrs. Bannion instead of the sergeant (34:33–35:32). Bertha Duncan is also destroyed by Bannion's doppelganger, Debby. Bannion's investigation into Tom Duncan's suicide leads him to suspect Bertha. She had discovered Tom's suicide note, hid it from the police, and used it to blackmail Lagana. Bannion knows that if Bertha dies the note will go public, and then "the big heat falls." Enraged by her silence and criminal collusion, he nearly strangles her (1:11:31–1:12:34). Later he confesses to Debby that he wishes he had killed her (1:15:14–1:15:20). Debby does it for him. After killing Bertha, Debby tosses a gun on the floor and Lang overlaps the gun with an image of Bannion standing alone on a street, linking Debby's action with Bannion's desires (1:20:46). Finally, Debby's actions on Bannion's behalf also have harsh consequences. She is killed by Stone. Debby's death restores moral order, but Lang's final image is cautious and grim. Back at the precinct, Bannion picks up the phone: there's a hit and run over on South Street. As he exits, Lang shows the circularity of crime and its cost. A huge poster on the office wall reads: "Give Blood, Now." It seems that the women in this dark noir have given more than their fair share. *The Big Combo*, Allied Artists' seedy B-noir directed by Joseph Lewis and photographed exquisitely by John Alton, opens with Susan Lowell splashed in slanting shadows as she runs through tunnels along a boxing ring (2:02–3:28). She's chased by two hitmen, Fanty and Mingo, who are hired by her Napoleonic lover, Mr. Brown (Richard Conte), to keep an eye on her. Cornered, she emerges and stops running. The hitmen, in Alton's lighting scheme, remain shapeless in the dark. Susan, centered in an almost spot-effect, looks stark, pale and naked. Alton's lighting imbues Susan's nakedness with the noir concerns of guilt and obsession. She's not a femme fatale, but a character who needs to be controlled and punished for transgressions. Lieutenant Diamond will be the heroic figure, bringing her back to respectability. Susan's guilt develops across scenes. Following the elegiac opening, she meets Mr. Audobon, an old family friend, at a posh restaurant (9:08–10:02). Cryptically, Mr. Audobon comments, "Well you look so different, Susan. Why, I hardly recognized you." As Susan and Mr. Audobon stroll across the dance floor, Susan, unable to run from herself, collapses, and admits that she's taken some pills. Later, at the hospital, Susan's made to feel worse by Diamond who harangues her for trying to commit suicide: "You think you're the bright respectable girl you were four years ago? You're not" (15:59–18:46). Although Diamond discusses suicide, the real undercurrent of his accusations concern what Susan and Brown do in the dark. Following the murder of Diamond's on again off again girlfriend Rita, Susan leaves Brown and provides the detective with information on the mysterious Alicia, Brown's estranged wife. Moments later, Susan, in front of the police, Diamond, and Alicia, admits that she was Brown's girl (1:14:39–1:17:43). Alicia admonishes and judges Susan: "Then why did you stay four years, why did you start?" But the film's ending liberates Susan from Brown's control and sexual power. Brown, who is responsible for the deaths of Rita, McClure, Dreyer, Fante, and Mingo and lived by the ruthless motto "first is first and second is nobody," is reduced to a nobody. As Brown paces inside the airport hangar and wonders where that "stupid pilot" is, Susan coolly lights a cigarette. Brown knocks the lighter free with a left hand, and then slaps her with his right. "I want to be seen," she says, and Brown threatens, "Don't try that again." Moments later, a police car pulls up, and Brown looks into the dark fog and retreats, sliding into a corrugated tin wall. Susan adjusts the car searchlight and shines it on Brown, blinding him. He can no longer order the universe, nor possess her. Moments later the hapless Brown is seized by the police, and Diamond and Susan, in backlit silhouette, exit the hangar, finding love in the dark recesses of film noir.

Further Reading

Clarens, Carlos (with Foster Hirsch). "The Syndicate." *Crime Movies: An Illustrated History of the Gangster Genre from D. W. Griffith to Pulp Fiction.* New York: De Capo Press, 1997. 234–258.

Crowther, Bosley. Review of *The Big Heat. New York Times* (October 15, 1953): 43.

Eisner, Lotte. *"The Big Heat." Fritz Lang.* London, 1977.

McArthur, Colin. *The Big Heat.* London: BFI Publishing, 1992.

Shadoian, Jack. "Focus on Feeling: 'Seeing' Through the Fifties." *Dreams and Dead Ends: The American Gangster/Crime Film.* Boston: MIT Press, 1977. 209–220.

DOUBLE BILL: NUCLEAR MELTDOWN AND DEATH BY TECHNOLOGY

The China Syndrome (1979) (PG) (W)

Setting: Los Angeles and Southern California, 1979

Director: James Bridges

Screenplay: Mike Gray, T. S. Cook, and James Bridges

Director of Photography: James Crabe

Cast: Jane Fonda (Kimberly Wells), Jack Lemmon (Jack Godell), and Michael Douglas (Richard Adams)

Availability: Columbia Tri-Star Home Video

Meltdown at Three Mile Island (1999) (Doc.)

Setting: Harrisburg, Pennsylvania, March 28, 1979–April 1, 1979

Director: Chana Gazit

Writer: Chana Gazit

Narrator: Liev Schreiber

Editor: David Steward

Availability: PBS Home Video

In the 1950s a barrel of oil cost around $3.00. By the 1970s, OPEC had upped the cost to $30. In response to this price hike utility companies sought alternative forms of energy, and nuclear power plants dotted the country. Unfortunately, the safety of nuclear energy could not be fully assured. *China Syndrome* asks what might happen if one of these reactors melted down. While doing a fluffy news story on the Ventana Power Plant for KXLA news, Kimberly Wells and her leftist camera man, Richard Adams, stumble across just such a crisis. A shudder vibrates the plant, and then they observe pandemonium unleashed in the control room. A *Watergate*-type coverup follows as the plant public relations department informs the media that it was only a minor accident and everything is under control. But Richard covertly photographs the incident, and then later projects his footage for two experts: a university physics professor and a nuclear engineer. They "might have come close to exposing the core," says the engineer as they huddle in a closet looking at the clandestine film (1:01:27). The physics professor explains the "China Syndrome": the fuel in the reactor heats up, melts the core, and spills into the earth. From there it eventually hits the water table and sends a radioactive cloud into the atmosphere. Such an event, the professor argues, could "render an area the size of Pennsylvania uninhabitable . . . not to forget the cancer that shows up later" (1:01:59). Kimberly, who has always wanted to cover real, hard news instead of the insipid features on singing telegrams or dancing whales that she is pigeonholed to report, confronts the plant's chief engineer Jack Godell with what she now knows. Jack, himself embroiled in a coverup conspiracy, decides to expose the truth: Kim and Richard had observed a near China Syndrome situation, and the plant is not safe. Jack has discovered that a contractor didn't fully check the wells, and that the pump valves now can't take the strain. At full power, one valve might break and the plant would explode. Jack finds his life is in danger for bucking the nuclear plant hierarchy. Eventually, because his warnings aren't heeded, Jack seizes control of the plant at gunpoint. His actions meet with tragic consequences, but perhaps his garbled message reaches television viewers. The film also has a strong feminist undercurrent. Kimberly's reporting of Jack's story proves that she *can* do hard news. But the film's greatest coup seems to lie in its presaging of world events. In a strange case of life imitating art, the fictive post-Watergate paranoia of *China Syndrome* became very real twelve days after the film's release when a real meltdown occurred in Harrisburg, Pennsylvania. For five days in March and early April 1979, the *Meltdown at Three Mile Island* gripped North America. This PBS documentary explores the eerie origins of the terror and the decisions made during the crisis. As in *China Syndrome* a flash of mechanical errors and misreadings led to a series of wrong choices made by a group of control room engineers (2:55–4:27). At first the plant's public relations department, led by Jack Irvine, played down the seriousness of the drama unfolding, assuring the public that all "injection systems are [now] functioning properly" (11:43). But the situation was serious in part because the Nuclear Regulatory Commission had been largely a promotional agency and hadn't assured nuclear plant safety. The valve that had failed at Three Mile Island had failed at eleven other plants. But the designer was never issued a warning, nor was anything ever done about the danger (19: 54). Thus surrounded by a faulty government agency and the plant's own double-talking PR reps, Governor Dick Thornbourgh felt there was no one he could trust. Two days later Thornbourgh's troubles were compounded. Accident rumors spread that radioactive gas had escaped from the plant and for forty-five minutes evacuation was recommended (24:07). Thornbourgh issued a limited evacuation order for pregnant women and preschool children. But more than a "limited" few left: 140,000 citizens evacuated in panic (30:21–31:21). Thornbourgh needed the help of a disinterested outsider, and President Carter ushered in smooth-talking southerner Harold Denton. But just as Denton was reassuring the citizenry of the safety of Harrisburg, engineer Roger Mattson contended that there was a hydrogen bubble above the heat core and the plant and the city could explode (35: 45–36:14). Another engineer, Victor Stello, disagreed with Mattson's findings and said that the plant was safe (40:12). Thornbourgh had to decide who to listen to and whether or not to evacuate half a million people. While deciding, President Carter, himself a nuclear engineer, arrived on the fifth day. In a grand display of executive strength, the president toured the plant and sent a strong message of security to Harrisburg's people (45:22–47:00). Later that day, Stello showed the errors in Mattson's calculations. This harrowing episode from the "American Experience" illustrates how close we came to an American disaster on a global scale. But more importantly, the meltdown at Three Mile Island and the fictive power of *China Syndrome* issued a strong warning: before we embrace new technology we must be assured of its safety.

Further Reading

Canby, Vincent. Review of *China Syndrome*. *New York Times* (March 16, 1979): C16.
Hatch, Robert. Review of *China Syndrome*. *The Nation* 228 (March 31, 1979): 347–349.
Jameson, Richard T. "China Is Near." *Film Comment* 15 (May 1979): 28–31.
McMullen, Wayne J. "*The China Syndrome*: Corruption to the Core." *Literature/Film Quarterly* 23.1 (1995): 55–62.

DOUBLE BILL: NUCLEAR WAR, ATOMIC ANNIHILATION

Dr. Strangelove (1964)

Setting: Washington, DC, and Russia, 1964
Director: Stanley Kubrick
Screenplay: Stanley Kubrick, Terry Southern, and Peter George

Director of Photography: Gilbert Taylor

Cast: Peter Sellers (Group Captain Lionel Mandrake, President Merkin Muffley, and Dr. Strangelove), George C. Scott (Gen. "Buck" Turgidson), and Sterling Hayden (Gen. Jack D. Ripper).

Availability: Columbia Home Video

Fail Safe (1964)

Setting: Washington, DC; Omaha; New York; Russia, 1964

Director: Sidney Lumet

Screenplay: Walter Bernstein

Director of Photography: Gerald Herschfeld

Cast: Henry Fonda (the president), Dan O'Herlihy (General Black), and Walter Matthau (Groeteschele)

Availability: Columbia Home Video

In 1964, just months removed from the Cuban Missile Crisis, *Fail Safe* and *Dr. Strangelove* explored the threat of nuclear annihilation. In the dramatic *Fail Safe*, a mechanical control room failure puts two superpowers on the nuclear precipice. The film explores how dangerously dependent we've become on technology. In the darkly comic *Dr. Strangelove*, an insane general issues the "Go Code" for an all-out nuclear attack on Russia. Here the error isn't mechanical, but human. We have become too dependent on placing power in the hands of the few. Both films are well made, incredibly paced, and suspenseful. In *Fail Safe*, Henry Fonda plays a soft-spoken president who acts responsibly in the face of terror. A mechanical failure, a faulty indicator that blipped during an alert, sends a go signal from Omaha to a group of Vindicator jets who have orders to bomb Moscow (36:08–39:27). One of the jets, wounded by Russian antiaircraft fire, can't be recalled. The president, to avoid nuclear war, phones the Russian Premier and assures him that "all I can tell you, it's an accident . . . it's not part of a general attack. . . . We take full responsibility" (59:45–1:04:32). The president assures the enemy of his sincerity by helping the Russian military locate and shoot down six of the attack wing jets. But one slips through and Moscow is devastated. In anticipation of this event, the president had made an Old Testament promise. He tells the Russians that if Moscow is bombed, he will in turn order a twenty-megaton bomb dropped on New York City. The latter plan upsets some of the president's cabinet, including Professor Groeteschele, a cold-hearted pragmatist. The professor, following the "Go" signal, suggests that we launch an all-out nuclear attack and obliterate the Russians. "Those who can survive are the only ones worth surviving," he reasons (1:16:24), converting himself into one of the very enemies the United States defeated in World War Two. Fortunately, his insane views aren't supported by the noble General Black, the president, or the majority of his staff. But because the east and west so fervently distrust each other, the film reasons that New York must be destroyed to save the world. The plot to *Dr. Strangelove* is strikingly similar to *Fail Safe*. A group of B-52s are issued a "go" code, several are recalled, some are shot down, but one snakes through Russian air space and drops an atomic bomb. But here, there are no sacrificial New Yorks. Order, in this bleak comedy, can't be restored. Instead, the entire planet is devastated as the American attack triggers a Russian doomsday device that sets off a series of nuclear blasts. The metaphorical orgasms that end the film are fitting. *Dr. Strangelove*'s humor, from the openly sexualized refueling of a B-52 (00:00–3:16), reveals a dysfunctional energy of sexual destruction. The crazed General Ripper (named, no doubt, after the sexual serial killer) orders the "go" code because of his own thwarted sex life. Shot in distorted low angle closeups and chomping a big, phallic cigar, Ripper expounds on his belief that fluoridation is a "commie plot" denying us our "purity of essence." Thus because he feels sapped of his essence after making love, all communists must be destroyed (56:50–57:06). But the real joy in this film is watching Peter Sellers play three different characters: the sex-obsessed Dr. Strangelove; the proper British officer, Mandrake, who cracks the recall code; and President Merkin Muffley, a sort of ineffectual Adlai Stevenson. Muffley must also deal with a pragmatist in his cabinet: the gung-ho General Buck Turgidson, who had earlier conflated sex with technology, shouting "blast off" while making love (14:30). Turgidson is a fundamentalist Christian figure who regards all communists as devils. Jazzed with a war load, Turgidson wants to annihilate the Russians since we've caught them "with their pants down" (32:21–34:15). Muffley, fed up with Turgidson's insane logic, refuses to be another Adolf Hitler. In a comic tour de force, Muffley/Sellers contacts Russian Premier Dmitry Kissoff to keep him apprised of the situation (39:40–44:46). The conversation, a comic inversion of similar scenes in *Fail Safe*, shows two men squabbling like boys. Moreover, the president's good-bye extends the arms race to an emotions race: "Don't say that you're more sorry than I am." In *Dr. Strangelove* crucial decisions are made by immature, oversexed men-children. Their irresponsibility leaves nothing left to preserve.

Further Reading

Burgess, Jackson. "The Anti-Militarism of Stanley Kubrick." *Film Quarterly* 18 (Fall 1964): 4–11.

Suid, Lawrence. "The Pentagon and Hollywood: *Dr. Strangelove or How I Learned to Stop Worrying and Love the Bomb* (1964)." *American History/American Film: Interpreting the Hollywood Image*, ed. John E. O'Connor and Martin A. Jackson. New York: Continuum, 1988. 219–235.

Thomas, Tony. *"Fail Safe." The Films of Henry Fonda*. Secaucus, NJ: Citadel Press, 1983. 177–179.

Wollscheidt, Michael G. *"Fail Safe." Nuclear War Films*, ed. Jack G. Shaheen. Carbondale: Southern Illinois University Press, 1978. 68–75.

DOUBLE BILL: "WE MUST GUARD AGAINST . . . THE MILITARY INDUSTRIAL COMPLEX"

The Manchurian Candidate (1962)

Setting: Korea, Manchuria, New York, Washington, DC, East Coast, 1952

Director: John Frankenheimer

Screenplay: George Axelrod

Director of Photography: Lionel Lindon

Cast: Frank Sinatra (Lt. Bennett Marco), Laurence Harvey (Sgt. Raymond Shaw), Angela Lansbury (Mrs. Iselin), and James Gregory (Senator John Iselin)

Availability: MGM/UA Home Video

Seven Days in May (1964)

Setting: Washington, DC, and El Paso, Texas, 1964

Director: John Frankenheimer

Screenplay: Rod Serling

Director of Photography: Ellsworth Fredericks

Cast: Burt Lancaster (Gen. James Mattoon Scott), Kirk Douglas (Col. Martin "Jiggs" Casey), and Frederic March (President Jordan Lyman)

Availability: MGM/UA Home Video

In 1960 departing President Dwight David Eisenhower in his address to the nation said that "we must guard against the acquisition of uncorrected influence whether sought or unsought of the military industrial complex." In a sixteen-month period between 1962 and 1964, director John Frankenheimer realized Eisenhower's anxieties of a threat to national security in two chilling paranoid thrillers. In *Seven Days in May*, Frankenheimer explored a possible coup by the Joint Chiefs of Staff. President Lyman (an Adlai Stevenson–type figure) has just signed a nuclear ban treaty with Russia. His inner circle disapproves of the treaty. The public, fearful of a Russian sneak attack, rate the president's approval at a lowly 29 percent. Colonel Jiggs also disapproves of the treaty, but he believes in the constitution (42:15). Gen. Matoon Scott, on the other hand, is not content with the electoral process. A supposed superpatriot, Scott organizes a secret coup. He has a group of soldiers, Ecom-Con, practicing military maneuvers in El Paso, Texas, and during an "alert" he plans to kidnap the president, seize telecommunications, and take over the country. Jiggs stumbles across the plan, a supposed Preakness betting pool, and approaches the president about his suspicions (33:52–43:56). The president acts quickly, refusing to attend the alert, and finds enough evidence to ask Scott and his group to resign. The president succeeds in quelling the coup, but he doesn't completely blame the Joint Chiefs for their threat to national security. "The real enemy is an age, a nuclear age that happens to kill man's faith and his ability to influence what happens to him," he reasons (1:35:25). Out of fear, people look for a strutting egoist like Scott. *Seven Days in May* warns us to be wary of the vast industrial complex, and presages what might happen should the military abuse the people's trust. *Manchurian Candidate*, made one year earlier, suggests that Senator Joseph McCarthy, a notorious "red baiter" and destroyer of many leftists' reputations, was actually a cog in a larger communist conspiracy bent on destroying America. The film is set against the backdrop of the Korean War. A crack group of American commandos are captured by the Chinese, drugged, and taken into Manchuria where they are brainwashed. One of their members, Sgt. Raymond Shaw, is converted into a superkiller. His killings are triggered by playing solitaire. Back in the United States, Lieutenant Marco, the leader of Shaw's platoon, has a series of nightmares in which he recalls the brainwashing session before a combined group of Chinese/Russian communists (11:11–17:16). He becomes suspicious of Shaw's Congressional Medal of Honor, his own testimony on Shaw's behalf, and he looks into the conspiracy. What he finds is truly disturbing. Shaw is being made into a killing machine so that he can assassinate a presidential hopeful, so vice presidential nominee, Senator Johnny Iselin, a red baiter modeled on Senator McCarthy, can seize the party nomination. Behind Iselin is his cold, brutal wife played with delicious deadliness by Angela Lansbury. She acts like an ultraconservative but is actually an agent of the Kremlin. Marco, as played by Frank Sinatra, is a joy to behold. Sinatra is at the peak of his Rat Pack hipster popularity, coolly ad-libbing while deprogramming Shaw during a game of solitaire: "So the red queen is our baby. . . . Listen, this is Marco talking. . . . 52 red queens are telling you it's over. . . . We're busting up the joint, we're taking out all the wires. . . . You don't work anymore. . . . Sorry, buster, the ball game is over" (1:47:21–1:48:21). But despite Marco/Sinatra's charisma, he is powerless to stop Shaw. Marco entrusts Shaw to find out what the grand plan is, but Raymond decides to act alone after discovering that his mother is behind it all. He kills her, Iselin, and himself. And thus, like Frankenheimer's *Seven Days in May* in which the president fires his Joint Chiefs of Staff without detailing his reasons to the public, this film simultaneously reveals and conceals a conspiracy. Film viewers know what almost happened, but the public in the filmic world has no idea how close the presidency came to being seized by a red menace. Thus, despite the poetic justice of these two films, we are left painfully pondering what covert operations, coverups, and near injustices and disasters we are never informed about.

Further Reading

Bernstein, Fred. "Director John Frankenheimer's *The Manchurian Candidate* Plays to a Full House after 26 Years." *People Weekly* 29 (May 16, 1988): 129–131.

Biskind, Peter. Review of *The Manchurian Candidate*. *The Nation* 246 (May 14, 1988): 691–692.

Carruthers, Susan L. "*The Manchurian Candidate* (1962) and the Cold War Brainwashing Scare." *Historical Journal of Film, Radio and Television* 18 (March 1998): 75–94.

Condon, Richard. *Manchurian Candidate*. New York: New American Library, 1959.

Crowther, Bosley. Review of *Seven Days in May*. *New York Times* (February 20, 1964): 22.

DOUBLE BILL: RACE TO THE MOON

The Right Stuff (1983) (PG)

Setting: Edwards Air Force Base; Cape Canaveral, Florida; Houston, Texas; Washington, DC; Australia, 1947–1963

Director: Philip Kaufman

Screenplay: Philip Kaufman

Director of Photography: Caleb Deschanel

Cast: Sam Shepard (Chuck Yeager), Scott Glenn (Alan Shepard), Ed Harris (John Glenn), Dennis Quaid (Gordon Cooper), Fred Ward (Gus Grissom), and Mary Jo Deschanel (Annie Glenn)

Availability: Warner Bros. Home Video

Apollo 13 (1995) (PG)

Setting: Cape Canaveral, Florida; Houston, Texas; outer space, 1970

Director: Ron Howard

Screenplay: William Broyles, Jr., and Al Reinert

Director of Photography: Dean Cundey

Cast: Tom Hanks (Jim Lovell), Bill Paxton (Fred Haise), Kevin Bacon (Jack Swigert), Gary Sinise (Ken Mattingly), and Ed Harris (Gene Kranz)

Availability: Universal Home Video

In the early 1960s President John F. Kennedy vowed to set a man on the moon by the end of the decade. In 1957, the Russians were the first to orbit a satellite around the earth. In early 1961, they set another first, rocketing the first man, Yuri Gagarin, into space. America couldn't lose the battle of space for it was regarded as a final frontier, a location to set up a weapons defense, or offense, and, in the paranoia of the times, set up a big stick of foreign policy. *The Right Stuff*, based on the book by Tom Wolfe, portrays the early days of the space program from the Edwards Air Force Base test pilots breaking the speed of sound to the original seven astronauts of the Mercury Program conquering space and orbiting the earth. Chuck Yeager was one of the top test pilots. Yeager is mythically portrayed as a combination cowboy and Icarus attempting to conquer the skies. When we first see his resolute figure, he rides past the X-1 experimental jet on a horse (vol. 1, 4:40–6:00). Later, on October 14, 1947, as he readies to break the sound barrier, one of his colleagues radios, "Put the spurs to her, Chuck" (vol. 1, 18:55–23:29). He's a space cowboy, and for years after setting the mark, Yeager becomes a gunslinger attempting to hold onto his records. Whenever a young pilot bests him, Yeager goes back up into the skies and sets a new record such as hitting Mach 2.5 on December 12, 1953 (vol. 1, 39:00–43:03). By the end of *The Right Stuff*, Yeager attempts to conquer a Russian altitude record of 114,000 feet. He reaches 104,000 when his jet stalls and he goes into an Icarus-like spin. He survives, but perhaps, ultimately, our technology can't conquer the skies (vol. 2, 1:24:55–1:34:52). The retelling of the Mercury Program from Gus Grissom's losing of a spacecraft in the ocean (vol. 2, 31:20–35:43) to John Glenn's famous orbital flight (vol. 2, 58:16–1:15:35) is a colorful reenactment of history. The highlights include the "Lab Rats" section in which the future astronauts are put through a battery of dehumanizing tests to see if they have the right stuff (vol. 1, 57:38–1:16:41). Ed Harris' performance as John Glenn is also a highlight. Glenn, at first, appears to be a no-nonsense, gung-ho type of American patriot set on besting the Russians in the space race (vol. 1, 1:21:16). But Harris humanizes Glenn by showing a tender, quiet side in scenes with his wife Annie, who has a stuttering handicap (vol. 1, 1:25:48–1:28:08). Later Glenn reassures his self-conscious wife that it's okay to refuse the media access to their home (vol. 2, 54:08–54:51). His respect for her integrity and emotions is one of the film's more quiet moments. Glenn is also a leader among the astronauts, insisting that they conduct themselves as role models for the nation (vol. 2, 5:40–5:53). He also organizes a mini-coup against the rocket scientists, demanding that the astronauts be allowed to "pilot" the Mercury spacecraft and to have a window to see out of it (vol. 2, 8:54–13:03). *Apollo 13*, set in 1970, is a triumph of a collective human will against the dangers of technology and nature. The film recreates a seven-day odyssey in which Jim Lovell and his crew (Fred Haise and Jack Swigert) experience a serious malfunction in space, have to abort their mission to the moon, and struggle to find some way to make it back to earth. The film is packed with tension as Lovell and his crew overcome obstacle after obstacle. First, after a serious bang and shimmy, they shut down the command module and move to the lunar module in order to preserve energy (57:20–1:07:30). Second, the scientists at Houston have to create a makeshift carbon dioxide filter so that the men in the lunar module don't asphyxiate themselves (1:28:07–1:33:28). Third, Ken Mattingly, the original navigator of the flight who was replaced, has to figure out a way, in the lunar module simulator, for the crew to reenter the earth's atmosphere. They'll need to reboot the command module from the lem, but they'll have to do it without shorting the entire system and going over twenty amps of power. Mattingly, through a series of steps in the simulator solves the riddle and it works in space (1:48:17–1:56:06). Fourth, and most miraculous of all, the command module has to reenter the earth's atmosphere at a precise angle or else risk heating up and disintegrating or bouncing back into space like a skipping stone. Lovell and his crew manually place the Apollo in the correct reentry path and survive. *Apollo 13* explores a period in history when following the moon shot of Apollo 11 the public was no longer interested in the space program, and proposed government cutbacks threatened NASA's existence. But the dignity displayed by Jim Lovell ("Gentleman, it's been a privilege flying with you" [2:04:48]) and his crew in the face of such horror transcended the public's disinterest and made this flight NASA's finest hour.

Further Reading

Asahina, Robert. Review of *The Right Stuff*. *The New Leader* 66 (November 28, 1983): 19–20.

Kroll, Jack. Review of *Apollo 13*. *Newsweek* 126 (July 3, 1995): 55.

Lovell, Jim and Jeffrey Kluger. *Lost Moon: The Perilous Voyage of Apollo 13*. Boston: Houghton-Mifflin, 1994.

Williams, Lena. "In Space, No Room for Fear." *New York Times* (July 19, 1995): C1, C4.

Wolfe, Tom. *The Right Stuff*. New York: Farrar, Straus & Giroux, 1979.

DOUBLE BILL: THE KOREAN WAR: OVER THERE AND HERE

The Steel Helmet (1951)

Setting: Korea, 1951

Director: Samuel Fuller

Screenplay: Samuel Fuller

Director of Photography: Ernest Miller

Cast: Gene Evans (Sergeant Zack), Steve Brodie (Lieutenant Driscoll), James Edwards (Corporal Thompson), Richard Loo (Sergeant Tanaka), William Chun (Short Round), and Harold Fong (the Red)

Availability: Burbank Home Video

I Want You (1951)

Setting: small town USA, summer 1950

Director: Mark Robson

Screenplay: Irwin Shaw

Director of Photography: Harry Strandling

Cast: Dana Andrews (Martin Greer), Dorothy McGuire (Nancy Greer), and Farley Granger (Jack Greer)

Availability: None

Samuel Fuller's *The Steel Helmet* is a gritty, uncompromising look at guerilla warfare. Early in the film, Sergeant Zack, sensing trouble, hits the dirt and returns fire, killing two supposedly innocent women stopping by a well. After tearing off their clothes he barks to his orphaned Korean sidekick, Short Round, "These red guerrillas dress like women, huh?" (8:28–9:39). Later after checking the belongings of a group of Korean peasants, Zack offers some advice to the hapless Lieutenant Driscoll: "He's a South Korean when he's running with ya. And he's a North Korean when he's running after ya" (28:18). His words suggest the same confusions American GIs experienced fifteen to twenty years later in Viet Nam. Along with articulating the dangers of guerilla fighting, and the difficulties in distinguishing between friends and foes, Zack also embodies the principle of survival. He seeks to keep his emotions in check. He labels the young boy "Short Round" after a bullet that doesn't go all the way because he doesn't want the kid "to go all the way" with him (6:00–8:19). Later when Short Round is killed by sniper fire, Sergeant Zack loses control, shoots a high-ranking prisoner of war, and irrationally shouts at the dying man, "If you die, I'll kill you" (1:09:04–1:10:13). After losing his calculated distance, Sergeant Zack is ineffective as a soldier and emotionally disoriented during the film's crucial battle scene. In *The Steel Helmet*, Fuller, a combat veteran and recipient of the Bronze and Silver Star, authentically captures the irrational chaos of war. He also makes some strong social statements on the racism blacks experienced back home (56:53–58:04) and that the Niseis suffered in internment camps during World War Two (59:13–1:01:27). *I Want You*, a cozy homefront film, questions America's complacency after World War Two. Martin Greer, a war veteran, runs a successful contracting business in a small town, but he feels that in a time of economic prosperity, "we all think we're on a holiday, but somebody, somewhere, knows the holiday is over" (39:41). That somebody is communism. Later, true to his convictions, Martin decides to re-up to help build runways and bridges for the war effort. He explains his decision to wife, Nancy: What is he going to tell his children when they ask "what were you doing, Daddy, when the world was shaking?" (1:28:28). Kid brother Jack Greer is also wanted by his country, but he lacks the responsibility of his older brother. Somewhat callow and embittered over being drafted, he expresses a perverse wish that everybody would drop some atomic bombs and get it all over with (49:03–50:58). Nancy is appalled that Jack wouldn't mind seeing the United States bombed with retaliation, and she orders him from her house. Jack changes his mind, goes to boot camp, and later apologizes to Nancy (1:18:09–1:18:28). Nancy embodies the strong, supportive homefront woman, and when she acknowledges Martin's need to help police the world, she sacrifices her happiness for a greater good. In the end, *I Want You* promotes the draft and a view of defending the world against the falling dominoes of communism. America must be in a state of perpetual readiness.

Further Reading

Crowther, Bosley. Review of *I Want You*. *New York Times* (December 24, 1951): 9.

Hatch, Robert. Review of *I Want You*. *New Republic* 125 (December 31, 1951): 22.

———. Review of *The Steel Helmet*. *New Republic* 124 (February 12, 1951): 22–23.

Server, Lee. *Film Is a Battleground*. Greensboro, NC: McFarland, 1994.

DOUBLE BILL: SCIENCE, THE COLD WAR MILITARY, AND CLOSED AND OPEN COMMUNITIES

The Thing from Another World (1951)

Setting: Anchorage, Alaska, 1951

Director: Christian Nyby

Screenplay: Charles Lederer

Director of Photography: Russell Harlan

Cast: Kenneth Tobey (Captain Hendry), Margaret Sheridan (Nikki), Robert Cornthwaite (Dr. Carrington), Douglas Spencer (Scotty), Dewey Martin (Crew Chief), James Arness (the Thing)

Availability: RKO Home Video

The Day the Earth Stood Still (1951)

Setting: Washington, DC, 1951

Director: Robert Wise

Screenplay: Edmund H. North

Director of Photography: Leo Tover

Cast: Michael Rennie (Klaatu), Patricia Neal (Helen Benson), Billy Gray (Bobby Benson), and Sam Jaffee (Dr. Barnhardt)

Availability: CBS/FOX Home Video

The Thing from Another World and *The Day the Earth Stood Still*, released six months apart in 1951, reflect opposing views on the Cold War. In *The Thing*, the military are the heroes protecting us from an invasion from the skies. The space monster, a dehumanized "supercarrot" bent on our destruction, allegorically represents 1950s fears of the Soviet Union. The monster is a type of vampire, draining our blood, and replacing us with a group of spore, pod-like offshoots of his own unthinking brutality. Science, in this battle for the rights of the individual, can't be trusted. The head scientist of the Anchorage team, Dr. Carrington, illogically believes that the monster is our superior because he exists outside of emotion (46:21–47:57). Against the orders of Captain Hendry, Carrington provides the creature with blood and raises its spores in a nursery. This nearly allows the monster to spread, like communism, and take over everyone. Fortunately, Captain Hendry and his men are up to the task of protecting democracy. Director Christian Nyby, who had worked as an editor under Howard Hawks, captures the Hawksian collective and the spirit of team unity. Captain Hendry's team have fun with each other and are more than "good enough" to destroy the monster. Nyby showcases their fighting spirit in a key scene in which Hendry's men, under the suggestion of Nikki, decide to set the monster afire (1:07:40–1:11:20). The scene, shot in a series of long takes, shows the men readying, grabbing gas cans, and checking the Geiger counter. When Nyby cuts away to isolated shots, he always ends the sequence with the singled-out figure rejoining the crowded frame of men. The teamwork theme is further reinforced during the attack. The monster stands at the apex of a triangular composition, threatening the enveloping men, but they hold their own and repel him. And even though the military fails to kill the monster, they establish in this scene the teamwork necessary to electrocute the monster in the film's finale. *The Thing* further benefits from eerie lighting, a charming performance by Margaret Sheridan as Captain Hendry's equal, and a mood of paranoia stylishly captured in the film's concluding warning: "Keep watching the skies!" The military in *The Day the Earth Stood Still* is the trigger-happy enemy and scientists are the ones to be trusted. In Robert Wise's film an alien scientist, Klaatu, asks us to live in peace and not to threaten the worlds of other planets with our proliferation of nuclear weapons. Klaatu performs a kind of 1950s police action, demanding in his "foreign policy" that the countries of earth join the community of planets, a world beyond our borders. In *The Thing*, the world is closed off; we are protecting our own way of life. In *The Day the Earth Stood Still*, we are asked to sacrifice our petty fears for the greater good. Wise captures our fears of the unknown well in an early scene featuring Klaatu walking the streets of downtown Washington, DC. As he briskly ambles at night, distorted stories in the newspapers and over the radio exaggerate the threat he poses (21:54–25:30). The military embodies these fears of difference, twice shooting the alien. The first time they shoot Klaatu, he is reaching for a gift that they mistake for a weapon (7:21–12:15). The second time, they shoot him in the back as he tries to return to his spaceship (1:16:08–1:16:16). Klaatu, unable to communicate with the military or the government, receives help from a naive, trusting boy, a mother (Patricia Neal), and the earth's greatest scientist (Dr. Barnhardt, an Einstein-type). Eventually, all three help Klaatu deliver his message to a gathering of scientists and news cameras. But that message, for a supposedly liberal film, is painfully conservative in its Teddy Rooseveltian might-makes-right ideology. Klaatu's people apparently hold the ultimate atomic big stick. And if we, democratic and communist countries, refuse to live in harmony and don't dispose of our nuclear arsenals, Klaatu's peacekeepers will reduce all of us to a "burned out cinder."

Further Reading

Hartung, Philip T. Review of *The Thing from Another World*. *Commonweal* 55 (May 18, 1951): 143.

Kawin, Bruce. "Children of the Light." *Film Genre Reader II*, ed. Barry Keith Grant. Austin: University of Texas Press, 1995. 308–329.

Review of *The Thing from Another World*. *Time* 58 (May 14, 1951): 110–111.

Sobchack, Vivian. "The Leaden Echo and the Golden Echo: The Sounds of Science Fiction." *Screening Space: The American Science Fiction Film*. New Brunswick, NJ: Rutgers University Press, 1980, 1997. 146–222.

FURTHER VIEWING

All the King's Men (1949)

Die Hard (1988) (R)

Earth vs. the Flying Saucers (1956)

Hunt for Red October (1990) (PG)

Invaders from Mars (1953)

Iron Giant (1999) (PG)

Korean War: The Complete Set (1999) (Doc.)

Murder at 1600 (1997) (R)

Peacemaker (1997) (R)

Race for the Superbomb (1999) (Doc.)

Seeing Red (1984) (Doc.)

Underworld USA (1961)

12

Viet Nam and the Things We Carry, 1954–Present

Apocalypse Now ◆ *Born on the Fourth of July* ◆ *China Beach*
Coming Home ◆ *Dear America: Letters Home from Vietnam*
In Country ◆ *Jacknife* ◆ *Jacob's Ladder* ◆ *Vietnam: A Television*
History ◆ Double Bill: *Anderson Platoon* and *Platoon*

Apocalypse Now (1979) (R)

Setting: Viet Nam and Cambodia, 1968

Director: Francis Ford Coppola

Screenplay: John Milius and Francis Ford Coppola

Director of Photography: Vittorio Storaro

Cast: Martin Sheen (Capt. Benjamin Willard), Marlon Brando (Col. Walter E. Kurtz), Robert Duvall (Colonel Kilgore), and Dennis Hopper (photojournalist)

Availability: Paramount Home Video

Apocalypse Now is a conflicted film. On the one hand, director Francis Ford Coppola's visual flair and dynamics capture the absurd horror and dehumanizing specter of the war. But conservative writer John Milius strikes a different pose. His screenplay argues that the real problem in Viet Nam wasn't that the war was immoral and meaningless but that the American approach to the war was wrong. We, as Kurtz attests to in his apocryphal story of the Viet Cong cutting off the inoculated arms of little children in order to maintain control over a village (2:11:31–2:15:01), needed to get outside of judgment. To win in Viet Nam, American GI's must become primordial men. Milius' racist screenplay suggests that the Viet Cong were more primordial than the American GIs and that the American GI was too Christian to get into that necessary mind set. As Kurtz says about the VC who hacked off the kids' arms, "If I had ten divisions of those men, then our troubles here would be over very quickly" (2:14:07). Willard, too, seems to share Kurtz's view. A special forces assassin, he distances himself from his fellow grunts, disgusted by their rock 'n' roll ways, drug use, and lack of commitment. During the USO Bunny show Willard stands arms folded, aloof from the clamor of the jazzed up GIs. As they storm the stage trying to touch the *Playboy* bunnies, Willard, in voiceover, philosophizes on the enemy's resolve: "Charlie didn't get much USO. He was dug in too deep or moving too fast. His idea of great R and R was cold rice and a little rat meat. He had only two ways home. Death or Victory" (1:07:40–1:08:06). American GIs, by contrast, are only into carnal pleasures and kicks. Coppola's view, or course, differs from Milius' jingoism. He undermines Kurtz by having Marlon Brando play the imperialist with an over-the-top bravado. Kurtz's pursuit of personal glory has clouded his judgment and Brando's girth suggests the evils of his excess. Similarly, Coppola's shrewd casting choices of Robert Duvall as a crazed Air Cav commander who enjoys napalming beachheads so that his boys can surf and Dennis Hopper as a hopped-up photojournalist and philosopher of incomprehensible dialectics furthers the ironic dissonances between the textual intentions of the director and screenwriter. Finally, Coppola's visuals become more hauntingly lurid and explosively expressionistic the farther Willard travels up river. Ultimately, Willard's descent into a visual nightmare of nihilism mirrors the absurdity of his and our purpose in Viet Nam. Viet Nam, we find, as the Doors forewarned us, is not only meaningless, but really is "the end."

Further Reading

Cahir, Linda Costanzo. "Narratological Parallels in Joseph Conrad's *Heart of Darkness* and Francis Ford Coppola's *Apocalypse Now.*" *Literature-Film Quarterly* 20.3 (July 1992): 181–187.
Morris, Margot. "Modernism and Vietnam: Francis Ford Coppola's *Apocalypse Now.*" *Modern Fiction Studies* 44.3 (Fall 1998): 730–766.
Tomasulo, Frank P. "The Politics of Ambivalence: *Apocalypse Now* as Prowar and Antiwar Film." *From Hanoi to Hollywood: The Vietnam War in American Film,* ed. Linda Dittmar and Gene Michaud. New Brunswick, NJ: Rutgers, 1990. 145–158.

Born on the Fourth of July (1989) (R)

Setting: Massapequa, Long Island, 1956, 1966, 1969; Cua Viet River, Viet Nam, 1967; Bronx Veterans Hospital, 1968; Villa Dulec, Mexico, 1970; Georgia, 1970; Republican National Convention, 1972; Democratic National Convention, 1976

Director: Oliver Stone

Screenplay: Oliver Stone and Ron Kovic

Director of Photography: Robert Richardson

Cast: Tom Cruise (Ron Kovic), Caroline Kava (Mrs. Kovic)

Availability: MCA/Universal Home Video

Oliver Stone's well-meaning melodrama of a veteran's mythical journey from the pastoral garden of the Massapequa suburbs to the horrors of Viet Nam and his eventual return home lacks complexity. The film begins with young Ron playing war games in his backyard, suggesting a cultural conditioning that would make him a victim of war (00:00–2:32). Then Stone portrays teenage Ron as a gung-ho high school student and wrestler who too easily believes in John F. Kennedy and the threat of the Red Menace (8:37–9:37; 14:34–16:39; 24:00–24:55). In Viet Nam, Ron is a John Wayne type, shouting at the enemy, acting with bravado, until he's wounded and paralyzed (41:27–41:36). Upon his return home, he's bitter and argues with his Bob Dylanesque brother, Tommy, about the war ("love it or leave it" [1: 07:46–1:08:22]), and dismisses his mother (a caricature of a devil-fearing fundamentalist) with a sexually frustrated tirade ("My penis!" [1:35:30–1: 38:09]). Eventually, he leaves home to revel in Mexico, returns to the United States as a committed activist, and finally in 1976 speaks at a the Democratic National Convention, for himself and all vets: "Just lately, I felt home. You know? Well, maybe, we're home" (2:17:30–2:17:37). Stone's story isn't fully earned. How Kovic becomes an activist is never explored. Later, in 1972 he praises the resiliency of the Vietnamese: they're "a proud peasant people who are fighting a war of resistance" (2:08:54–2:11:27). These words of antiwar protest seem insincere, or spoken by someone other than Kovic. But there are some great cinematic moments that resonate truths. When the paralyzed Ron returns home and speaks at a veteran's parade, he suddenly loses the thread of his thought (1:12:21–1:14:08). We're doing our best, we're going to win, he says, but in the distance a baby cries and he can no longer speak. The baby represents both the Vietnamese children he killed in a village massacre and the child he can no longer have because of his wounds (1:58:57–2:05:16). Ron's visit to Georgia and the family of a GI he accidentally killed also carries great moral weight. The scene is not in Kovic's book but the emotional impact is overwhelming. (1: 58:57–2:05:16). There he painfully reveals how the sun glared that day. "It was late. . . . Babies were killed by mistake . . . I was confused . . . scared. I think I was the one who killed your son." The story of Billy's death from friendly fire releases Ron of his guilt. But in telling the story, Stone opens up a larger nexus of guilt, one in which the U.S. government not only covers up horrors of war, but perpetuates false truths of heroism, and is thus indicted.

Further Reading

Canby, Vincent. Review of *Born on the 4th of July*. *New York Times* (December 20, 1989): C15.

Ebert, Roger. Review of *Born on the 4th of July*. *Chicago Sun Times*, www.
     chicagosuntimes.com
Hoberman, J. Review of *Born on the 4th of July*. *Village Voice* (December 26, 1989):
     99.

China Beach (1988) (W) (TV)

Setting: Danang, Viet Nam, 1967.

Director: Rob Holcomb

Screenplay: John Sacret Young

Director of Photography: Charles Minsky

Cast: Dana Delany (Lt. Colleen McMurphy), Nan Woods (Cherry White), and Chloe
Webb (Laurette Barber)

Availability: Warner Home Video

This pilot for the sixty-two-installment series *China Beach* offers profound
insight into the women of the Viet Nam war (some 50,000 served). Army
nurse Lt. Colleen McMurphy, who has just a few days left on her tour of
duty, has seen too many soldiers die. That pain has caused her to distance
herself from the war. At one point, she walks out of the operating room
with two corpses on different gurneys and engages in playful banter with a
pilot, seemingly oblivious to the carnage (9:00–9:55). She also denies her
femininity within the "in country" war zone, labeling herself "just one of
the guys" (19:40). But McMurphy's calm belies pent-up emotions. Later,
safe and alone in her Quonset hut, Nurse McMurphy X's out November
23, 1967, on her calendar as she counts down the days until her departure
from Viet Nam. Suddenly the marker leaks on her hand. The ink spots
become a visual correlative for blood, and McMurphy can't wipe them away
fast enough as she desperately squeezes her hands and tries to remove the
damn spots (22:50–23:34). McMurphy has another private breakdown a
few days later as she struggles to remove her bloody scrub (34:37–36:00).
Desperately flailing, she crashes into a series of lockers before heaving it.
Just hours later, she meets a young Red Cross aide from Iowa, Cherry, who
feels naive and childlike for crying. "You're a new guy," McMurphy says,
but not with disdain. "Be glad that you can cry. . . . Do it while you can"
(38:08). McMurphy has lost her innocence through war, and her story becomes the search to regain feeling and to reconnect with those around her.
The person to reach McMurphy is the one disconnected from the unit.
Laurette, an orphan and USO singer, encourages McMurphy, who is about
to return stateside, to perform as a backup singer for her show. That moment is magical. Dana Delany, in an acting tour de force, dances in a se-
quined miniskirt and false wig, looking simultaneously stunning and halting
as she struggles with the dance steps to a Supremes' song. Her unit, however, recognizes her and applauds her performance. Their gleeful responses

don't eroticize but humanize. In a slow motion closeup, she cries, recognizing her own compassion and commitment to them (1:20:09–1:22:47). The next day, she decides not to come home, but to stay in Danang. "I have an even bigger family here," she affirms, as helicopters whir in the distance.

Further Reading

Auster, Albert. "Reflections of the Way Life Used To Be: *Tour of Duty, China Beach* and the Memory of the Sixties." *Television Quarterly* 24.4 (Fall 1990): 61–69.

Hanson, Cynthia A. "The Women of *China Beach*." *Journal of Popular Film and Television* 17.4 (Winter 1990): 154–163.

Rasmussen, Karen. "*China Beach* and American Mythology of War." *Women's Studies in Communication* 15.2 (Fall 1992): 22–51.

Vande Berg, Leah R. "China Beach, Prime Time War in the Postfeminist Age: An Example of Patriarchy in a Different Voice." *Western Journal of Communications* 57.3 (Summer 1993): 349–366.

Coming Home (1978) (R) (W)

Setting: Southern California and Hong Kong, 1967–1968

Director: Hal Ashby

Screenplay: Waldo Salt and Robert C. Jones (based on a story by Nancy Dowd)

Director of Photography: Haskell Wexler

Cast: Jane Fonda (Sally Hyde), Jon Voight (Luke Martin), Bruce Dern (Capt. Bob Hyde), Penelope Milford (Vi Munson), and Robert Carradine (Billy Munson)

Availability: MGM/UA Home Video

Winner of several Academy Awards, *Coming Home* seems to be a product of 1960s activism. Jane Fonda represents a woman coming into social consciousness. Initially unaware of the horrors of the war, the mousy Sally naively supports her husband's jingoistic fervor and dresses herself in straight-haired 1950s conformity. Later, while working as a volunteer at a VA hospital, she accidentally rams into the cart of a paraplegic, Luke Martin, sending his urine bag bursting on the floor (18:31–19:27). "Just take care of me," he howls as orderlies strap and sedate him. Later Luke, a former high school star athlete, expresses his anger at Sally's seeming lack of connectedness to the war (31:50–32:47). Sally eventually with his help becomes more compassionate and caring about the plight of the men around her. Her friendship with Luke blossoms into a love affair. For the first time, she experiences an orgasm and her transcendence through love is captured by Ashby in a liberal outlook that goes beyond Sally's braless outfits and frizzed hair (1:27:42–1:28:47). Luke, too, in his relationship with Sally is changed from self-centered bitterness about his wounds to a desire to stop the mindless killing and maiming in Viet Nam. After being unable to save the stressed-out Billy Munson from killing himself, Luke chains himself to the gates of the local Marine recruiting center to try to prevent more Americans from dying in war or in its posttraumatic aftermath (1:15:52–1:17:45). In the end, Luke becomes a messianic figure, traveling to high school auditoriums and preaching against recruitment and the horrors of war: "It ain't like it is in the movies. . . . I have killed for my country . . . and I don't feel good about it" (2:03:16–2:04:00). *Coming Home*'s seeming 1960s activism is really grounded in the politics of the personal. Sally and Luke are moved to activism by the deaths and injuries suffered by loved ones.

Further Reading

Blake, Richard. "The Revolution Is Forever." *America* 138 (March 18, 1978): 211.
Emerson, Gloria. "Gloria Emerson Comes Home." *Ms.* 6 (May 1978): 27–29.
Selig, Michael. "Boys Will Be Men: Oedipal Drama in *Coming Home*." *From Hanoi to Hollywood: The Vietnam War in American Film*, ed. Linda Dittmar and Gene Michaud. New Brunswick, NJ: Rutgers, 1990. 189–202.

Dear America: Letters Home from Vietnam (1987– 1988) (PG-13) (Doc.)

Setting: Viet Nam, early 1960s–1973

Director: Bill Couturie

Writers: Richard Dewhurst and Bill Couturie

Director of Photography: Michael Chin

Editor: Stephen Stept

Availability: HBO Home Video

Bill Couturie's tribute to the American GI in Viet Nam is a stunning documentary that relies on raw images and emotion to make us experience life in a grunt's boots. The opening montage over Credence Clearwater Revival's stirring protest song, "Fortunate Son," establishes the outlook. As John Fogerty screams "It ain't me," Couturie edits images of soldiers firing M-16s and others lying on stretchers, waiting to be evacuated to MASH units. The rock soundtrack blisters and punches an empathetic mood. Later, the Rolling Stones' "Gimme Shelter" snakes over a "Search and Destroy" montage of GIs arriving in "Hueys," hitting the "LZ," "chasing Charlie," and lighting a thatched hut with a Zippo (24:52–26:41). Here the Stones' thump provides a bright counterpoint to the darkness of war, suggesting a soldier's need to be rescued and saved from perpetrating such acts. Combined with the thumping music are the vocal talents of thirty-three actors. Stars such as Robert De Niro, Robin Williams, and Michael J. Fox breathe life into the words of veterans collected in Bernard Edelman's original source book. One particularly haunting moment occurs as PFC Raymond Griffiths (Fox) wonders if his girlfriend is faithful, and if he will be lucky enough to make it out of Viet Nam. A quick graphic suddenly informs us that he was killed a few weeks later, and then editor Stephen Stept freeze-frames Griffiths' prom picture (31:07–33:00). Couturie loves these men. His film praises them for doing their duty. They are normal, everyday Americans, not apolitical dupes. Several soldiers tell television reporters that they want to go home (40:48). "I'd like to see all this end," says another (1:04:43). "I feel I'm at the bottom of a great sewer," says a third (1:07:21). If anyone is the film's antagonist, it's the generals. In one telling clip, General Westmoreland shakes hands with the troops, attempting to boost their morale, while a voiceover informs us that "Most men believe we won't win the war" (35:28). The generals can't achieve victory in Viet Nam, and later, we discover that their whole military policy is illogical and cruel. At a press conference, General Wheeler assures the media that nuclear weapons won't be used to save Khe Sanh, but a prior graphic undercuts his assurances: the U.S. Air Force dropped the equivalent of five Hiroshima bombs on Viet Nam (42:10). Because Couturie's goal is to revise the stereotype of the "baby-killing" U.S. soldier, he glosses over images that run contrary to his snapshots of normalcy. Atrocities such as the My Lai massacre get little attention: thirty-six seconds of screen time (1:06:04–1:06:40). Drug problems and racial tensions among soldiers are also unfortunately erased from this record of cultural memory. Such reflections could have added depth and complexity to *Dear America*'s already arrestingly powerful mosaic of the personal.

Further Reading

Dornfeld, Barry. "*Dear America*: Transparency, Authority, and Interpretation in a Vietnam War Documentary." *From Hanoi to Hollywood: The Vietnam War in American Film*, ed. Linda Dittmar and Gene Michaud. New Brunswick, NJ: Rutgers, 1990. 283–297.

Edelman, Bernard, ed. *Dear America: Letters Home from Vietnam*. New York: Pocket Books, 1985.

Johnson, Brian D. "Second Glances: Documentaries Salvage Truth from History." *Maclean's* 101 (October 3, 1988): 54E.

In Country (1989) (R) (W)

Setting: Hopewell, Kentucky, 1989

Director: Norman Jewison

Screenplay: Frank Pierson and Cynthia Cidre

Director of Photography: Russell Boyd

Cast: Emily Lloyd (Samantha Hughes), Bruce Willis (Emmett Smith), and Joan Allen (Irene).

Availability: Warner Home Video

Based on the novel by Bobbi Ann Mason, in this film teenager Samantha Hughes searches for the identity of her father, Dwayne, who died in Viet Nam before she was born. She lives with her uncle, Emmett, who is also a Viet Nam–era veteran, but he refuses to reveal his wartime experiences to her. Her grandparents and remarried mother also resist Sam's search for meaning, but eventually they all help her, and she reaches a deeper understanding of her father and of what other veterans went through in country. Director Norman Jewison captures the spirit of Sam's search by often photographing her running through the town, and cleverly playing off the history of her boyfriend (everyone knows him as the boy that made a series of jump shots against a cross-state rival) with the buried history of Viet Nam that no one (vets or town citizens) cares to talk about. In her quest for knowledge, Sam discovers her father's letters to her mother (18:20). As she reads them, she is appalled by some of the implied horror of his narratives. Much later she makes an overnight camping excursion to the town bog where she attempts to experience Viet Nam. After awaking "in country," she finds Emmett sitting next to her (1:30:30–1:35:30). Emmett has post-traumatic flashbacks and may suffer from Agent Orange poisoning, but he also has a sense of humor and a deep compassion. When Sam confesses that she doesn't like her father anymore, Emmett asks her "who the hell are you to judge him?" (1:32:30). Then he opens up, telling her that after being in country and seeing friends killed, you no longer care, you just "quit feeling." In tears, he reveals his inner turmoil. "I have a hole in my heart. I can't get it back" (1:35:30). Sam learns through Emmett's pain what it means to be a veteran. Through Emmett she forgives and loves her father. The film ends with a touching tribute to her father, as Sam, her grandmother, and Emmett visit the Viet Nam Veterans Memorial in Washington, DC, and share an epiphany that honors all the men of the war.

Further Reading

Corliss, Richard. Review of *In Country*. *Time* 134 (October 2, 1989): 90.
Edelstein, Richard. Review of *In Country*. *New York Post* (September 15, 1989): 21.
James, Caryn. Review of *In Country*. *New York Times* (September 15, 1989): C6.
Mason, Bobbi Ann. *In Country: A Novel*. New York: Harper and Row, 1985.

Jacknife (1988) (R) (W)

Setting: Connecticut, 1988
Director: David Jones
Screenplay: Stephen Metcalfe

Director of Photography: Brian West

Cast: Robert De Niro (Megs), Kathy Baker (Martha Flanagan), and Ed Harris (Dave Flanagan)

Availability: HBO Home Video

David Jones' *Jacknife* is a warm film that helps rehabilitate the image of the Viet Nam War–era veteran. Veterans Megs and Davey have readjustment troubles, but they are presented as fully realized human beings, and the arc to Stephen Metcalfe's screenplay is therapeutic. Davey, embarrassed about his own wartime fears, denies the past. He tells his sister that Megs was never his friend in order to mask his own guilt and pain over his inaction in Viet Nam and the loss of his friend Bobby. Megs, known as Jacknife in his younger days for his reckless truck driving, always has a twinkle in his eye while talking with Martha, but behind the charm rests a repressed wildness. Megs arrives at Davey's unannounced, rouses him from bed, and insists they go fishing. While fishing, Megs falls in love with Davey's sister Martha, played with a strong vulnerability by Kathy Baker. Their romance seems unlikely (she's a high school biology teacher; he's a grease monkey), but through knowing each other they grow. Martha, who never went to the prom while a high school student, is accompanied by Megs to the prom now as a high school chaperone. With Megs, she opens up sexually and deepens her understanding about the war and the problems of the returning veteran, including her brother's. Megs, through his relationship with Martha finds contentment and peace. Their relationship also enables Megs to reach Davey. During Megs and Martha's prom date and dance, Jones frequently crosscuts to Davey arguing and drinking in a bar (1:15:22–1:21:50). The crosscut links the three and suggests a repression in Martha's life: her fear for her brother's life has held her back emotionally and sexually. Eventually, Jones combines the crosscuts as Davey arrives at the school, and in a rage shatters the athletic trophy case. Earlier, Megs had been sexually frustrated by Martha. She had refused his passionate kisses, and he smashed his hand through a window in her house. She told him that she liked the kiss, and then she took him to a hospital, and upon their return home, they made love as a kind of therapy (1:00:23–1:07:00). Now, as Davey lashes out violently, Megs therapeutically heals him. Megs releases the film's repressed inner story. He tells about being wounded in Viet Nam and how he heard Davey reject him, shouting to their friend Bobby, "Don't go back, Jacknife's dead." But Bobby did go back and he was killed attempting to rescue the wounded Megs. Megs' angry confession releases Davey's guilt. Later, Davey sincerely apologizes to his sister for ruining her prom date (1:32:18–1:32:41), and goes to vet counseling wearing Bobby's Red Sox hat, and admitting, "the three of us were friends. . . . I was the scared one" (1:35:33–1:35:50). He reclaims his friend Jacknife, and Jones returns to a final crosscut sequence that suggests Davey's acceptance of his sister's sexual identity.

Mixed with his words of self-healing are images of further healing as Megs drives out of town, pulls over, and then returns to Martha's front door where he stands on the porch waiting.

Further Reading

Ebert, Roger. Review of *Jacknife*. *Chicago Sun Times* (March 24, 1989): www.suntimes.com

Kempley, Rita. Review of *Jacknife*. *Washington Post* (March 24, 1989): www.washingtonpost.com

Selig, Michael. "From Play to Film: *Strange Snow*, *Jacknife*, and Masculine Identity in the Hollywood Vietnam Film." *Literature/Film Quarterly* 20.3 (July 1992): 173–180.

Jacob's Ladder (1990) (R)

Setting: Mekong Delta, 1971; New York City, 1975?

Director: Adrian Lyne

Screenplay: Bruce Joel Rubin

Director of Photography: Jeffrey L. Kimbal

Cast: Tim Robbins (Jacob Singer), Elizabeth Pena (Jezzie), Danny Aiello (Louis), Patricia Kalembar (Sarah), Matt Craven (Michael Newman), and Macaulay Culkin (Gabe)

Availability: Carolco Home Video/LIVE Home Video

Jacob's Ladder, an unsettling film that was underappreciated by the popular critics upon its initial release, captures the paranoia and feeling of dislocation experienced by Viet Nam veterans. The film thwarts our expectations. Scenes set in Viet Nam are juxtaposed with Jacob's life as a postal carrier in New York. But the Viet Nam scenes aren't posttraumatic flashbacks; instead the scenes in New York are a projected future, an existence that Jacob has yet to experience, but instead fantasizes about as he lies dying in the fields of Viet Nam, on a helicopter, and later in a MASH unit. In effect, the majority of the film takes place in Jacob's mind. This mindscreen creates an impermanence and lack of rational order. The stability of a healthy domestic life doesn't truly exist. Jacob's relationship with his lover Jezzie, his ex-wife Sarah, and his three sons are visionary, not real. Does he even have any sons? Does he really know a Jezzie? Did he divorce Sarah? Was he ever married? Jacob's logical incoherence, smattered with images of demonic presences, resonates a deeper mood shared by most Viet Nam veterans, a mood of always feeling like they're back in the jungle and never at home. Added to this swirl of biographical haziness is a paranoia-conspiracy plot in which Jacob suspects he and his outfit were victims of some kind of scientific testing. As the paranoia plot unfolds, Jacob is beaten by government men, the army denies his existence, and his lawyer and fellow GIs eventually refuse to pursue their case. Caught in a coverup conspiracy, Jacob finally finds answers from Michael, a chemist. In an underground New York tunnel, Michael freely admits to the military experiments he had conducted in Viet Nam (1:33:52–1:36:41). Michael developed Jacob's Ladder, an LSD-like hallucinogen, sprinkled in K-rations, that converted supposedly "soft" soldiers into aggressive, primordial killers. But the drug has a wicked side-effect: it removes conscience, and the men in Jacob's platoon killed each other. Lyne captures this horrific moment in a brilliant piece of inventiveness. He closes off an earlier absent reverse shot of Jacob being bayonetted (7:11), and reveals, much later, that his attacker was one of his platoon friends (1:38:39). Unfortunately, this closed reverse shot suggests that the war is about us and only us. Moreover, the ending of the film suggests a further kind of erasing of history. Jacob returns home in a cab, and ascends the stairs with his dead son, Gabe (did he ever have a son?), and into a bright light. Like the biblical figure in *Genesis*, *Jacob's Ladder* now signifies a communion with God, and here his soul crosses over. In death Jacob lets go. Earlier, Louie, a chiropractor and angelic figure, spoke the film's central message, telling Jacob that the demons he sees are really angels freeing him from the earth (1:24:00–1:25:14), and that he must let go of material concerns. On a larger allegorical level, if the United States also lets go and reconciles itself to Viet Nam, then are we too angelically cleansed?

Further Reading

Christopher, Renny. *"Jacob's Ladder." Vietnam War Films*, ed. Jean-Jacques Malo and Tony Williams. Jefferson, NC: McFarland, 1994. 218–224.

Fry, Carrol, Robert Craig, and Ken Jurkiewicz. "Three Viewers Viewing: A Viewer-Response Symposium on *Jacob's Ladder*." *Literature-Film Quarterly* 26 (July 1998): 220–234.

Rubin, Bruce Joel. "Jacob's Chronicle." *Jacob's Ladder*. New York: Applause Screenplay Series. 147–98.

Vietnam: A Television History (1983) (Doc.)

Setting: Viet Nam, 1860–1980s; United States, 1950s–1983

Directors: Judith Vecchione, Elizabeth Deane, Austin Hoyt, Andrew Pearson, Martin Smith, Bruce Palling, and Richard Ellison

Writers: Judith Vecchione, Elizabeth Deane, Austin Hoyt, Andrew Pearson, Martin Smith, Bruce Palling, Richard Ellison, and Marilyn Hornbeck Mellowes.

Cameras: Donato Boltiglione, John Gordon, Jean-Claude Larrieu, John Packwood, Gerry Pinches, Dick Williams, Jean-Marie Esteve, Boyd Estrus, Carol Poletti, Peter Hoving, Murdoch Campbell, Joseph Vitagliano, Jerry Hogrewe, Werner Bundschuh, Kevin Burke, Dick Currance, Jon Else, Wayne Miller, Judy Isola, and Hiro Narita

Narrator: Will Lyman

Editors: Eric W. Handley, Carl Hayward, Eric Neudel, Ruth Schell, Julian Ware, Glen Cardino, Paul Cleary, Jonathan Marys, Daniel Eisenberg, and Mavis Lynn Small

Availability: American Experience/PBS Home Video

This thirteen-hour, seven-volume documentary provides a solid, well-balanced historical contextualization of the Viet Nam conflict. Whereas most Hollywood films see Viet Nam through western eyes, this series provides a broader, more complex outlook. Volume one explores the roots of the war and studies how the Vietnamese have fought a 2,000-year guerilla-style war for independence. The French colonized Viet Nam in the 1860s, pacified it by 1885, and even sent home postcards featuring the severed heads of Vietnamese resistant fighters (12:28–12:39). In 1941, the Viet Minh were founded by Ho Chi Minh who organized guerilla bases and urged the peasants to resist. Ho Chi Minh was a fervent nationalist who wanted to reunify his country, and he succeeded in retaking Hanoi from the Japanese in 1945 (32:30–40:13). But in the South, after the war, the British helped the French maintain colonial power. The French declared the southern part separate from the north (vol. 1, 1:01:54). By 1950, the United States supported the French imperial efforts, shipping over 150 million dollars worth of aid in planes, tanks, and napalm (vol. 1, 1:16:18). Following France's collapse at Dienbienphu (vol. 1, 1:26:30–1:40:12), Ho Chi Minh's allies, the Russians and Chinese, undercut him at the Geneva Accord of 1952. There, Viet Nam was divided into two chunks, and there were promises of a national election for reunification in two years (vol. 1, 1:52:40). But the United States had no intention of allowing Minh's government to gain a foothold in the south; instead, the United States tried to control the region through a "policing action" and setting up a series of "puppet" governments to represent their own interests. Volume two looks at America's involvement in Viet Nam and how it grew out of a fear of falling dominoes and the spread of communism. President Johnson committed 3,500 Marines on March 8, 1965. By year's end 200,000 were sent (vol. 2, 1:26:47–1:30:44). Surprisingly, the series is sympathetic to LBJ (much maligned for his foreign policy decisions). Early on, the president realized that he couldn't win in Viet Nam because of the VC's commitment to independence and their guerilla fighting style, but he feared becoming the only president to lose a war (vol. 2, 1:33:10–1:41:56). He tried to find other options. He even suggested using American aid to convert the Mekong Delta into a kind of Tennessee Valley Authority, providing water and modernized power for all of the Vietnamese, if only Ho Chi Minh "would be reasonable" and keep the two countries separate (vol. 2, 1:34:10). But Minh, wanting to reunify his country, wasn't about to make such deals. Volume three explores the insane horror of the war from a Vietnamese perspective. Nguyen Bay discusses the atrocities perpetrated on his people by American GIs (27:22–38:

00). Grenades were indiscriminately thrown into village huts, animals were slaughtered, and the ears of the dead were shot off. "They seemed to hate us." This volume also looks at the horror inflicted by the U.S. Air Force in their Operation Rolling Thunder (vol. 3, 1:14:20–1:23:30). As one Vietnamese woman says, "I didn't see any guerillas being killed. Just villagers" (vol. 3, 1:22:03). Moreover, in this volume the series suggests that the American effort in Vietnam was doomed to failure because of its predictability and ineffectualness. Dr. Ton That Thung remembers how bombs were always dropped at 10 A.M., just after breakfast, and at 3 P.M., just after lunch. The surgeons and nurses got used to the patterns and would work from 5 A.M. to just shortly before 9 or 10 (1:48:06–1:48:57). Volume four looks at the meaning of the Tet Offensive for American television audiences. Although the Marines won that battle, the perception back home was that we couldn't win the war (vol. 4, 26:07–40:43). After Tet, Congress demanded a deescalation and withdrawal of forces from Viet Nam. Volume six analyzes the homefront protest. Martin Luther King, Jr., protested the war because it diverted necessary domestic funding for America's disadvantaged peoples (7:22–7:47). Students, too, protested the war as immoral and unjust. In 1967, 50,000 students marched on the Pentagon, and by late 1967 a majority of Americans thought the war was a mistake (vol. 6, 14:47–16:44). In 1968, violence broke out between Chicago police and demonstrators outside the Democratic National Convention. These protests and Nixon's reaction to them helped him claim the presidency. He spoke a tough rhetoric—"This a nation of laws . . . [and I promise to] enforce the law" (vol. 6, 32:12–32:25)—and this rhetoric appealed to conservative patriots. Perhaps this volume's most fascinating aspect belongs to the veterans who felt changed by the war and, in turn, became committed to activism and protest. John Kerry, a lieutenant in Viet Nam, said, "We weren't gaining any territory, we weren't winning the hearts and minds of anybody . . . we were simply doing a very macho kind of public demonstration of our presence" (vol. 6, 49:33–51:02). He was forever changed, and several decorated vets are shown flinging away their medals on the steps of the Capitol (vol. 6, 51:42–52:42). "Legacies," the final volume in the series, complicates the communist victory by looking at what the fall of Saigon in 1975 meant for Southeast Asia. In Cambodia peace meant death under Pol Pot and the Khmer Rouge regime (vol. 7, 21:52–23:57). In South Viet Nam, 1.5 million Vietnamese had to settle on poor farming land. Another 700,000 fled to America as political refugees. And in America, Viet Nam became part of our national consciousness. Today congressmen and senators demand that our foreign policy decisions never create a second Viet Nam. But such future mistakes appear unavoidable. The PBS documentary suggests that we have yet to learn any firm lessons about our reasons for being in Viet Nam, and our policies of postcolonialism and "police" intervention in communist-run countries.

Further Reading

Corry, John. "The Tet Offensive in Vietnam." *New York Times* (November 8, 1983): C15.
———. "13-Part History of Vietnam War on PBS." *New York Times* (October 4, 1983): C18.
Herring, George C. *America's Longest War: The United States and Vietnam, 1950–1975*. New York: John Wiley & Sons, 1979.

DOUBLE BILL: VIET NAM AND THE RULES OF ENGAGEMENT

Anderson Platoon (1967) (Doc.) (M)

Setting: An Khe, 1966

Director: Pierre Schoendorffer

Writer: None listed

Director of Photography: Dominique Merlin

Sound: Raymond Adams

Narrator: Pierre Schoendorffer

Availability: Public Media Video

Platoon (1986) (R)

Setting: Viet Nam, near Cambodia, 1967–1968

Director: Oliver Stone

Screenplay: Oliver Stone

Director of Photography: Robert Richardson

Cast: Charlie Sheen (Chris Taylor), Tom Berenger (Sgt. Bob Barnes), Willem Dafoe (Sergeant Elias), and Mark Moses (Lieutenant Wolfe)

Availability: Orion Home Video

French filmmaker Pierre Schoendorffer's documentary accurately captures Viet Nam's rules of engagement. Schoendorffer, a veteran of the French conflict in Dienbienphu, admires soldiers. He photographs them shaving, bathing, huddling in the rain (19:47–20:33), reading letters (26:37–28:21), and singing soulful blues as laments for home and for the deaths of fellow GIs (15:42–17:24). He also reveals the drudgery of a grunt's life in a clever montage of soldiers struggling through jungles, set to Nancy Sinatra's "These Boots Are Made for Walking" (9:37–11:21). But Schoendorffer's greatest accomplishment is his understated revelations of combat. In Viet

Nam there were no clear objectives (hills to be taken, bridges to be blown up). Instead, soldiers were dropped by helicopter into a VC area, searched for the enemy, and then were evacuated out. In Viet Nam there was also no clear demarcation of the enemy. Twice Schoendorffer shows Lieutenant Anderson's platoon entering a village and trying to find an invisible enemy. The second time, they find a cache of ammunition in a basket, but the only people visible are old men, women, and children (45:20–51:22). A suspected VC sympathizer is found and taken away but there's no real confidence that the platoon has pacified the village and made it safe. Finally, Schoendorffer's battle scenes capture a mood of swirling dislocation. His use of canted framing and handheld cameras raises our level of anxiety. The enemy in Viet Nam is invisible, blending into the landscape. American GIs can only hunker down to escape from sniper fire (57:43–1:03:46). American filmmaker Oliver Stone, too, looks inside the dynamics of a platoon in his feature-length film. Stone's film is less romantic. His focus on the rules of engagement is more internal as two sergeants, Barnes and Elias, fight for the wills of the young men under their charge. Barnes is a lifer. His men drink whiskey, listen to country music, and believe in the military. Elias believes that the United States is going to lose this war and he just wants to survive. His group listens to rock and soul music and smokes dope to loosen up. Within his group is a spirit of integration and friendship among blacks, whites, and Latino soldiers (29:41–32:01). Thrown into this platoon is a young volunteer, Chris Taylor. Taylor quit college because he didn't feel it was right for him to avoid the war, and he's also looking for a way to authenticate his existence. In Viet Nam, he is taught by Sergeants Elias and Barnes, his surrogate fathers, how to be a soldier. From them, he eventually understands the moral ambiguities of the war. The film has several great battle scenes, but Stone's crowning moment occurs when Barnes enters a village and instead of rounding up suspects like Lieutenant Anderson does, he summarily executes two villagers (45:05–58:33). Barnes is upset because two of his men have been killed (one by a VC booby trap; the other by a guerilla fighter). The ineffectual Lieutenant Wolfe does nothing to stop Barnes' carnage, but Elias, a crusading man of justice, intervenes before Barnes can execute a child. Taylor, attentively watching, admires Elias' courage, and moments later he stops several of his men from raping an under-aged Vietnamese girl. "You just don't get it, do you?" he shouts. "She's a fucking human being" (57:09). But ultimately, Taylor's humanity and moral imperatives become a synthesis of his two fathers. After discerning that Barnes had shot Elias in order to stop a court-martial from proceeding, Taylor decides to "frag" Barnes. Thus, he learns from Elias to have compassion and to be responsible, but he also learns from Barnes to be brutally cold. Within the rules of a platoon, Taylor discovers that society's notions of law and order don't necessarily apply.

Further Reading

Attanasio, Paul. Review of *Platoon*. *The Washington Post* (January 16, 1987): B1.
Beck, Avent. "The Christian Allegorical Structure of *Platoon*." *Literature-Film Quarterly* 20.3 (July 1992): 213–222.
Canby, Vincent. Review of *Platoon*. *New York Times* (December 19, 1986): C12.
Corliss, Richard. "*Platoon*: Viet Nam, the Way It Really Was on Film." *Time* 129 (January 26, 1987): 54–61.
Sturken, Marita. "Reenactment, Fantasy, and the Paranoia of History: Oliver Stone's Docudramas." *History and Theory* 36 (December 1997): 64–79.

FURTHER VIEWING

The Boys in Company C (1978) (R)

Casualties of War (1989) (R)

The Deer Hunter (1978) (R)

Full Metal Jacket (1987) (R)

Good Morning Vietnam (1987) (R)

Hamburger Hill (1987) (R)

Heaven and Earth (1995) (R)

Rambo: First Blood, Part II (1985)(R)

Walking Dead (1995) (R) (M)

13

The Counterculture
Rebellion and the Quest for
Authenticity, 1961–Present

Alice Doesn't Live Here Anymore ◆ *Billy Jack* ◆ *Boys Don't Cry*
Dazed and Confused ◆ *Easy Rider* ◆ *The Graduate* ◆ *Harlan*
County, USA ◆ *The Heart Is a Lonely Hunter* ◆ *The Hustler*
The Last Detail ◆ *Medium Cool* ◆ *The Outsiders* ◆ *Taxi Driver*
Thelma & Louise ◆ *Two-Lane Blacktop* ◆ *Double Bill:*
Woodstock and *Gimme Shelter*

Alice Doesn't Live Here Anymore (1974) (PG) (W)

Setting: Monterey, California, 1947; Socorro, Phoenix, and Tuscon, Arizona, 1974

Director: Martin Scorsese

Screenplay: Robert Getchell

Director of Photography: Kent L. Wakeford

Cast: Ellen Burstyn (Alice Hyatt), Mia Bendixsen (Alice, age eight), Alfred Lutter (Tommy Hyatt), Lelia Goldoni (Bea), Harvey Keitel (Ben), and Jodie Foster (Audrey)

Availability: Warner Bros. Home Video

Martin Scorsese's *Alice Doesn't Live Here Anymore* reworks *The Wizard of Oz* story into a feminist context. Made during the women's rights era, and on the cusp of campuswide women's studies classes, Scorsese's tender film explores a woman's quest for identity and meaning. Alice (played with wonderful vitality and realistic nuance by Ellen Burstyn) is a product of 1960s suburbia. She has surrendered her dreams and allowed herself to be protected by an overbearing, unappreciative husband. But when her husband dies in a truck accident, she and her twelve-year-old son must fend for themselves, and they do so admirably. She leaves the dull, bleached whiteness of Socorro, Arizona, to pursue a career as a singer. Her ultimate dream is to sing her way home to Monterey, where she claims to have been happy as a child. But this desire is troubled by Scorsese's opening sequence. There, Scorsese shows us a Monterey that wasn't a home of pleasant dreams, but a setting of possible repression. Twenty-seven years ago young Alice walked in a red-washed landscape that vaguely resembled Dorothy's home in Kansas. Alone, Alice stopped by a white picket fence, looked at the red sky, contemplated her parents, and cursed, "Blow it out their ass" (1:49). On her quest to return home, Alice first stops in Phoenix. There she's accosted by a bar manager who demands that she turn around. "You want to look at my face. I don't sing with my ass," she snaps. A jump cut follows, as Alice kicks at a slammed door in frustration (30:42). A woman, it seems, has to parade her looks to be successful. Later, Alice earns a job at a rival bar, after impressing the manager with her breathy versions of "Where or When" and "Gone with the Wind." At the club she meets Ben and has an affair. But she later discovers that not only is he married, he is also violently abusive (49:57–52:16). After witnessing Ben's rage, Alice and her son leave Phoenix for Tuscon, and she gives up singing to support herself through waitressing at Mel's Diner. There she falls in love with a rancher, David. But following an argument with David, in which he hit the undisciplined Tommy (a faint echo of Ben's violence), Alice walks out and tells her coworker Flo, "I don't know how to live without a man" (1:36:19). But maybe in the end, she learns. The film, like many art films of that period, concludes with a series of unresolved issues: Will Alice and David become a couple again? How will Tommy deal with the loss of his father, his own burgeoning anger, and adolescent angst? Will Tommy and street urchin Audrey (played with sweet malice by Jodie Foster) team up at school and wreak more havoc? Whatever happens, Alice has learned to no longer yearn for the past. Unlike Dorothy Gale of Kansas who learns that happiness is in one's own backyard, Alice doesn't need to return to Monterey. There's a world beyond her old backyard, and she could be happy in the present, a self-determined woman, "living here" (1:41:29).

Further Reading

Braudy, Susan. "Bang! A Little Gift from Hollywood." *Ms.* 7 (January 1975): 34–37.

Kael, Pauline. "Woman on the Road." *The New Yorker* 50 (January 13, 1975): 74–82.

Lourdeaux, Lee. "Martin Scorsese in Little Italy and Greater Manhattan." *Italian and Irish Filmmakers in America: Ford, Capra, Coppola and Scorsese.* Philadelphia: Temple University Press, 1990. 217–266.

Billy Jack (1971) (PG)

Setting: the Southwest, 1971

Director: Tom Laughlin

Screenplay: Tom Laughlin and Delores Taylor

Directors of Photography: Fred Koenekamp and John Stephens

Cast: Tom Laughlin (Billy Jack), Delores Taylor (Jean Roberts), Clark Howat (Sheriff Cole), David Roya (Bernard Posner), Bert Freed (Posner), and Kenneth Tobey (Deputy)

Availability: Ventura Home Video

In 1971, actor/writer/director Tom Laughlin unleashed his alter-ego, Billy Jack, on American audiences. Billy first appeared in the 1966 American International film *The Born Losers*, but *Billy Jack* was Laughlin's breakthrough. For people born between 1946 and 1966 Billy Jack signified alienation from the status quo. Half Native American and a former Green Beret who hated the Viet Nam War, Billy is an environmentalist, holding stewardship over the land. In an arresting opening sequence, Billy rides out of the forest and stops businessman Posner and his crooked deputy sheriff from poaching wild mustangs. He calls them liars and says that "when the policemen break the law there isn't any law" (7:44). Along with defending the land and exposing police corruption, Billy also protects an alternative, Montessori-type school run by Jean, his close friend and soul mate (played by Laughlin's real-life wife, the understated and talented Delores Taylor). At the school, Jean states that the children pursue their own learning. There are no drugs allowed, everyone carries their own load and has to create something positive, something that makes them proud of their own history and past (13:26–14:33). The status quo, the town's parochial authorities and education board, feels threatened by the school and wants to shut it down. That fear leads to violence from which Billy must protect the students. In a wonderfully choreographed action sequence, Billy arrives at an ice cream parlor to see several Native Americans degraded. The parlor's proprietor refused to serve them ice cream, and Bernard Posner, the son of the powerful business figure, poured flour on them to make them "white." Billy enters, and in a series of quick glances, sizes up the kids, and then says in a voice rising in anger, "When I see this girl . . . so degraded . . . I just want to go berserk!" And in a series of lightning karate moves he sends Posner flying through a plate glass window (25:30–31:10). Such action sequences led several critics to unfairly dismiss the film as ludicrous propaganda, promoting peace through violence. But Billy's disrespect for white-collar authority, combined with his distaste for war, his stewardship over the land, and his love for the alternative school, captivated audiences in 1971. Moreover, Billy Jack's mythology, linked to Native American traditions and philosophy—"Being Indian isn't a matter of blood. It's a way of life" (1:38:48)—was very appealing to whites looking for alternative paradigms. The film also appealed to Native Americans. Even though they didn't see themselves on the screen, they did see a white actor, Laughlin, respecting the rights of difference and those of the counterculture. Holed up in a stone cottage, Billy fights it out with authorities and only surrenders after they promise ten years of noninterference with the alternative school and agree to give Jean a ten-year contract as director. As Billy is taken away in handcuffs, the kids in the film, and those in the movie theater, raise triumphant fists, saluting a brother.

Further Reading

Casuso, Jorge. *The Amazing Story Behind the Legend of Billy Jack.* (Spiral bound). California: Tom Laughlin, 1999.

Cooper, Arthur. "Big Jack for Billy Jack." *Newsweek* 81 (March 26, 1973): 81.

Kael, Pauline. Review of *Billy Jack. The New Yorker* 47 (November 27, 1971); 148–152.

Rosenzweig, Sidney. "The Dark Night of the Screen: Messages and Melodrama in the American Movie." *American Quarterly* 27 (1975): 88–98.

Siminoski, Ted. "The Billy Jack Phenomenon: Filmmaking with Independence and Control." *Velvet Light Trap* 13 (Fall 1974): 36–39.

Boys Don't Cry (1999) (R) (W)

Setting: Lincoln and Falls City, Nebraska, 1992–1993

Director: Kimberly Peirce

Screenplay: Kimberly Peirce and Andy Bienen

Director of Photography: Jim Denault

Cast: Hilary Swank (Brandon Teena/Teena Brandon), Chloe Sevigny (Lana Tisdel), Peter Sarsgaard (John Lotter), and Brendan Sexton III (Tom Nissan)

Availability: 20th Century Fox Home Video

Kimberly Peirce's heart-breaking story *Boys Don't Cry* reexamines issues of sexual identity that films in the post–Production Code era (1934–1967) wouldn't dare tackle. As a matter of fact, mainstream Hollywood today shies away from such material. But this independent gem is a stunning variation on the *Romeo and Juliet* theme of doomed love. *Boys Don't Cry* is based on the true story of Brandon Teena/Teena Brandon, a twenty-one-year-old Nebraska woman who passed as a man and dated women who found him sexually alluring. In Falls City he falls in love with Lana, but when his "deception" is uncovered by Lana's friends, John Lotter and Tom, he is brutally raped and then later murdered, a victim of a hate crime. John and Tom cram sexual identity into narrow boxes (male/female; heterosexual/ "dyke"). But Brandon fits neither of these categories. Brandon is a man trapped in a woman's body. He's a transgendered character. Painfully, Brandon wraps his breasts with sensor bandage, stuffs a sock down his pants, wears his hair short, and participates in male acts of bravado, such as bumper skiing off of the back of a truck, in order to "fit in." Academy Award winner Hilary Swank plays Teena with a wonderful androgynous quality. She has a boyish grin, hangs her hands on her jeans pockets like a guy, and walks with a James Dean gait. She's alluring and beautiful as she conveys a character playing out his own dream vision of himself. But because John and Tim felt duped by such a fantasy, they brutally desire to redefine Brandon as a "woman." Thus, they rape and then destroy him. By contrast, Lana, Brandon's lover, views gender identity in much more fluid lines. She's not offended by Brandon's complexity. While making love with Brandon (with the aid of a concealed dildo), she notices Brandon's cleavage but says nothing (58:36–1:00:41). Later, when Brandon, in jail, tells Lana that his identity is all very complicated, Lana affirms their love. "I don't care if you're half monkey or half ape. I'm getting you out of here" (1:11:49–1:12:59). Lana loves Brandon for Brandon's sensitivity. Moreover, Lana never refers to Brandon with a female pronoun. Even after John and Tom yell at Brandon, "Are you a girl or not?" and take him to the bathroom and expose his female genitalia for Lana to look at, she shouts back, "Leave *him* alone" (1: 22:17–1:23:34). Eventually, just prior to Brandon's murder, the two lovers make out in full awareness of each other's identities. That moment powerfully affirms this film's revolutionary love story.

Further Reading

Johnson, Brian D. "Sex, Love and Human Remains: Pushing the Envelope with Gender Bending, Sensual Healing and Nights of the Living Dead." *Maclean's* 112 (November 1, 1999): 68.

Loos, Ted. "A Role within a Role: A Girl Who Became a Boy" (interview with Hilary Swank). *New York Times* (October 3, 1999): 25.

Maslin, Janet. "Sometimes Accepting Identity Means Accepting Fate, Too." *New York Times* (October 1, 1999): B10.

Thomas, Dana. "Walk Like a Man, Talk Like a Man: Revisiting the Real-Life Murder of Brandon Teena." *Newsweek* 134 (October 11, 1999): 85.

Dazed and Confused (1993) (R)

Setting: Texas, 1975

Director: Richard Linklater

Screenplay: Richard Linklater

Director of Photography: Lee Daniel

Cast: Jason London (Randall "Pink" Floyd), Adam Goldberg (Mike), Marissa Ribisi (Cynthia), Wiley Wiggins (Mitch), Ben Affleck (O'Banion), and Nicky Katt (Clint)

Availability: MCA/Universal Home Video

Richard Linklater's coming-of-age masterpiece looks at the generation after the counterculture movement. In films such as *Diner* and *American Graffiti* innocence on the edge of experience was explored as characters lost their naivete in an America about to explode with Viet Nam, the Civil Rights Movement, and the Women's Movement. But *Dazed and Confused*, set in

May of 1975, occurs in the aftermath of these experiences (including the trauma of Watergate). The high school youngsters are no longer idealistic, but lost, confused, and searching for meaning in a world that has gone yuppie and appears even more conservative than the 1950s. As Cynthia puts it: "The 50s were boring. The 60s rocked. And the 70s. Oh, my God. They obviously suck. Maybe the 80s will be radical" (1:17:17–1:17:28). The kids are waiting for something to happen, for something to matter. Rather than fight the draft (Viet Nam ended in April) or protest injustices, the issues have become much more personal and local. Randy "Pink" Floyd, a star football player, defends his libertarian rights by refusing to sign a football coach's pledge that demands that he not hang around with a "loser" crowd and smoke pot. Mitch, a junior high grad, worries about getting paddle-whupped by two-time senior O'Banion, and once he is whupped he fits in with the faster high school kids by drinking, smoking pot, and kissing another ninth grader. Michael, aka Bernstein (named after the famed Water-gate reporter), refuses to partake in rituals that dehumanize ninth grade girls (20:10–24:30). He wonders how the whole community can support such nonsense as the "air raid," in which the girls are squirted with ketchup, mustard, and an assortment of other condiments. As he searches for his own masculine identity, Mike tackles Clint at an all-night party (1:22:08–1:23:10). Mike loses the fight but gains self-esteem. Set against a pulsing rock soundtrack, featuring songs by Aerosmith, *Dazed and Confused* captures the look (the 70s big hair, the flared pants, the neon orange cars) and feeling (the desire to "party down" all night, the emphasis on personal desires and pleasures, and the rambling, episodic aimlessness) of the era. Pleasantly, Linklater offers no easy solutions to the youthful ennui. Instead, *Dazed and Confused* echoes *Two-lane Blacktop* in its circular plot structure and love for the open road, as a group of kids ride off into the highway's vanishing point looking for an Aerosmith gig.

Further Reading

Corliss, Richard. Review of *Dazed and Confused*. *Time* 142 (October 11, 1993): 83–84.

Speed, Lesley. "Tuesday's Gone: The Nostalgic Teen Film." *Journal of Popular Film and Television* 26 (Spring 1998): 24–32.

Thompson, Ben. Review of *Dazed and Confused*. *Sight and Sound* 4 (October 1994): 39–40.

Easy Rider (1969) (R)

Setting: Mexico, Los Angeles, Southwest, the South, New Orleans

Director: Dennis Hopper

Screenplay: Peter Fonda, Dennis Hopper and Terry Southern

Director of Photography: Laszlo Kovacs

Cast: Peter Fonda (Captain America), Dennis Hopper (Billy), Phil Spector (Connection), Jack Nicholson (George Hanson), Toni Basil (prostitute in New Orleans), and Karen Black (Karen)

Availability: Columbia Tri-Star Home Video

This visually challenging buddy-buddy film searches for the meaning of freedom and never finds it. Captain America and Billy are two chopper-riding pals who buy drugs from the Mexicans and sell them to an American capitalist for a high profit. With their capital, the two mavericks seek the open road of America, yearning for something new. They're the modern cowboys, riding bikes instead of horses across the frontier. Director Dennis Hopper drives this theme home in a subtle scene in which Captain America changes a tire while a group of ranchers simultaneously shoe a horse (9:07–9:57). And like cowboys, Captain America and Billy sleep around campfires. Their image of freedom scares the mainstream, and they can't get rooms in motels (6:43–9:18). George Hanson, a lawyer that Cap and Billy pick up following a stay in a county jail, says that people are scared "of what you represent." It's hard for onlookers to face the "freedom" of Cap and Billy, because their own identities "are bought and sold in the market place" (1:09:58–1:10:32). But what is the film's definition of freedom? On their journey, Cap and Billy hang at a commune (26:30–42:05), skinny dip with two girls (40:32–41:06), celebrate the glories of grass (in a seemingly shocking, prodrug ad [55:08–1:01:44]), drop acid and frolic with two prostitutes in the French Quarter of New Orleans (1:14:12–1:27:47). Filmically, Hopper challenges the notions of traditional cinema. Occasionally, the narrative pauses, as several pre-MTV videos are spliced into the film, including the classic "Born to Be Wild" title sequence, and the comical "So You Wanna Be a Bird" number, with Jack Nicholson flapping his arms on the back of a chopper (52:02–54:01). Hopper's French Quarter sequence combines rapid-fire images with the offscreen voice of a young girl saying her catechism to momentarily transform a Hollywood film into a bizarrely artful experimental piece. Sadly, Cap and Billy's search for freedom ends with frustration. They experience a variety of hedonistic pleasures on their journey, but they don't find any larger spiritual meaning to their quest. Perhaps that's why, near the end, Cap shakes his head and disappointedly tells Billy, "We blew it."

Further Reading

Costello, Donald P. "From Counterculture to Anticulture." *Review of Politics* 34 (1972): 187–193.

Greenfield, Jeff. Review of *Easy Rider*. *Esquire* 96 (July 1981): 90–91.

Larner, Jeremy. "From *Easy Rider* to *Dirty Harry*." *Dissent* 36 (Winter 1989): 109–112.

Polt, Harriet R. Review of *Easy Rider*. *Film Quarterly* 13 (Fall 1969): 22–24.

Thompson, Frank. Review of *Easy Rider*. *American Film* 15 (November 1990): 55–56.

The Graduate (1967) (W)

Setting: Southern California, 1967

Director: Mike Nichols

Screenplay: Calder Willingham and Buck Henry

Director of Photography: Robert Surtees

Cast: Dustin Hoffman (Benjamin Braddock), Anne Bancroft (Mrs. Robinson), Katharine Ross (Elaine Robinson), and Murray Hamilton (Mr. Robinson)

Availability: New Line Home Video/Columbia Tri-Star

The Graduate was the number one box office hit of 1968, amassing over $50 million in revenues. A song from the film, "Mrs. Robinson" by Simon and Garfunkel, topped the charts for four weeks. What made this adult comedy about a love triangle involving a twenty-year-old college grad, a fifty-something housewife, and her college-age daughter so popular? By the late 1960s the average filmgoer was 23 to 24, and *The Graduate* spoke to the dislocated and educated. The film's antihero, Benjamin Braddock, is at loose ends. He has just finished four years of college and in an era of political turmoil and Viet Nam he doesn't know what to do with his future. The film's opening reflects nothingness. As Benjamin rides an escalator and stands on the right side of the frame, the rest, three-quarters of the composition, remains a blank void (00:00–2:28). Later, as Benjamin hides in the darkness of his room, director Mike Nichols crops Dustin Hoffman's face to suggest that he's drowning in a fish tank (2:50–3:02). In a way, Benjamin is drowning. His parents pressure Benjamin to conform to the world of business. "Plastics," Mr. McGuire utters at a party for the grad, is the future (5:51). The very word "plastics" imbues McGuire's business advice with the false and impure. Later, during his twenty-first birthday party, Benjamin is humiliated by his father who forces him to model scuba equipment for their circle of friends. Alienated by the experience, Benjamin sinks to the bottom of the pool and sits there (20:53–24:32). The above adult world is a mixed-up one of cocktail parties, business ease, and insincere prattle. The gap between those over and those under thirty is strongly reinforced by the insensitivity of Benjamin's parents, and thus alienated the graduate drifts into an affair with Mrs. Robinson. Mrs. Robinson was regarded by many in 1967 as a cold-hearted seductress. Afterall, she leads Benjamin into a world of sexistentialism where nothing matters but sex. But Mrs. Robinson, in retrospect, is a very sympathetic character. She too is alienated. During the first seduction, she confesses that she's neurotic (11:04) and an alcoholic (11:35). Later in a haunting bedroom conversation she reveals to Benjamin how hollow her life has been (45:33–54:48). She married her husband because of an unplanned pregnancy. The marriage forced her to give up her study of art history. Pent up in suburbia and sexually frustrated (she and her husband keep separate rooms), Mrs. Robinson is underappreciated and has never found her full identity in life. Unfortunately, her personal frustrations make her jealous of her daughter's freedoms, and she acts injudiciously toward Elaine. Once Elaine falls in love with Benjamin, Mrs. Robinson tries to destroy her daughter's happiness by forcing her to marry a smothering, randy frat boy. Fortunately, Elaine, in a moment of nonconformity, breaks from her parents' designs and leaves her groom in a post-wedding-service haze. Whereas Benjamin rejected the restrictive world of business, Elaine rejects the restrictive world of the suburban housewife. Together, on a bus, the two trend-setters light out for new, uncharted territory.

Further Reading

Armstrong, Marion. "The Curtain Is Belated." *The Christian Century* 85 (February 21, 1968): 38.

Brackman, Jacob. "Onward and Upward with the Arts: *The Graduate*." *The New Yorker* 44 (July 27, 1968): 34–66.

Farber, Stephen and Estelle Changas. Review of *The Graduate*. *Film Quarterly* 21 (Spring 1968): 37–41.

Kauffmann, Stanley. Review of *The Graduate*. *The New Republic* 158 (February 10, 1968): 20, 37.

Webb, Richard Charles. *The Graduate*. New York: New American Library, 1963.

Harlan County, USA (1976) (Doc.) (W)

Setting: Brookside, Harlan County, Kentucky, 1973–1975

Director: Barbara Kopple

Writer: None listed

Directors of Photography: Tom Hurwitz, Kevin Keating, Flip McCarthy, Phil Parmet, and Hart Perry

Editors: Nancy Baker, Mirra Bank, Lora Hays, and Mary Lampson

Availability: First Run Features

Directed by twenty-six-year old Barbara Kopple, *Harlan County USA* documents a thirteen-month mining strike in Brookside, Kentucky, and pays stirring tribute to the hard-working miners and their politicized wives. The miners, wanting their union contract ratified, are fighting for higher wages and safety in the mines. As one graphic states, in 1975 coal profits were up 170 percent but the miners' wages rose only 4 percent (3 percent less than the cost of living) (31:27). In terms of safety, Kopple edits together a miniessay on black lung disease (35:52–40:22). An old miner, who can barely breathe, offers a testimony on the disease. But an attorney for Duke Power refuses to acknowledge that such risks exist. Kopple dramatically undercuts the attorney's authority by editing his false assurances with a follow-up sequence featuring Dr. Hawley Wells, Jr. Wells holds up desiccated lung tissue and dramatically shouts, "This is one of your brothers' lungs. And this is what it looks like at autopsy." He crushes the lung into a powder: "And this is why he died." The miners' cause is just, but Duke Power wants to maintain its feudal system and refuses to acknowledge the workers' right to unionize. Some of the real grit in Kopple's story comes from her courageously daring artistry. In true *cinema verité* style, she lives with her subjects, shoots scenes in low levels of light, and confronts danger. Kopple, as documentarian, stands up to Basil Collins, a "gun thug" (51:07–52:20), and takes her own place on the picket lines where violence teeters (1:10:04). Kopple's cameras are there when gun thugs open fire on the crowd (1:04: 06–1:05:25), and she later inserts herself into the film, presenting a warrant to sheriff Billy G. Williams to arrest Collins (1:09:43–1:12:32). But the real strength of her film is twofold: First, Kopple strings together a thematic motif of folk songs that conflate the 1930s with the 1970s and suggest that history is circular. Nothing for the miner has changed from the bloody riots of the 1930s to the injustices of the 1970s. In one brilliant sequence, Kopple shows how history repeats itself (11:57–14:57). An old miner recalls working ten-hour days at ten years of age for six and a half cents an hour. As a child he was whipped by an overseer for not picking slate fast enough, and when the miners went on strike, the government acted as the power company's "muscle man." While the miner talks, Kopple cuts to still images of children working under horrid conditions and newsreel footage of national guardsmen pushing strikers back with rifles, armored cars, and tanks. On the voiced-over "muscle man," Kopple graphically matches the image of an armored 1930s tank with the movement of a right-to-left police car (14: 52). In the 1970s, the company still has its muscle man, and it's still a form of the government. The second strength of the film is Kopple's portrayal of the miners' wives, particularly leaders Lois Scott and Sudie Crusenberry. These two women organize meetings, lead the discussion, fight for the miners' contract, reconcile riffs in the group's solidarity, and make sure that women are on the picket line every day. Their moment of triumph occurs when they stand down the scabs, refusing to let them cross the line to work, and force Sheriff Williams to turn Basil Collins back (1:09:43–1:12:32). Ultimately the contract is ratified but at a price (a young man is killed on the picket line). As the men return to work, Kopple, off camera, says in a plaintive voice, "Have a safe day" (1:40:15). The words seem almost insignificant and yet they are infused with a gentle, caring, and respectful dignity for the men and women she admires and films.

Further Reading

Allen, Robert C. and Douglas Gomery. "Case Study: The Beginnings of American Cinema Verité." *Film History: Theory and Practice*. New York: McGraw Hill, 1985. 213–241.

Friedman, Samuel R. "Which Side Are You On?: The Brookside Mine Strike in Harlan County, Kentucky, 1973–74." *Contemporary Sociology* 10 (January 1981): 154–155.

"Harlan County, USA" Utne Reader 41 (September/October 1990): 147.

The Heart Is a Lonely Hunter (1968) (W)

Setting: Selma, Alabama, 1968

Director: Robert Ellis Miller

Screenplay: Thomas C. Ryan

Director of Photography: James Wong Howe

Cast: Alan Arkin (John Singer), Sondra Locke (Mick), Stacy Keach (Blount), Percy Rodriguez (Dr. Copeland), and Laurinda Barrett (Mrs. Kelly)

Availability: Warner Bros. Home Video

This quiet, subtle film, based on the novel by Carson McCullers, beautifully portrays the life of a deaf mute in Selma, Alabama. John Singer travels to Selma to be close to his friend, Spiro Antonapoulos, who has been institutionalized. There he befriends several locals: Blount, a tough ex-sailor turned carny; Doctor Copeland, a black doctor who dislikes whites; and Mick, a fifteen-year-old girl who loves music and seeks a future beyond Selma. In his relationships with all of these people, John gives more than he receives. For Blount, he finds a medical doctor to help him (30:14–30:40) and becomes an attentive listener (he reads lips) (34:50–36:22). But Blount never does play the promised return chess game with John (50:02–50:51). With Dr. Copeland, John opens up the doctor's closed humanity to white people (40:35–41:33) and helps reconcile him to his daughter Portia (1:55:22). But the doctor isn't able to comfort John in his loneliness after Spiro dies. With Mick, we see the greatest influence of John's humanity. Initially, Mick regards John as a "dummy" taking over her room (16:23). But her immaturity wanes once John connects with her needs. One night, he follows her on the streets of Selma and watches her sit on a fire escape, listening to a classical concert that she can't afford to attend (43:35–44:58). He walks over to a sign that lists the featured symphonies and writes down the titles (45:02–47:07). The next day, he buys the records, and when Mick comes home from school she hears them playing. Later, she tries, in one of the film's most splendidly touching moments, to reveal to John what the music sounds like by relying on images that he can understand. The symphony's solemn section is like old ladies in a line, the quiet, faster section is like water running down a hill (58:12–1:01:32). Unfortunately, Mick's life is stifling. Her father's broken hip hasn't mended properly, and her mother insists that Mick quit school to support the family. Mom's despair suggests that perhaps she has fallen out of love with her husband (1:40:00–1:41:09). Mick, troubled by these harsh realities, retreats to John's room where she cries on his lap, seeking consolation (1:43:44). But sadly she cannot console John. After Spiro's death, John commits suicide. Mick and Dr. Copeland visit his grave site, where Mick confesses that "He was always there when I needed him [but I was never there for him]" (2:01:32). It seems that no one in town knew of John's friendship with Spiro. He had never communicated that aspect of his life, and thus his motivations for death are left shrouded in mystery. But the effect John had on the living is the haunting beauty of this wonderful story.

Further Reading

Gilliatt, Penelope. "Eye for Affliction." *The New Yorker* 44 (August 3, 1968): 72–74.

Knight, Arthur. Review of *The Heart Is a Lonely Hunter*. *The Saturday Review* 51 (August 10, 1968): 43.

McCullers, Carson. *The Heart Is a Lonely Hunter*. Boston: Houghton-Mifflin, 1940.

The Hustler (1961)

Setting: New York City; Louisville, Kentucky, 1961

Director: Robert Rossen

Screenplay: Sidney Carroll and Robert Rossen

Director of Photography: Eugen Shufftan

Cast: Paul Newman (Fast Eddie Felson), Jackie Gleason (Minnesota Fats), Piper Laurie (Sara Packard), George C. Scott (Bert Gordon), and Murray Hamilton (Oames Findley)

Availability: 20th Century Fox Home Video

"Do you think I'm a loser?" Fast Eddie Felson asks his girlfriend, Sara, halfway through *The Hustler*. His concept of self is tied deeply into playing pool, hustling to be the best. When he challenged the greatest pool player in the world, Minnesota Fats, to a series of games in the Ames pool hall in New York, Eddie wasn't content with just winning $10,000 (the goal of his manager, Charlie). He wasn't going to quit until Minnesota Fats said that the game was over (27:32–27:52). For Eddie, pool isn't about money. Instead, pool embodies a code of ethics, a style to live by, and a deep spiritual meaning. When he explains all this to Sara, how a pool stick becomes an extension of himself as he plays, she calls him a winner (1:24:04–1:26:31). She senses his passion for the game and how it transcends him. Eddie's decision to make pool his life transforms him into an antiestablishment figure. He's a drifter, a beat-poet type, finding kicks in a game. Early on in his matches against the fat man, Eddie declares, like a disciple of Jack Kerouac, that "This is my table, man. I own it" (22:01–22:26). And he does, for a while. But because of his immaturity, he underestimates his seasoned opponent, gloating in victory over Minnesota Fats (33:38). After twenty-four hours, Eddie's disrespectful laughter ends as the fat man finds a second wind and roundly defeats the brash newcomer. Eddie, in a bourbon and smoke-filled haze, wonders why the game has not ended on his terms. Desperate to regroup and to be the best, Eddie eventually teams up with Bert, a promo man, gambler, and underworld figure who is dead inside. As he learns to master pool, Eddie, through neglect, loses Sara. Following her suicide, a distraught Eddie shows up in Ames for a return game with Minnesota Fats. There, in a moment of sad self-recognition, he confesses his love for Sara. He couldn't say this while she was alive, but now in a moment of bitter irony he expresses his repressed emotions in a dingy-lighted hall full of strangers. "I traded her in for a pool game," he cries (2:11:57). Then in the smoke-streaked hall, Eddie masters the fat man quickly. Having lost in love, Eddie gains a small measure of self-esteem by being the best that day. In the film's final moment, the integrity and poetry of pool are affirmed through the players' mutual respect. Eddie pauses and glances at his opponent: "Fat Man. You shoot a great game of pool." Minnesota Fats nods and welcomes Eddie into the game's honor roll: "So do you, Fast Eddie."

Further Reading

Crowther, Bosley. Review of *The Hustler*. *New York Times* (September 27, 1961): 35.

Review of *The Hustler*. *Time* 78 (October 6, 1961): 74.

Zinman, David. *"The Hustler." Fifty Grand Movies of the 1960s and 1970s.* New York: Crown Publishers, 1986. 37–40.

The Last Detail (1973) (R)

Setting: Norfolk, Virginia, Washington, DC, Boston, and New Hampshire, 1973

Director: Hal Ashby

Screenplay: Robert Towne

Director of Photography: Michael Chapman

Cast: Jack Nicholson (Billy "Badass" Badduskey), Otis Young (Mulhall), Randy Quaid (Seaman Meadows), Carol Kane (prostitute), and Michael Moriarty (Marine duty officer)

Availability: Columbia Tri-Star Home Video

Set against the backdrop of Viet Nam, *The Last Detail* is an absurdist buddy-buddy film in which two shore-patrol lifers escort a naive seaman to naval prison. When they hear about this "shit detail," the lifers (Billy "Badass" Badduskey and Mulhall) assume that they are escorting a violent killer. Instead, their mission is to take a poor kleptomaniacal schmuck to prison for stealing $40 from a polio contribution box (4:35). Since Seaman Meadows stole from the Master-of-Arms' personal pet charity project, he's going to serve eight years. At a time when Americans were dying in Southeast Asia, *The Last Detail* reveals the harsh hierarchy within the military. How a few funds missing from a polio contribution box can signify so much is ludicrous. Initially, Badduskey and Mulhall deny Meadows his humanity. They want to rush him to prison and spend the remainder of the per diem and their leave time on themselves (6:00). But upon meeting the naive Meadows, they feel for the kid. First, Badduskey removes Meadows' handcuffs (10:47), and then he tells him, "They really stuck it to you, kid" (16:22). In Washington, Badduskey deliberately misses the connecting train to Boston (23:44). He decides to treat Meadows to a joy ride and to become his father figure. During the trip, Badduskey allows Meadows to visit his mother (45:33), and later in Boston takes him to a prostitute. At first, the overexcited, virginal Meadows prematurely ejaculates while she bathes him. On a second go around with her, he succeeds (1:23:24–1:25:22). Afterward, Meadows has a poignant conversation with Badduskey, in which he acknowledges that sex probably didn't mean much for her, but it did for him (1:25:22). Meadows no longer sees the world so naively. In the end, he learns another brutal lesson. Badduskey worries about Meadows serving time in Portsmouth. "Marines are really assholes, you know that," he tells Mulhall (1:31:17). Just then, Meadows makes a desperate break for freedom. Badduskey identifies with the kid, but he stays painfully in character, chasing the young seaman and violently subduing him (1:32:26–1:34:59). The violent moment is filmed by Ashby in long shots by herky-jerky handheld cameras that suggest the erratic unfairness of it all.

Further Reading

Bingham, Dennis. " 'As Staging of the Father': Nicholson and Oedipal Narrative in *The Last Detail* and *Chinatown*." *Acting Male: Masculinities in the Films of James Stewart, Jack Nicholson, and Clint Eastwood*. New Brunswick, NJ: Rutgers University Press, 1994. 117–135.

Bookbinder, Robert. *"The Last Detail." The Films of the Seventies*. Secaucus, NJ: Citadel Press, 1982. 79–81.

Canby, Vincent. Review of *The Last Detail. New York Times* (February 11, 1974): 50.

Sarris, Andrew. "The Salty Way to Naval Prison." *Village Voice* (February 7, 1974): 61–62.

Medium Cool (1969) (R)

Setting: Chicago, 1968

Director: Haskell Wexler

Screenplay: Haskell Wexler

Director of Photography: Haskell Wexler

Cast: Robert Forster (John Cassellis), Verna Bloom (Eileen), and Peter Bonerz (Gus)

Availability: Paramount Home Video

"Watch out Haskell, it's real," shouts an assistant to director, writer, and camera operator Haskell Wexler. Wexler's camera shakes slightly as the Illinois National Guard lobs tear gas at a group of frustrated students in Chicago. The combination of startling visuals mixed with the director's actual name blends documentary realism and Hollywood fiction into a new 1960s hybrid. *Medium Cool*, set against a backdrop of violence (the funeral for Robert F. Kennedy, the riots outside the 1968 Democratic Convention, Viet Nam, and urban ghetto anger), critiques the medium of television news for being too dispassionate. The medium is cool in a dual sense. It vividly captures images with verve and style, but it prepackages those images in such a way as to depoliticize them. That alienation between medium and reality spills over to the film's protagonist, John, a camera man. Early in the film, John and his sound recordist pal stop by a mangled automobile. They film the driver pinned behind the wheel, and then finally call in an ambulance (00:00–2:18). Later, during the funeral for Robert F. Kennedy, John fails to comment on the assassination or the mood of the people. Instead, he envies how the other channel's crews set up their cameras so quickly. In one of the film's brilliant set pieces of social critique, John visits a group of black activists and learns how distant he is from their reality (46:35–53:40). The activists don't appreciate how the news portrays urban violence as chaotic. Instead, the violence needs to be placed within a larger social context that understands the black experience. The activists accuse John and the news of not being "black enough" (51:58). John can't visit a ghetto for fifteen minutes and understand a sensibility that has taken three hundred years to develop (51:46). But John is eventually moved toward feeling experiences outside the camera. First, he falls in love with a displaced woman from Appalachia and her thirteen-year-old son. Second, he becomes enraged when he finds himself implicated in a larger conspiracy. John's footage has been handed over by the station to the FBI and local police to help arrest protesters. As for his girlfriend, she can't make sense or fit into the counterculture of the 1960s. In a strange, almost mini-essay entitled "America's Wonderful," the two of them attend a jarring psychedelic dance (1:20:56–1:23:50). The music is full of a loping edgy grunge and dissonant lyrics like "What's there to live for? Who needs the Peace Corps? I'm completely stoned!" She stiffly walks through the room, her body an upright contrast to dancers curving and gyrating under skittering strobic flashes. Overall, Wexler suggests that meaning is relative and there are no definitive truths. As he self-reflexively ends *Medium Cool*, Wexler turns the camera on himself, blurring the lines between reality (the aftermath of the Chicago riots) and fiction (Haskell Wexler, the camera operator and director, centering a story around a real event). "I honestly don't know what real is," Wexler said in a 1969 interview. "Sometimes the rehearsed controlled thing seems more 'real' than the real thing."

Further Reading

De Muth, Jerry. "Life in the U.S.A." *Christian Century* 86 (November 19, 1969): 1487.

Gilliatt, Penelope. "Getting Warm." *The New Yorker* 55 (September 13, 1969): 143–144.

Kauffmann, Stanley. Review of *Medium Cool*. *The New Republic* 161 (September 20, 1969): 20, 34.

Kenny, Glenn. Review of *Medium Cool*. *Entertainment Weekly* 273 (May 5, 1995): 76–77.

The Outsiders (1983) (PG)

Setting: Tulsa, Oklahoma, 1967

Director: Francis Ford Coppola

Screenplay: Kathleen Knutsen Rowell

Director of Photography: Stephen H. Burum

Cast: C. Thomas Howell (Ponyboy Curtis), Matt Dillon (Dallas Winston), Ralph Macchio (Johnny Cade), Diane Lane (Cherry Valance), and Darren Dalton (Randy Anderson)

Availability: Warner Bros. Home Video

In 1967 S. E. Hinton's *The Outsiders*, a story set in Oklahoma concerning the rigid structures in society that separate the high-class socials from the lower working class greasers, changed the course of the young adult novel. Her artistry brought realism, complexity, and acclaim to an underdeveloped genre. In *The Outsiders* Hinton struck a chord with seventh and eighth grade students. Her story has plenty of action (three violent deaths, several rumbles, and a burning church rescue), but what students identify with is the outsiders' status. For many seventh and eighth graders school life becomes Balkanized: Jocks, Popular Girls, Nerds, and so forth are all separated into their own cliques. Identity is defined by a set of ritualized codes and prejudices. Francis Ford Coppola's fine adaptation of Hinton's novel strongly pursues this aspect to the book. After having a wonderful drive-in talk with greaser Ponyboy Curtis, Cherry Valance, a soc, has to return to her defined role. Apologetically, she says, "If I see you at school, and I don't say hi, please don't take it personal, okay?" (17:22). Later, she sadly confesses that her obligation to the soc's won't allow her to visit a dying Johnny in the hospital. Ponyboy understands, smiles, and tells her that the sun sets on the south side socs and the north side greasers equally (1:09:10–1:09:34). Randy, the best friend of the murdered Bob Sheldon, doesn't understand the social divisions and turmoil. In the quiet of his car, Randy confesses to Ponyboy that despite Johnny's murder of Bob he admires Johnny for rescuing those kids trapped in the church. "I just don't know anything anymore, I guess" (58:51). Confused and conflicted by the codes that separate socs from greasers, Randy is conspicuously absent from the fist-to-fist rumble near the end of the film (1:13:13–1:17:14). Ponyboy, too, can't understand it all, but he matures. Sensitive and able to share moments of sincerity with various socs and greasers alike, Ponyboy "stays gold." In a letter that Johnny wrote shortly before he died from extreme burns, he told Ponyboy, "It's worth saving those kids. Their lives are worth more than mine. They have more to live for." And having read Robert Frost's "Nothing Gold Can Stay," Johnny says that Ponyboy's love for sunsets is gold. "Keep it that way, it's a good way to be. There's still lots of good in the world. Tell Dally, I don't think he knows" (1:26:00–1:28:22). Johnny dies content. He's made up for killing Sheldon by sacrificing himself for the kids in the burning church. Johnny's friend Dallas, however, dies broken and lost. After Johnny's death, Dallas falls into nihilism, robs a convenience store, and confronts the police with an empty gun. Ponyboy stands between the idealism and nihilism of these two characters. He can no longer be gold, in the sense of innocent or naive. Nor can he become lost like Dallas. Instead, Ponyboy stays gold by not giving up, by not falling into cynicism and despair. With new knowledge, he walks into the sunset.

Further Reading

Canby, Vincent. Review of *The Outsiders*. *New York Times* (March 25, 1983): C3.

Corliss, Richard. Review of *The Outsiders*. *Time* 122 (April 4, 1983): 78.

Hinton, S. E. *The Outsiders*. New York: Viking Press, 1967.

"Librarian and Students Inspire Filming of *The Outsiders*." *American Libraries* 14 (May 1983): 313.

Taxi Driver (1976) (R)

Setting: New York City, 1975

Director: Martin Scorsese

Screenplay: Paul Schrader

Director of Photography: Michael Chapman

Cast: Robert De Niro (Travis Bickle), Jodie Foster (Iris), Harvel Keitel (Sport), and Cybill Shepherd (Betsy)

Availability: Columbia/Tri-Star Home Video

Travis Bickle represents a fringe figure who can't fit into society and thus reacts violently against that which he doesn't understand. Bickle, a Viet Nam vet, doesn't know much about music (Kris Kristofferson? [26:48–27:19]), politics (he has no concept of presidential hopeful Charles Palantine's platform [20:20–23:25]), or slang expressions (phrases like "moonlighting" [4:21] and "how's it hangin'?" [16:19–16:27] confuse him). On a date with the sultry Betsy, he takes her to a porno theater (33:35–36:53). She's appalled and storms out just as the porn-film begins. This "is about as exciting to me as saying let's fuck," she says with disgust (36:10). Her rejection fuels his anger, his need to do something. Following Betsy's rejection, Travis plans to assassinate Palantine, the presidential candidate. His reasons are never explored. When those plans are thwarted by Secret Service agents, Bickle with a cathartic rush, races his cab to rescue twelve-year-old Iris from her pimp, Sport, and his gang of gangsters. There he succeeds, and winds up a New York city hero. Cynical, perverse, and morbid, *Taxi Driver* is an incredible film that forces us into the crazed sensibilities of an unreliable narrator. In this regard, the film itself was a product of the counterculture, creating an outsider whose goals spectators couldn't easily identify with. Of course, Bickle's rage did strike a chord with the John Hinckleys and other violent-prone outsiders. Moreover Bickle's rage against the city—"Someone should just flush the whole thing down the fucking toilet" (30:01)—and his desires to see a "real rain come and wash all the scum off the streets" (6:00–6:29) strongly code Bickle as a racist. Often he stares at blacks in the street, his eyes filled with the same rage John Wayne had toward Native Americans in *The Searchers* (1956) (46:00–46:13). Later, he uncompromisingly kills a black youth who had been robbing a Mom and Pop convenience store (1:08:40–1:09:46). Overall, Robert De Niro's outstanding performance is one part edgy menace and three parts charm, and his classic macho staredown in the mirror ("You talkin' to me?") portrays Bickle's need to be seen and noted (1:06:00–1:07:14). And, sadly, he is.

Further Reading

Dempsey, Michael. Review of *Taxi Driver*. *Film Quarterly* 29 (Summer 1976): 37–41.

Kael, Pauline. "Underground Man." *The New Yorker* 51 (February 9, 1976): 82+.

Lourdeaux, Lee. "Martin Scorsese in Little Italy and Greater Manhattan." *Italian and Irish Filmmakers in America: Ford, Capra, Coppola and Scorsese*. Philadelphia: Temple University Press, 1990. 217–266.

Quart, Leonard. "A Slice of Delirium: Scorsese's *Taxi Driver* Revisited." *Film Criticism* 19 (Spring 1995): 67–71.

Thelma & Louise (1991) (R) (W)

Setting: Southern California and the southwest, 1991

Director: Ridley Scott

Screenplay: Callie Khouri

Director of Photography: Adrian Biddle

Cast: Geena Davis (Thelma) and Susan Sarandon (Louise)

Availability: MGM/UA Home Video

Thelma & Louise expands on the buddy-buddy tradition by incorporating a female, riot girl perspective into the mix. The mix, how two women become outlaws within an unjustly male-dominated society, is stirred nicely by Callie Khouri's insightful script and Ridley Scott's sensitive direction. Thelma is married to an ogre of a husband, a salesman who yells at her and expects her to serve only his needs (3:01– 5:30). Louise works at a diner and needs a vacation to sort out her problems with her boyfriend. Together, they hit the road for fun, but after a stop at a roadside bar and grill where Thelma is nearly sexually assaulted, their world changes dramatically (18:12–22:11). Louise rescues Thelma from the redneck rapist, and in a rage kills the attacker. Aware that the two of them won't stand much of a chance before a male-dominated legal system (Thelma was seen dancing with the attacker prior to the shooting), Louise suggests that they drive to Mexico. On the road, the repressed Thelma has a transformation. She has meaningful sex with a drifter, and robs a gas stop so that she and Louise can eat. She even holds a gun to a police officer's head and tells him to treat his wife and kids "nice." "My husband wasn't sweet to me. Look at how I turned out," she says, half-facetiously (1:40:20). Later Thelma also blows up a misogynist trucker's rig (1:52:40–1:52:57). Louise's transformation doesn't appear as dynamic, but it is just as important. She comes to grips with the rape she suffered years ago in Texas and finds true companionship with Thelma (1: 35:14–1:35:57). In the end, like *Butch Cassidy and the Sundance Kid*, Thelma and Louise are surrounded by police, but the outlaws refuse to surrender. Transcending gender norms, and the limitations of a heterosexist society, they kiss each other, grip hands and run their 1966 T-Bird off a cliff into the Grand Canyon. Scott ends with a *Butch and the Kid* freeze frame that stamps the women into history.

Further Reading

Billson, Anne. Review of *Thelma & Louise*. *New Statesman & Society* 159 (July 12, 1991): 33.

Greenberg Harvey R., Carol J. Clover, Albert Johnson, Peter N. Chumo II, Brian Henderson, Linda Williams, Leo Braudy, and Marsha Kinder. "The Many Faces of *Thelma & Louise*." *Film Quarterly* 45 (Winter 1991): 20–31.

Schickel, Richard. "Gender Bender: A White-hot Debate Rages over Whether *Themla & Louise* Celebrates Liberated Females, Male Bashers, or Outlaws." *Time* 137 (June 24, 1991): 52–56.

Taubin, Amy. "Road Work" (an interview with Ridley Scott). *Sight and Sound* 1 (July 1991): 18–19.

Two-Lane Blacktop (1971) (R)

Setting: U.S. highways from Los Angeles to Memphis to Washington, DC, 1971

Director: Monte Hellman

Screenplay: Rudy Wurlitzer and Will Corry

Director of Photography: Jack Deerson

Cast: James Taylor (The Driver), Warren Oates (GTO), Laurie Bird (The Girl), and Dennis Wilson (The Mechanic)

Availability: Anchor Bay Home Video

According to Universal Studio publicity, *Two-Lane Blacktop* was a film without a beginning, middle, or end, and that label accurately fits this existentially absurdist, rootless story about drag-racing drifters. The drifters (two in a 1955 Chevy, one in a 1970 Pontiac GTO, and a girl who hops between both camps) affirm meaning by racing each other across America's backroads for each other's "pinks." The film's existential absurdism reworks Albert Camus' variation on the myth of Sisyphus, whereby we seek meaning by pushing a rock up a hill. We know that the rock will keep rolling down the hill, and that we'll have to push it up again and again, but that's all there is to life, to joyfully push. Monte Hellman's stunning cult film set against a context of turmoil (political assassinations, the hippie movement, and Viet Nam) suggests a similar absurdity, but now Sisyphus isn't pushing rocks but racing automobiles. None of the characters can communicate with each other. Their world is full of silences or they hide behind gear talk. "They got some muscle here," Mechanic says, sizing up the dragging competition in a small town. " '70 'Cuda . . . Roadrunner . . . '32 Ford with a 427" (15: 33). When the characters do break through silences to discuss a world beyond automobiles, nobody runs on the same octane. Driver tells Girl about the wonders of cicadas, how they sleep for seven years, grow wings, "fuck and then die." "We've got a better life haven't we?" he muses. She's not sure about his intended irony, and moments later decides, "You bore me" (32:19–33:37). GTO, also can't communicate. He tells Driver about his past woes as a television producer, but Driver cuts him off before he can finish. "It's not my problem," he says (54:41). Ultimately, the film's ending suggests a circularity to *Two-Lane Blacktop* that further resembles Sisyphus' rolling rock. As GTO picks up two servicemen, he tells them his philosophy and a story that inverts the very film we've been watching: "I won it [the GTO] flat out. I was driving a '55 stock Chevy across country and I got in a race with this GTO for pink slips. I beat the GTO by three hours. Of course, the guys in the GTO couldn't drive worth a damn. But I'll tell ya one thing. There's nothing like building up an old automobile from scratch and wiping out one of these Detroit machines. That'll give ya a set of emotions that'll stay with you. . . . Those satisfactions are permanent" (1:37:47–1:39:03).

Further Reading

Cocks, Jay. "Wheels: Hi Test." *Time* 98 (July 12, 1971): 44–45.

Gelatt, Roland. Review of *Two-Lane Blacktop*. *Saturday Review* 54 (July 17, 1971): 14.

Gilliatt, Penelope. "Split." *The New Yorker* 47 (July 10, 1971): 55–56.

DOUBLE BILL: ROCK 'N' ROLL
DIALECTICS: IDEALISM VERSUS NIHILISM

Woodstock (1970) (R)

Setting: Woodstock, New York, 1969

Director: Michael Wadleigh

Editors: Jere Huggins, Thelma Schoonmaker, Martin Scorsese, Michael Wadleigh, Stanley Warnow, and Yeu-Bun Yee

Directors of Photography: Don Lenzer, David Myers, Richard Pearce, Michael Wadleigh, and Al Wertheimer

Cast: Joan Baez (as herself); Roger Daltrey, Pete Townsend, John Entwistle, and Keith Moon (as The Who); Jimi Hendrix (as himself); and Country Joe McDonald (as himself)

Availability: Warner Bros. Home Video

Gimme Shelter (1970) (PG)

Setting: New York City, Georgia, and Altamont Motor Speedway, San Francisco, 1969

Directors: Albert Maysles, David Maysles, and Charlotte Zwerin

Editors: Joanne Burke, Ellen Giffard, and Kent McKinney

Directors of Photography: George Lucas, Albert Maysles, and David Maysles

Cast: Mick Jagger, Keith Richards, Mick Taylor, Charlie Watts, and Bill Wyman (as the Rolling Stones)

Availability: Abcko Home Video

In 1969, the dialectics of rock 'n' roll—the power to transform and destroy (idealism versus nihilism)—were center stage. In the heat of summer there were three days of peace in Woodstock, New York, as a host of wonderful acts converted a small village into a city of 500,000 idealists seeking a new mecca. Later, in December, rock hosted a much darker party as the Rolling Stones, rock's bad boys, played a free concert at Altamont Motor Speedway in San Francisco that ended up with four dead. Rock has always held an antiestablishment ethos with respect to the ruling class, and in the 1960s rock became the sound of protest, underscoring youth's disenfranchisement from the policies of Johnson and Nixon and the Viet Nam war. In *Woodstock*, the film's attitude toward this disenfranchisement is portrayed positively. Idealistic youths frolic naked in the water, make love in the bushes, slide around in the mud, and enjoy joints with each other, but overall they live in harmony during the festival. The music further reinforces the distance between those in power and those on the fringes. And what music! A pregnant Joan Baez sings about her imprisoned husband and the rights of work-

ing stiffs across the United States (vol. 1, 48:40–52:42); The Who capture
the spirit of alienation in their rousing *Tommy* classic "We're Not Going to
Take It" (vol. 1, 55:13–1:00:02); Country Joe and the Fish, strongly supported by the fans, sing the ultimate Viet Nam–era protest song, "Fixin' to
Die Rag" (vol. 2, 23:56–27:12); and Jimi Hendrix explosively ends the
concert with his simultaneously transforming and annihilating, feedback-
filled version of the "Star Spangled Banner" (vol. 2, 1:10:17–1:19:20).
Gimme Shelter, by contrast, looks upon the Rolling Stones' fans with contempt. Every cutaway shows Stones followers storming the stage when they
shouldn't, walking around stoned and naked, or gyrating toplessly to music
(47:22–56:50). Innocence is missing from this film, and the fans have no
voice. Instead, *Gimme Shelter* suggests that rock's bad boys made a pact
with the devil in allowing the Hell's Angels "to police" their gig. In Woodstock, the kids policed themselves; in Woodstock West, as Altamont was
nicknamed, the Angels forced the issue of violence. Told in a retrospective
mode, *Gimme Shelter* has Mick Jagger and the Stones watching on a steenback machine the finished cut of their documented U.S. tour that started
in New York and ended in San Francisco. During the viewing Jagger is
transformed. He watches the Stones do several of their classic tracks ("Jumping Jack Flash" [1:10–4:42], a bluesy "Satisfaction" [10:02–15:11], and a
heavily riffed "Sympathy for the Devil" [1:08:52–1:17:04]) before screening
the violence that erupted during "Under My Thumb" at Altamont (1:19:
58–1:23:03). Violently, a group of overzealous Angels shove back the
crowd, and then one member knifes a black man for knocking down his
bike. The violent context is established early in the film, as the biker chillingly tells talk radio, "When they started messing with our bikes, they started
it . . . and they got got" (6:47–8:19). The film ends with Jagger and the
viewers participating in the stabbing that was only alluded to in the film's
opening. The resulting mayhem leaves us and the usually loquacious Jagger
stunned. He exits the steenback room, emotionally exhausted, as the camera
closes in to a freeze frame of his sad and traumatized face. In just five months
Woodstock's summer of peace, love, and hope was no more.

Further Reading

Cocks, Jay. "Apocalypse '69." Review of *Gimme Shelter*. *Time* 96 (December 14,
    1970): 101.
Fager, Charles E. "Creeping Corruption." Review of *Woodstock*. *The Christian Cen-
    tury* 87 (June 10, 1970): 733–734.
Gelatt, Roland. "Was This Trip Really Necessary?" Review of *Woodstock*. *Saturday
    Review* 53 (April 18, 1970): 42–43.
Gilliatt, Penelope. Review of *Woodstock*. *The New Yorker* 56 (April 11, 1970): 161+.
Kael, Pauline. "Beyond Pirandello." Review of *Gimme Shelter*. *The New Yorker* 46
    (December 19, 1970): 112–115.

FURTHER VIEWING

Bullitt (1968) (PG)

Cutter's Way (1981) (R)

Dirty Harry (1971) (R)

Don't Look Back (1967) (Doc.)

Forrest Gump (1994) (PG-13)

Kurt and Courtney (1998) (R) (Doc.)

Long Kiss Goodnight (1996) (R) (W)

Midnight Cowboy (1969) (R)

Ms. 45 (1981) (R) (W)

Night of the Living Dead (1968) (R)

Putney Swope (1969) (R)

Rock N Roll High School (1979) (PG)

Shadows (1962) (M)

Sudden Impact (1984) (R)

14

Watergate, Political Cynicism, and Hope, 1972– Present

All the President's Men ◆ *The American President* ◆ *Arlington Road*
Bob Roberts ◆ *Dead Man Walking* ◆ *Donnie Brasco* ◆ *Double
Jeopardy* ◆ *Fight Club* ◆ *Girl 6* ◆ *Lethal Weapon* ◆ *Parting Glances*
sex, lies, and videotape ◆ *Silence of the Lambs* ◆ *Silkwood*
The Thing ◆ *Traffic* ◆ *Twelve Monkeys* ◆ *Wag the Dog*

All the President's Men (1976) (PG)

Setting: Washington, DC, 1972–1974

Director: Alan J. Pakula

Screenplay: William Goldman

Director of Photography: Gordon Willis

Cast: Dustin Hoffman (Carl Bernstein), Robert Redford (Bob Woodward), Hal Holbrook (Deep Throat), Jason Robards (Ben Bradlee), and Jane Alexander (the bookkeeper)

Availability: Warner Bros. Home Video

In the days prior to President Nixon's reelection, *Washington Post* reporters Carl Bernstein and Bob Woodward cover what seems to be a minor break-in at the Democratic National Party Headquarters at the Watergate hotel. But when they follow a trail of money that sponsored the five burglars, it leads from the Committee to Re-Elect the President (CREEP) to White House insiders and the president himself. Nixon was a shoo-in to defeat George McGovern in 1972, but his abuses of power from wire taps to the leaking of false stories on presidential hopefuls Edmund Muskie and Ted Kennedy showed an obsessive and paranoid man. Watergate was probably the crowning incident—following on the assassination of John F. Kennedy and failed policies in Viet Nam—that created a mood of distrust of the government and despair in our institutions. This white-knuckle thriller adds to that malaise by presenting the good-guy newspaper reporters versus bad-guy security advisers and crooked politicians dialectic. The reporters are often photographed in the brightly lit *Washington Post* offices (22:16–23:18; 59:29–1:00:52), and even though ceilings hang over them, they don't oppressively drape the reporters like Billy Wilder's images of IBM office ceilings imply in *The Apartment*. In the world of the *Post*, these reporters, led by the gruff and avuncular Ben Bradlee, are allowed to pursue the bright light of truth. Outside, where Woodward has noir-lit secret meetings in underground parking lots with informant Deep Throat (36:56–40:53; 1:46:00–1:47:13), or when Bernstein gathers information in the dim-lit home of a CREEP bookkeeper (played by Jane Alexander) (1:15:01–1:21:09), the world is treacherous, a national security state run amok. The reporters even discover, late in the film courtesy of Deep Throat, that their lives are in danger. But the reporters push on. When other papers doubt the validity of their findings, Bradlee insists that the *Post* "stand by our boys" (2:05:03). Ultimately, director Alan J. Pakula's final montage—a series of machine-gun typewriter taps listing the names of the guilty and Nixon's resignation—implies that the reporters brought down the White House administration. But what the film's dialectic removes from its narrative is the role played by those within government who helped bring down a crooked government. Senator Sam Ervin's select committee was instrumental in holding the first Watergate hearings and discovering the existence of the White House tapes, and Judge John J. Sirica was an important icon, assuring the public of truth and honesty when we least expected it. Sirica made it clear that the president would be forced to turn over those tapes. Of course, Hollywood films simplify stories for purposes of narrative economy, but in this case the simplification unfortunately only furthers a cynical divide that citizens, in a post-Watergate period, all too freely embrace between themselves and their government.

Further Reading

Bernstein, Carl and Bob Woodward. *All the President's Men*. New York: Simon and Schuster, 1974.

Canby, Vincent. Review of *All the President's Men. New York Times* (April 12, 1976): 36.

Elliot, William R. and William J. Schenck-Hamlin. "Film, Politics and the Press: The Influence of *All the President's Men*." *Journalism Quarterly* 56 (Fall 1979): 546–553.

Leuchtenburg, William E. *"All the President's Men." Past Imperfect: History According to the Movies*, ed. Mark C. Carnes. New York: Henry Holt, 1996. 292–295.

The American President (1995) (PG-13)

Setting: Washington, DC, 1996

Director: Rob Reiner

Screenplay: Aaron Sorkin

Director of Photography: John Seale

Cast: Michael Douglas (President Andrew Shepherd), Annette Bening (Sydney Ellen Wade), Martin Sheen (A. J. MacInerney), Michael J. Fox (Lewis Rothschild), and Richard Dreyfuss (Senator Bob Rumson)

Availability: Warner Bros. Home Video

In the post-Watergate era most political films critique America's over-commitment to national security or question the honesty of those in the oval office, but this film does neither. Director Rob Reiner and screenwriter Aaron Sorkin clearly admire the characters they've created—liberal-minded President Andrew Shepherd; tough, clear-thinking advisor A. J.; idealistic press secretary Lewis Rothschild; and the gritty but lovable lobbyist Sydney Ellen Wade—and respect the office of the presidency. Weeks prior to ree-lection, Shepherd is ahead in the polls by a wide margin and, in order to hold on to the power he has, decides to push through a flimsy piece of crime legislation to appear "tough on crime." Unfortunately, the legislation doesn't go after handguns or semiautomatic weapons. But Shepherd's de-sires for reelection are turned upside down once the widower falls in love with lobbyist Wade, and he promises her to push forward legislation to cut fossil fuels by 20 percent if she can garner twenty swing votes for him. During their love affair (highlighted by the couple dancing at a White House reception, a Cinderella-goes-to-the-ball moment [38:00—39:52]), Wade is attacked in the media by conservative presidential hopeful Bob Rumson. Rumson implies that she's the "President's mistress," a "whore" who up-ends "family values." Isn't she cavorting with the president while Shepherd's twelve-year-old daughter sleeps just down the hall? Rumson's character-assassination team also uncovers a photograph of college student Wade burning a flag, and uses this to question her patriotism and expose her ACLU-driven liberal values (1:09:15–1:09:39; 1:14:52–1:16:58). Shepherd, despite the pleading of his cabinet, refuses to enter into a character debate with Rumson, and his numbers dip in the polls. He also can't get the votes he promised Wade for her fossil fuel legislation because several congressmen don't want to associate with a "loser." Here *American President* echoes the problems of the left in the Reagan years. Labeled liberal ACLU card–carry-ing members (as was Michael Dukakis in 1988), the left refused to stand up for what they believe, to defend why liberalism is important, or how the ACLU protects the Bill of Rights. Instead, the left failed to counter these charges and allowed the right, until the Clinton era, to define the parameters of the debate. But in Sorkin and Reiner's story, President Shepherd, in a resounding moment of redemption, does define himself and his cause (1: 38:52–1:43:43). After losing the love of Wade, he regains her respect and his own by going before a national television audience and setting his record straight. "Yes, I'm a card-carrying member of the ACLU. Why aren't you, Bob?" After supporting the Bill of Rights and the Constitution, he then accuses Rumson of running a campaign based on fear and hate: "He's interested in two things: making you afraid of it, and telling you who's to blame for it." He also confesses that he's only loved two women in his life— one he lost to cancer, the other he lost because he was "so busy keeping my job, I forgot to do my job." But now he's going to act presidential. He is throwing out the phony crime legislation bill, pushing ahead with the fossil fuels bill, and, as the camera tracks in to a tight closeup, he promises to debate Rumson head on with a war-like declaration: "My name is Andrew Shepherd and I am the president."

Further Reading

Kauffmann, Stanley. Review of *American President*. New Republic 213 (December 18, 1995): 28.
McCarthy, Todd. Review of *American President*. *Variety* 361 (November 6, 1995): 71.
Travers, Peter. Review of *American President*. *Rolling Stone* (November 30, 1995): 76.

Arlington Road (1999) (R)

Setting: Washington, DC; Virginia, 1996–1999

Director: Mark Pellington

Screenplay: Ehren Kruger

Director of Photography: Bobby Bukowski

Cast: Jeff Bridges (Michael Faraday), Tim Robbins (Oliver Lang/William Fenimore), Joan Cusack (Cheryl Lang), Hope Davis (Brooke Wolfe), Mason Gamble (Brady Lang), and Spencer Treat (Grant Faraday)

Availability: Sony/Screen Gems Entertainment

A child walks down the middle of a street, his eyes unfocused. An American history professor, driving home, stops his car, runs toward the child, and finds a dazed boy, his left thumb blown away, his hand charred (00:24–3: 43). He rushes the child to the hospital, shouting to the ER crew, "I don't know his name!" Moments later he meets the boy's parents, and discovers they're his neighbors, the Langs. Their son, Brady, was supposedly bundling together a group of fireworks and they exploded. Professor Michael Faraday bonds with the gregarious Langs and wonders how come he never got to know their names sooner (7:28–8:04). But how much do we really know our neighbors? That's the gripping question underlying this thriller of paranoia. In the early 1990s, terrorists bombed the UN building, and in 1995 Timothy McVeigh bombed a government center in Oklahoma City. Professor Faraday talks about these types of cases in his class on American terrorism, and he's convinced that none of these terrorists acted alone (20:43–25:02). They were part of a wider conspiracy, but the media and state officials want us to believe in the one suspect theory so that we'll "have our security back." But the world, according to the professor, is not secure, and he eventually finds that insecurity in his neighborhood. Brady Lang's blown off hand is the first clue of many that says all is not normal next door. The Langs are terrorists, a cold masquerade of the all-American couple from the Midwest. As Faraday investigates them, he discovers a right wing extremist group—with power to tap phones and orchestrate mass destruction against the government—in his midst. But Faraday is powerless to stop them. First, he enlists the aid of his girlfriend, but she fears that the stress of having lost his FBI wife (in a Ruby Ridge–type of failed raid on a survivalist and his family) has pushed Michael past the point of paranoia. When she does discover the truth—Oliver Lang's tie-in with a delivery courier service bomber—Brooke is headed off by Cheryl Lang and murdered. Her death is disguised as an accident. When Faraday seeks the FBI's help, his son is kidnapped by Lang, and the professor is forced into silence. In the end, our safety is again falsely secured as the media seeks quick closure to the blowing up of the FBI building in Washington. The conspiratorial actions of a group of dangerous terrorists led by Lang are blamed on one man, the "increasingly erratic" professor, who through a sick twist of fate becomes the unwitting accomplice to the very disaster he had tried to avert.

Further Reading

Atkinson, Michael. Review of *Arlington Road. Film Comment* 35 (May 1999): 84+.
Lane, Anthony. Review of *Arlington Road. The New Yorker* 75 (July 19, 1999): 98–99.
McCarthy, Todd. Review of *Arlington Road. Variety* 374 (March 22, 1999): 35.

Bob Roberts (1992) (R)

Setting: Pennsylvania, 1990–1991

Director: Tim Robbins

Screenplay: Tim Robbins

Music: David Robbins and Tim Robbins

Director of Photography: Jean Lepine

Cast: Tim Robbins (Bob Roberts), Giancarlo Esposito (Bugs Raplin), Alan Rickman (Lukas Hart III), and Gore Vidal (Senator Brickley Paiste)

Availability: Artisan Home Entertainment

What if singer/songwriter Bob Dylan were a right wing political candidate? That's one of the stunning questions *Bob Roberts*, a pseudo-documentary about a 1990 senatorial campaign, asks. Roberts is a corrupt politician who runs a crooked campaign, but because of his pop personality—he's had several albums on the charts—and his supposedly free-wheeling persona, he appeals to the greed and self-interest of the young. His songs, a sham of leftist politics, an inversion of the pleas of Woody Guthrie, Dylan, and Bruce Springsteen, eschew collective needs and goals for personal wealth and wants. With lyrics such as "Some people will work, some simply will not" (1:26–3:04), "This land was made for us, this land was made for me" (13: 21–13:26), "string 'em [drug dealers] up from the highest tree, without a trace of sympathy" (28:34–29:58), and "they complain, and complain, and complain, and complain . . . no one's gonna hand you opportunity" (45: 03–47:40), Roberts sets forth his "rebel conservative" agenda of intolerance, avarice, and a desire to dismantle the welfare state. When questioned about his politics, Roberts hides behind a smug façade, demanding that the reporters be objective, and if they aren't he issues *ad hominem* attacks. He accuses a black reporter, Kelly Noble, of being a communist after she defends the social protests of the 1960s (6:56–10:52). For Roberts, social protest is an anathema, a disregard for our law and institutions. But Roberts himself breaks the law, and that is one of the film's deeper ironies. He makes money off of shady business deals, and he stole money targeted for inner city rebuilding to help finance a war in Central America. Nobody seems to care about this darkness around Roberts except for an underground reporter, Bugs Raplin, who can't get anyone to listen to him. Even incumbent senator Brickley Paiste, who detects a faint smell of sulphur around Roberts, can't counteract Roberts' allegations against his campaign (Roberts' camp has accused Paiste of having an affair with a teenage girl). The left is powerless against the hate-mongering of the extreme right. In the end Roberts wins election by feigning his own attempted assassination, surrounded by the likes of Lukas Hart III—a CIA type who led covert operations in Central America.

Further Reading

Cooper, Marc. "Tim Robbins: Rocking the Establishment." *Mother Jones* 25 (January/February 2000): 82–83.

Kauffmann, Stanley. Review of *Bob Roberts*. *New Republic* 207 (October 5, 1992): 34–35.

Travers, Peter. Review of *Bob Roberts*. *Rolling Stone* (September 17, 1992): 101–102.

Dead Man Walking (1995) (R) (W)

Setting: New Orleans and Angola, Louisiana, 1988–1994

Director: Tim Robbins

Screenplay: Tim Robbins

Director of Photography: Roger Deakins

Cast: Susan Sarandon (Sister Helen Prêjeán), Sean Penn (Matthew Poncelet), Raymond J. Barry (Mr. Delacroix), R. Lee Ermey (Clyde Percy), Celia Weston (Mary Beth Percy), Lois Smith (Helen's mother), and Scott Wilson (Chaplain Farley)

Availability: Polygram Home Video

Dead Man Walking is a powerful film with a dual purpose: The first is to educate the masses against the horrors of capital punishment, and the second is to tell the compelling story of Sister Helen Prêjeán, who overcomes her fears and the doubts placed on her by society's patriarchal structures in order to help a condemned man find his own dignity and ultimately grace. Sister Helen (played with a marvelous mix of quiet righteousness, love, and gentle anguish by Susan Sarandon) is a strong woman who brings redemptive love to Matthew Poncelet, a rapist and murderer who is on death row in Angola, Los Angeles. Sister Helen at first isn't sure if she is qualified to handle Matthew's consultations. While visiting Matthew in prison she experiences patronizing commentary from the chaplain, who wonders why she's not wearing a habit and accuses her of pursuing her own "morbid fascination" (5:52–7:01). The prison guards, too, feel as if this is no place for a "lady." Even her own family has doubts that she is doing the right thing—they fear that she is in over her head and that she has enough work to do in her assigned community (24:09–25:28). But perhaps the greatest questions about her involvement are raised by her own community, a black ghetto in Louisiana, and the parents of the two victims (high school sweethearts who were killed brutally in some backwoods). The members of Sister Helen's congregation—children and parents—don't appreciate her involvement with a man who told television reporters that he admires Adolf Hitler and wishes to be a domestic terrorist (54:01–55:17). The Percys and Delacroixs—the parents of the murdered—chastise her for not counseling them (32:01–33: 50), for not siding with the victims, and for fighting Matthew's death sentence (36:01–40:04; 44:57–53:54). Both sets of parents want Matthew executed so that they can gain closure. The scenes in which they confront Sister Helen are powerfully balanced—director Tim Robbins presents their passion and pain with a level-handed touch. The parents of the victims aren't reduced to brutal stereotypes. We can understand their needs, even if we don't agree with them. Sister Helen, despite these obstacles, does what she believes in her heart to be right. She becomes Matthew's spiritual advisor, helping him see the faulty logic in his racism (42:18–43:43) and bringing him together with his mother and brothers (1:19:10–1:22:16). But the greatest gift she gives him is love. Prior to his execution, she sings him a hymn of redemption, and her kind words and face grant him the strength to face honestly his own demons. Moments away from execution, Matthew finally owns up to what he did. He confesses to Helen about killing the Delacroix boy and raping Hope Percy (1:34:27–1:40:29). He says he was too weak to stand up to his accomplice, and that he is sorry for what he did. His confession sets him free. Sister Helen calls him a son of God, and Matthew, appreciating her love and compassion, cries, "No one ever called me a son of God before" (1:37:21). The film ends with Matthew's execution—a haunting and informative scene in which Robbins details the execution of a crucified Poncelot with a crosscut sequence of what Matthew and Vitello did to Hope and DelaCroix in the woods. The juxtaposition of images sends a clear message: both types of murder (individual and state sanctioned) are brutal and wrong.

Further Reading

Friedman, Leon. Review of *Dead Man Walking*. *Films in Review* 47 (March/April 1996): 58–59.

Grundman, Roy and Cynthia Lucia. "Between Ethics and Politics: An Interview with Tim Robbins." *Cineaste* 22 (1996): 4–9.

Kemp, Philip. Review of *Dead Man Walking*. *Sight & Sound* 6 (April 1996): 43–44.

Prejean, Helen. "Letter from Death Row: Execution of Dobie Williams in Louisiana." *America* 180 (February 13, 1999): 24–29.

Donnie Brasco (1997) (R)

Setting: New York City and Florida, 1978–1979
Director: Mike Newell
Screenplay: Paul Attanasio
Director of Photography: Peter Sova
Cast: Johnny Depp (Joe Pistone/Donnie Brasco), Al Pacino (Lefty Ruggiero), Anne Heche (Maggie Pistone), and Michael Madsen (Sonny Black)
Availability: Columbia Tri-Star Home Video

"You know something? I got him. I got my hooks in the guy," Joe Pistone boasts with a smile to his fellow FBI operative, Tim Curley, early in this film about identity and subterfuge (18:37–18:41). But the confidence is short-lived. While infiltrating the Mafia and collecting evidence against Sonny Black's organization, Pistone begins literally to lose himself in his alter ego, smooth-talking jewel man Donnie Brasco. As he loses himself he identifies with the man he's helping to bring down, Lefty Ruggiero, a small time operator who has "twenty-six hits under his belt." Ultimately, it's Lefty who gets his hooks into Joe/Donnie. He becomes a surrogate father, teaching Donnie the ways of the mob. He shows him how to carry his money in a roll, the semantic distinctions between "friend of mine" (a connected guy) and "friend of ours" (a made guy) (15:04–16:27). He also tells Donnie to lose the mustache and the jeans ("this isn't a fucking rodeo"). Donnie/Joe genuinely comes to care for Lefty. He is welcomed into his home, witnesses Lefty's tribulations with a drug-addicted son, and shares in several horrifying experiences: a gangland murder in a garage (1:31:18–1:36:16) and a brutal beating in a Chinese restaurant (43:53–47:10). But Lefty's hooks are most deeply felt by Donnie because the mobster vouched for him in front of the gang. "I went on record with you. Nobody can touch you. I'm your man," Lefty smiles. "Anything happens, I'm responsible" (23:13–23:59). That responsibility hits Donnie deeply. If he pulls out of the operation, Donnie will be signing Lefty's death sentence, or as he confesses to his wife, in a tension-filled scene, "I can't breathe anymore. And if I come out of this Lefty dies" (1:44:09–1:48:36). His identity with the mob is complete: "I'm not becoming like them, Maggie. I am them." But before he can save Lefty and extricate himself from the mission, the FBI drops in and breaks up the subterfuge. Lefty is eventually wiped out by the mob for trusting Donnie. Director Mike Newell follows up Lefty's exit to go see "a guy" (his hit) with an elliptical edit of Joe, in FBI gear, firing bullets into a target. The edit—Lefty versus a hail of target bullets—strongly suggests that Joe is responsible for Lefty's death (2:00:54–2:01:29). The film ends with a mock ceremony in which Joe is decorated by the FBI for his mission. The presenter mispronounces Pistone's last name, fostering a lack of sincerity to the festivities. During the ceremony, Joe's head hangs, his body stooped with dejection. Joe's transformation into the very type of man he's trying to destroy blurs the lines between good and evil. In a post-Watergate era the line between the FBI and the mob seems to be very thin indeed.

Further Reading

Doherty, Thomas. Review of *Donnie Brasco*. *Cineaste* 23 (1997): 42–43.
Kaufman, Debra. "Domino Lends Impressionistic Edge to *Donnie Brasco*." *American Cinematographer* 78 (May 1997): 22+.
Wrathall, John. Review of *Donnie Brasco*. *Sight & Sound* 7 (May 1997): 40–41.

Double Jeopardy (1999) (R) (W)

Setting: Seattle; San Francisco; Evergreen, Colorado; and New Orleans, 1994–1999

Director: Bruce Beresford

Screenplay: David Weisberg and Douglas Cook

Director of Photography: Peter James

Cast: Ashley Judd (Elizabeth, Libby Parsons), Tommy Lee Jones (Travis Lehman), Bruce Greenwood (Nick Parsons/Simon Ryder/Jonathan Devereaux), and Annabeth Gish (Angela Green)

Availability: Paramount Home Video

In film noirs of the 1940s and 1950s, women were often portrayed as deceptively dangerous black-widow figures who destroyed men. Bruce Beresford's *Double Jeopardy* inverts and revises that paradigm. Nick Parsons is corrupted by the business world and bent on his own self-preservation and pleasure. Libby Parsons, his loyal housewife, is the film's hero. Like many a 1940s noir hero, she is caught in a web of forces beyond her control. When her husband, Nick—who is embroiled in an embezzlement scandal—suddenly disappears from their romantic sailing ship, she is indicted for his murder: Nick is not dead, but he has deviously framed his wife so that he can escape scandal and start his life anew with his lover Angela Green and his son. Nick is pure evil. Not only does he make love to his wife hours before his duplicitous exit (7:28–8:33), he also plants damaging evidence against her, including a desperate SOS distress call sent to the coast guard that is played at Libby's trial (16:24–18:18). Of course, Libby is found guilty of murder and sentenced. At first she believes that her husband was truly killed, but when she tries to contact her missing son in San Francisco, and finds out that Nick is alive, she dedicates herself—mirrored through a rigid exercise regiment—to getting even (25:05–27:32; 29:48–30:25). Thus, the title of the film has two meanings: Libby's need to avenge her husband's crime, and her longing to regain custody of her son. Libby is strong and savvy enough to achieve both. She tracks Angela down through the internet, and then (when she discovers that Angela died in an "accident"), she hunts down Nick through an art dealership (he recently sold a Kandinsky and is now living in New Orleans). With a parole officer after her, played with a mix of hard-edged and sleepy aplomb by Tommy Lee Jones, Libby confronts Nick, now Jonathan Devereaux, in the Poeseque domain of the French Quarter of New Orleans. The auction scene, where she first reemerges before her husband, is pure brilliance (1:09:42–1:12:50). As she buys him on the fundraising auction block, the usually hammy host, Nick/ Jonathan, loses his faux Southern charm in her haunting presence. His face even breaks with spasms of guilt. After purchasing him, she deliberately embarrasses him in front of everybody, by first asking for a kiss and then not letting him deliver, and brutally asking in front of a crowd, "How long were you and Angela fucking before you decided to get rid of me?" Then she demands the return of her son. Devereaux promises to deliver him tomorrow, but instead he double-crosses her again and buries her alive in a coffin. But she returns (she blows the coffin hinges apart with a concealed gun) and with the help of officer Lehman, who is now convinced of her innocence, proves her husband's guilt, regains custody of her child, and wins her own much-deserved freedom.

Further Reading

Drosu, Alexandra. "Ashley Judd in *Double Jeopardy*." *In Style* 6 (September 1, 1999): 306.

Koehler, Robert. Review of *Double Jeopardy*. *Variety* 376 (September 20, 1999): 86.

Smith, Kyle. "Jeopardy Winner: A Butt-Kicking Bookworm, *Double Jeopardy*'s Ashley Judd Emerges from Naomi's and Wy's Shadow." *People Weekly* 52 (October 25, 1999): 81+.

Fight Club (1999) (R)

Setting: New York City, 1999

Director: David Fincher

Screenplay: Chuck Palahniuk and Jim Uhls

Director of Photography: Jeff Cronenweth

Cast: Edward Norton (the narrator), Brad Pitt (Tyler Durden), and Helena Bonham Carter (Marla Singer)

Availability: Regency/20th Century Fox Home Video

Midway through David Fincher's evocative *Fight Club*, Tyler Durden tells the men gathered for a series of underground boxing matches that "we're all working jobs that we hate so that we can buy shit we don't need." Durden expresses how white-collar men feel: they've lost their identity. They, unlike previous generations, haven't experienced a "great war" or the "Great Depression." Because we lack collective purpose, Durden says "We're very pissed off" (1:10:38–1:11:54). His angst and frustration echoes a growing concern with maleness in a post–World War Two age. The men of Fight Club, living with political correctness, gender wars, and economic prosperity, can't define themselves in traditional ways. But in Fight Club they can. There, the brutal bouts return them to primordial impulses. In the ring, they're free of societal constraints and white-collar conformity. The narrator, who forms the club with Durden, had previously lived a constrained life. He couldn't sleep at nights, and he sought support groups (feigning various ailments) in order to feel connected. His job, too, required mindless conformity. The Narrator's supervisor always wore the same cornflower blue tie on Tuesdays (4:46), and at home, the lack of vitality continued. The furniture in the Narrator's apartment—chosen from a catalog—further mirrors a lack of individualism (5:06–6:01). But once he meets Durden, the Narrator rejects the past in order to "evolve" into an ideal man. He even moves into Durden's dilapidated house in order to escape the trappings of possessions. Together, the Narrator and Durden recruit into Fight Club similarly frustrated men. Eventually the club evolves into "Project Mayhem," a domestic terrorist organization bent on destroying the office buildings of the major credit card companies in order to remove the tools of capitalism that enslave men with style over substance. Surprisingly we discover, in another one of Fincher's typical plot twists, that Durden isn't a real character, but an extension of the Narrator's psyche. Durden—with his James Dean looks, sculpted muscles, and sexual virility—represents an ego-ideal for everything that the Narrator wants to become. And the Narrator's version of a superior self, Durden, blends smoothly with men needing to transcend office world limitations. In the end, as office buildings explode and crumble around him, the Narrator looks on dispassionate but pleased. Fincher rams home the transformation with a subliminal edit. Running briefly over the Narrator and Marla Singer's embrace is a cropped shot of a rather large penis (2:16:28), suggesting that in these acts of violence and revenge, the Narrator's masculinity is restored.

Further Reading

Crowdus, Gary. "Getting Exercised Over *Fight Club*." *Cineaste* 25 (Fall 2000): 46.
Faludi, Susan. "It's *Thelma and Louise* for Guys: Beneath the Violent Surface of the Controversial Film *Fight Club* Is a Surprising Message about How to Be a Man Today." *Newsweek* 134 (October 25, 1999): 89.
Travers, Peter. Review of *Fight Club*. *Rolling Stone* 824 (October 28, 1999): 113–114.

Girl 6 (1996) (R) (M) (W)

Setting: New York City and Hollywood, 1996

Director: Spike Lee

Screenplay: Suzan-Lori Parks

Director of Photography: Malik Hassan Sayeed

Cast: Theresa Randle (Girl 6/Judy), Spike Lee (Jimmy), Peter Berg (Bob Regular), Michael Imperioli (Scary Caller #30), and Jacqueline McAllister (Angela King)

Availability: Fox Home Video

Spike Lee's edgy film examines the life of a black actress in New York City. She believes that she is not beautiful and, suffering from low self-esteem, becomes a phone sex operator in order to gain personal control and economic power. Ultimately, she conquers her insecurities and finds her own rich identity. Before becoming Girl 6, Judy auditions for a film in New York and the casting director demoralizes her. He doesn't let her finish her dramatic monologue, and insists that because the role oozes sexuality he needs "to see your breasts." She unbuttons, reveals herself, and, embarrassed, leaves the audition (3:26–7:18). Shortly after the debacle, her manager and her acting coach dump her because they feel she isn't "serious" about her craft (8:26; 10:06–12:17). Fed up with being exploited by racism and sexism, Girl 6 becomes a phone sex operator to meet her economic means and, more importantly, to give herself an actorly lifestyle (she performs for clients' libidos). As a phone sex operator, she's in control. Her neighbor Jimmy fears that Girl 6 is getting lost in a fantasy world of performance (in one shot/reverse shot sequence with her ex-husband she exhibits four phone sex alter egos [1:13:48–1:14:38]), and he's right. Girl 6, immersed in her power over others, believes there is truth in Bob Regular's fantasy. When Bob says he really wants to meet her at Coney Island, she arrives as "Lovely Brown," expecting to see him (1:04:47–1:07:56). As she waits by the boardwalk, he never arrives, and Girl 6 discovers that the line between real and fantasy perhaps ought not be crossed. Moreover, Girl 6's need to perform, to be in control, reveals a darker side, a dislike for herself. As a phone sex operator she often has to play at being "white," thus denying her own beauty. Girl 6's poor self-image is further mirrored in her infatuation and identification with Angela King, a nine-year-old girl who fell down an elevator shaft. Girl 6 bandages her own head like King's, follows her story on the newscasts, and keeps her photograph taped to the wall. Director Lee makes the low self-esteem connection in a surreal montage sequence. During a conversation with a Scary Caller #30 who enjoys making women scream with fear, Lee photographs—by slowly tracking in and simultaneously reverse zooming—Theresa Randle as if she's falling down an elevator shaft (1:28:34–1:34:21). Like the injured King, she's injuring herself in abusive relationships. But after escaping from the darkness of Scary Caller #30, Girl 6 reaches a catharsis. She visits Angela, bearing a gift, and moves on with her life. She calls herself Judy again, and heads to Hollywood. There, at another audition, she meets another sleazy executive who cavalierly says, "We need to see your tits." But instead of being embarrassed like she was in New York, Judy has new-found confidence. She strongly refuses. "Enough's enough," she says, and drops the script to the floor while striding out of the office. Moments later, she strolls across Dorothy Dandridge's star on the walk of fame in Hollywood (Dandridge played the sultry temptress in *Carmen Jones*) and heads to Grauman's Chinese Theater to watch herself in *Girl 6*. Lee's ending opens the text up. Black women like Theresa Randle are beautiful, and they don't have to succumb to playing stereotyped hot mamas like their predecessors did. It's time for new roles and new identities.

Further Reading

Fitzgerald, Sharon. "Spike Lee: Fast Forward." *American Visions* 10 (October/November 1995): 20–24+.

Hooks, Bell. "Women in the Sex Industry in Spike Lee's *Girl 6*." *Sight and Sound* 6 (June 1996): 18–20+.

Klawans, Stuart. Review of *Girl 6*. *The Nation* 262 (April 26, 1996): 35–36.

Morgan, Joan L. "Theresa's Time." *Essence* 26 (April 1996): 72–74+.

Lethal Weapon (1987) (1998 director's cut) (R) (M)

Setting: Los Angeles, 1987

Director: Richard Donner

Screenplay: Shane Black

Director of Photography: Stephen Goldblatt

Cast: Mel Gibson (Detective Sgt. Martin Riggs), Danny Glover (Detective Sgt. Roger Murtaugh), Gary Busey (Mr. Joshua), Mitch Ryan (the General), Darlene Love (Trish Murtaugh), and Traci Wolfe (Rianne Murtaugh)

Availability: Warner Bros. Home Video

Lethal Weapon is a buddy-buddy film that inverts the usual paradigm of stable white hero and the wild and/or comical ethnic sidekick. Detective Roger Murtaugh is African American and a figure of family loyalty and stability. He has just turned fifty and has a few years left before he retires from the Los Angeles Police Department when suddenly he's teamed up with a crackshot cop, Martin Riggs, who has just lost his wife and is dangerously suicidal. When a gunman attacks a group of grade school children, Riggs obliviously walks right out into the playing field, at great risk to himself, and levels his gun, killing the shooter (12:22–14:02). Later, as a drug bust goes bad, Riggs, in the arms of one of the dealers, orders the police to shoot (16:32–19:50). The dealer, stunned at Riggs' apparent lack of concern for his own life, is unnerved, and Riggs explosively disarms him. After they're teamed up to track down a drug baron, the General, and his lieutenant Mr. Joshua, Murtaugh has problems with Riggs' recklessness and quickly discovers that his partner isn't feigning madness but really is on edge and desires to "eat a bullet" (40:15–41:37). Murtaugh wants out of the partnership, but after Riggs saves his life at a poolside siege (47:02–47:54), Murtaugh invites Riggs to his home for dinner (48:48–52:21). This interlude becomes the film's central moment of redemption. In the warmth of Murtaugh's house, Riggs begins to feel human again. "You've got a helluva nice family there," he says (55:38). Here, buddy-buddy conventions are inverted. Both cops are Viet Nam veterans. Murtaugh, as a happily married family man, differs from typical representations of black men and single parent families in films. Riggs' intensity and edgy insanity isn't a product of the Viet Nam war (he is not suffering post-traumatic stress disorder). Instead, his state of mind was brought about through the death of his wife. Thus Shane Black in his creation of Riggs has it both ways: a crazed Viet Nam vet who isn't crazy because of war trauma. Together the two cops forge an alliance that moves Riggs closer to feeling like an integrated member of society (this too inverts the usual paradigm of minority groups trying to join the mainstream; in Black's script, Murtaugh *is* the mainstream). During their quest, they have to tackle a renegade group of Viet Nam veterans. After taking out the bad guys, Riggs is cured. He gives the bullet he had intended "to eat" to Murtaugh as a Christmas gift. "I'm not crazy," he says. "I know," his partner realizes.

Further Reading

Ames, Christopher. "Restoring the Black Man's *Lethal Weapon*: Race and Sexuality in Contemporary Cop Films." *Journal of Popular Film and Television* 20.3 (1992): 52–60.

Fiorillo, C. M. Review of *Lethal Weapon*. *Films in Review* 38 (May 1987): 299–300.

Wiley, Bess. "*Lethal Weapon*: New Look for Old Theme." *American Cinematographer* 68 (April 1987): 52–54+.

Parting Glances (1986) (R)

Setting: New York City, 1986

Director: Bill Sherwood

Screenplay: Bill Sherwood

Director of Photography: Jacek Laskus

Cast: Richard Ganoung (Michael), John Bolger (Robert), Steve Buscemi (Nick), and Kathy Kinney (Joan)

Availability: First Run Features

This episodic, gay-themed film is a quiet love story of loss. Robert and Michael, long time partners, are breaking up, and as Michael deals with the dissolution of his partnership with Robert, he also comes to grips with the illness of his first lover, Nick Spangler, a rock 'n' roll musician who is dying from AIDS. At first Michael thinks that Robert is being transferred to Africa on the implicit instructions of his company, but in a cab ride, he discovers that Robert wants out. "It was my decision," he says, their relationship has "gotten too settled. Predictable" (28:06). Michael is stunned, but perhaps the real reason Robert wants to leave their relationship is that he, too, struggles with Nick's illness and can't bear being around to watch him deteriorate. Michael accuses him of this directly, late in the film (1:09:27–1:10:38), but he too seems scared of Nick. While helping fix a meal in Nick's apartment, Michael accidentally cuts his finger on a knife and asks Nick, with a worried intonation to his voice, "Have you used that knife, lately?" (14:24–15:00). Throughout the film, Michael often tells others that they should visit Nick some time, but they all seem to avoid him. In contrast to the older gay community which has become cautious are the young callow Republican gays, such as Peter, who seem oblivious to the epidemic. At a party Peter tells Nick that Michael won't respond to his sexual advances and irresistible charms. "If he's worried about catching you know what, it won't come from me," he brags (51:48–51:53). Peter opts for a euphemism—he can't even use the word "AIDS," but director Bill Sherwood (who died of the disease in 1990) is suggesting a position somewhere between the two extremes (blind disregard for AIDS versus ostracizing those who have the disease). Michael strikes the right balance. Although worried about possibly contracting HIV, he cares a lot for Nick and remains his friend, visiting him frequently. Nick was Michael's first lover. He helped Michael discover his sexual identity when he was just a young student from the Midwest attending NYU. In one of the film's most touching scenes, Michael tells Nick that he has only been in love once in his life—"with you" (1:16:22). Together they cry. Ultimately, *Parting Glances* is a story about saying goodbye, but it also transcends forthcoming death by valuing and affirming life in the face of a deadly disease.

Further Reading

Burns, Robert. "Skeletons in the Closet: Paradox, Resistance, and the Undead Body
    of the PWA (People with AIDS)." *College Literature* 24 (February 1997):
    263–279.
Kopkind, Andrew. Review of *Parting Glances*. *The Nation* 242 (March 8, 1986):
    283–284.
Vilanch, Bruce. "Best and Worst." *The Advocate* 713–714 (1996): 99–109.

sex, lies, and videotape (1989) (R) (W)

Setting: Baton Rouge, Louisiana, 1989

Director: Steven Soderbergh

Screenplay: Steven Soderbergh

Director of Photography: Walt Lloyd

Cast: James Spader (Graham Dalton), Andie MacDowell (Ann Bishop Melaney),
Peter Gallagher (John Melaney), and Laura San Giacomo (Cynthia Patrice Bishop)

Availability: Columbia Pictures Home Video

The granddaddy of Independent Cinema, *sex, lies, and videotape* has a rather
simple plot: Ann, a sexually repressed woman who obsesses over "all the
garbage," is unaware of her husband's affair with her sister. But the plot is
enriched by the arrival of Graham who changes Ann's outlook. Graham
can't get close to women. Because of a past failed relationship, he's impotent
in the presence of a woman. In order to fulfill his sexual needs, he videotapes
women talking about sex, and then later masturbates in privacy. This plot
wrinkle makes *sex, lies, and videotape* truly unique, for it directly focuses on
the relationship between women and the camera, or more importantly, how
the female body is eroticized through the male gaze. Ann, who was dreading
Graham's arrival, finds herself attracted to his artiness. She appreciates his
open-faced honesty, but is at first unaware of his controlling gaze. When
they first converse around her table, Graham indirectly eroticizes her, asking
her questions as if she were one of his video subjects. "How do you like
being married. What about it do you like?" (12:29–13:57). As he asks about
her exhibitionist sister Cynthia, he does slightly apologize, "I'm sorry, I'm
prying again" (16:07). Later, over lunch, Ann tells Graham that "sex is
overrated," and he tells her that he's impotent. As they talk honestly, Ann's
husband is breaking his marriage vows by having sex with Cynthia. Soderbergh's crosscut between open talk and clandestine sex is arresting (19:42–
27:50). In the next few days, Ann visits Graham in his rather sparse
apartment and finds a large collection of videos (33:58–38:56). "Why do
these tapes all have women's names on them?" She confronts his fetish, but
he doesn't run from her questioning. Instead, he openly tells her about his
voyeurism, how the interviews about sex help him achieve climax. Ann is

stunned by his fetish and at a loss for words. But days later, after discovering her husband's affair with Cynthia, Ann revisits Graham—and they have a joint catharsis (1:09:02–1:13:19; 1:17:10–1:32:23). She realizes that "life is shit," and that her husband is a "bastard." Then she troubles Graham's voyeurism, demanding that he make a video of her. Graham, at first, chivalrously refuses. She's not in a "normal frame of mind," and because he likes her he doesn't want to eroticize her. But she insists and on tape confesses that she's never had an orgasm and that she's thought about having sex with Graham. Graham, during the interview, confesses that he too has thought about having sex with her. Through the medium of video, he's able to express himself more directly. But as he opens up his feelings, Ann controls the interview, asking Graham personal questions about his failed relationship with Elizabeth. "What was the problem?" Then she grabs the camera, interrogates him about his voyeurism, and he admits, "I don't have the slightest idea who I am." Ann drops the camera to her chest—no longer photographing him and thus showing Graham respect and dignity and, indirectly, how the gaze is a heterosexual male preoccupation. She wants to help him, and tells him "you've got a problem." Graham at first denies it, and then sheepishly smiles, "You're right. I've got a lot of problems." From there, the two of them break the gaze, move to the couch, shut off the video camera, and enfold each other in an embrace of sexual and therapeutic healing.

Further Reading

Grant, Edmond. Review of *sex, lies, and videotape*. *Films in Review* 40 (October 1989): 482–483.

Jacobson, Harlan. "Steven Soderbergh: King of Cannes, Truth or Consequences (An Interview)." *Film Comment* 25 (July/August 1989): 22–24+.

Jaehne, Karen. Review of *sex, lies, and videotape*. *Cineaste* 17.3 (1990): 38–40.

Seidenberg, Robert. *American Film* 14 (April 1989): 76–77.

Silence of the Lambs (1990) (R) (W)

Setting: Quantico, Virginia; Baltimore; Memphis; Washington, DC; Belvedere, Ohio; and Calumet City, Illinois, 1990

Director: Jonathan Demme

Screenplay: Ted Tally

Director of Photography: Tak Fugimoto

Cast: Jodie Foster (Clarice Starling), Anthony Hopkins (Dr. Hannibal Lecter), Scott Glen (Jack Crawford), and Ted Levine (Jame Gumb/Buffalo Bill)

Availability: Criterion

Jonathan Demme's brilliant thriller has all of the fineries of the slasher genre, including grisly murders, an Ed Gein–type of cannibal (Hannibal Lecter), and a "Final Girl" sequence in which the heroine is stalked by the psycho killer, but the film's strength rests in its complex characterization of Clarice Starling. Starling, a fledgling FBI agent, wants to track down a serial killer to work through her own personal demons. As a child Clarice lost her father, a marshall, when he was killed trying to stop a robbery. Young Clarice was then sent to a relatives' ranch in Montana, where one morning she awoke to faint screams—the slaughtering of the spring lambs (53:88–57:39; 1:09:23–1:13:39). Horrified, she grabbed a lamb and fled, only to be caught later and to have her lamb slaughtered. Now, working for the FBI and under the "guidance" of Hannibal, a captured vicious serial killer, she rescues a senator's daughter (a surrogate for the lamb), and in the process puts to rest her past traumas. Along with this therapeutic theme, *Silence of the Lambs* also tells the story of a woman negotiating her space within a predominantly male world. In the opening sequence, Clarice runs through an FBI obstacle course (00:27–3:09). As she conquers each physical test, Clarice shows a tenacious ability to make it in the FBI's male realm, but as she runs, the tracking camera stalks her, suggesting that she's not only running toward a future (becoming a qualified FBI agent) but also running from a past (the slaughter of the lambs, the death of her father, and her working class, Southern origins). While working on the case, Clarice has to further negotiate her female sexuality around Dr. Chilton and Hannibal, who falls in love with his young "intern." But her supervisor, Jack Crawford, is perhaps, in his patronizing commentary, the film's worst offender. First he manipulates her to get evidence from Hannibal. Later when she questions his motives, he argues that preserving her innocence before Lecter was the only way that she would ever have got in good with the killer. As he explains his position, Demme photographs eyeline matches of Clarice looking at the back of Crawford's head (37:00–38:19). The shots suggest the shadiness of her supervisor, as well as Clarice's need for male approval. Clarice, through her hard work, detective smarts, and following Hannibal's leads, ultimately gets that approval. In a stunning crosscut cheat (three locations: the FBI in Calumet City, Illinois; Buffalo Bill in his basement; Clarice in Belvedere, Ohio) Demme has us believing that the FBI's SWAT team is about to bust in on the serial killer in Illinois, but he is in Ohio, and when he answers the doorbell, Clarice, and not the all-male SWAT team, is at the door (1:43:00–1:49:54). Vulnerable and alone, Clarice quickly realizes that the homeowner is Buffalo Bill, and she tries to arrest him. He flees, shuts off the power, and in night vision goggles tracks her down. But Clarice is not another one of his victims. She's a strong woman and she emerges victorious.

Further Reading

Garrett, Greg. "Objecting to Objectification: Re-viewing the Feminine in *Silence of the Lambs.*" *Journal of Popular Culture* 27 (Spring 1994): 1–12.

Rainer, Peter. Review of *Silence of the Lambs*. *American Film* 16 (November/December): 56.
Robbins, Bruce. "Murder and Mentorship: Advancement in *Silence of the Lambs*." *boundary 2* 23 (Spring 1996): 71–90.
Travers, Peter. Review of *Silence of the Lambs*. *Rolling Stone* (March 7, 1991): 87–88.

Silkwood (1983) (R) (W)

Setting: Rural Oklahoma and Midland, Texas

Director: Mike Nichols

Screenplay: Alice Arlen and Nora Ephron

Director of Photography: Miroslav Ondricek

Cast: Meryl Streep (Karen Silkwood), Kurt Russell (Drew Stephens), Cher (Dolly Pelliker), and Craig T. Nelson (Winston)

Availability: Anchor Bay Home Video

In 1983, ABC Pictures promoted *Silkwood* with the following tag line: "On November 13, 1974, Karen Silkwood, an employee of a nuclear facility, left to meet with a reporter from the *New York Times*. She never got there." The tagline suggests that the film is a thriller, a blend of *All the President's Men* and *China Syndrome* in its mixing of corporate coverups with a story about a dangerously unsafe work environment. Karen is a lab analyst at a Kerr-McGee plant in Oklahoma where she obliviously mixes plutonium with uranium oxide (0:00–4:48). She's unaware of any danger until she is contaminated (38:01–39:01). Although the film is full of paranoia and intrigue, the heart of the story is a woman's coming to knowledge and power. Karen is initially presented kibbutzing with her fellow workers, flashing those who annoy her, and having a good time with her lover, Drew. But she's apolitical and not in charge of her surroundings. She's even dominated by her ex-husband. When she plans to take the kids on a weekend getaway, he says, "You should have talked to me," and only lets her have them for the afternoon (13:40–14:52). At the plant, too, she's controlled by Kerr-McGee who refuses to inform its workers of the real dangers in their midst. After being exposed to radiation, Karen's life changes. Quickly she's detoxed. Men shove her down a hall and scrub her in a shower. Afterward, while tensely smoking a cigarette, she incredulously asks, "What happened?" Perversely, the event empowers her. She reads up on the dangers of plutonium—exposure can cause cancer and genetic defects. Her quest for safety leads her to helping form a company union. Unfortunately, as she becomes more involved in the union, her relationship with Drew becomes strained. He doesn't know how to handle her expanding intellect and consciousness, but she sacrifices love for the greater pursuit. Inside the union, Karen feels a moral imperative to make working conditions at Kerr-McGee safer. After being reassigned to metalography, she discovers that Winston is removing spots from photographic negatives (49:41; 1:04:49–1:06:42). The spots could reveal defects in the plant's welds and fuel rods. A whole state could be wiped out in a nuclear holocaust if those components are not up to specifications. Karen decides to take this information to the *Times*, and her honorable quest leads to her death.

Further Reading

Doherty, Thomas. Review of *Silkwood*. *Film Quarterly* 37 (Summer 1984): 24–26.
Kaufman, Joanne. "Abandoned by Mom, Karen Silkwood's Children Struggle with a Complex Legacy." *People Weekly Anniversary Issue* (March 15/22, 1999): 224–226.
Korman, Kenneth. Review of *Silkwood*. *Video* 19 (July/August 1995): 72+.

The Thing (1982) (R)

Setting: Antarctica, 1982

Director: John Carpenter

Screenplay: Bill Lancaster

Director of Photography: Dean Cundey

Cast: Kurt Russell (J. R. MacReady), A. Wilford Brimley (Blair), David Clennon (Palmer), and Keith David (Childs)

Availability: Universal/MCA Home Video

In the post-Watergate era, Hollywood genre films bifurcated into two types. Some films, such as the romantic comedies of the 1980s and 1990s and the action-oriented *Star Wars* and Indiana Jones trilogies, longed for a more innocent period of idealism and nostalgia. Others, such as the psychological thrillers à la *Seven* and the horror films of Wes Craven, presented darker visions of lost ideals. John Carpenter's *The Thing* combines the two. It is indebted to the past (reworking Howard Hawks' 1951 sci-fi classic), and inverts it. In Hawks' *The Thing*, a group of Air Force pilots band together to fight an invading monster and destroy it. The trust and strength of the collective triumphs. In Carpenter's reworking that trust is gone. What was a strength in 1951 has become a weakness, as the monster, a shape-shifting, guerilla-war type of alien invades the crew in Antarctica and divides them. When we first see the monster, he is disguised as a husky dog running across snow-swept dunes of the Antarctic (2:34–10:52). A pursuit helicopter shoots repeatedly at the dog, and the sequence filmed in extreme long shot makes the entire episode seem strange and alienating. After the pilots are killed, the dog is taken in by MacReady's group and then morphs into a tentacle-whipping monster. One of the group's scientists, Blair, discovers that the monster can spread like a virus to all the men, and that its body parts remain contagious even after death (41:25–43:26). Blair also tells

MacReady to watch Clark, since he was alone with the dog for an extended period of time before it morphed, and thus he sets in motion the mood of doubt and conspiracy engulfing the crew (55:47). In 1951, Captain Hendry and his men surrounded the monster and set him ablaze with an arc of electricity. In 1982, MacReady, the spiritual leader of the team, has to tie up his fellow men (one of them might be the monster) and then perform a blood test (1:18:25–1:26:29). Through the blood test he discovers that Palmer is one of the enemy, but as Palmer's replica morphs into an alien form, MacReady must face him alone because his possible allies are all roped. It's a strong revisionist statement by Carpenter on how the spirit of collectivism sadly disappears during the Reagan era. But MacReady ultimately does act for collective good. In the end, in order to stop the monster from spreading his virus-like plague throughout the world, MacReady destroys the monster (disguised as Blair), the camp, and possibly himself for the greater good.

Further Reading

Billson, Anne. *The Thing*. London: BFI, 1997.

Jones, Kent. "John Carpenter's American Movie Classic." *Film Comment* 35 (January 1999): 36.

McCarthy, Todd. "What Hawks Discarded Back in Carpenter *Thing* Re-do." *Variety* 303 (July 29, 1981): 28.

Morrison, Michael A. "A Few Remarks about a Couple of *Things*: Hawks and Carpenter Reconfigure Campbell." *Other Dimensions* 1 (Summer 1993): 9–18.

Traffic (2000) (R) (M)

Setting: Mexico; Columbus, OH; San Diego, CA; Cincinnati, OH; La Jolla, CA; Washington DC; El Paso, TX, 2000

Director: Steven Soderbergh

Screenplay: Stephen Gaghan

Director of Photography: Peter Andrews

Cast: Benicio Del Toro (Javier Rodriguez), Jacob Vargas (Manolo Sanchez), Tomas Milian (General Arturo Salazar), Luis Guzman (Ray Castro), Don Cheadle (Montel Gordon), Miguel Ferrer (Eduardo Ruiz), Michael Douglas (Robert Wakefield), Erika Chistensen (Caroline Wakefield), Alec Roberts (David Ayala), and Catherine Zeta-Jones (Helena Ayala)

Availability: USA Home Entertainment

Steven Soderbergh's Academy-award winning *Traffic* borrows the best elements from television's *NYPD Blue* and *Homicide*—the mix of multiple story lines, ambiguous character motivations, and life's complexities with a wild style that weds old-fashioned story telling with jump cutting and herky-jerky hand-held camera movements—to tell a gripping story about the "war on drugs" that offers no easy answers to a problem that may affect up to 25 percent of the U.S. population. Screenwriter Stephen Gaghan quilts together four compelling story lines. Honest Mexican cop Javier and his partner Manolo are caught in the middle of a drug cartel war. They perform their jobs honestly, but are manipulated by a corrupt Mexican general into doing his bidding. A pair of Drug Enforcement Agency operatives (Montel and Ray) work undercover in a dangerous neighborhood of San Diego, attempting to bring down a drug lord (David Ayala) by forcing one of his business partners (Ruiz) to testify against him. Ayala lives in the upscale suburb of La Jolla and is arrested for drug distribution. His naïve and somewhat pampered wife, Helena, quickly adapts to life without her husband, taking over his business and, in the film's most chilling complexity, orders the assassination of police informant, Ruiz. And finally, Robert Wakefield is appointed the president's new drug czar, but soon discovers his position compromised and complicated by his 16-year-old daughter's drug addiction. All of these pieces quilt together a story of futility about America's war on drugs. Robert's life changes soon after he discovers Caroline's addiction, and following her escape from rehab, Robert, like John Wayne looking for his niece in *The Searchers*, travels into a demi-monde to bring her back (1: 57:46–2:01:10; 2:02:35–2:04:30). Upon her rescue, Robert realizes that the drug war rhetoric doesn't work when you have to prosecute your own family. He quits his position and visits Caroline's rehab classes in order to listen and understand (2:17:58–2:19:41). Ayala, with the help of his wife's cold machinations, is eventually freed from drug trafficking charges and returns to a swank party in the suburbs. DEA agent Montel learns that his war on drugs is futile. Ruiz, prior to being poisoned to death, tells Montel, "Your whole life is pointless" (2:06:22–2:06:42). According to Ruiz, all Montel achieves in arresting him is allowing another drug cartel to move in and claim the informant's business. The cycle of drugs moving from Mexico into the United States will continue. Javier's story offers glimmers of hope. After Javier and Manolo discover that Madrigal, a notorious drug runner, is still alive, Manola wants to inform to the DEA so that he can earn a bundle of money. Javier initially discourages him: "We're going to keep our mouths shut" (1:12:50–1:14:28), but after his partner is murdered in the desert, Javier works in concert with the DEA to have Salazar and Madrigal arrested. Javier's motivations are not for personal gain (as are his partner's). Instead, he seeks to honor his friend's memory and to provide the youth of Mexico with a safe place away from drugs. As Javier sits in yellow-orange night light watching Mexican kids playing baseball, Soderbergh suggests that recreational alternatives for youths might be the best way to minimize the drug war's casualties.

Further Reading

O'Hehir, Andrew. Review of *Traffic*. *Sight & Sound* 11 (February 2001): 53–54.

Shargel, Gavin. Review of *Traffic*. *The New Leader* 84 (January/February): 35–37.

Smith, Gavin. "Hired Gun." *Film Comment* 37 (January/February 2001): 26–29, 31.

Twelve Monkeys (1995) (R) (W)

Setting: Baltimore, 1990, 1996; Philadelphia, 1996; and sometime in the near future

Director: Terry Gilliam

Screenplay: David Peoples and Janet Peoples

Director of Photography: Roger Pratt

Cast: Madeleine Stowe (Dr. Kathryn Railly), Bruce Willis (James Cole), Brad Pitt (Jeffrey Goines), and David Morse (Dr. Peters)

Availability: Universal Home Video

Twelve Monkeys is a powerful film that deals with a combination of fears. What if an AIDS-like virus were to spread across the planet because a postapocalyptic nut (a scientist) believes in setting it free and precipitating our destruction? Kathryn Railly is a noted psychiatrist—she has written an award-winning book—and when she first meets patient James Cole in 1990, she's sympathetic to his troubles, but she believes him to be irrational and mentally disturbed. Cole tells her and a panel of doctors that he comes from the future, and his mission is to find a virus that in 1997 will wipe out 5 billion people. There will be few survivors, and those who do survive will live in a hermetically sealed environment underground. Railly listens to Cole, lets him make an important phone call, but ultimately she has him consigned to a mental ward. Cole can't be heard, but after a violent incident in which he is confined to solitary and magically disappears, some of her self-assurance about him wears thin. Flash forward six years: Railly is giving a lecture on pestilence, the Bubonic plague, AIDS, and chemical warfare. Afterward, she is kidnapped outside her car, and the man insists on listening to rock 'n' roll music. Where he comes from it apparently doesn't exist. Suddenly, Railly discovers it is Cole, and she drives in tears, afraid of what might happen to her. Cole elaborates on his mission: to steal the virus in its pure form before it mutates in just a few months and destroys the world. Although he ties her to a bed, he doesn't hurt her. As they travel to Philadelphia together in search of the "Army of the 12 Monkeys" she continues to work under a rational assumption: "He's been living in a meticulously constructed fantasy world." But after a series of strange events (a meeting with the Army of the 12 Monkeys; Cole's leg wound being caused by a World War One bullet; Cole appearing in a World War One photograph that Railly owns; and Cole knowing, ahead of everyone else, that a child trapped in a well wasn't really trapped—he was just playing a prank), Railly is forced to reassess Cole and her finely constructed rational views. She commits to him both metaphysically and emotionally, believing that Cole is a time traveler and that he is trying to save the planet from destruction. But, of course, no one else on the planet—doctors, scientists, and the police—believe in Railly and Cole's quest. Railly, because she's a woman, ultimately isn't listened to. That lack of faith seals our planet's doom. The two are powerless to stop the assistant of the Nobel Prize–winning Dr. Goines from spreading contagion throughout the world. There aren't enough checks on the medical establishment, and at the airport, the two fugitives have to take matters into their own hands, with tragic consequences for all.

Further Reading

Morgan, David. "Extremities on the Set of Terry Gilliam's *Twelve Monkeys*." Sight & Sound 6 (1996): 18–21.
Pizzello, Stephen. "*Twelve Monkeys*: A Dystopian Trip Through Time." *American Cinematographer* 77 (January 1996): 36–44.
Rayner, Richard. "Bruce Willis Moonlights." *The New York Times Magazine* (May 14, 1995): 20–23+.

Wag the Dog (1997) (R)

Setting: Washington, DC, 1996
Director: Barry Levinson
Screenplay: Hilary Henkin and David Mamet
Director of Photography: Robert Richardson
Cast: Robert De Niro (Conrad Breen), Dustin Hoffman (Stanley Motss), Woody Harrelson (Willie Schumann), and Kirsten Dunst (Tracy Lime)
Availability: New Line Home Video

Eleven days prior to reelection the president of the United States is swarmed with controversy. A Firefly girl has accused him of sexual dalliance in the oval office. In order to save his presidency and to deflect negative campaign momentum, the president enlists the help of Conrad Breen to create a new issue of urgency. Breen, a genius of subterfuge, teams with Hollywood movie mogul, Stanley Motss, and Motss' team of clever writers and collaborators to create a war with Albania. (The Albanians have the bomb.) Motss and Breen fabricate images of a war-torn Albanian woman fleeing across a bridge as she hugs a white cat, and her city is bombarded by zealous nationalists (29:36–35:53). The images run on CNN and are broadcast to the United States and around the world. The woman, a Hollywood actress wannabe, was actually filmed against a blue wall holding on to a Tostitos bag. When the CIA tries to stop the story—they know that the war doesn't exist—Breen smooth talks them into the story's necessity (39:31–44:44): if there are no enemies, there is no need for a CIA. They go along with the fake threat to national security in order to secure their jobs. But then the president's chief rival, Senator Neal, learning of the subterfuge, refuses to tell the public the truth. Instead, he strikes a deal with the CIA and on national television says that the conflict is over. Motss, refusing to be one-upped, cleverly comes up with a second act to the story (49:19). A U.S. sergeant, Schumann, was trapped behind enemy lines, and our boys are trying to bring him back. To milk the viewing audience for sympathy, Motss arranges for an image of Schumann to be broadcast on television. The missing veteran is seen wearing an old commando sweater, inscribed in Morse code with "Courage Mom" (58:48–1:01:14). Motss' team works audience emotions better than a Cecil B. DeMille biblical epic. They follow up the power of the image by writing a moving speech for the president and concocting a Gulf War echo of the yellow-ribbon-around-the-tree campaign, involving a bunch of old shoes (1:02:32–1:04:40). This film is a stunning satire. It received a lot of critical following because its theme—of what those in power will do to hold onto it—seemed prescient upon its release: *Wag the Dog* debuted just as President Clinton's Monica Lewinsky scandal was coming to national prominence. Clinton, similar to the president in the film, did bomb terrorist sites in Afghanistan and in Sudan as the scandal escalated. What is of even greater interest, and was perhaps overlooked in the context of the Clinton impeachment hearings, is how this film lambastes the media. In an attempt to get stories, the media follow a series of hierarchical sources (the president, the Joint Chiefs of Staff, a White House press secretary), but what if those sources are lying? Throughout the film, the media are manipulated by Breen and Moss and, thus duped, are powerless to stop the unfolding series of false innuendo and outright lies.

Further Reading

Alter, Jonathan. "Clinton's Houdini Act." *Newsweek* 131 (February 9, 1998): 52.
Bruni, Frank. Review of *Wag the Dog*. *New York Times* (August 21, 1998): A12.
Levinson, Barry. "We Were Just Kidding." *Newsweek* 131 (February 9, 1998): 51.
Siskel, Gene. Review of *Wag the Dog*. *TV Guide* 47 (January 23–29, 1999): 18.

FURTHER VIEWING

The Accused (1988) (R) (W)

Boogie Nights (1997) (R)

Clueless (1995) (PG-13) (W)

Dangerous Minds (1995) (R) (W)

Dave (1993) (PG-13)

Dick (1999) (PG-13)

Down for the Barrio (1998) (R) (M)

E.T.: The Extra-Terrestrial (1982) (PG)

Gas, Food, Lodging (1992) (R) (W)

Magnolia (1999) (R)

Men in Black (1997) (PG-13) (M)
New Jack City (1991) (R) (M)
Norma Rae (1979) (PG) (W)
Philadelphia (1993) (PG-13)
The Player (1992) (R)
The River (1984) (PG-13)
Seven (1995) (R)
The Sixth Sense (1999) (PG-13)
Streetwise (1998) (R) (Doc.)
Twister (1996) (PG-13) (W)
Waiting to Exhale (1995) (R) (M) (W)

Appendix 1: Multicultural Films

Air Force (1943)

America and the Holocaust: Deceit and Indifference (1994)

Amistad (1997)

Anderson Platoon (1967)

Angels with Dirty Faces (1938)

The Autobiography of Miss Jane Pittman (1974)

Baseball (1994)

Beloved (1998)

Boyz 'N' the Hood (1991)

Corinna, Corinna (1994)

The Crimson Kimono (1959)

Dances with Wolves (1990)

The Defiant Ones (1958)

Devil in a Blue Dress (1995)

Do the Right Thing (1989)

Eat a Bowl of Tea (1989)

Ellis Island (1997)

Eyes on the Prize (1986, 1990)

The GI Bill: The Law that Changed America (1998)

Girl 6 (1996)

Glory (1989)

The Godfather (1972)

The Godfather II (1974)

Hester Street (1974)

Incident at Oglala (1992)

In the Heat of the Night (1967)

Intruder in the Dust (1949)

The Irish in America: From the Emerald Isle to the Promised Land (1996)

Lethal Weapon (1987)

The Life and Times of Rosie the Riveter (1980)

Lilies of the Field (1963)

Malcolm X (1993)

Malcolm X: Make It Plain (1994)

Matewan (1987)

Mayor of Hell (1933)

Mississippi Burning (1988)

The Patriot (2000)

Pleasantville (1998)

Posse (1993)

Quiz Show (1994)

The Rat Pack (1998)

Rosewood (1997)

The Searchers (1956)

The Shawshank Redemption (1994)

Smoke Signals (1998)

Thomas Jefferson (1997)

Thousand Pieces of Gold (1990)

Thunderheart (1992)

A Tree Grows in Brooklyn (1945)

The Way West (1995)

Zoot Suit (1981)

Appendix 2: Woman-centered Films

Alice Doesn't Live Here Anymore (1974)
All That Heaven Allows (1955)
The Apartment (1960)
The Autobiography of Miss Jane Pittman (1974)
The Ballad of Little Jo (1993)
Beloved (1998)
The Big Combo (1955)
The Big Heat (1953)
The Big Sleep (1946)
Bonnie and Clyde (1967)
Boys Don't Cry (1999)
Bringing Up Baby (1938)
China Beach (1988)
The China Syndrome (1979)
Coming Home (1978)
Corinna, Corinna (1994)
Courage Under Fire (1996)
Dance, Girl, Dance (1940)
Dead Man Walking (1995)

Double Jeopardy (1999)

Eat a Bowl of Tea (1989)

Fly Girls (1999)

Footlight Parade (1933)

Girl 6 (1996)

Gold Diggers of 1933 (1933)

Gone with the Wind (1939)

The Graduate (1967)

Harlan County, USA (1976)

The Heart Is a Lonely Hunter (1968)

Hester Street (1974)

The Hudsucker Proxy (1994)

In Country (1989)

It Happened One Night (1934)

Jacknife (1988)

The Last Picture Show (1971)

The Life and Times of Rosie the Riveter (1980)

Marked Woman (1937)

Meet Me in St. Louis (1944)

Mildred Pierce (1945)

My Reputation (1946)

Our Town (1940)

Outrage (1950)

Raw Deal (1948)

Reds (1981)

sex, lies, and videotape (1989)

Shadow of a Doubt (1943)

Silence of the Lambs (1990)

Silkwood (1983)

So Proudly We Hail (1943)

Thelma & Louise (1991)

Thousand Pieces of Gold (1990)

To Kill a Mockingbird (1962)

A Tree Grows in Brooklyn (1945)

Twelve Monkeys (1995)

Wings (1927)

General Index

Abbott, George, 88
ACLU, 283–84
Adams, Evan, 190
Adams, Jack, 160–61
Adams, John Quincy, 2
Adams, William P., 119
Addy, Wesley, 212
Ades, Lisa, 47
Adoree, Rene, 79–80
Aerosmith, 262
Affleck, Ben, 261
African Americans: all black unit during Civil War, 13; black cowboys in *Posse*, 23–23; destruction of Rosewood, 52–53; double-voiced discourse in *Do the Right Thing*, 181–83; G.I. Bill opens doors for, 134; horrors of the Diaspora, 2; inner-city black-on-black crime, 177–78; Jackie Robinson integrates baseball, 65; lack of opportunity in the 1950s, 178–79; legacy of slavery, 3; lynching of, 22, 53, 71, 186–87; Malcolm X recovers black pride, 197–98; "passing" in *Devil in*

a Blue Dress, 96–97; Reconstruction and, 3, 176; role in Revolutionary War, 4–5; Sidney Poitier articulates blackness, 181; slavery, 1, 2, 11, 176; stereotypes in *Gone with the Wind*, 15; travails of Sammy Davis, Jr. and the Rat Pack, 73–74. *See also* Civil Rights
Agent Orange, 248
Ahern, Daniel, 113
Aidman, Charles, 191
AIDS, 189, 295, 303
Aiello, Danny, 182, 250
Akins, Claude, 24, 55
Alamo, The, 139, 223
Albert, Eddie, 126
Alberti, Maryse, 192
Aldrich, Robert, 126–27, 212–13
Alexander, Jane, 281
Alexie, Sherman, 190
Alford, Phillip, 111
Ali, Muhammad, 185
All-American Girls Professional Baseball League, 65

Title Index

About the Author

GRANT TRACEY, an Assistant Professor of English at the University of Northern Iowa, teaches film studies and creative writing. His short stories have appeared in a variety of publications, and he is also fiction editor for the *North American Review*.